A Shared Vision

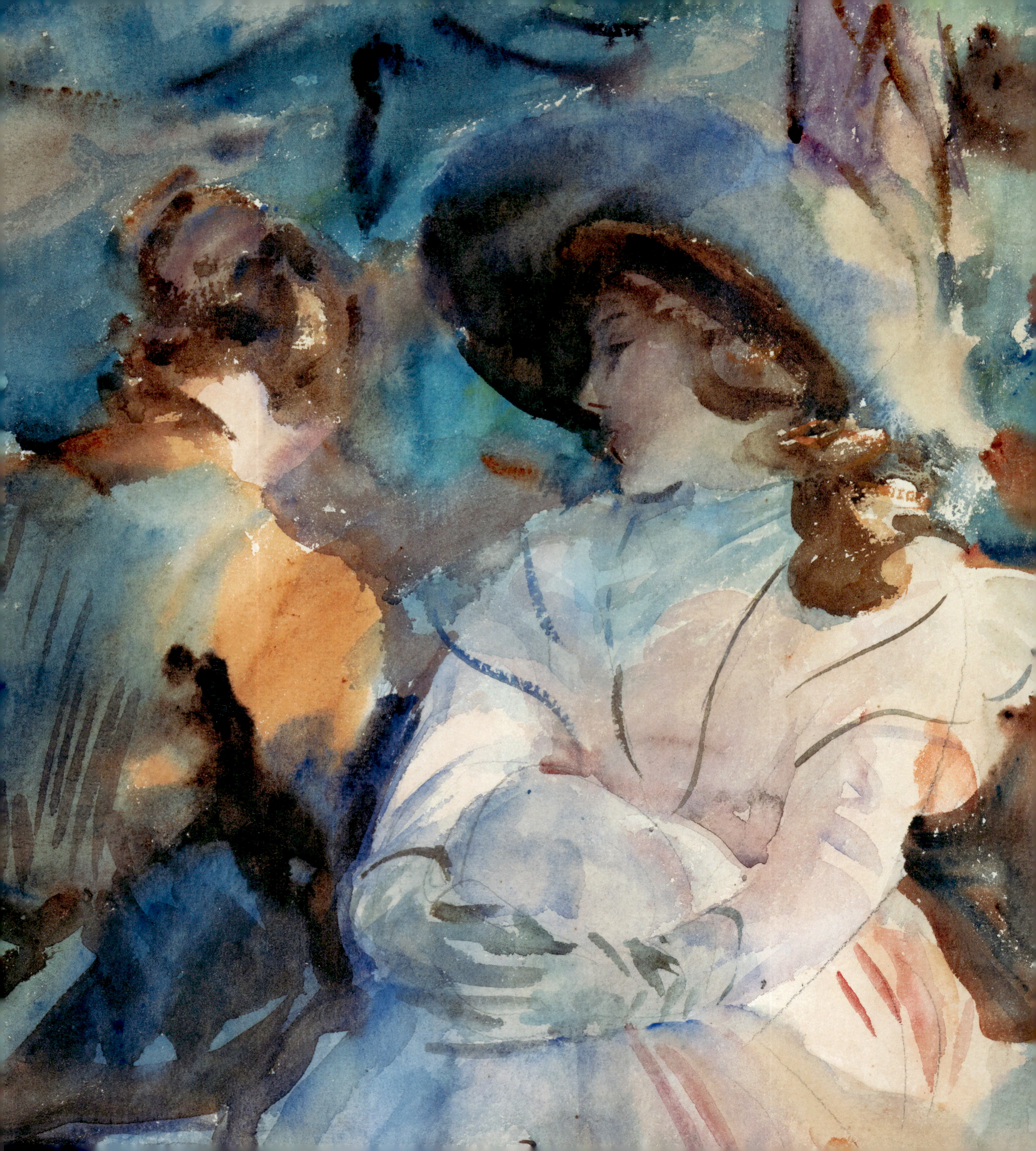

A Shared Vision

The Macon and Joan Brock Collection of American Art

Corey Piper, Editor

WITH CONTRIBUTIONS BY

Lloyd DeWitt

JR (Jennifer R.) Henneman

Stephanie L. Herdrich

Susan A. Hobbs

Leo Mazow

Erin Monroe

Carolyn Swan Needell

Lauren Palmor

Jennifer Stettler Parsons

Chelsea Pierce

Corey Piper

Scott A. Shields

Tashae Smith

AND A PREFACE BY

Joan Brock

CHRYSLER MUSEUM OF ART

DISTRIBUTED BY THE UNIVERSITY OF VIRGINIA PRESS

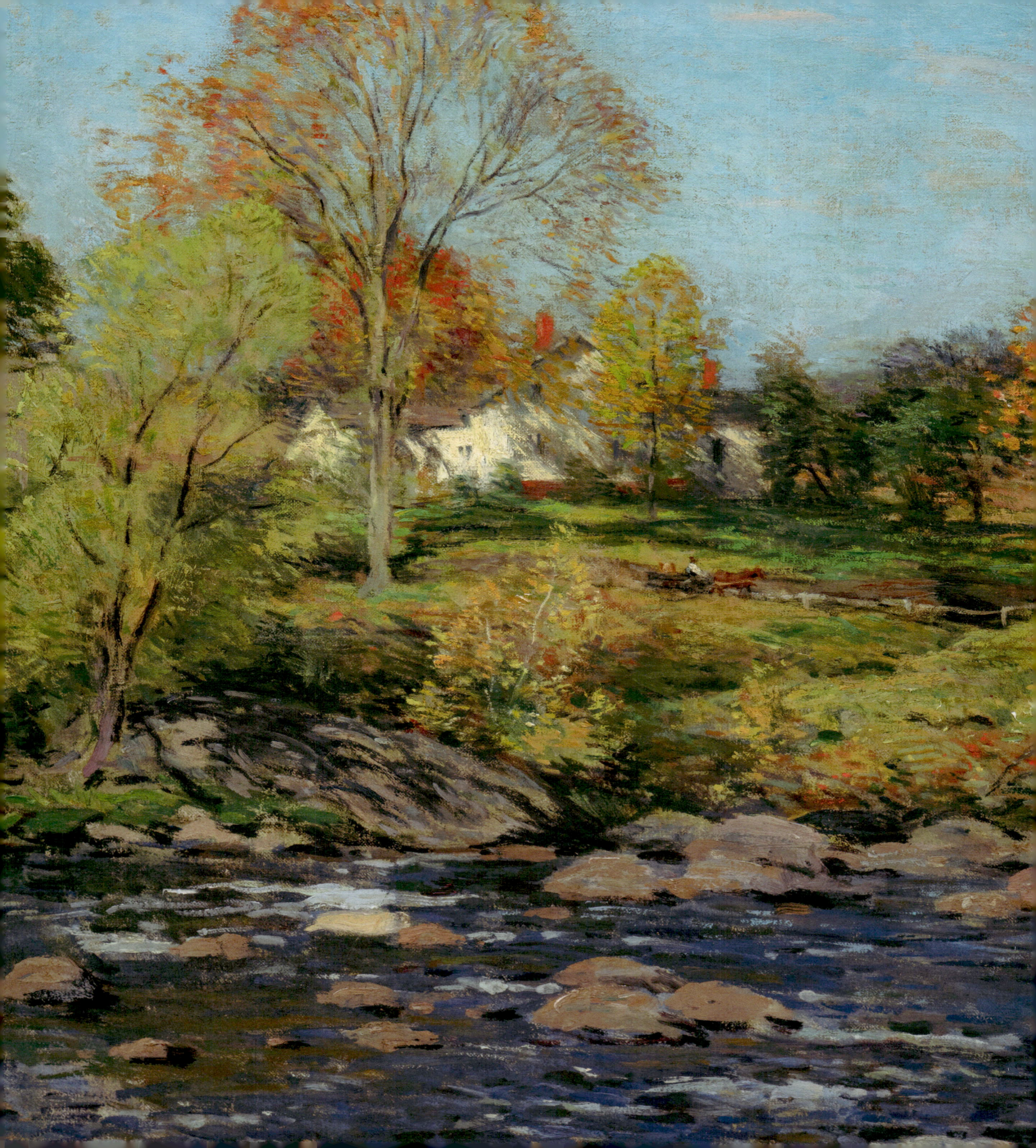

Contents

Director's Foreword

IN 1971 WALTER P. CHRYSLER, JR., and Jean Outland Chrysler initiated a series of gifts that transformed the Norfolk Museum of Arts and Science into the Chrysler Museum of Art. This new museum would have much greater ambitions and a more deeply felt impact on the community. Indeed, the scope and caliber of the collections placed the fledgling institution on a national and international stage. Over the decades the Museum has been fortunate to receive many additional important gifts of art, as well as financial support that has improved and expanded our buildings. Macon and Joan Brock were among the generation of community leaders who recognized the importance of the Chryslers' gifts and were determined to carry their example forward.

The Brocks' commitment to the Chrysler has lasted decades. In the 1980s they started as museum members at the $60 level. Joan joined the Board of Trustees in 1998 and, in 2002, became the first woman to chair the Board. After she completed her two full terms, Macon followed and served for eight years. In that period they helped shepherd the Museum through an array of challenges and opportunities and helped build a stronger and more robust organization. They always believed in the essential importance of art and learning, which are at the heart of everything the Chrysler does. They have been philanthropic leaders in creating important endowments, supporting vital building needs, and assisting in the acquisition of many works of art.

Macon and Joan made long-term commitments. In American art they saw a need to further the program at the Museum by endowing a permanent curator of American art and establishing the Brock Endowment for American Art. This supported recent groundbreaking exhibitions like *Thomas Jefferson, Architect*; *Americans in Spain*; *Alma Thomas: Everything is Beautiful*, and others, and ensured that the Chrysler would always be a site of original scholarship and exciting programming in American art.

The gift of fifty American paintings, drawings, and prints is the most important addition to the Museum's collection since Walter and Jean's donation.

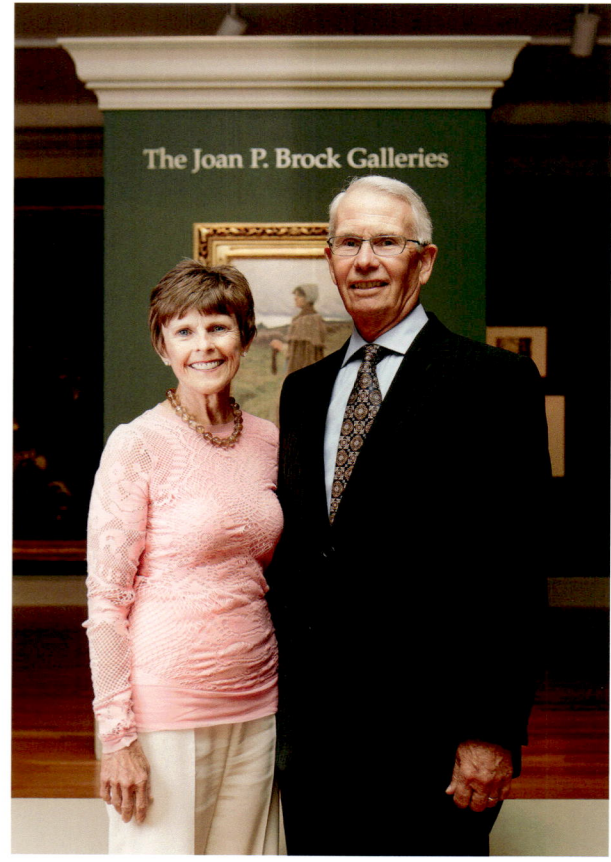

Joan and Macon Brock at the Chrysler Museum of Art, 2011.

Carefully selected with rigor and taste, these works will expand and fill out the Chrysler's current collection. As Corey Piper, the Brock Curator of American Art, explains in his thoughtful essay for this publication, it will allow for new discoveries and developments in thinking about American art. The catalogue's incisive entries, contributed by a distinguished group of art historians, affirm the significance, dynamism, and scholarly potential inherent in the Brock Collection. In addition to the works of art destined for the Chrysler, this volume includes the entirety of the American art collection assembled by Macon and Joan in order to fully document and survey their achievements as collectors.

Macon and Joan's connection to the Museum has been rooted in the art, the deep connection with beauty and great works of art, but also the understanding that art has the power to transform, delight, and inspire. As a result, the Chrysler Museum remains vibrant, and our collection is now growing very significantly because of their vision. I am sincerely appreciative of their commitment, foresight, and generosity. The positive effects of their philanthropy will be felt for generations.

ERIK H. NEIL, PHD
The Macon and Joan Brock Director
Chrysler Museum of Art

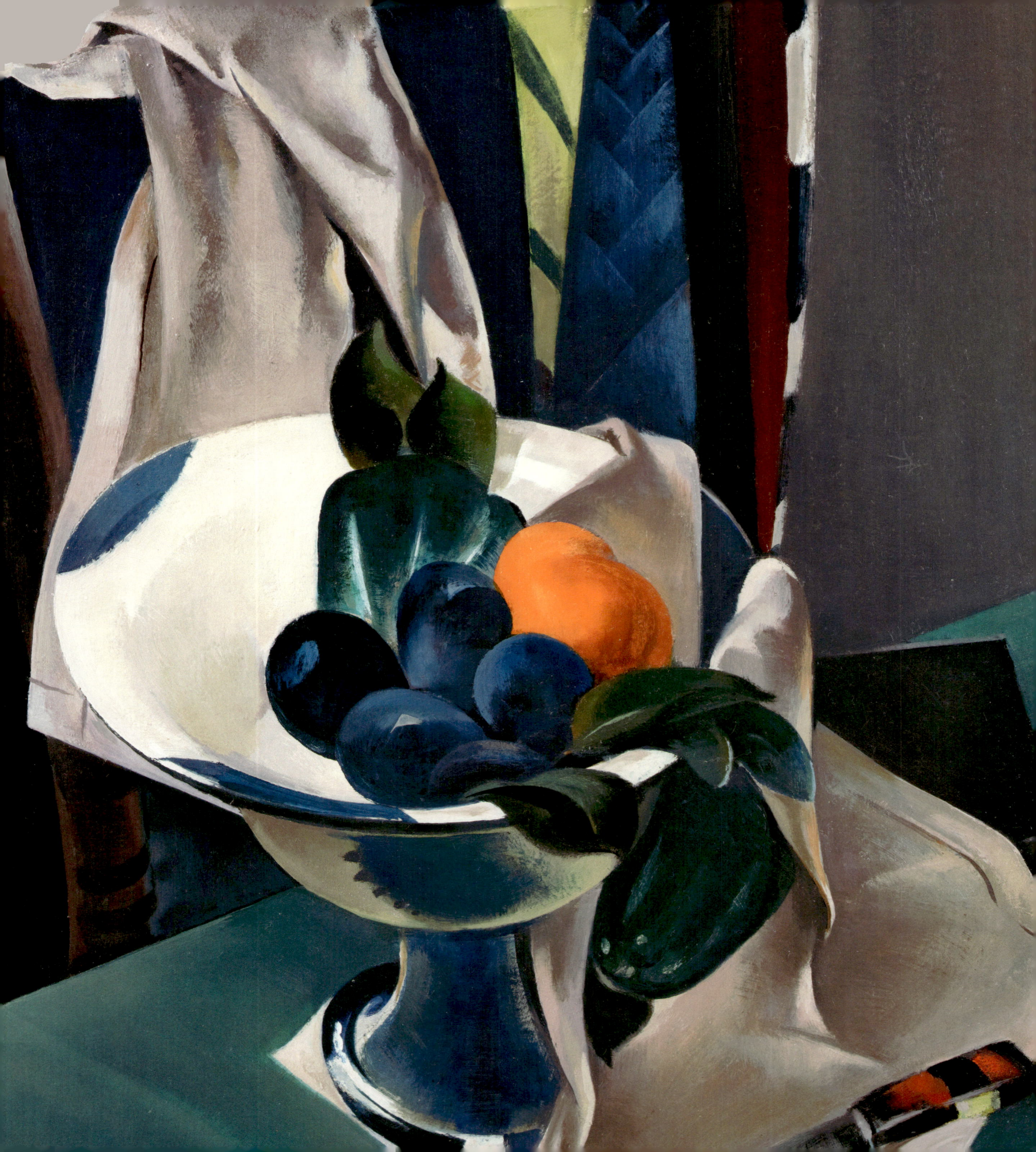

A Shared Vision

Joan Brock

MY HUSBAND AND I EMBARKED on our odyssey into the world of art as young adults at the Boardwalk Art Show in Virginia Beach. We knew next to nothing about art at the time—we couldn't tell good from bad, recognize a particular painter's work, or pick an impressionistic piece from an abstract—but we had so much fun wandering the boardwalk at that annual Oceanfront festival. The sun was bright, the breezes sweeping ashore from the Atlantic refreshing, and scores of artists and their tents lined the beach for blocks. We especially enjoyed talking with the artists and coming away with insights into what drove them to create.

Every so often, Macon and I came upon a piece that stopped us. Often we couldn't say why—its use of color, perhaps, or an intriguing story that seemed to whisper from the canvas. Whatever the reason, we felt a shift while viewing these paintings. They involved us. Over the years several of them moved from the boardwalk to the walls of our home and office.

Macon and I had known each other since the eighth grade. We were best friends as well as partners in life; we shared everything. So it's no surprise, looking back on the joys we experienced at the beach, that together we were drawn to become members of Norfolk's Chrysler Museum. I later became a docent there, leading tours for children from the region's schools. That experience, and the training I received at the Museum, instilled in me a hunger to deepen my understanding of art, so I enrolled in the Master of Arts program at Old Dominion University; I earned my degree at age forty-nine, under the guidance of Dr. Linda McGreevy. Macon, a voracious reader with a wide range of interests, became a student of my studies, vicariously enjoying the fruits of my education.

By then the company we cofounded, Dollar Tree, had grown from a few tiny outposts to a retail juggernaut. Macon was in charge of merchandising, so he crisscrossed the globe looking for products to sell in our stores. I would often accompany him. Together we explored Vietnam, Italy, Portugal, China, India, and Brazil, too many countries to recount. We'd make it a point to stop at art fairs in these far-flung locales on the hunt for small, inexpensive pieces to serve as mementos of our travels. We covered the walls of a room with them. Stepping into the space, we'd be flooded with memories of our adventures together.

And in that, we discovered the joy of collecting. The art we bought overseas, like those early pieces we'd found on the boardwalk, had their own stories, their own messages to tell. But each piece also told part of *our* story—bound up in each painting, drawing, or sculpture were the circumstances of our having acquired it, the memories of a day, a journey, a chapter in our lives. Each was a layered record of experience: the artist's, the subject's, and our own.

In time our business became successful beyond reason. Our children grew up and left home, and we decided we wanted to live on the beach. We found a wonderful old home that had been owned by a single family since 1917. The Cooke Royster Cottage was, despite its modest name, a grande dame of a house—a shingled mansion wrapped in two-story porches, rising from the dunes on the North End of the Virginia Beach Oceanfront (fig. 1). Restoring it to its original splendor was a rewarding challenge, but it took time—enough time to reflect that it would be fitting to fill it with art that reflected the period when it was built. And so we began thinking seriously about American art of the early twentieth century.

Not long after that, Macon and I were in London, having dinner at Heathrow Airport as we waited for a departing flight, when we noticed a celebration underway at the next table. We struck up a conversation with the couple there, learning they had recently sold several American paintings to Michael Owen, an art gallery on New York's Upper East Side. Our interest piqued, we visited the gallery on our next trip to New York. We loved meeting Michael and left his place with our first American painting, a 1921 work by Raymond Perry Rodgers Neilson.

So began our love affair with American art. Many an art dealer aided and abetted our quest; Mr. Thomas Colville, in particular, shepherded us through the art-buying process, sharing his years of experience and knowledge. We sought advice from the curators at the Chrysler, dealers, and auction houses. We were good students. We gradually grew into detectives of sorts, digging into each of the various paintings that called to us—learning about the artist's life and how the painting fit into the whole range of their work and exploring what it said about the time in which they produced it. Everything about the process was exciting, fascinating, and fun. And as he had on his merchandising safaris for Dollar Tree, Macon loved the thrill of the hunt.

Into each painting we embedded our own memories. We would spend hours debating where to hang each piece and, as our collection grew, which should hang next to which. We had lots of wall space, and after the renovation of the house was complete, we expanded our collection to include art that was painted before the turn of the last century. We also added contemporary glasswork to the mix, as we had come to appreciate that art form through our exposure to the Chrysler's collection (fig. 2).

What we found, as we passed years in the company of this magnificent art, was something that's probably old hat to artists and their agents but which

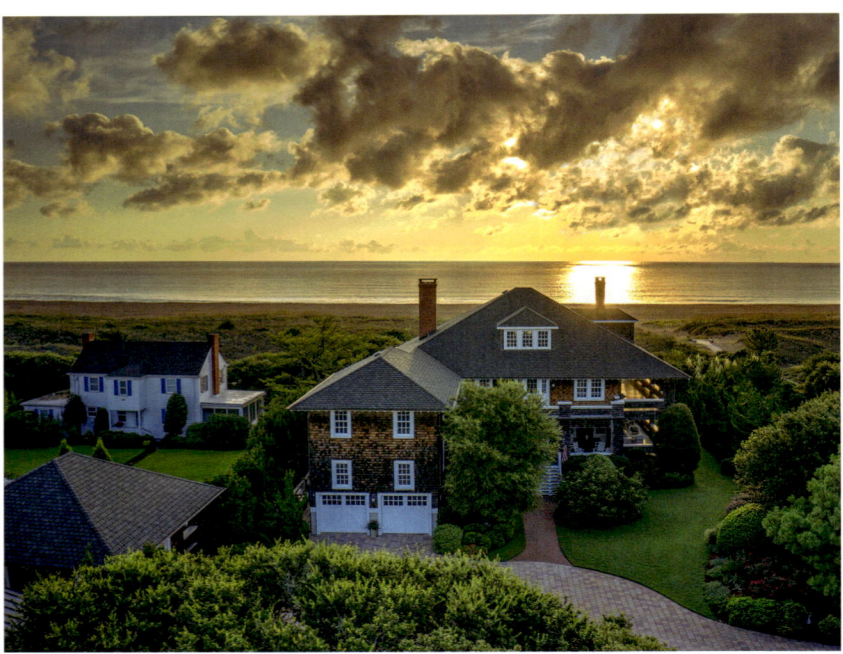

FIG. 1 Exterior view of the Brocks' home, the Cooke Royster Cottage, 2022. Photograph by John Wadsworth

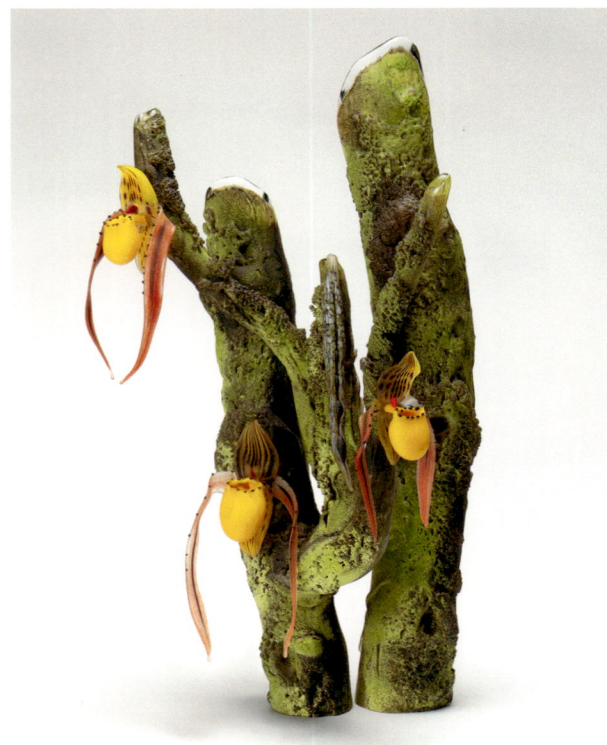

FIG. 2 Debora Moore, American, b. 1960. *Yellow Lady Slipper*, 2008. Blown and hot-worked glass, 25½ × 13 × 12 in. Chrysler Museum of Art, Gift of the Macon and Joan Brock Collection of American Art, 2021.22

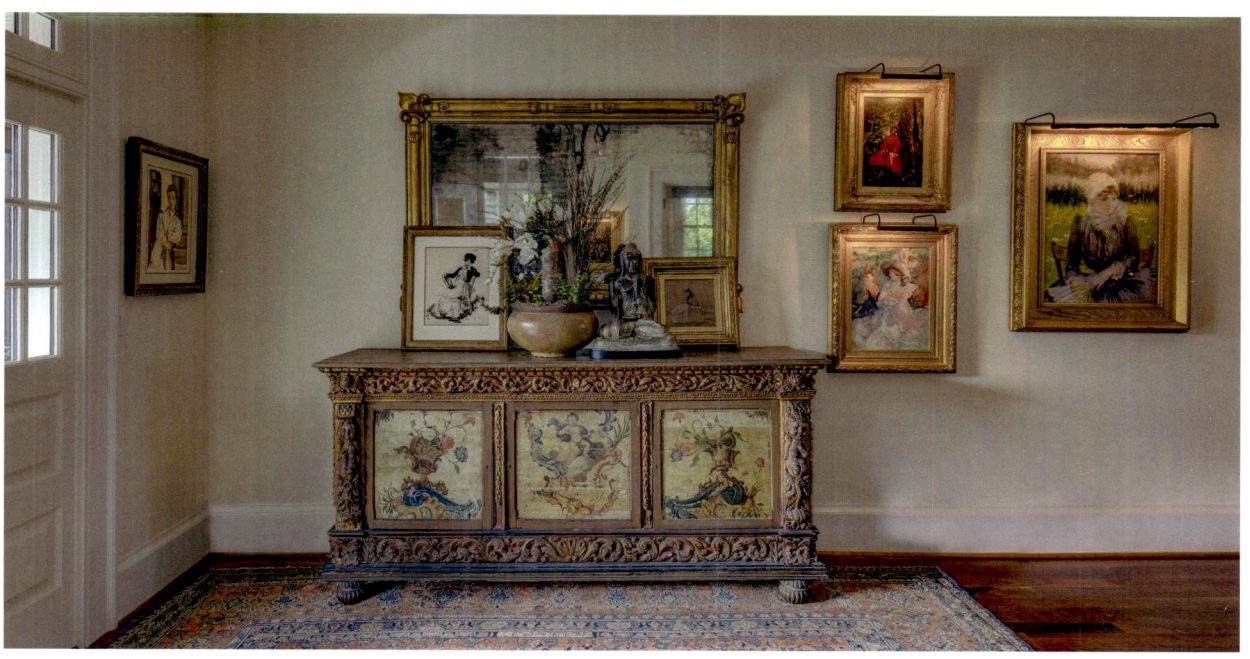

amounted to an almost daily revelation to us: That art might be an investment, but it's unlike any other—it's an investment that pays dividends in pleasure every time your eye falls upon it (fig. 3). It thus offers rewards that cannot be measured in dollars and cents.

When I'm asked about my favorite pieces, two immediately come to mind. From the moment we saw it, both Macon and I loved the Charles Sprague Pearce painting that graces the cover of this book. We were in New York visiting the annual American Art Fair with Bill Hennessey, the Chrysler Museum's director. Bill approached us, exclaiming there was a painting we had to see, and took us to a piece that, indeed, instantly grabbed our hearts. Even its frame was gorgeous and original to the painting. We bought it without the slightest hesitation.

Another painting that immediately spoke to us was the William Merritt Chase pastel titled *At Her Ease*, in which Chase used his wife as his model. Chase's fascination with Japanese-inspired design is evident—his subject is clad in a blue kimono, for starters—and the painting's deceptive simplicity masks a story that's left for the viewer to decipher. I have my own ideas about what that story might be. And, of course, Macon and I have our own stories woven into our love for the piece as well.

Today I look back with pride and gratitude at the collection we built together before my beloved husband passed away in 2017. My heart brims with appreciation not only for the merits of the art itself but for the personal memories each piece evoked in us. Collecting these paintings has been an incredible journey, and we both enjoyed every minute of it.

We were fortunate to be in a position to have amassed these great works and feel genuinely privileged to share our deep love of them with the Chrysler Museum. I am confident they will bring joy and enlightenment to all who behold them. More than anything, I hope that in years to come, the Museum's visitors find pleasure in the stories they tell and leave with their own stories entwined with those of the work—that they'll carry something of these masterworks with them and leave a little piece of themselves behind.

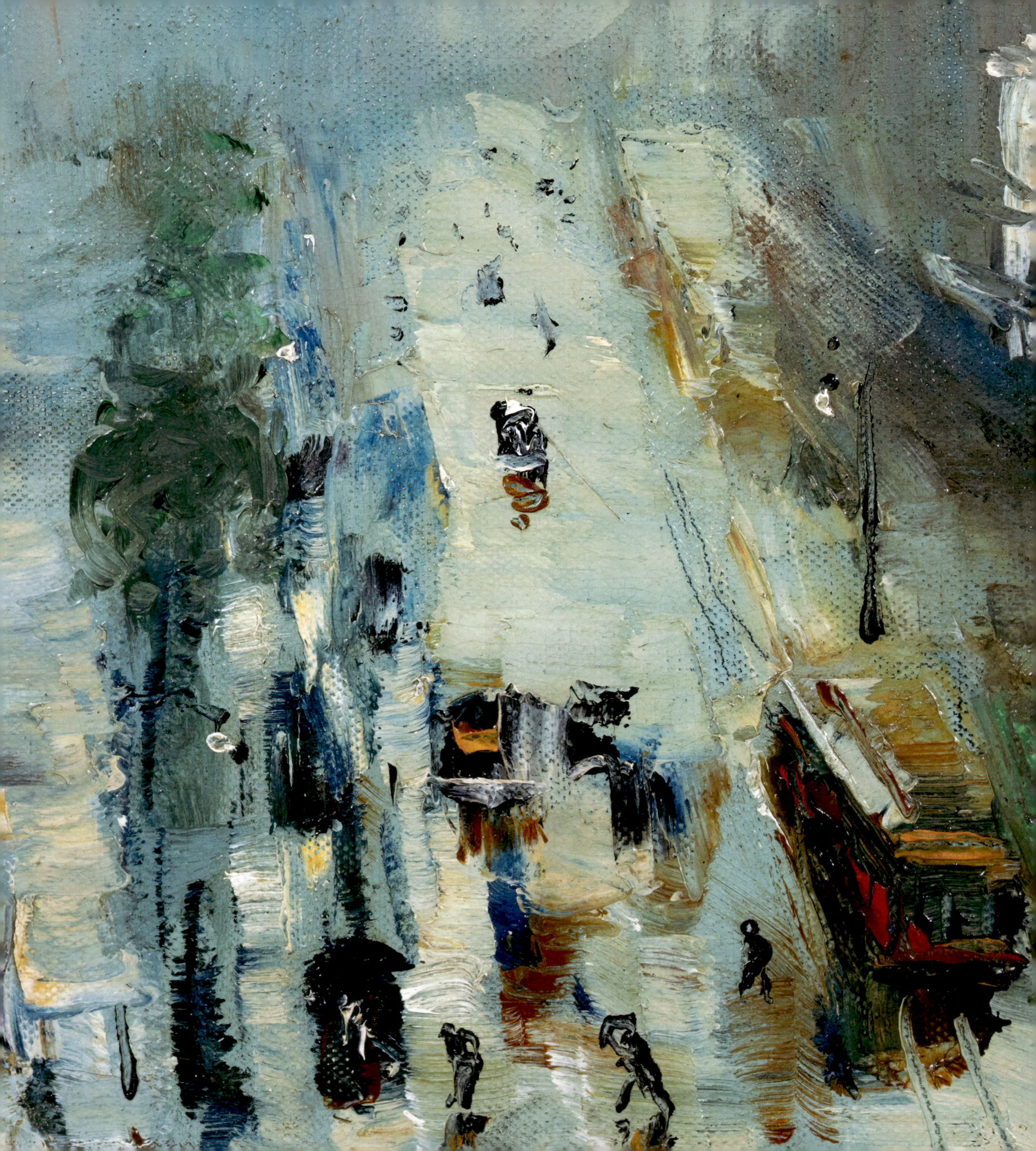

Introduction

Corey Piper

ALL COLLECTIONS, WHETHER COMPILED by grand museums or formed by private collectors, have the effect of compressing time and rearranging distance. Disparate artists and artworks are suddenly linked across the years, while long epochs and movements are coalesced along a single wall or across just a few pages within a catalogue. The Brock Collection spans around one hundred years, from just before the Civil War to the heights of the Cold War and the Civil Rights Movement. Encompassing fifty-seven artists and more than seventy-five works of art, the Brock Collection encapsulates an era of rapid transformation in the visual arts, an evolution parallel with the tectonic shifts in American political and social life during the same period. While the collection necessarily reflects the choices made by collectors Macon and Joan Brock, in its focus on the work of artists of a shared nationality across the course of a pivotal century, it offers keen insights into the aesthetic and social forces that shaped the course of American art history.

Across its varied entries, this catalogue offers a close examination of the individual works of art contained within an expansive collection. Rather than a linear survey, or encyclopedic compendium of the history of American art, the groupings of objects form clusters or constellations of artworks that probe connections between the artists during their time and beyond. In these groupings resonances and affinities reveal themselves, demonstrating the interconnectedness of artists with varying aesthetic interests and political concerns. Artists with shared aesthetic foundations at a certain point in their careers often diverged in style or subject matter. However, one can frequently find points of connection in work created at different phases of their lives, despite the separations of time and distance. Take, for example, the case of two artists found within the Brock Collection, John Singer Sargent and James Carroll Beckwith. The artists first formed a close friendship as young art students in the studio of the esteemed French painter Carolus-Duran. Beckwith captured the intensity of the studio in a lively sketch which depicts Sargent working at his easel alongside another American painter, Frank Fowler (fig. 1).[1]

Beckwith and Sargent thrived under the progressive tutelage of Carolus-Duran, who emphasized painting over drawing, and working with oil and brush, directly from nature. The works featured in the Brock Collection by these artists date from long after their student years and are separated by more than two decades. They chart the different paths that each artist followed to artistic maturity after concluding their intense training period together. Beckwith's *The Grey Gown* (p. 41), created in Normandy following his student years in Paris, reflects the artist's early exuberance at working out of doors. The drawing's ambitious scale for a work in pastel hints at the leading role the artist would play in American progressive art circles, including the foundation of the Society of Painters in Pastel. The three works by Sargent chart the artist's move away from the portraiture and official patronage that sustained his reputation following his experiences in Carolus-Duran's studio. Sargent's watercolors and oils demonstrate an increasingly direct and personal approach to his subjects. The painterly flourish deployed in works like *Olives at Corfu* (p. 72) reveals a glimpse of the artistic foundations that continued to connect Sargent to his friend and former classmate despite the divergent trajectories of their careers.

As a collection focused on American art, the artists in the Brock Collection are united generally around a common nationality. Rather than an essential characteristic, national identity among these artists functioned as a category (among many others such as gender, race, and class) that could be performed through a variety of means to achieve a range of professional and personal objectives. This catalogue includes artists born in the United States, as well as those originally from Britain, Germany, Sweden, Poland, and elsewhere. While some artists born in the United States, like James Jebusa Shannon or James McNeill Whistler, settled permanently abroad, others, like Rockwell Kent, traveled widely but invariably returned to a permanent home in the United States. Even those whose biographies are more firmly rooted within the United States, like Charles Burchfield or Edgar Payne, still engaged with art and stylistic trends from abroad like Impressionism and Fauvism. Across the century, people traveled with increasing ease, allowing artists of relatively modest means to access great collections, and especially training, abroad. Moreover, a modern and sophisticated art media flourished in the United States over the century that allowed artists and the public more broadly to develop greater fluency in art from international sources, particularly progressive currents in Europe.

By the latter decades of the nineteenth century, adolescent cultural institutions like the National Academy of Design, and offshoots like the Society of American Artists and Art Students League, offered a wealth of education and exhibiting opportunities to American artists. Still, nearly all of the artists in this catalogue traveled abroad to Europe for formal training or self-guided study. In Europe, American artists strove to prove themselves in more cosmopolitan circles and bolster their résumés for collectors back home who valued European sophistication above all. The parallel imperatives to both demonstrate fluency with the most up-to-date European styles, and embody a "national" spirit or character, drove a dynamic creative tension that pushed American art in exciting new

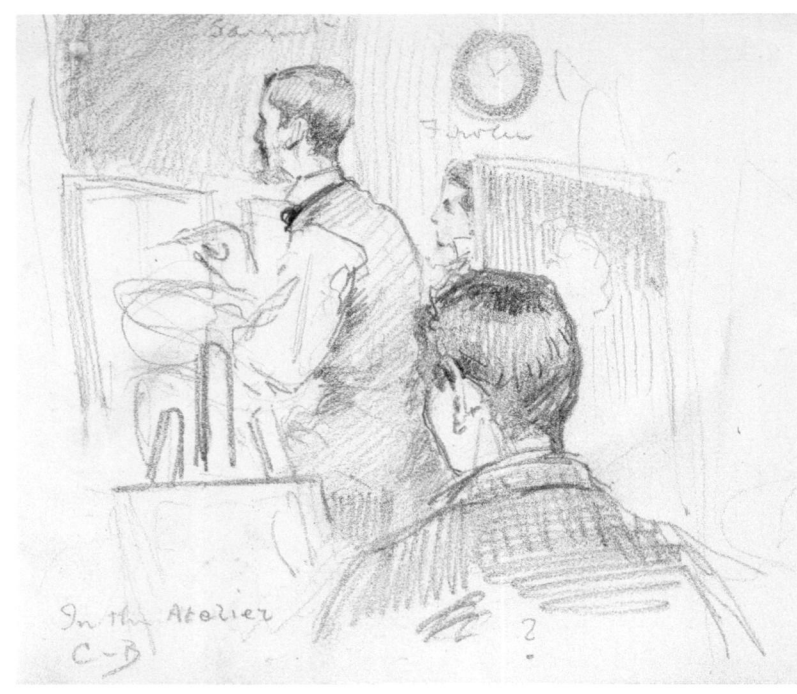

FIG. 1 James Carroll Beckwith, *In the Atelier of Carolus-Duran*, 1874–76. Graphite on ivory paper, 3 13/16 × 4¼ in. New-York Historical Society, Gift of the National Academy of Design, 1935.85.2.245

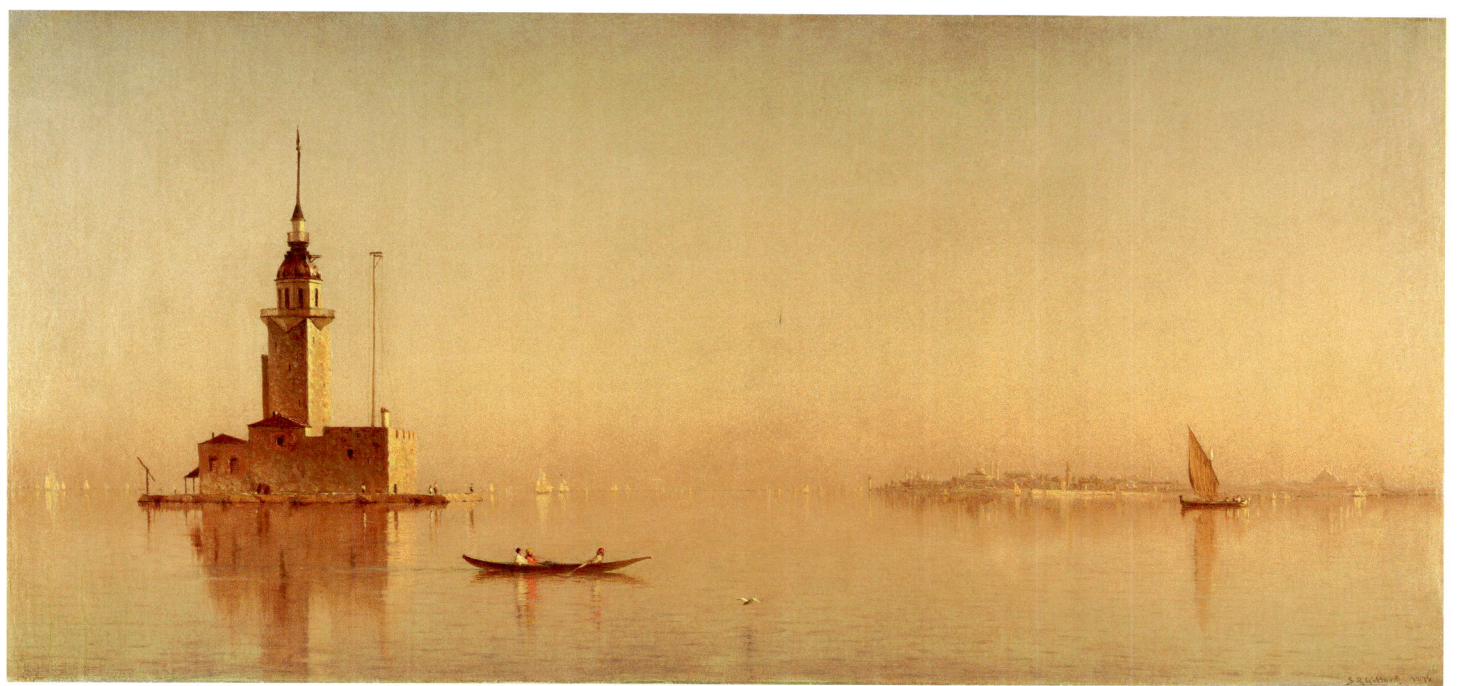

FIG. 2 Sanford Robinson Gifford, *Leander's Tower on the Bosporus*, 1876. Oil on canvas, 19 1/16 × 39 1/8 in. Harvard Art Museums/Fogg Museum, Bequest of Mrs. William Hayes Fogg, 1895.716

directions. Painters like Sanford Robinson Gifford, a leader of the quintessentially "American" Hudson River School, traveled widely in Europe and the Mediterranean and subsequently developed a distinct style of painting that could equate the disparate landscapes of New York in *Tappan Zee* (p. 25) and the Ottoman Empire in *Leander's Tower on the Bosporus* (fig. 2). Though the architecture and topography vary slightly, the compositional format and pictorial language used to depict the American and Near-Eastern landscapes appear nearly identical. This push-pull dynamic continued to propel American artists and critics through the early decades of the twentieth century. Marsden Hartley's *Volupté* (p. 131), painted in New Mexico in the midst of the artist's deep engagement with the Southwestern landscape, also carries markers of his embrace of European Modernism. While he was displaced from Europe due to the conflict of World War I, the painting bears traces of his engagement with the European avant-garde, with its references to the work of Henri Matisse and Paul Cézanne.[2]

The entries in this volume follow a general chronological order, which proceeds from the mid-nineteenth through the mid-twentieth centuries. Rather than a strict chronology, works sometimes appear out of temporal order to group artists and artworks that belong to broad movements or address similar aesthetic concerns. The entries begin around the era of the Civil War, when the National Academy of Design served as the key venue in the promotion of a national school of landscape painting. Two key figures of this movement, Gifford and John Frederick Kensett mark the transition from the dominance of landscape painting to the postbellum years in which more varied styles and subjects competed on the walls of the Academy. Figure and genre painters like John George Brown, Seymour Joseph Guy, and Winslow Homer all found success at the National Academy.

Through the 1870s the artists that followed, like William Merritt Chase, Charles Sprague Pearce, and Julian Alden Weir, challenged the authority and conformity of the National Academy. These artists honed their craft in Europe and wore their hard-earned international accolades as badges of honor back home. The Brock Collection is particularly rich in chronicling episodes of American artists abroad around the turn of the twentieth century. In addition to expatriates and inveterate travelers, the catalogue includes numerous examples of artists who lived and worked in the artists' colony at Giverny, like Mary Fairchild MacMonnies, Willard LeRoy Metcalf, Karl Albert Buehr, and others. The entries also shed light on the experience of women artists who sought training and professional opportunity in Europe. Helen Corson Hovenden and MacMonnies enrolled at the progressive Académie Julian in Paris and found success exhibiting at the Salon, while Mary Cassatt participated in the groundbreaking Impressionist exhibitions and forged an innovative and highly personal style in her paintings and prints.

Eventually the challenge posed by forward-thinking artists, steeped in European styles, fractured the National Academy's power and influence within the American art establishment. In 1898 several artists banded together to form the Ten American Painters, who mounted their own exhibition away from the more conservative National Academy. The group's organizers included several artists found in the Brock Collection, including John Henry Twachtman, Childe Hassam, and Weir. Twachtman's highly impressionistic *Spring* (p. 97) was included in the group's first exhibition at Durand-Ruel Galleries in New York. In Boston painters like William McGregor Paxton and Frank Weston Benson, trained in Europe and enamored of old master painters, formed their own loosely organized movement. The Boston School, as it came to be known, embraced tradition in terms of subject matter and composition while they also welcomed more painterly approaches borrowed from Impressionism and other progressive modes.

As impressionist-inspired styles became more widely accepted in the United States, subsequent generations challenged the new status quo. Young and brash Realist painters like George Bellows and George Luks joined together with fellow artists to form "The Eight," a group united less by a shared style and more by their commitment to ushering in a new avant-garde. American painters like Max Weber and Hartley, who engaged the most up-to-date modern styles they encountered in Europe, like Cubism and Fauvism, propelled American Modernism even further. At the dawn of World War I, the Armory Show introduced European Modernism to a wide American audience and also showcased the work of the United States' own progressive artists like Arthur B. Davies, Leon Kroll, Charles Sheeler, and many other artists included in this catalogue. Through the twentieth century, American painting diverged in numerous directions, many of which are traced through the works in the Brock Collection. Thomas Hart Benton and Reginald Marsh helped give rise to a social realist style known as Regionalism, while other painters like Kent or John Whorf defied easy categorization into a defined school or movement. Through World War II, the works in the Brock Collection by Milton Avery, Sally Michel Avery, and Fairfield Porter chart the persistence of representation in painting, despite the overwhelming turn toward abstraction in American art.

In addition to artists grouped by period, style, and movement, the catalogue also contains focused explorations of works linked by media and subject matter. A group of dazzling pastels by Chase, Beckwith, Weir, Whistler, and Thomas Wilmer Dewing illustrates the important role that this media had in linking progressive-minded artists at the end of the nineteenth century. The revival of pastel among American artists and audiences culminated in the establishment of the short-lived but influential Society of Painters in Pastel. Similarly, works in watercolor by Homer, Sargent, and Burchfield demonstrate the central importance of the medium, from the establishment of the American Watercolor Society in 1866 to the rise of American Modernism in the twentieth century.

Several key subjects recur throughout the catalogue, demonstrating the persistence of particular themes throughout the history of American art. Perhaps most heavily represented in the Brock Collection are depictions of elegant women engaged in leisure or contemplation, a motif the art historian Zachary Ross dubbed the "Woman at Home."[3] This proved an enduring subject matter throughout the Gilded Age, and several artists like John White Alexander, Paxton, and Dewing made it a specialty. The Brock Collection also traces the course of American landscape after the decline of the Hudson River School, including key examples of American Impressionism. Artists who traveled in France, like John Leslie Breck, Metcalf, and Hassam, translated the lessons they learned from the French Barbizons and Impressionists to depictions of bucolic American scenery and even urban streetscapes. The catalogue also features a selection of landscape painters who settled in and focused on the American West, including Edgar Payne, William Wendt, and Granville Redmond. Among the twentieth-century works, still life features as an important venue for exploring principles of Modernism, which was embraced by a diverse slate of artists, including Hartley, Sheeler, Porter, and Jane Peterson. These artists' devotion to the genre demonstrates the persistence of still life as a critical subject for painters through the twentieth century and a vehicle for experimentation.

The Brock Collection was formed in Hampton Roads, Virginia, close to the Chrysler Museum of Art, where Macon and Joan Brock served for many years as volunteers, leaders, and supporters. From the Museum's founding as the Norfolk Museum of Arts and Sciences, American art played an important role as a pillar of the institution's permanent collection.[4] Early gifts from the Norfolk Society of the Arts and other local supporters added works by contemporary American artists like Helen Maria Turner, Daniel Chester French, and Walter Emerson Baum, and in 1946 the Museum received its largest bequest to date, comprised of paintings and drawings by American artist Susan Watkins. Through the next several decades, the American collection grew with key additions in a piecemeal fashion. The acquisition of important works by Charles Willson Peale, Jasper Francis Cropsey, Chase, and other major figures of American art bolstered the collection and established American art as a vital component of the Museum's collection.

Walter P. Chrysler, Jr.'s, transformative gift in 1971 affirmed the central importance of American art to the Museum's collection. While his appreciation of American art developed later than his taste for European Modernism and old masters, Chrysler possessed unusual foresight. American art was not widely sought after by major collectors or given serious weight by academic and museum institutions until later in the 1970s when the Bicentennial spurred a revival of interest in historical American art. Chrysler's gift elevated the stature of American art at the Museum and for the first time allowed for the presentation of a broad survey of American art history from the colonial period through World War II. Canonical artists and movements dominated, with heavy emphases on colonial portraiture, antebellum genre scenes, Hudson River School landscape, the Ashcan School, and Regionalism. In his various leadership roles at the Museum in subsequent years, Chrysler continued to build the American collection, adding works by Thomas Cole, Homer, and John Singleton Copley, among others.

The Brock Collection complements and supplements the Chrysler's American art holdings in fascinating and compelling combinations that elevate the overall stature of the Museum's collection. For example, as a pendant with the Chrysler's majestic Albert Bierstadt, *The Emerald Pool* (fig. 3), Kensett's *Bash Bish Falls* (p. 23) depicts a similar type of geologic feature, a rocky mountain pool, but provides a counter to the sublime grandeur that sometimes dominates the perception of the Hudson River School. Kensett's landscape instead revels in the minute and infinite complexity of detail found in nature. Together, the two works illustrate the range of pictorial modes American landscape painters employed in their exploration of the United States' natural bounty. Likewise, the Brock Collection's Bellows, *Upper Broadway* (p. 117), builds upon a strong group of work by the artist at the Chrysler. While the Museum's collection includes examples of Bellows's figure painting, landscapes, and even a World War I scene, it lacked an urban setting, a signature subject on which the artist's reputation was first established as a promising Realist painter.

In addition to refining the collection's strengths, the Brock Gift brings completely new dimensions to the Chrysler's American art holdings, adding media and movements not previously present in the collection. These include artists

FIG. 3 Albert Bierstadt, *The Emerald Pool*, 1870. Oil on canvas, 76½ × 119 in. Chrysler Museum of Art, Bequest of Walter P. Chrysler, Jr., 89.59

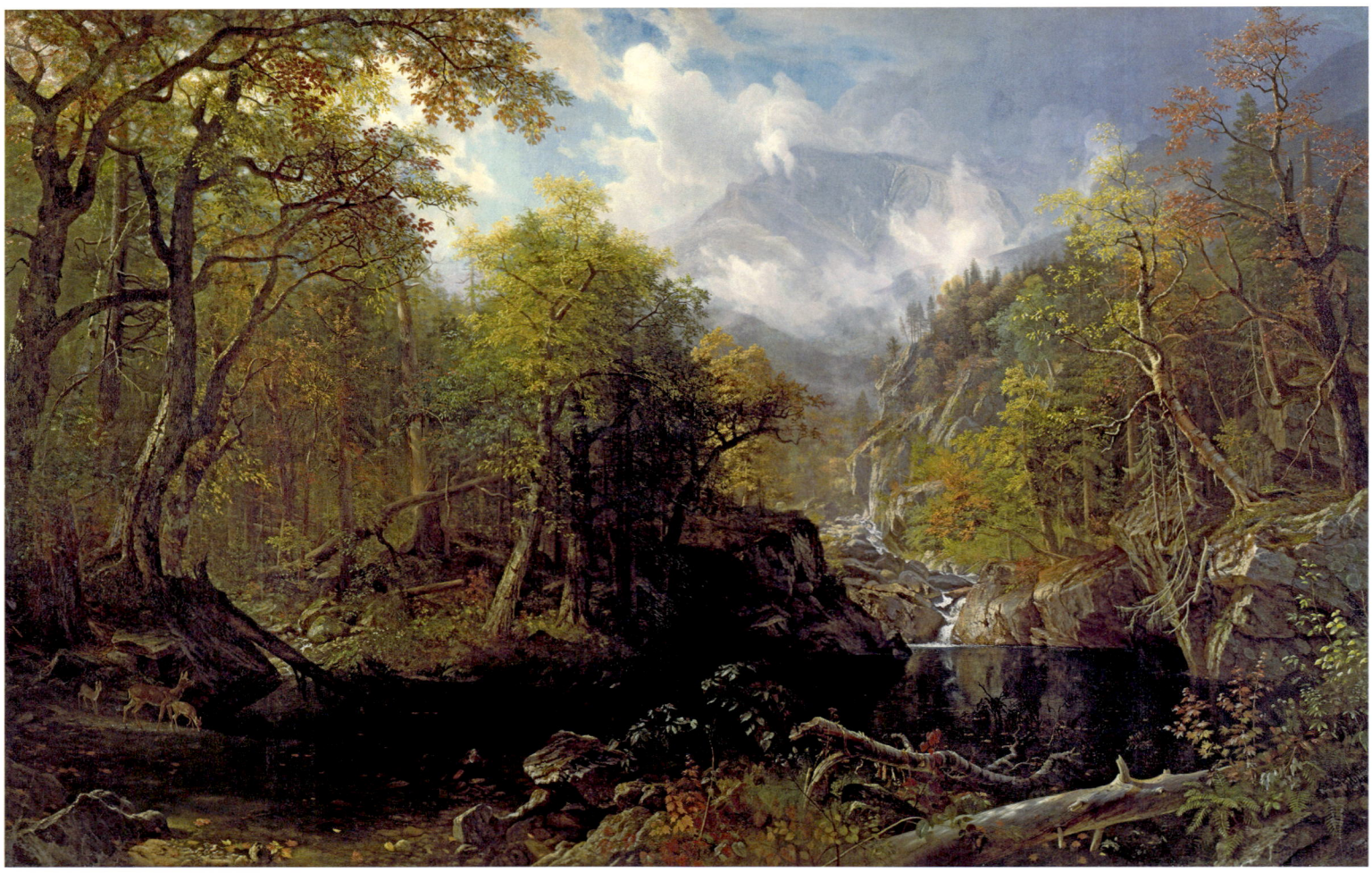

associated with the Aesthetic Movement, as well as American Modernists like Hartley and Weber. The Brock Collection is particularly strong in works on paper. Key artworks help illustrate the rise of both watercolor and pastel as important media in American art, where leading artists like Homer, Sargent, and Whistler made some of their most experimental and captivating works. In all, the Brock Gift will add nineteen completely new artists to the Chrysler's collection, as well as artwork in new media by another ten artists. Throughout the catalogue, the works the Brocks have given and promised to the Chrysler are indicated in the credit lines found with the entries and in the checklist. This selection, crafted from a collection of museum-quality works, was designed to complement and enhance the Museum's American art program by avoiding duplication, filling in key gaps, and adding superlative works by artists already found within the collection.

As collectors, Macon and Joan Brock exercised great discipline and prudence in assembling a collection that both traced the contours and probed the interstices of a focused period of American art history. The esteemed art historians who authored the insightful commentaries throughout this catalogue build upon a legacy of scholarship in American art at the Chrysler, one that has been greatly enhanced by the generosity of the Brocks. The gift of many of these works to the Chrysler Museum of Art attests to the Brock's keen foresight in building a collection for the benefit of the public in Hampton Roads and beyond.

1. Roberta J. M. Olson, *Drawn by New York: Six Centuries of Watercolors and Drawings at the New-York Historical Society* (London: D Giles Limited, 2008), cat. no. 120i, 358.

2. See Chelsea Pierce's entry in this volume. The title *Volupté* is likely a reference or homage to Matisse's *Luxe, Calme et Volupté* (1904; Musée d'Orsay, Paris). For the foundational account of the relationship between American artists and Europe during the period, see Wanda M. Corn, *The Great American Thing: Modern Art and National Identity, 1915–1935* (Berkeley: University of California Press, 1999).

3. Zachary Ross, "Rest for the Weary: American Nervousness and the Aesthetics of Repose," in *Women on the Verge: The Culture of Neurasthenia in Nineteenth-Century America* (Palo Alto, CA: The Iris and B. Gerald Cantor Center for the Visual Arts at Stanford University, 2004), 21–35. The literature on the subject of Gilded Age artists' fascination with female subjects is extensive. For selected readings, see Bailey Van Hook, *Angels of Art: Women and Art in American Society, 1876–1914* (University Park: Pennsylvania State University Press, 1996); Beverly Gordon, "Women's Domestic Body: The Conceptual Conflation of Women and Interiors in the Industrial Age," *Winterthur Portfolio* 30, no. 1 (Spring 1995): 281–99; and Martha Banta, *Imaging American Women: Idea and Ideals in Cultural History* (New York: Columbia University Press, 1987).

4. For a history of the American Art Collection at the Chrysler, see Martha N. Hagood, "American Art at the Chrysler Museum," in Martha N. Hagood and Jefferson C. Harrison, *American Art at the Chrysler Museum: Selected Paintings, Sculpture, and Drawings* (Norfolk, VA: Chrysler Museum of Art, 2005), 15–17.

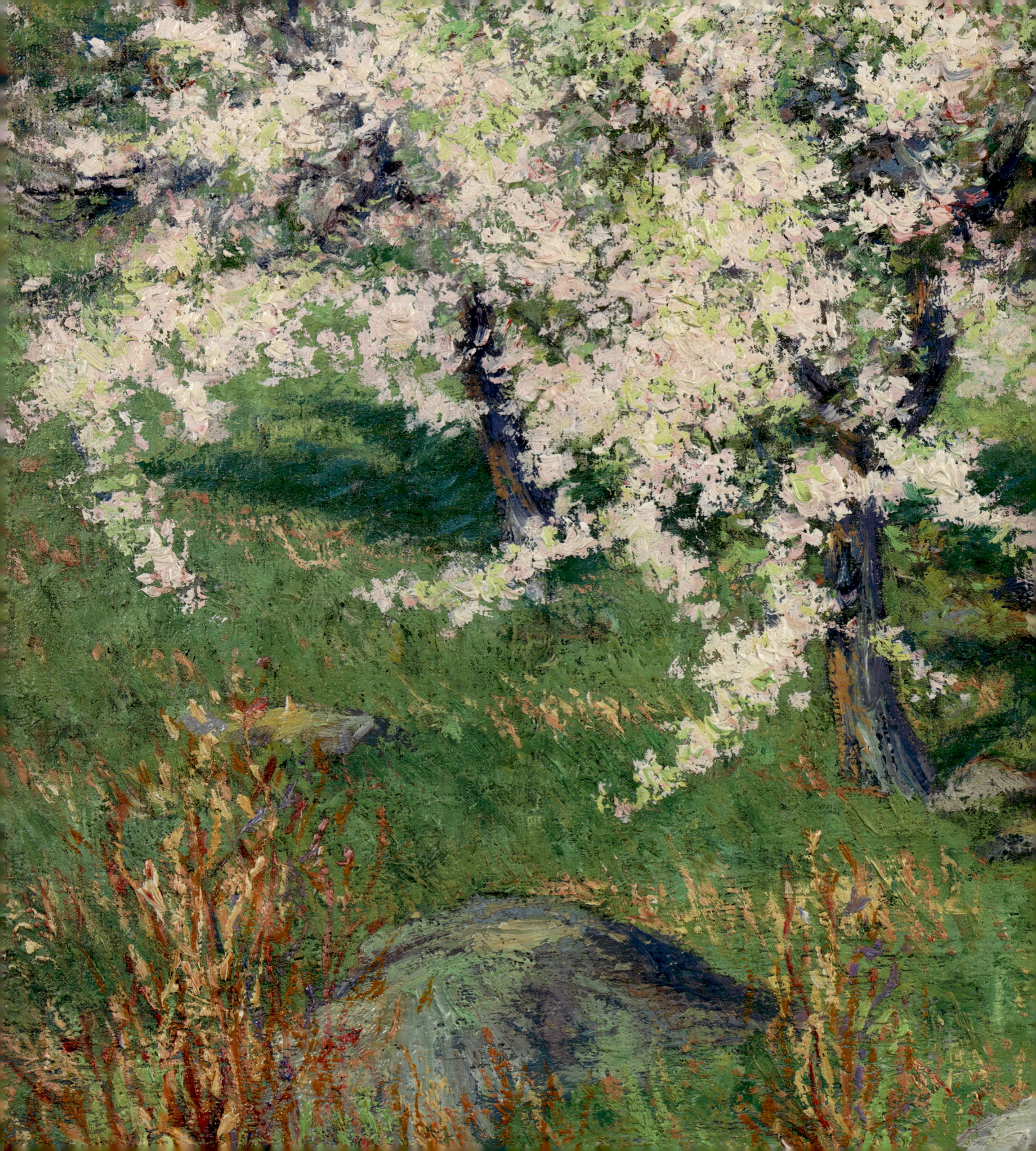

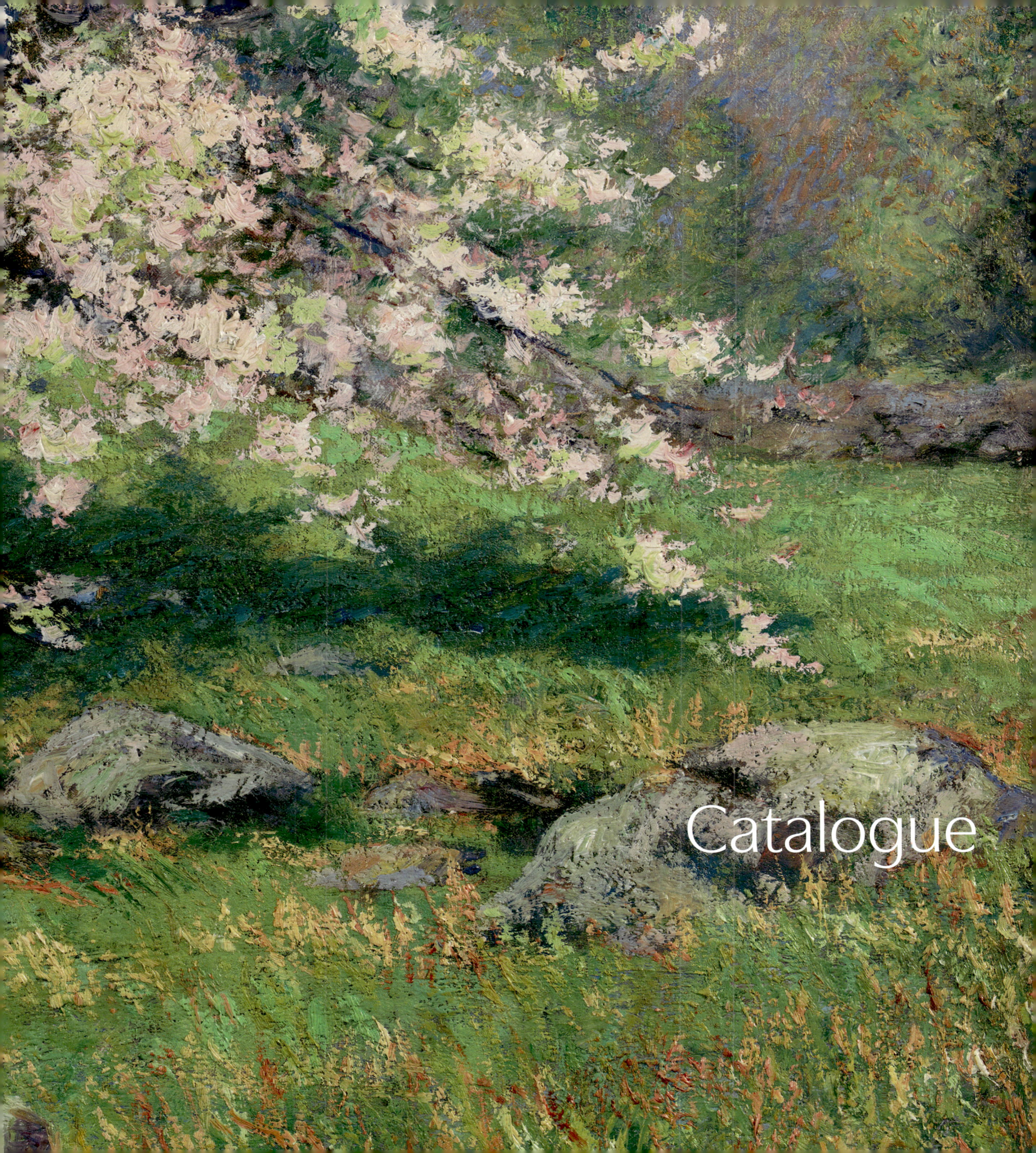

Catalogue

John Frederick Kensett
AMERICAN, 1816–1872

Bash Bish Falls, ca. 1860

Oil on canvas

18 × 22¼ inches

Gift of the Macon and Joan Brock Collection of American Art, 2023.4.2

DURING THE 1850S AND 60S, John Frederick Kensett captured the landscape around western Massachusetts's Bash Bish Falls many times, making it one of the most frequent subjects in his art.[1] Located around 120 miles north of New York City, other artists associated with the Hudson River School, including Asher B. Durand, also painted the site. A popular tourist destination, the falls offered a wealth of natural visual delights as the mountain stream of Bash Bish Brook carves its way westward, creating a dramatic gorge and numerous cascades and mountain pools. Though the scene in Kensett's *Bash Bish Falls* appears completely devoid of figures, the artist has included a rustic footbridge spanning the chasm in the distance, a picturesque acknowledgment of the site's frequent human visitors.

Kensett chose a vantage point among the stream's lower falls rather than focusing on the more imposing vertical drop of the canyon's largest waterfall, which offered the most dramatic attraction for visitors to the site (fig. 1). His view instead revels in the abundance of varied natural forms and the experiential effects of being fully immersed in nature. An author of an 1855 travelogue described the delightful mingling of sights and sounds to be found among the falls: "It was a glorious spot there, underneath the old hills, with the precipices towering away into the heavens on every side and the torrent ringing the while in your ear a low deep monotone."[2] This painting also differs in its horizontal orientation from most of Kensett's other depictions of Bash Bish Falls, which are oriented vertically to accentuate the steep drop of the falls or the towering walls of the valley. Beyond adding a bit of variety to the composition of a subject the artist depicted over and over again, the reorientation of the frame allowed Kensett a more expansive view of the geology of the site and the dense foliage that envelops the rocky stream.

Among American landscape painters, Kensett had long been singled out by critics as a precise and accomplished painter of rock forms. In 1850 a critic for the *Literary World* proclaimed, "As a painter of rocks we know of no one superior to Kensett."[3] In a period in which the understanding of the processes that shaped the earth's elemental features was rapidly developing, his keen interest in the intricacies of geologic structures resonated with both popular and scientific audiences attuned to such details. Kensett's geologic fascinations were shared by many of his fellow Hudson River School artists, as well as European artists ranging from John Ruskin to Gustave Courbet.

The massive rock forms that flank the stream and pool in *Bash Bish Falls* showcase Kensett's skill at translating the multifaceted surfaces and immense mass of stone to painted canvas. In 1858 the artist sent eight paintings to the Annual Exhibition of the National Academy of Design, including another, earlier version of *Bash Bish Falls* (National Academy of Design Museum). In *The Crayon* a critic hailed Kensett's ability to balance the seemingly infinite details of nature, writing, "His perception of the poetry and harmony of nature . . . is remarkably subtle and delicate."[4] Rather than merely a study of geology, the more expansive composition of the Brocks' *Bash Bish Falls* presents a vision of an interconnected nature, which inspires awe through the interplay between water, rock, plants, and trees, rather than an emphasis on a single dominant natural feature.

COREY PIPER

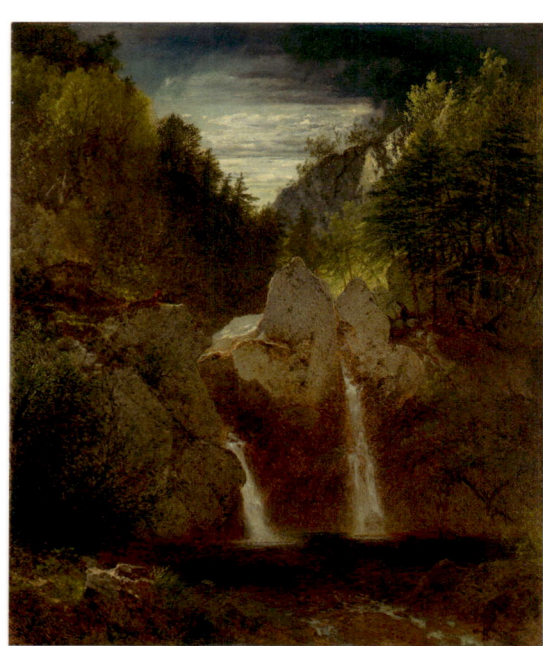

FIG. 1 John Frederick Kensett, *Rocky Pool, Bash Bish Falls*, 1865. Oil on paper, 30 × 25 in. Yale University Art Gallery, Estate of James W. Fosburgh, B.A. 1933, M.A. 1935, 1979.13.2

1. See examples at the Museum of Fine Arts, Boston, National Academy of Design Museum, Yale University Art Gallery, The Butler Institute of American Art, and Lyman Allen Art Museum, among others.

2. J. T. Headley, "Bash-Bish Falls," *Christian Parlor Magazine* (May 1, 1855), 114.

3. "The National Academy," *Literary World* 6 (April 27, 1850): 423.

4. "Sketchings," *The Crayon* 5 (May 1858): 146.

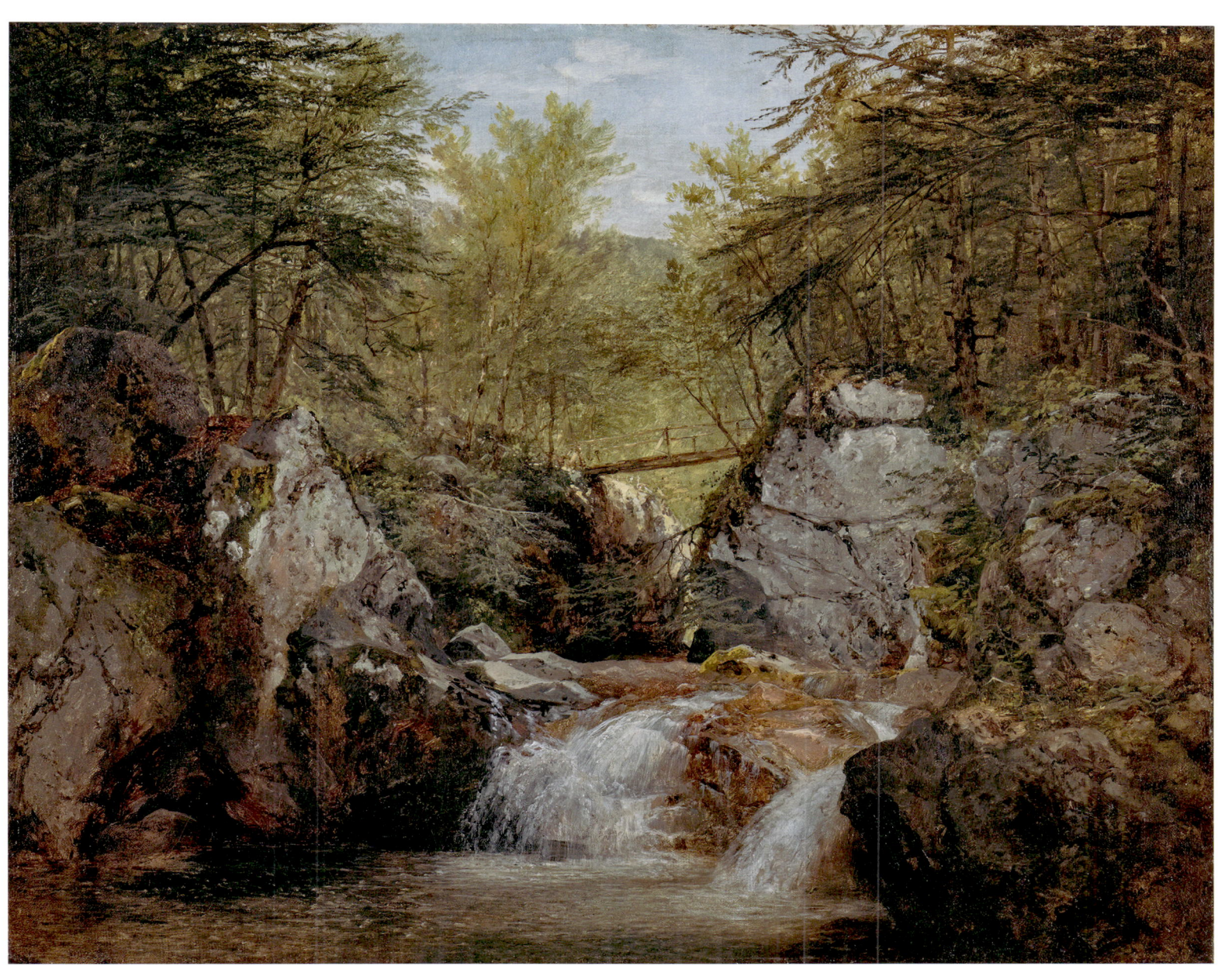

Sanford Robinson Gifford

AMERICAN, 1823–1880

Tappan Zee, 1879–80

Oil on canvas

17¼ × 36¼ inches

Promised Gift of the Macon and Joan Brock Collection
of American Art

THE PLACID STRETCH of New York's Hudson River at Tappan Zee is situated around thirty miles north of Manhattan, where the river expands to a width of nearly two miles. In *Tappan Zee* Gifford takes this expanse as his principal subject, using the broad, horizontal canvas to explore the subtle effects of light and color of the roseate sky reflected upon the nearly still water. Amidst the exploration of color and atmosphere, only a few areas of greater detail can be found around the margins. At right a narrow sliver of land, dotted with autumnal trees and gently animated by the steam rising from a slow-moving train, reaches into the water. The distant boats, with their white sails reflecting the angle of the early morning light, are framed by the imposing cliffs of the Palisades along the river's western banks. A large void of water and sky forms most of the composition's center, punctuated by a simple skiff with two fishermen aboard.

Despite its lake-like appearance here, the Hudson River served as a bustling commercial artery for New York and the nation for much of the nineteenth century. The opening of the Erie Canal in 1825 positioned New York City at the nexus of the United States' waterborne transportation network. By the time of Gifford's depiction in the late 1870s, the railroad had largely supplanted ships as the primary avenue of conveyance for goods and travelers along the river. For the group of landscape painters who came to be known as the Hudson River School, the Hudson offered a pathway to landscape subjects that many audiences embraced as emblematic of the natural bounty, rugged spirit, and noble character of the American nation. In turn the scenes of wilderness and sublime landscapes from New York, New England, the western United States, and beyond were eagerly consumed by metropolitan audiences in New York and other growing American cities.

As artists and tourists traversed the Hudson to more distant locales like the Catskills and the Adirondacks, the river itself remained a compelling subject for Gifford. Ten years earlier he had pictured nearly the same stretch in *An Indian Summer's Day on the Hudson—Tappan Zee* (1868; private collection).[1] Among his Hudson River views, *Tappan Zee* was singled out as one of his "Chief Pictures," a group of works that the artist identified as his most significant and exemplary paintings.[2] In images like this one, Gifford distinguished himself from many of his peers among American landscape painters, like Albert Bierstadt or Frederic Edwin Church, who reveled in the precise and naturalistic description of detail.

Gifford died not long after completing this canvas in 1880, succumbing to a relatively brief but intense malarial infection. This painting was included in the monumental memorial exhibition mounted at the Metropolitan Museum of Art the following year. In the introduction to the catalogue, the artist John Ferguson Weir eulogized his friend Gifford and his unique landscape vision. In a passage that could readily apply to Gifford's late work *Tappan Zee*, Weir wrote, "He recognized in the landscape that its expression, for him, rested mainly in its atmosphere. He rendered this atmosphere palpably, with very subtle sympathy, with great delicacy."[3] For an artist with a long and varied career—Gifford served in the Union Army during the Civil War and traveled widely throughout Europe and the United States—it was the painter's simple clarity of vision and radically restrained approach to compositions like this one that endured as a truly distinctive contribution to American landscape art.

COREY PIPER

1. See no. 46 in Kevin J. Avery and Franklin Kelly, eds., *Hudson River School Visions: The Landscapes of Sanford R. Gifford* (New Haven, CT: Yale University Press, 2003), 190–91.

2. See Ila Weiss, *Poetic Landscape: The Art and Experience of Sanford R. Gifford* (Newark: University of Delaware Press, 1987), 327–30.

3. John Ferguson Weir, *A Memorial Catalogue of the Paintings of Sanford Robinson Gifford, N.A.* (New York: The Metropolitan Museum of Art, 1881), 9.

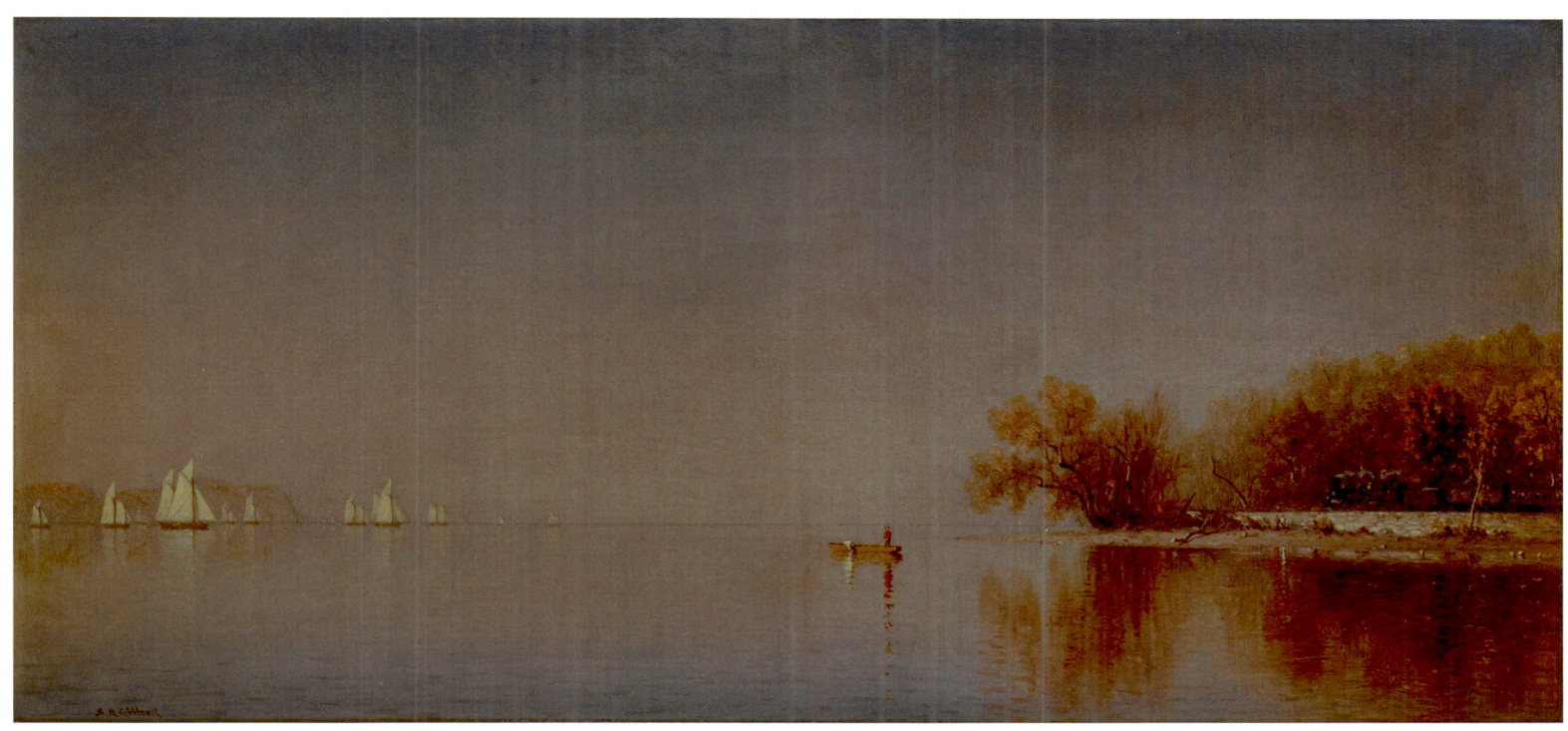

John La Farge
AMERICAN, 1835–1910

Flowers in a Lacquer Bowl, 1861

Oil on canvas

13½ × 22½ inches

Promised Gift of the Macon and Joan Brock Collection
of American Art

AT THE TIME OF HIS DEATH, American artist and decorator John La Farge had gained a towering reputation as a man of considerable artistic talent and intelligence. "He was our sole 'Old Master,' our sole type of genius that went out with the Italian Renaissance," effused his biographer Royal Cortissoz.[1] La Farge was a true creator, experimenting and innovating in a wide range of artistic fields: painting, illustration, stained glass, and design (fig. 1). Born in New York, La Farge had a cultured upbringing that included embarking on a grand tour of Europe in 1856, as well as a brief stint in the Paris atelier of artist Thomas Couture. After the death of his father, La Farge felt able to leave an unsatisfactory career in law and devote himself entirely to the pursuit of art. He eventually settled in Newport, Rhode Island, briefly studying with William Morris Hunt before moving on to teach himself independently.

Still life paintings show La Farge "at his best and most beguiling."[2] This theme was one that the artist continued to paint throughout his lifetime, and it was his central focus in the 1860s and again in the 1880s. La Farge treated his subject with a softness and mystery that was at odds with the crisp techniques used by most of his contemporaries working in the still life genre, creating a sense of atmosphere with loose brushwork and strong color.[3] The sensuous beauty and quiet mystery with which La Farge rendered his still lifes make them as arresting today as they were during his lifetime. A student of the artist remarked, "One feels that all flowers yielded their most intimate beauty and expression, told a secret to this wizard hidden from every other painter."[4]

Flowers in a Lacquer Bowl represents the first tabletop still life La Farge ever produced, and it demonstrates the artist's early interest in capturing light and air that anticipated the European Impressionists.[5] The canvas was painted in the dining room of his Newport home, on a drop-leaf table placed near a window; "instead of arranging my subject, which is the usual studio way, I had it placed for me by chance, with any background and any light."[6] The wide, shallow lacquer bowl is shadowy beneath a spread of cut greenery and flowers with clusters of tiny blossoms in hues of purple, red, and white.[7] A white curtain is pulled back from a window, simultaneously reflecting the room's own light onto the tabletop and revealing a hazy view of the garden landscape outside.

The atmospheric and deep-toned painting *Hollyhocks* is considered one of La Farge's most dramatic nature-in-nature compositions.[8] Delicate white and red flowers stretch on thick stalks toward the sky, the sense of verticality and dynamism heightened by the tall and narrow field of the panel itself. The subject matter and composition, as well as notions of design and space, take their inspiration from Japanese prints by Hokusai, Hiroshige, and others that La Farge began to collect in the early 1860s. The moody coloration—with its deep, shadowy greens—and the decorative details of La Farge's work also reflect his early fascination with the aesthetic sensibilities of the British Pre-Raphaelites.

La Farge focused again on still life painting in the early 1880s, this time choosing to experiment with the new medium of watercolor over traditional oil paint. Watercolor allowed him to investigate further the theories of color and light that so interested him. Viewed intimately and in isolation, the bright white blossom in *Water Lily with Green and Red Pads* emerges from an inky background. For most of his works, he selected flower species based upon formal interests alone rather than for their symbolic meanings; the water lily, however, was an exception.[9] For La Farge, the water lily had "a mysterious appeal such as comes to us from certain arrangements of notes of music."[10]

CAROLYN SWAN NEEDELL

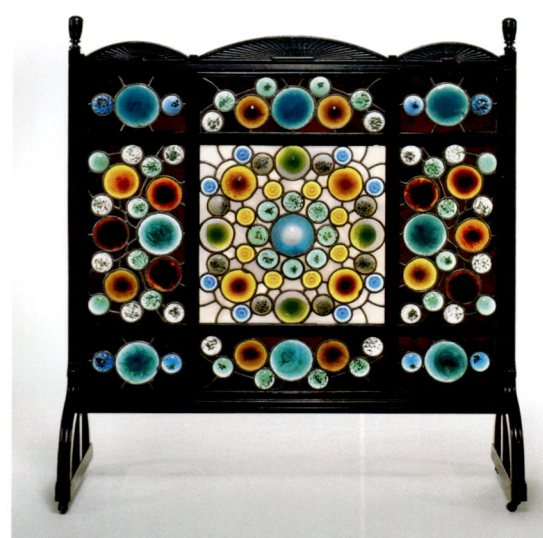

FIG. 1 John La Farge, *Fire Screen*, ca. 1880–85. Leaded opalescent glass with painted wood, 40 × 36¼ × 13 in. Chrysler Museum of Art, Gift of Walter P. Chrysler, Jr., 74.26.1

1. Royal Cortissoz, *John La Farge: A Memoir and a Study* (New York: Houghton Mifflin Company, 1911), 261.

2. James L. Yarnall, *Nature Vivante: The Still Lifes of John La Farge* (New York: The Jordan-Volpe Gallery, 1995), 7.

3. Kathleen A. Foster, "The Still-Life Painting of John La Farge," *The American Art Journal* 11, no. 3 (1979): 4–37; 13.

4. Maria Oakey Dewing, "Flower Painters and What the Flower Offers to Art," *Art and Progress* 6 (1915): 255–62.

5. Yarnall, *Nature Vivante*, 13; Foster, "The Still-Life Painting of John La Farge," 5.

6. Cortissoz, *John La Farge*, 66.

7. The flowers are rendered without great specificity, perhaps including violets or pansies and lilacs. Yarnall, *Nature Vivante*, 115 and cat. 5.

8. Yarnall, *Nature Vivante*, 54 and 118, cat. 13.

9. Foster, "The Still-Life Painting of John La Farge," 13.

10. Cortissoz, *John La Farge*, 135.

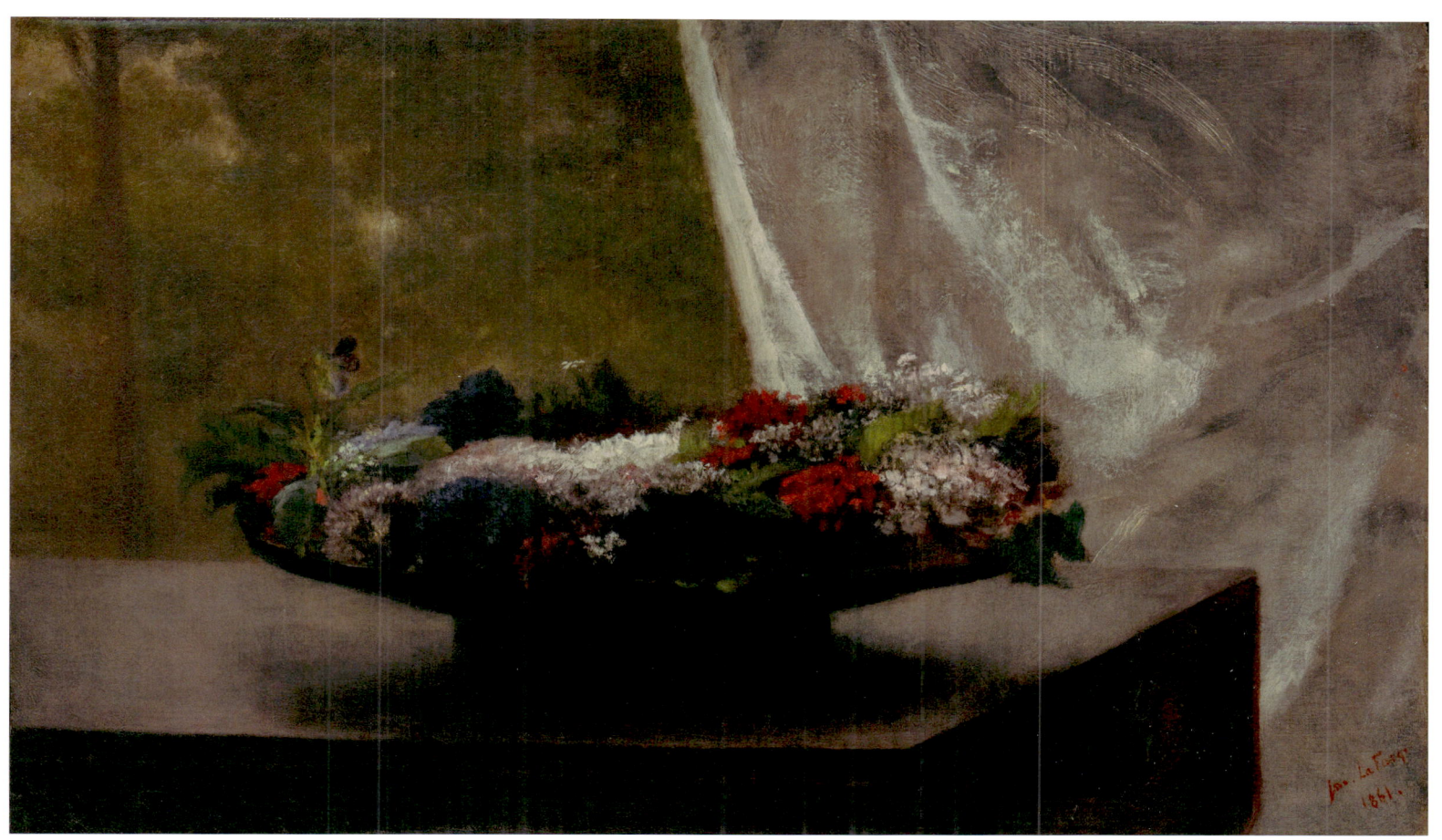

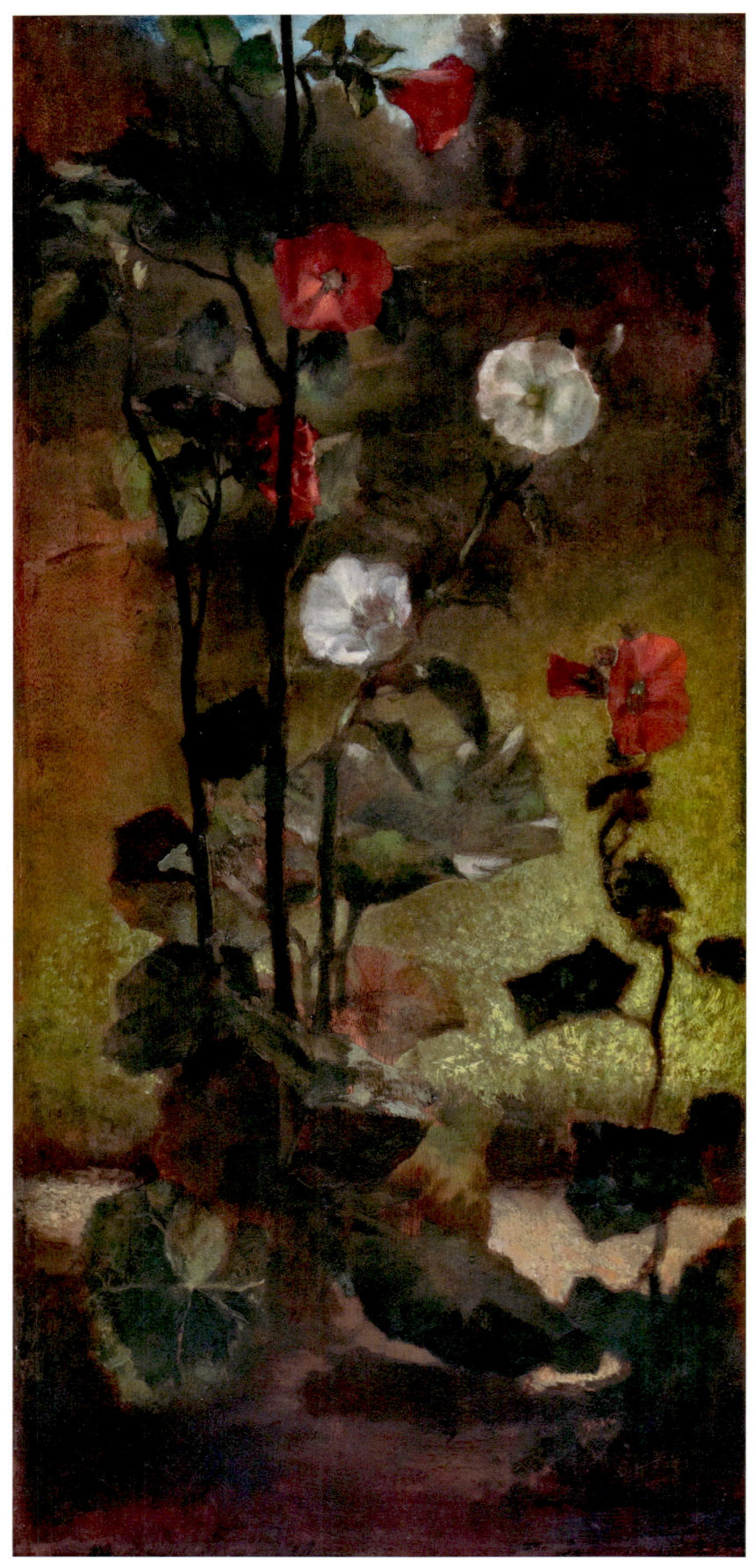

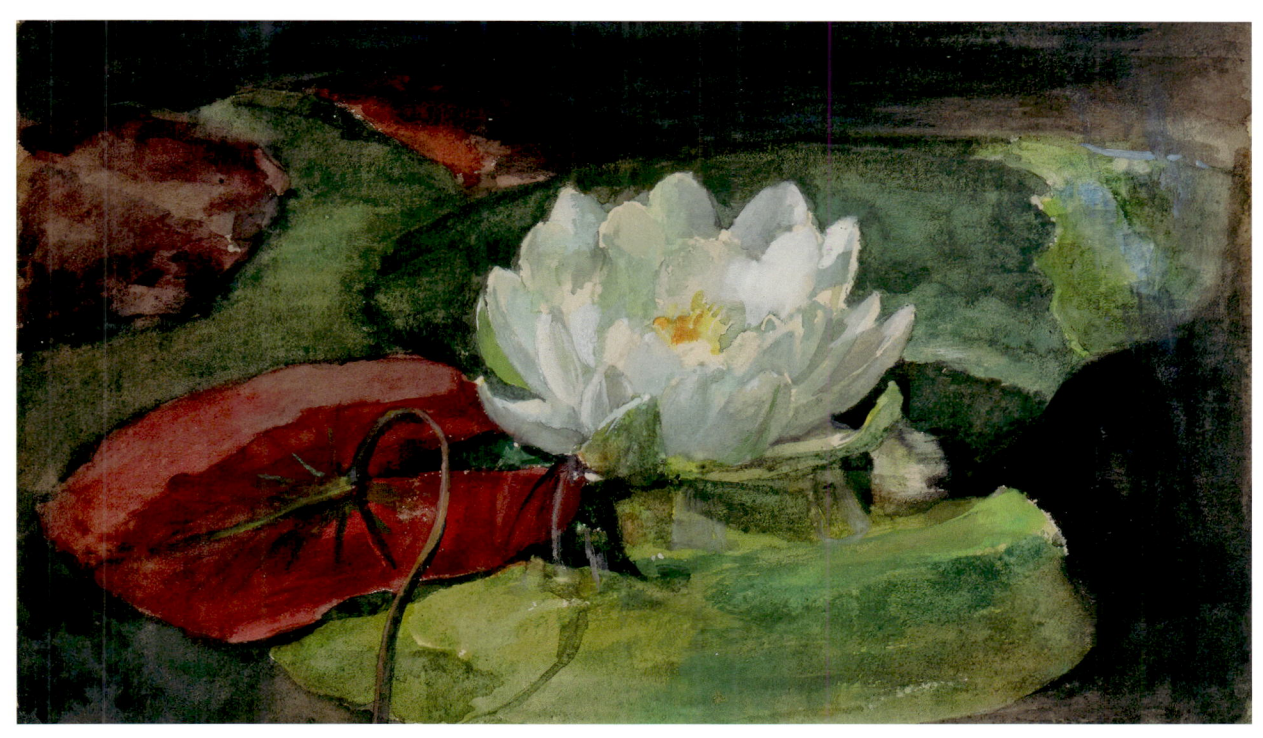

Hollyhocks, 1863
Encaustic on panel
34⅛ × 15⅝ inches

Promised Gift of the Macon and Joan Brock Collection of American Art

Water Lily with Green and Red Pads, ca. 1883
Pencil, watercolor, and gouache on heavy wove paper
Sight: 5½ × 9½ inches; sheet: 11¾ × 15½ inches

Gift of the Macon and Joan Brock Collection of American Art, 2023.4.3

Seymour Joseph Guy

AMERICAN, 1824–1910

The Big Catch (Say! Not Too Fast!), ca. 1862

Oil on canvas

9¼ × 12¼ inches

ONE OF THE MOST commercially successful painters of the later nineteenth century, English-born Seymour Joseph Guy was renowned in his lifetime for his genre paintings of American childhood. A contemporary profile described his favorite subjects as "incidents in children's lives," a theme he took up around 1861 and which he may have begun exploring through his friendship with artist John George Brown, who began painting genre scenes a few years prior.[1] Guy described his method: "I paint up a simple story, trying to get into it as much beauty as possible from color, light, and shade—as much beauty of every sort as it will admit."[2] Guy's "simple stories" usually depicted children indoors, engaged in activities with rich visual and narrative potential. His vision of childhood centered on innocence and playfulness, often within interiors that featured the trappings of comfortable, middle-class family life. Guy's aesthetic and sentimental glorification of youth struck a chord with some of the most eminent collectors of the era, including Samuel P. Avery, William H. Vanderbilt, and Thomas B. Clarke.

Guy rejoiced in designing compositions and narratives that captured moments of childhood action and drama. *The Big Catch (Say! Not Too Fast!)* interprets one such moment in the life of a young boy: he wears a dressing gown and stands up in his crib, perhaps playing alone in his room past his bedtime. The two titles that have been given to the work suggest the two different games he may be engaged in: "*The Big Catch*" implies that he is pretending to reel in a large fish—he holds a stick resembling a fishing rod in his right hand while pulling in the "catch" with his left. The second title, "*Say! Not Too Fast!*" indicates that he may be fantasizing about driving a horse and cart, with his stick standing in for a driver's whip and his left hand pulling on the "horse's" reins.

The Big Catch (Say! Not Too Fast!) features some of Guy's distinctive techniques, including a smooth, lacquered finish, an effect he achieved using carefully layered glazes. Like many of his best-known domestic genre pictures, this work also demonstrates Guy's ability to construct a dramatic lighting scheme, which produces a stark contrast between the boy's nursery and the darkened hall outside his door.

Period interest in both angling and hansom cabs support the two possible themes of the boy's imaginative play. In the mid-nineteenth century, fishing was deemed an acceptable pastime for all and crossed many social lines; it was a hobby that required little by way of equipment or training and was enjoyed by people of all ages, genders, and social classes.[3] The boy in Guy's picture would have also been very familiar with hansom cabs, the horse-drawn carriages that were then commonly found throughout New York City. While playing in his room at night, his imagination could have easily enabled him to enact either scenario.

Works like *The Big Catch (Say! Not Too Fast!)* suggest Guy's genuine commitment to his subject: painted with empathy and care, it offers a sympathetic view into the world of childhood. It is precisely this sensitivity that led one contemporary reviewer to declare of a similar composition, "Nobody but a father could have made such a painting as this."[4]

LAUREN PALMOR

1. Bruce Weber, "Seymour Joseph Guy," *The Magazine Antiques* 174, no. 5 (November 2008): 144.

2. George William Sheldon, *American Painters: With One Hundred and Four Examples of Their Work Engraved on Wood* (New York: D. Appleton and Company, 1881), 68.

3. Donald G. and Irene Kmet Wetherell, *Useful Pleasures: The Shaping of Leisure in Alberta: 1896–1945* (Regina: John Deyell Company, 1990), 180.

4. "The Academy Exhibition," *The Art Journal* New Series, 5 (1879): 159.

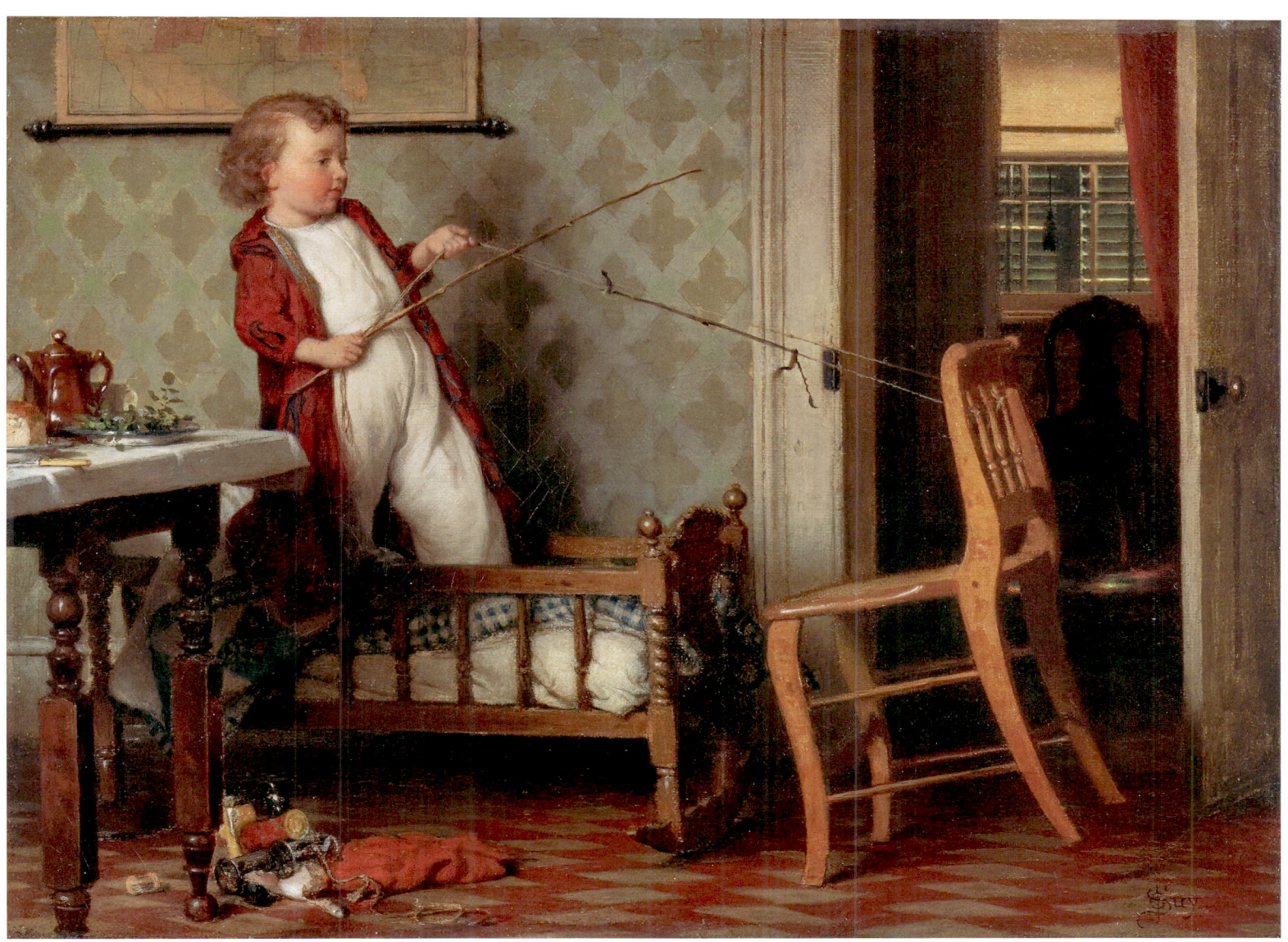

John George Brown

AMERICAN, 1831–1913

Resting in the Woods (Girl Under a Tree), 1866

Oil on canvas

18 × 12¼ inches

Promised Gift of the Macon and Joan Brock Collection of American Art

ALTHOUGH JOHN GEORGE BROWN is most identified with his images of urban, working-class children, he laid the foundations for his career with picturesque paintings of boys and girls in the American countryside. Brown's turn toward the subjects of childhood and nature likely stemmed from his personal life and surroundings. He had married in 1855, and his daughters Charlotte and Isabelle were born in 1860 and 1863. In addition, around late 1862 or early 1863, Brown moved to Fort Lee, New Jersey, a rural community on the Hudson River across from New York City, where he kept a studio in the famous Tenth Street Studio Building.[1] These factors might help explain why Brown may have felt compelled to paint children in nature, playing in forest interiors or resting beneath the trees.

Brown's interest in painting girls in forest settings was also influenced by American Pre-Raphaelite painters like William Trost Richards, who, through the late 1850s and early 1860s, painted richly patterned, realistic tapestries of light and foliage on forest floors (fig. 1). Brown responded intensely to the "truth to nature" practiced by American followers of the Pre-Raphaelite movement, and his own interest in Realism was strengthened as a result.

Resting in the Woods is often invoked as a prime example of Brown's achievements in the rural genre and his integration of Pre-Raphaelite influences. Featuring dappled light and realistic details, the painting depicts a young girl within a forest interior. Looking beyond the frame, she appears thoughtful and dreamy, her gaze averted as she poses between a large, lichen-covered boulder and the trunk of an old tree. The girl's pink dress stands out against the colors and textures of the forest floor—the pink cotton contrasts with the rough bark, green moss, and cool stone, and the folds of her skirt echo the deep furrows of the bark.[2] Her accessories are closely studied, and Brown renders the fine details of her black, laced leather boots and woven straw hat.

One of a series of works Brown painted on the theme of young girls in woodland settings, *Resting in the Woods* is often interpreted as a statement on the end of childhood innocence, the transition to womanhood, and our connection with the natural world. Although the artist would later earn the most recognition for his sentimental, urban storytelling pictures, *Resting in the Woods* demonstrates his ability to study individual character, the textures of natural surfaces, and complex patterning of light.

Brown's country scenes led to early commercial success: in the late 1860s, he saw increased interest in reproductions of his work, and between 1868 and 1870, six of his paintings were reworked as chromolithographs, four of which offered examples of his achievements as a painter of girls resting and playing outdoors.[3] The dissemination of these prints attests to Brown's aims, as he described them to an early biographer, "I want people a hundred years from now to know how the children that I paint looked."[4]

LAUREN PALMOR

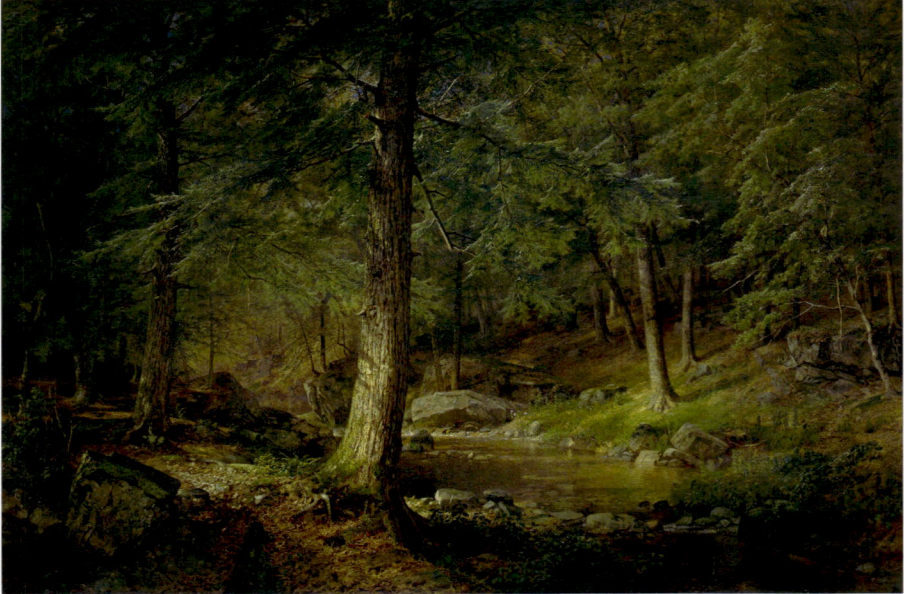

FIG. 1 William Trost Richards, *Forest Scene*, 1875. Oil on canvas, 27¼ × 40 in. Chrysler Museum of Art, Bequest of Edward J. Brickhouse, 84.499

1. Barbara Dayer Gallati, "Family Matters: Artists and Their Model Girls," in *Angels and Tomboys: Girlhood in Nineteenth-Century American Art*, ed. Holly Connor Pyne (Newark, NJ: Newark Museum, 2012), 60.

2. Martha J. Hoppin, *The World of J. G. Brown* (Chesterfield, MA: Chameleon Books, 2010), 46.

3. Martha J. Hoppin, *Country Paths and City Sidewalks: The Art of J. G. Brown* (Springfield, MA: George Walter Vincent Smith Art Museum, 1989), 10–11.

4. George William Sheldon, *American Painters: With One Hundred and Four Examples of Their Work Engraved on Wood* (New York: D. Appleton and Company, 1881), 141.

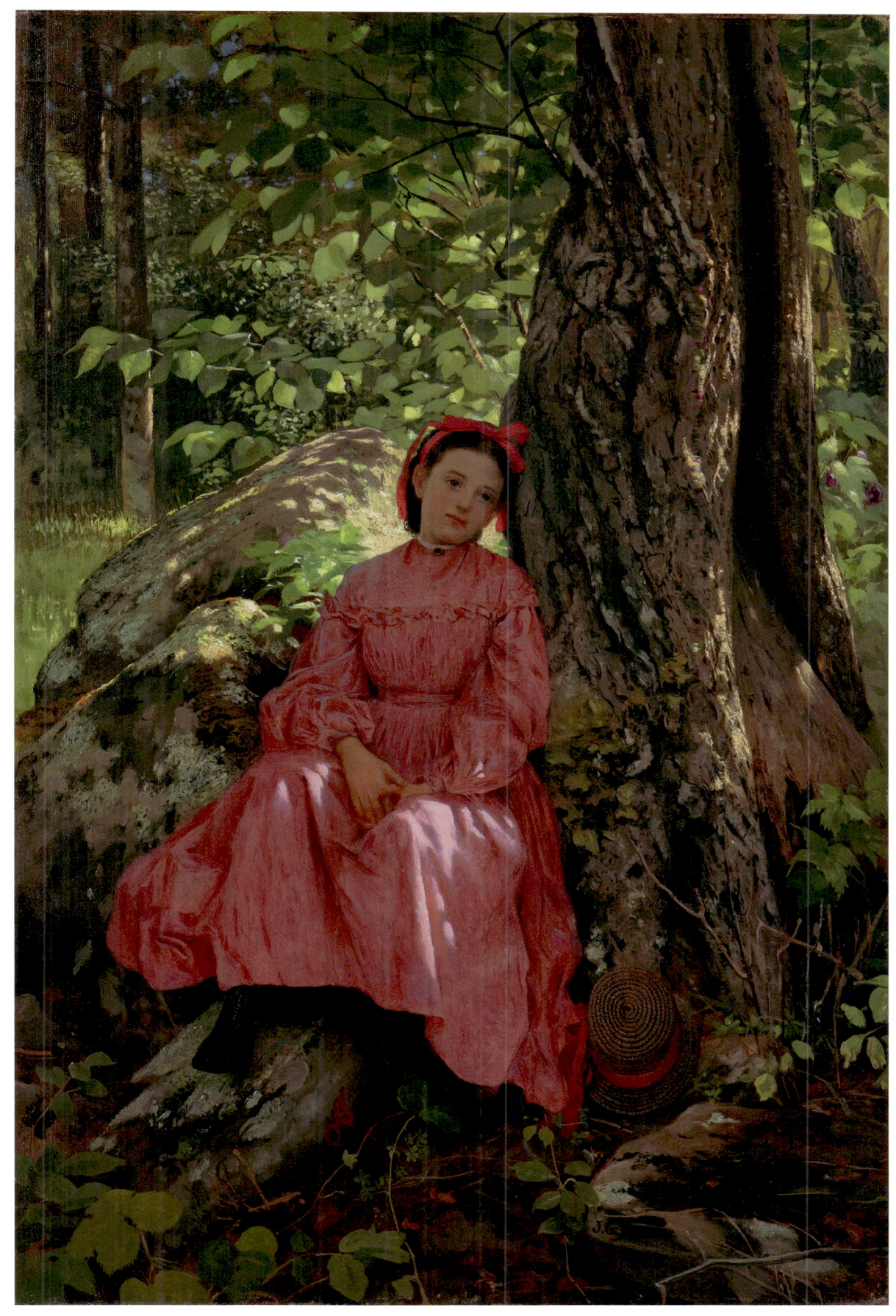

Winslow Homer

AMERICAN, 1836–1910

Portrait of Elizabeth Loring Grant, 1866
Charcoal, chalk, and pencil on paper
10 × 10 inches

Promised Gift of the Macon and Joan Brock Collection
of American Art

AFTER COMPLETING AN APPRENTICESHIP in a commercial lithographer's shop in Boston, Winslow Homer moved to New York City in 1859. He earned a living producing illustrations for contemporary periodicals while taking painting lessons at the National Academy of Design. During the Civil War, he traveled to the front lines in Virginia as an artist-correspondent for *Harper's Weekly* magazine. Homer was deeply affected by the experience of war and created his first significant oil paintings based on observations made at the front. His years as an illustrator taught him to distill narrative detail into potent images that transcended anecdotal storytelling. During the late 1860s and 1870s, he focused on contemporary American life and depicted deliberately nostalgic rural scenes and thoughtful explorations of difficult histories, including a series of paintings on the lives of the formerly enslaved in Reconstruction-era Virginia.

Throughout his career, Homer grappled with the theme of humans' relationship with the natural world. In the 1880s and after, he made the sea the subject of his art at the rugged village of Cullercoats on the North Sea in England and at his home in Prouts Neck, Maine. He painted the arduous labors of North Atlantic fisherfolk and the relentless power of the ocean under varying conditions of weather and light and across the seasons. Multiple trips to the Caribbean yielded dazzling watercolors that hint at complicated histories of colonization and empire. By the 1890s his art ruminated on ever more universal themes as he grappled with his own mortality. At his death, he was lauded as the quintessential painter of American life and landscape.

Homer honed his skills as a draftsman while working as an illustrator for almost two decades. His careful drawings often reveal his roots in that profession while serving as preparatory works for his paintings. Homer seems to have presented this delicate portrait sketch of family friend Elizabeth Loring Grant to the sitter as a gift. Seated on a step, she is rendered in a pensive pose, averting her gaze as she rests her chin in her hand. Homer concentrated on her voluminous skirt, indicating the folds with white highlights. According to a note by the sitter, she was fourteen years old when this drawing was made: "Taken on Uncle Wm. Wellington Mead's front door steps at the Little Cottage, Belmont, Massachusetts, 1866."[1] Homer described the details of this setting with pale graphite, showing a curving leafy vine at left and horizontal lines of shutters in the background.

Homer's family had moved to Belmont, a western suburb of Boston, in 1858, and the artist returned there frequently to visit his family and friends. In 1866 he seems to have spent most of the summer in Belmont, where he made at least two drawings of Grant.[2] Here she wears a distinctive pillbox hat, a style that would appear in drawings and paintings of other women in the period. His portrait of Grant seems closely related to a female type that he painted in various settings into the 1880s. Homer depicted the "modern" American woman indulging in the trendy pastime of croquet, enjoying leisure at the shore or in the mountains, or working as a teacher.

For Homer the 1870s were a period of experimentation. He developed his skills in watercolor as he explored a range of subjects in his art. With the founding of the American Watercolor Society in 1866, the medium gained prominence in the United States as artists had new venues and audiences for their work. Homer successfully exhibited and sold his watercolors and eventually gave up his work as an illustrator. *Girl with a Letter* reflects his increasing proficiency in the medium. The figure is carefully drawn—especially her face, framed by her curly bangs—while her dress is painted with layered passages of blue. In the background, broad washes of pigment foreshadow the fluidity that would become a hallmark of this style. The young woman has paused from reading her letter, which seems to glow with reflected light at the center of the composition. The carved chair and red-tasseled pillow provide a hint of color and decorative detail amidst the spare setting and subdued tones. In a series of works made around this time, Homer embraced Aestheticism, and watercolors such as *Girl with a Letter* emphasize beauty over narrative detail.

Homer saw watercolor as central to his art and used it to explore the same themes that preoccupied him in oil during his career. When he famously declared, "You will see, in the future I will live by my watercolors," he acknowledged the income that would sustain him but also seemed to prophesize their role in securing his reputation as one of the greatest American painters of all time.[3]

STEPHANIE L. HERDRICH

1. See Lloyd Goodrich and Abigail Booth Gerdts, *Record of Works by Winslow Homer, 1867 through 1876*, vol. 1 (New York: Spanierman Gallery, 2005), 364–65, cats. 289–290. Homer made two drawings of Grant in the summer of 1866. Gerdts explains that the inscription describing this portrait sketch (cat. 290) is on the back of the other drawing (cat. 289), which shows Grant seated, leaning against a tree trunk.

2. See note 1.

3. Quoted in Lloyd Goodrich, *Winslow Homer* (New York: Published for the Whitney Museum of American Art by Macmillan Company, 1944), 98.

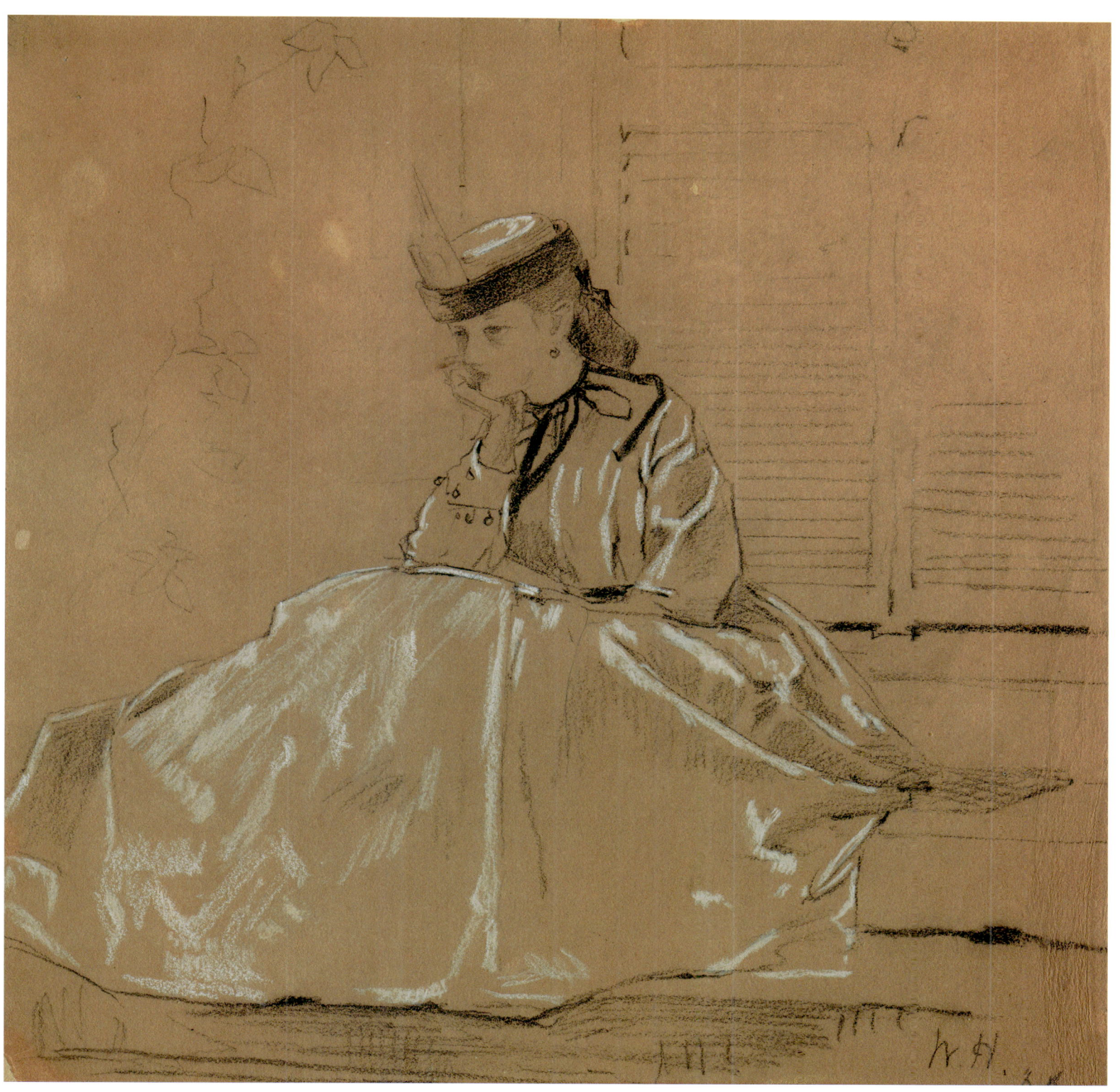

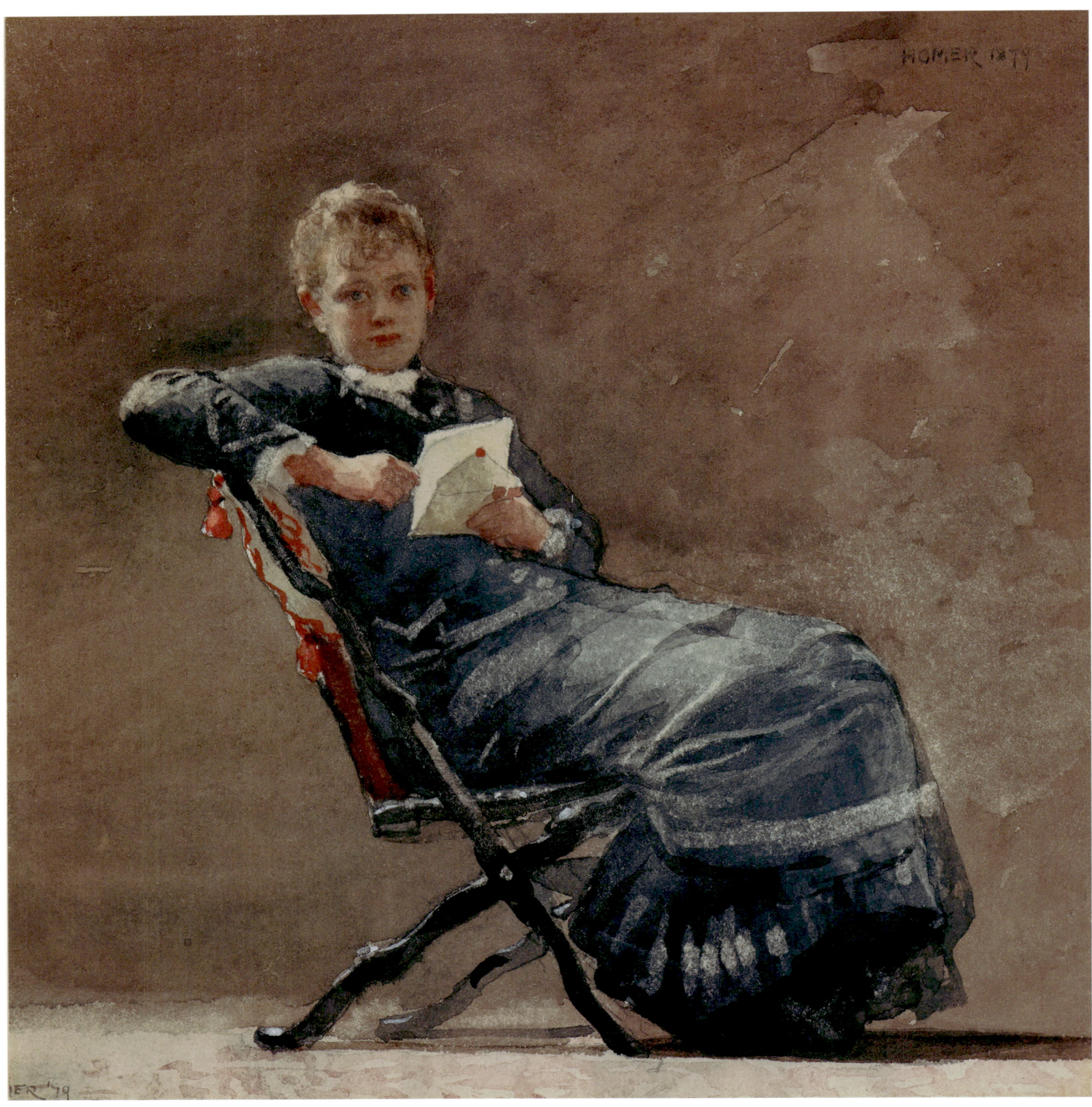

Girl with a Letter, 1879
Watercolor on paper
8½ × 8½ inches

Promised Gift of the Macon and Joan Brock Collection
of American Art

Charles Sprague Pearce

AMERICAN, 1851–1914

Young Lady with Flowers, ca. 1875–80

Oil on canvas

13 × 10 inches

Promised Gift of the Macon and Joan Brock Collection of American Art

LIKE MANY AMERICAN ARTISTS in the late nineteenth century, Charles Sprague Pearce traveled to France for academic training in the art capital of Paris. However, few others adapted as fully to life in France as Pearce, who settled permanently in Auvers-sur-Oise on the rural outskirts of the city. Though critics and writers back in the United States counted him among the group of notable American painters working abroad, as his career developed, his attention focused on the annual Salon and other measures of professional success within the French art establishment. Likewise, he found stylistic models among leading French academic painters, in particular his teacher Léon Bonnat and later Jules Bastien-Lepage, whose peasant subjects and rural themes Pearce echoed in his later work.

Pearce enrolled at Bonnat's independent atelier in 1873, shortly after his arrival in Paris. A famed painter and influential teacher, Bonnat had won many accolades at the Salon and taught numerous students who went on to acclaimed careers, including Americans like Thomas Eakins and John Singer Sargent. Just a few months after arriving in France, Pearce left for Egypt along with fellow American painter Frederick Arthur Bridgman. The destination was a logical one for ambitious young artists, as themes drawn from the Near East were wildly popular at the Salon and featured prominently in the work of Bonnat, who had recently traveled to Egypt as an official representative at the commemoration of the opening of the Suez Canal.[1]

Pearce's first successes at the Salon and other important venues like the Royal Academy in London and the Centennial Exposition in Philadelphia, featured scenes of the Near East and biblical subjects, drawing upon the experiences of his travels. The association with his prominent teacher eased entrée into such circles but after a time began to weigh upon the artist. In 1882 when Pearce exhibited *Lamentations over the Death of the First-Born of Egypt* at the Museum of Fine Arts, Boston, one critic generally praised the work but at the same time proclaimed, "It is easy to imagine that when Mr. Pearce finally escapes from the influence of Bonnat he will paint really great pictures (fig. 1)."[2]

Around 1880 Pearce embarked on a series of portrait heads of elegant young women, a more modern subject seemingly designed to distinguish himself from the associations with his teacher. These enchantingly up-to-date young women recall fashionable painters like the Belgian Alfred Stevens, well known for his depictions of stylish women in eclectic interiors. *Young Lady with Flowers* offers a particularly striking example of the genre. The young woman's sideward glance provides just the slightest hint of flirtatiousness, while the shimmery fabric and brilliant gold background showcase the artist's command of modern painterly effects. Pearce exhibited a group of these female heads at the 1882 exhibition of the Pennsylvania Academy of the Fine Arts, where they attracted positive attention for the marked shift in the artist's approach toward more contemporary and buoyant subjects. Such paintings propelled the artist's reputation beyond the encumbrance of his earlier teacher, marking him as a more modern spirit who one critic distinguished for his "tender regard for the beauties of every-day life."[3]

COREY PIPER

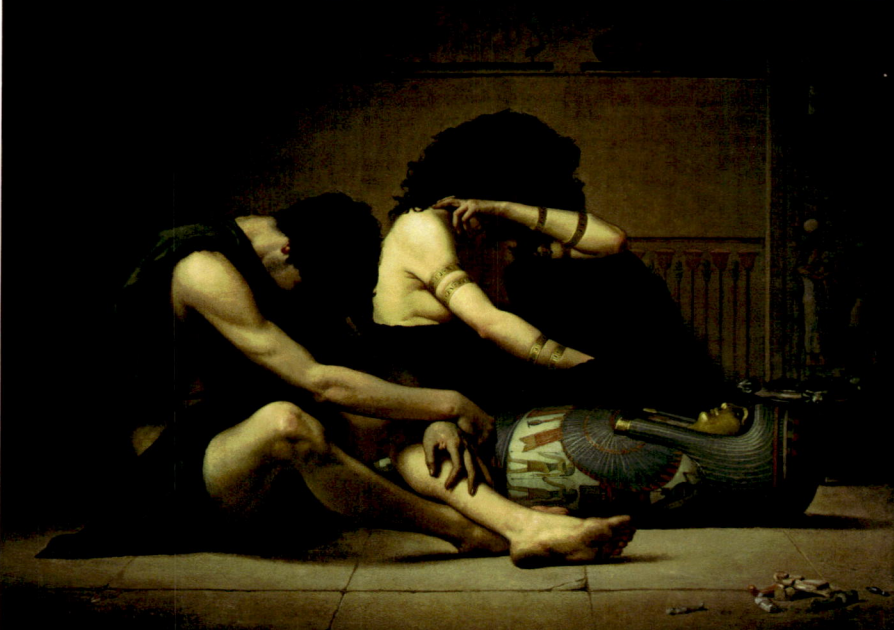

FIG. 1 Charles Sprague Pearce, *Lamentations over the Death of the First-Born of Egypt*, 1877. Oil on canvas, 38½ × 51½ in. Smithsonian American Art Museum, Museum purchase, 1985.28

1. Mary Lublin, *A Rare Elegance: The Paintings of Charles Sprague Pearce (1851–1914)* (New York: Jordan-Volpe Gallery, 1993), 12.

2. "Fine Arts," *The Independent* (June 22, 1882), 8.

3. "Gallery and Studio: Charles Sprague Pearce," *Art Amateur* 10 (December 1883): 5.

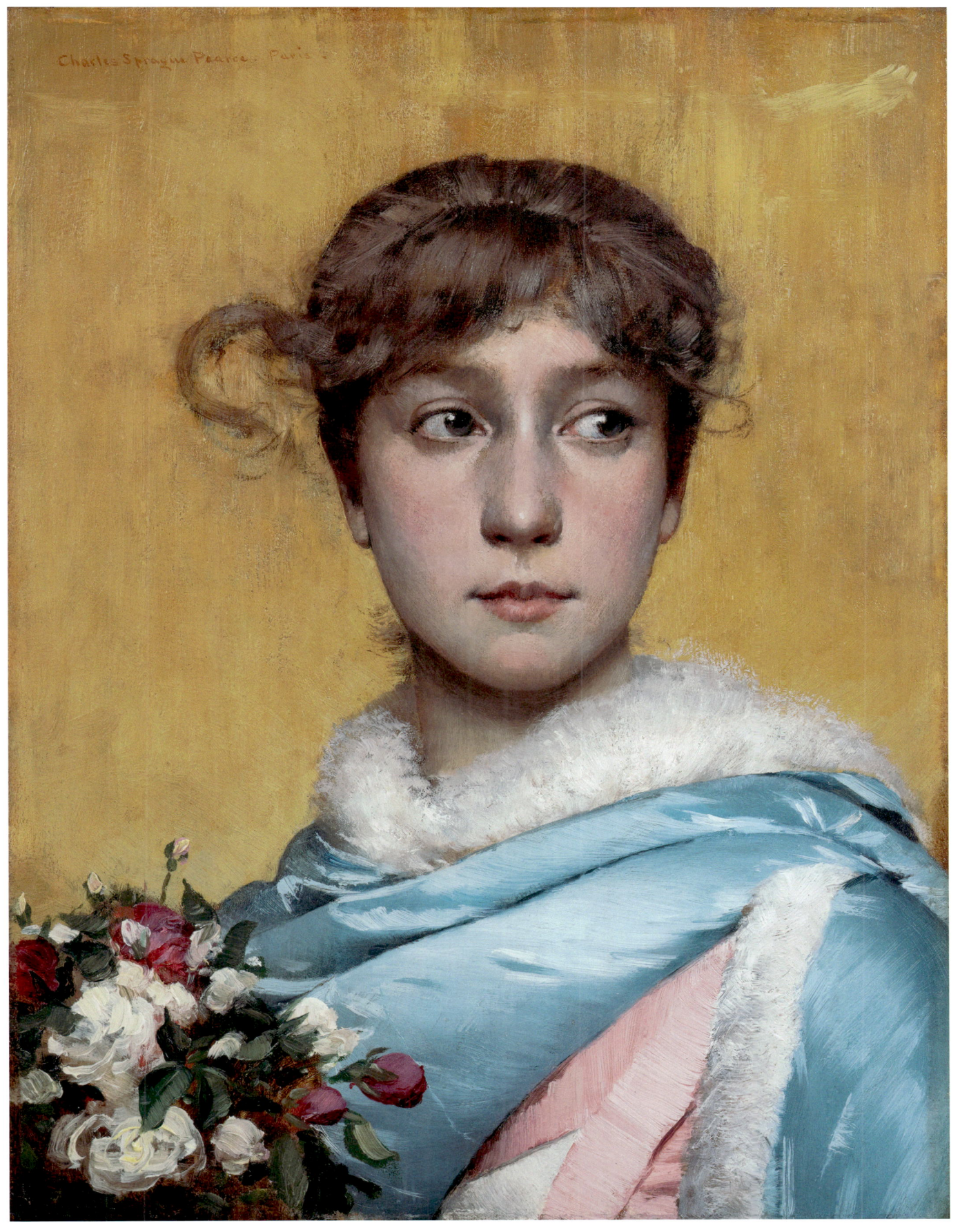

James Carroll Beckwith

AMERICAN, 1852–1917

The Grey Gown, 1882

Pastel on paper

32 × 24½ inches

Promised Gift of the Macon and Joan Brock Collection
of American Art

DURING A CAREER that straddled the turn of the twentieth century, James Carroll Beckwith exemplified the experience of American artists who traveled to Europe in pursuit of academic training and returned embracing stylistic innovations pioneered by the independent avant-garde. Beckwith's cosmopolitanism, along with his rich network of connections among American artists, earned him adulation among the art public in the United States. By the end of the nineteenth century, he achieved recognition as one of the chief proponents of a lively manner of painting steeped in European sophistication that came to dominate the American art world of the Gilded Age.

Beckwith grew up in modest circumstances in Chicago and moved as a teenager to New York City, where he studied at the National Academy of Design. However, it was his first journey to Europe in 1873 that fully set him upon his professional path. After a brief visit to England, Beckwith arrived in Paris, where he later recounted, "My real Art life began."[1] He enrolled in the studio of the brash young French teacher Carolus-Duran, a popular atelier for American students, including John Singer Sargent, who forged a close friendship with the slightly older, but less worldly Beckwith. The two artists progressed apace under Carolus-Duran's guidance, which emphasized working in oil and building form with color over a strict foundation of drawing.

In 1878 Beckwith returned from his European sojourn and took up a teaching post at the newly formed Art Students League in New York alongside William Merritt Chase. Just a year after his return to the United States, Beckwith again set sail for Europe, inaugurating a regular pattern of travel to the continent. He spent the summers of 1881 and 1882 working in Andé, a small French town in Normandy situated along the Seine between Paris and Rouen. Beckwith was joined there by a small colony of French and American artists who enjoyed a rather idyllic existence exploring the relatively new pictorial freedom afforded by painting *en plein air*.

During that second summer, Beckwith hired two ballet dancers to travel to Andé and serve as models, Céline, and Marguerite, the likely subject of *The Grey Gown*. The time spent working in Normandy invigorated Beckwith. With a practice rooted in a strong academic foundation of drawing from the model, the experience of working more rapidly out of doors offered him greater freedom to explore the effects of color, light, and a looser approach to the application of paint. He produced two works closely related to *The Grey Gown*, a pencil drawing of Marguerite and an oil painting.[2]

It seems only natural that Beckwith would explore the same subject through the medium of pastel, as at that same time he was engaged, along with Chase and other artists like Robert Frederick Blum, in the founding of the American Society of Painters in Pastel. Beginning in 1884 the group held a total of four exhibitions devoted to elevating the status of pastel among the American art public. Beckwith exhibited in all four of the Society's exhibitions, showing *The Grey Gown* in the final iteration in 1890, where one critic singled it out as "very interesting."[3] Critics largely celebrated the Pastel Society exhibitions for the fresh works they brought to the public, but ultimately they could not sustain interest among a crowded field of artistic attractions, and the group folded after this final show.

COREY PIPER

1. J. Carroll Beckwith, unpublished manuscript, *Souvenirs and Reminiscences*, 1917, 19. James Carroll Beckwith papers, Archives of American Art, Smithsonian Institution, Washington, DC.

2. For the drawing, James Carroll Beckwith, *Margot [Marguerite]*, 1882. New-York Historical Society, Gift of the

National Academy of Design, 1935.85.3.26. For the painting, see Pepi Marcheti Franchi and Bruce Weber, *Intimate Revelations: The Art of Carroll Beckwith (1852–1917)* (New York: Berry-Hill Galleries, 1999), illus. 9, 84.

3. "The Pastel Exhibition," *Art Amateur* 23 (June 1890): 4.

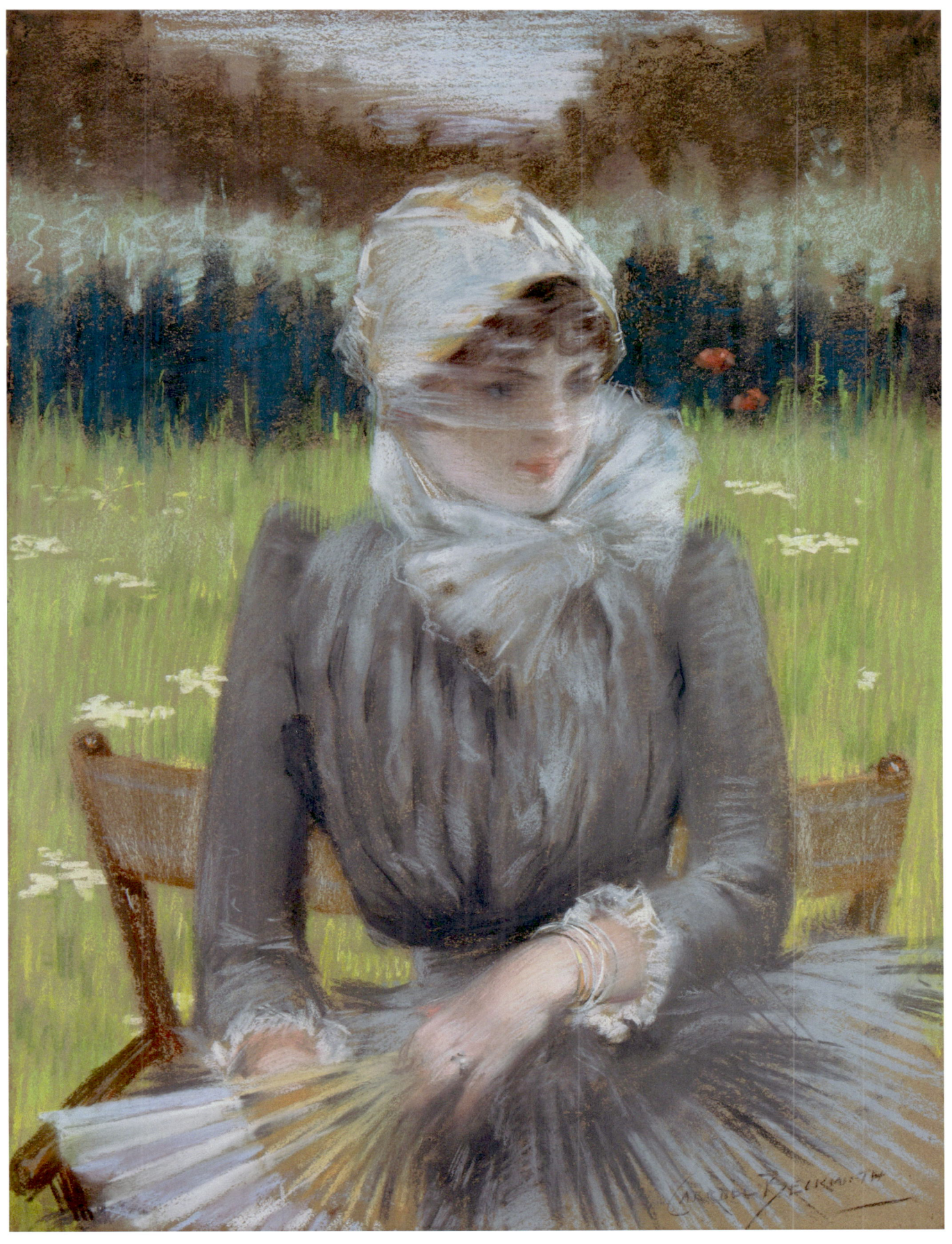

William Merritt Chase

AMERICAN, 1849–1916

Spanish Roma Girl, ca. 1881–84

Ink and gouache on paper, mounted to card

18¼ × 13 inches

Promised Gift of the Macon and Joan Brock Collection of American Art

BORN IN INDIANA IN 1849, William Merritt Chase studied painting in Indianapolis briefly before enrolling at the Royal Academy in Munich, Germany, in 1872. Inspired by the great art of the past, he was determined to forge a modern American art and returned to New York City six years later, in 1878. He positioned himself at the center of the art world, acquiring a prominent studio in Greenwich Village in the famed Tenth Street Studio Building—a hub for the era's great artists—and joined progressive art organizations and social networks in the city. As a painter, he worked in diverse media and across genres but was known for genteel portraits and picturesque landscapes. He became one of the most influential art teachers in the United States in the late nineteenth century, instructing a generation of American painters—notably Georgia O'Keeffe, Marsden Hartley, and Joseph Stella, among others—at prominent institutions across the country. In 1891 he established the Shinnecock Art School on Long Island, New York, and painted there each summer, moving away from the dark palette he had embraced in Munich toward sparkling outdoor light and impressionist practice. He carefully cultivated his artistic identity as a stylish cosmopolitan—he was attentive to his appearance as an elegant *maître* and curated his studio with eclectic objets d'art and trinkets that he collected on his travels, all of which earned him a reputation as a sophisticated tastemaker.

"My God . . . I'd rather go to Europe than go to heaven," Chase famously proclaimed when offered an opportunity to study abroad.[1] Throughout his life, he was enamored with the art and culture of the continent and traveled there frequently. Prompted in part by a commission he received in 1881 to create illustrations for an article in *Scribner's Magazine*, he visited Spain for at least three consecutive summers from 1882 to 1884. This vivid ink painting of a Spanish Roma woman is similar in style and subject to some of the illustrations that would appear in the article "Street Life in Madrid" (1899).[2] Though inspired by his travels and the vogue for Spanish culture during

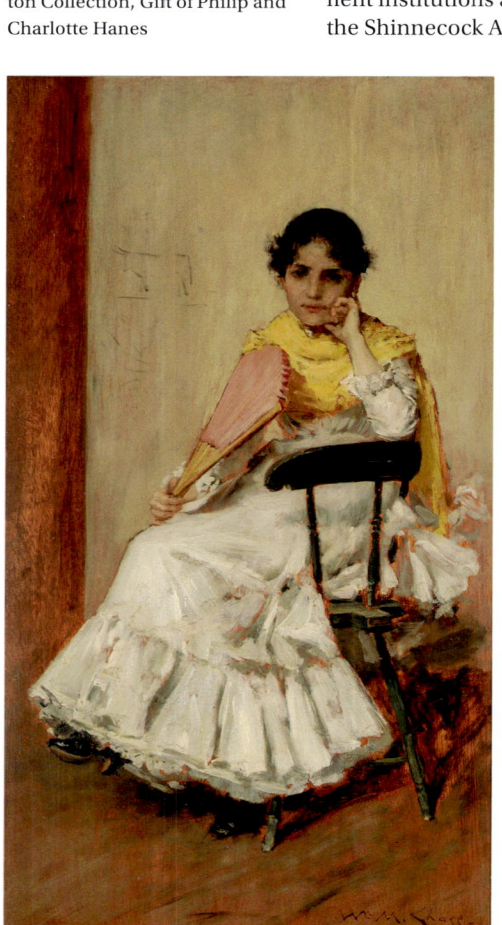

FIG. 1 William Merritt Chase, *Spanish Girl in White*, ca. 1886. Oil on panel, 26¾ × 15¼ in. Wake Forest University, Middleton Collection, Gift of Philip and Charlotte Hanes

this era, the painting may have been made in his New York studio—contrived as a charming image of a picturesque foreign land for audiences in the United States. The model leans back in a straight chair as she props a tambourine in her right hand against her thigh, her chin resting on her left hand. Her dark hat, bolero-style jacket, and sash evoke Spanish dress generally. The details of her face are obscured in shadow and, although it is difficult to confirm, related works from this period suggest that the model may be Alice Gerson, Chase's future wife (they married in 1886), who frequently posed for him (fig. 1).[3] *Spanish Roma Girl* was considered significant enough to include in the artist's first solo exhibition, held at the Boston Art Club in 1886, which was deemed a huge success.[4]

Across his oeuvre Chase made women the subject of his art—painting them in elegant portraits, refined rural and urban landscapes, and genre scenes, reflecting their evolving roles in society in the decades after the American Civil War. *Woman in White Satin* seems to bridge the gap between the past and the present, portraiture and anecdote. Here a model seen in profile wears an elaborate ruffled collar and white dress, likely contrived from studio props to suggest a historicizing costume. Her draped overskirt and train cascade to the floor in fluid passages of paint suggesting the lush textiles of grand manner portraits. She clutches a closed fan in her right hand—a symbol of sophisticated cosmopolitan taste and refinement. With an eye to the past, the artist incorporated lessons learned from Dutch and Spanish old masters. The spare setting and monochromatic background, for example, recall portrait formulas derived from artists like Velázquez.

While Chase paid homage to the old masters, he also embraced progressive practices and techniques. In 1882 he formed the Society of Painters in Pastel with his friend and traveling companion, artist Frederick Blum.[5] Though pastel was not a new medium for American or European artists, it was gaining attention among the Impressionists in France, and Chase was probably exposed to diverse works while traveling across the continent in the early 1880s. Chase believed that pastel should be considered on par with oil painting. His fledgling pastel society held four exhibitions in the 1880s, and he exhibited prominently in each one, producing a significant body of appealing work in the medium.

The dazzling pastel *At Her Ease* depicts Chase's wife, Alice, reclining on a bench in his studio, wearing a pale blue kimono with a contrasting red sash. Chase painted several portraits of Alice in this kimono around the time

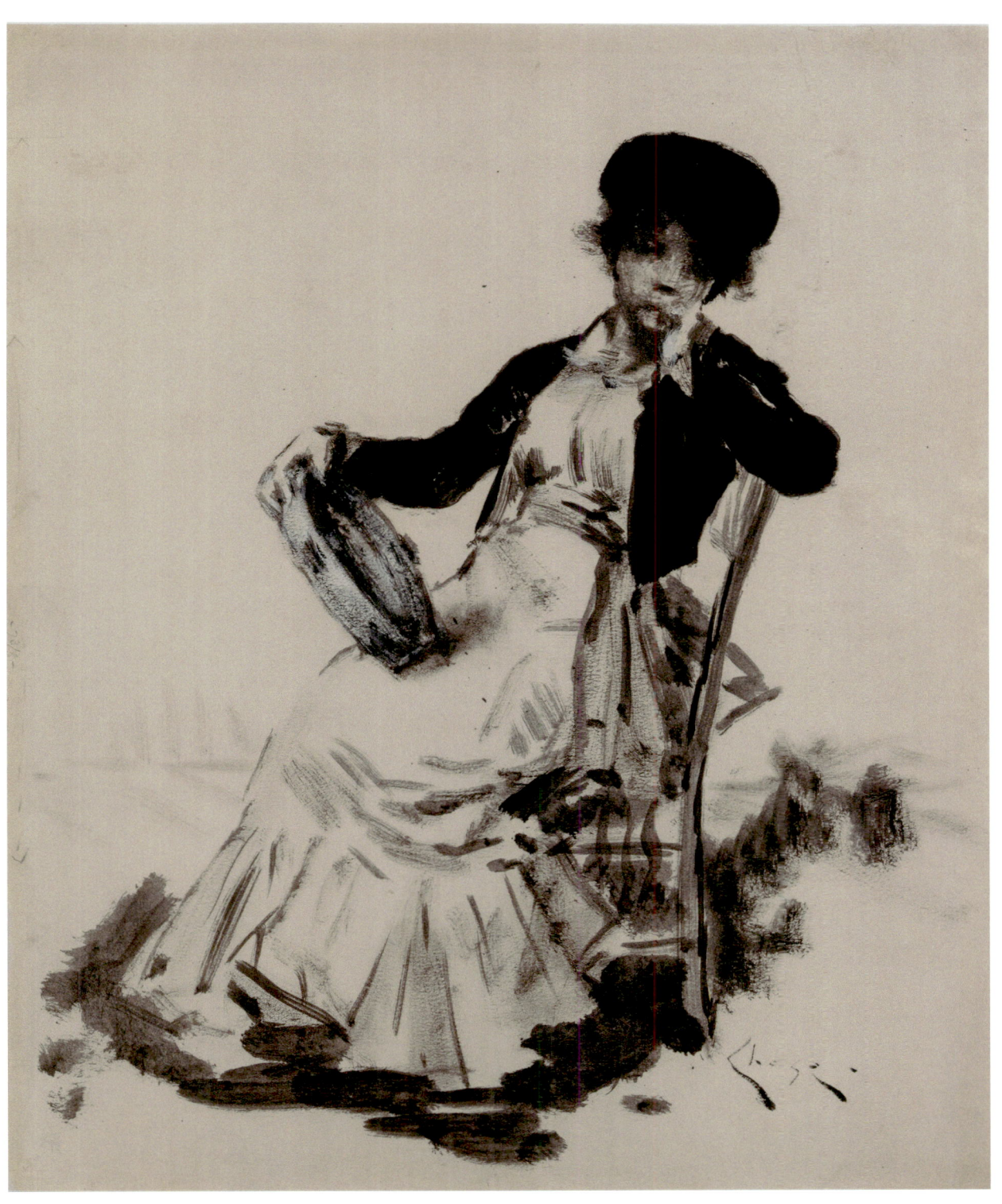

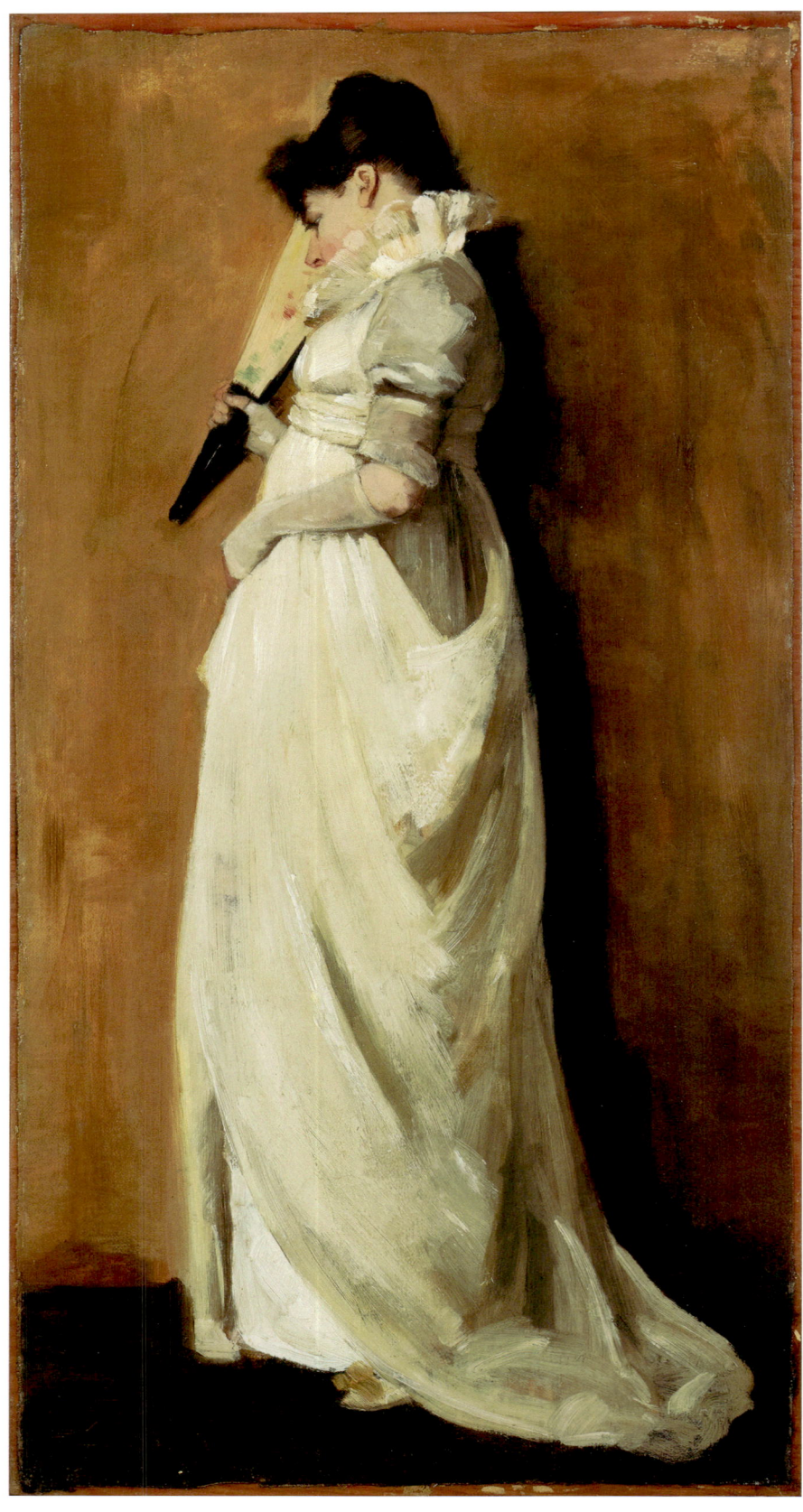

Woman in White Satin, ca. 1885
Oil on canvas, mounted on wood
22 13/16 × 11 11/16 inches

At Her Ease, ca. 1889
Pastel on panel
10½ × 16 inches

Promised Gift of the Macon and Joan Brock Collection
of American Art

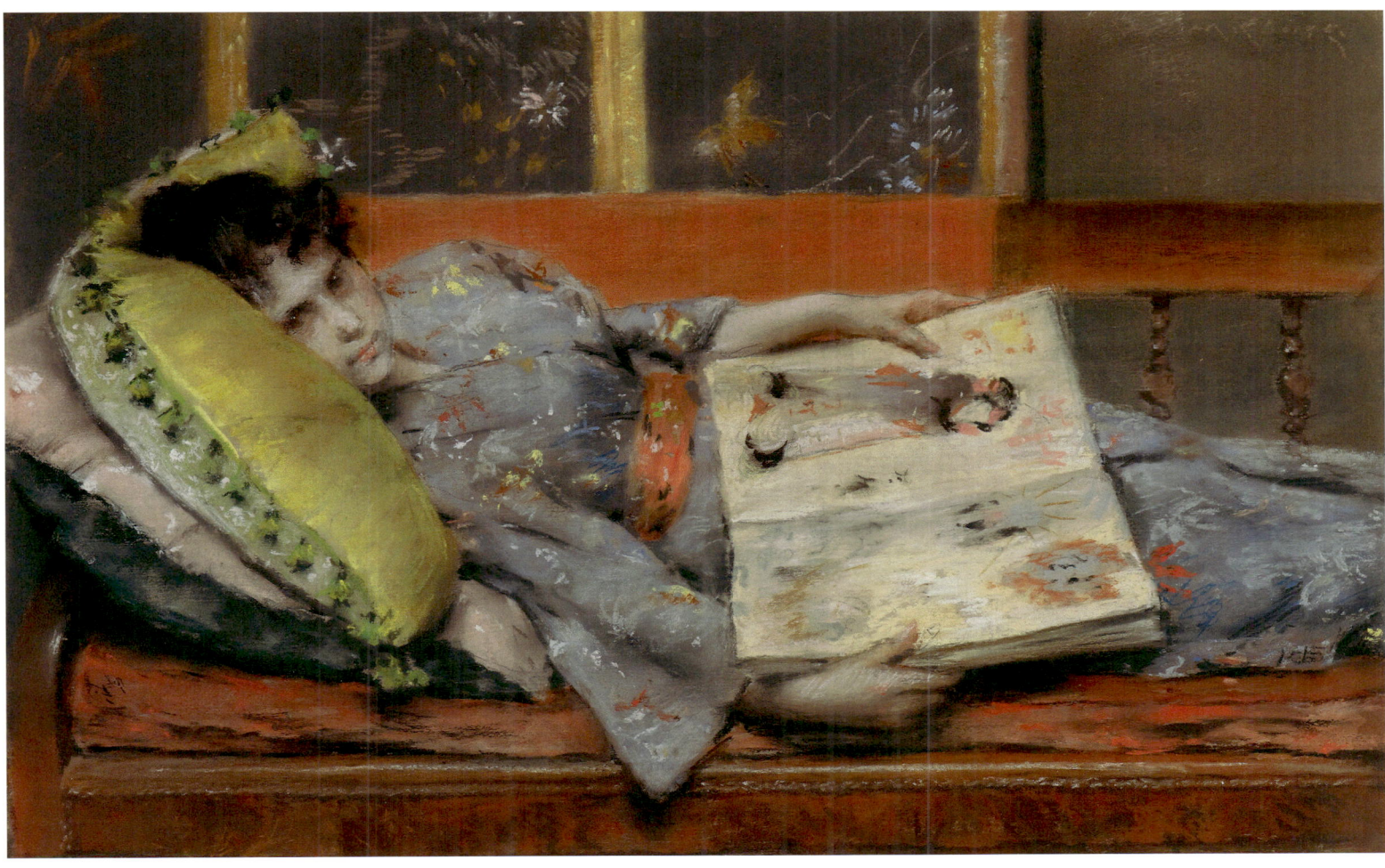

of their marriage in 1886, and decorative details seen here reappear in other images of the studio. Here Chase focuses on Japanese design elements—in addition to the kimono, she holds a book of Japanese prints on her lap and an Asian screen appears in the background—signifiers of the artist's refined sensibilities. He creates an intimate composition within a narrow horizontal format as Alice's body extends across the paper near the picture plane. Propped upon plush pillows, she turns away from her book and gazes directly at the artist and, by extension, at us—the viewer—and we are inserted into this tender moment between the artist and his wife.

Chase exploits a vibrant palette, highlighting the play of patterns and colors from the kimono, the sash, the book, and the screen. The sharp contrast between the pale tones of the kimono and the vivid yellow-green pillow and red cushions, lushly rendered, reveals his technical virtuosity in the medium. Chase conveys the tactility of the diverse textiles—silks, satins, and plush velvets—with the inherent creaminess of the pastel. Set in his studio, a space central to his artistic identity, he created a sensitive portrait of his beloved wife and a personal image of refined elegance.

STEPHANIE L. HERDRICH

1. "Janitor Brother Tells How Chance Aided W. M. Chase," *Indianapolis Star* (March 25, 1917) quoted in Elsa Smithgall et al., *William Merritt Chase: A Modern Master* (Washington, DC : The Phillips Collection; in association with Yale University Press, 2016), 17.

2. The illustrations were published in the article, Susan N. Carter, "Street Life in Madrid," *Century Magazine* 19 (November 1889): 32–41. For images of the illustrations, see Ronald G. Pisano et al., *The Complete Catalogue of Known and Documented Work by William Merritt Chase (1849–1916)*, Vol. 1: *The Paintings in Pastel, Monotypes, Painted Tiles and Ceramic Plates, Watercolors, and Prints* (New Haven, CT, and London: Yale University Press, 2006), 72.

3. The oil, *Spanish Girl in White* (ca. 1886; Wake Forest University), also shows Alice seated in

a chair wearing a similar white dress (though holding a fan and wearing a yellow shawl). In the painting *A Tambourine Player; Mrs Chase as a Spanish Dancer* (ca. 1886; Montclair Art Museum), Alice modeled for the figure wearing the same white dress and yellow scarf while playing a tambourine. See Brandon K. Ruud et al., eds., *Americans in Spain: Painting and Travel, 1820–1920* (New Haven, CT: Yale University Press, 2021), 150–61.

4. Chase originally exhibited this work with the title *Spanish Gypsy Girl*, terminology that is now understood to be racist and harmful. In 1887 the work was sold in Chase's studio sale in New York.

5. For more on Chase's work in pastel, see Marjorie Shelley, "Assimilating Modernism: The Pastel Technique of William Merritt Chase," in Pisano et al., *William Merritt Chase*, 97–111.

Julian Alden Weir

AMERICAN, 1852–1919

The Window Seat, 1889
Pastel, charcoal, and pencil on paper
Sight: 13¼ × 17½ inches

Gift of the Macon and Joan Brock Collection
of American Art, 2023.4.4

A MEMBER OF A DISTINGUISHED FAMILY of artists, Julian Alden Weir forged a career at the intersection of academic tradition and artistic innovation. Weir's father, Robert Weir, served for more than four decades as a professor of drawing at the US Military Academy at West Point. This background likely encouraged his son's pursuit of an academic education rooted in figure drawing at France's prestigious École des Beaux-Arts, where he enrolled in 1874. There his training was concentrated on drawing from antique casts and the live model. This academic foundation perhaps explained Weir's initial revulsion upon encountering the Impressionists, whose work he viewed at the Third Impressionist Exhibition in 1877, which he declared "worse than the Chamber of Horrors."[1]

Nevertheless, Weir maintained an open mind artistically and continued to supplement his academic training with more modern approaches that included experimenting with loose brushwork and painterly effects, as well as painting out of doors. Like other progressive American artists, Weir also worked in pastel, a medium that had recently been revived and invigorated by the work of Impressionists like Mary Cassatt and Edgar Degas. Weir was a founding member of the American Society of Painters in Pastel and exhibited his first works at the group's second exhibition in 1888. The organization was formed to promote the vitality of the medium of pastel in the United States, and for Weir the impetus to work in this lively and direct medium proved transformative. Throughout the 1880s he embraced many of the tenets of Impressionism that he once scorned, aided by the opportunity afforded by media like pastel and watercolor, which allowed him to work in color directly from nature.

The pensive figure seated in the simple, sunbathed interior of *The Window Seat* is the artist's wife, Anna, captured during the summer of 1889 when the couple traveled to the Isle of Man off the coast of England. The restrained but psychologically charged study of a figure in an interior marks a departure from much of Weir's work in pastel, which to this point had largely focused on landscape. The monotone setting and stripped-down subject allowed for a subtle exploration of gradations in the shades of white and gray and the effects of light and shadow upon the texture of the space. When the work was shown in the fourth and final exhibition of the Pastel Society, critics' attention focused on this aspect in particular, with one writer praising the "graceful modulation of white tones," while another found fault in the variation of tones, which they called "too alike in quality."[2]

The Window Seat marked a moment of artistic and personal inflection for Weir. He created the work shortly following the death of his father and a year after the loss of the couple's infant son. Less than three years later, Anna herself passed away following the birth of the couple's daughter, Cora. During this period of personal tumult and loss, Weir honed his artistic approach, incorporating a wider array of sources from avant-garde artists like Édouard Manet to his father's former student, James McNeill Whistler. By the end of the century, Weir established a position as a leading progressive voice among American artists. In 1898 he joined with John Henry Twachtman, Childe Hassam, and others to form the group known as the Ten American Painters, which opposed the rigid structure and traditionalism of the National Academy of Design and other more conservative institutions. The artist who began his career steeped in academic principles and bristling at the innovations of Impressionism helped usher in a revolution in the American art establishment that paved the way for even more radical departures of the Ashcan School and American Modernists.

COREY PIPER

1. Julian Alden Weir, Letter to Robert Weir and Susan Weir, April 15, 1877, in Dorothy Weir Young, *The Life and Letters of J. Alden Weir* (New Haven, CT: Yale University Press, 1960), 123.

2. "The Painters in Pastel," *New York Sun* (May 17, 1890), 6; and "The Pastel Exhibition," *Art Amateur* 23 (June 1890): 4.

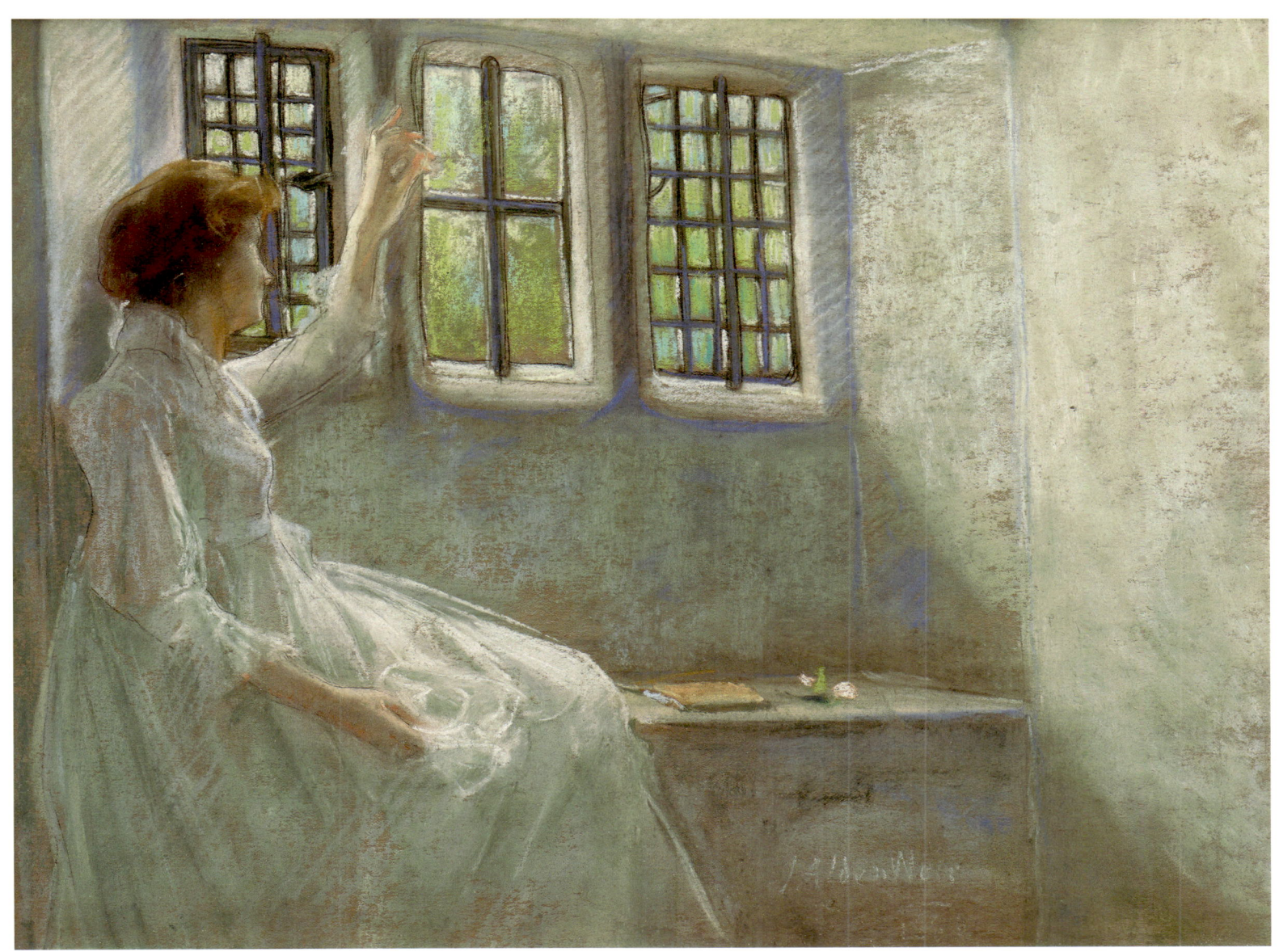

James McNeill Whistler

AMERICAN, 1834–1903

Mother and Child, ca. 1890

Pastel on brown paper, laid down on board

11 × 7⅛ inches

Gift of the Macon and Joan Brock Collection
of American Art. 2023.4.10

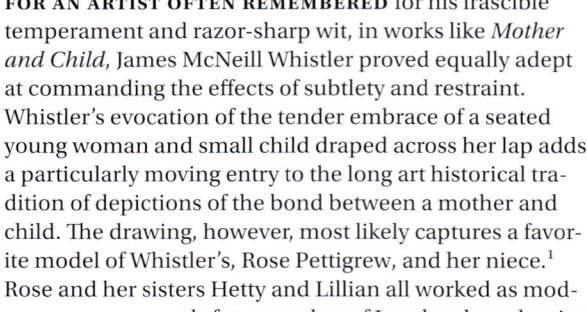

FIG. 1 James McNeill Whistler, *Bead Stringers*, 1880. Crayon and pastel on brown paper, 10⅞ × 4⅝ in. Freer Gallery of Art, Smithsonian Institution, Gift of Charles Lang Freer, F1905.124a-b

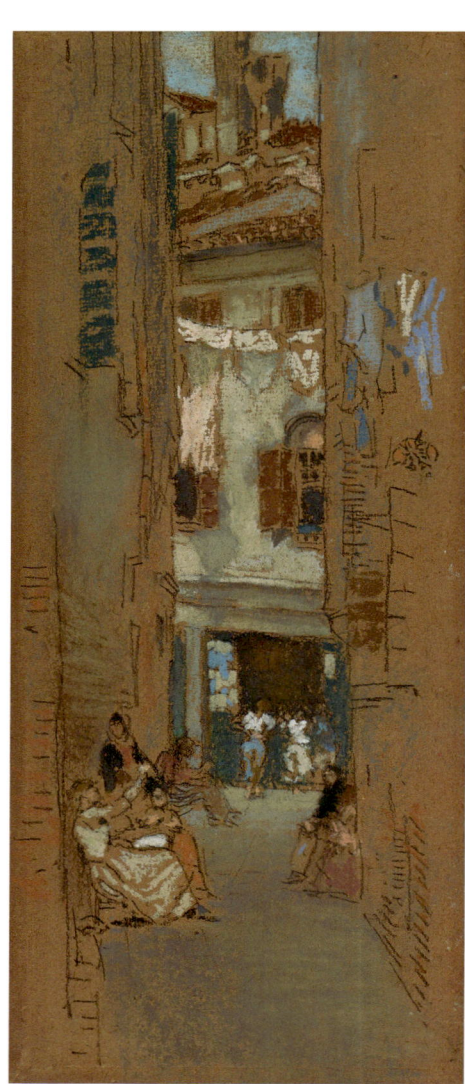

FOR AN ARTIST OFTEN REMEMBERED for his irascible temperament and razor-sharp wit, in works like *Mother and Child*, James McNeill Whistler proved equally adept at commanding the effects of subtlety and restraint. Whistler's evocation of the tender embrace of a seated young woman and small child draped across her lap adds a particularly moving entry to the long art historical tradition of depictions of the bond between a mother and child. The drawing, however, most likely captures a favorite model of Whistler's, Rose Pettigrew, and her niece.[1] Rose and her sisters Hetty and Lillian all worked as models for a number of London-based artists, including John Everett Millais, William Holman Hunt, and Whistler.[2]

At the height of Whistler's fascination with Rose Pettigrew, she modeled for the artist on a near-daily basis and posed for a series of related drawings depicting her holding the young child. As he repeatedly returned to the motif, Whistler clearly felt that he had achieved something lofty in these understated yet powerfully moving drawings. In 1891, after visiting an exhibition at the Paris gallery of Paul Durand-Ruel, Whistler wrote to his wife, Beatrice, scoffing at the efforts on display by Renoir and Degas, and proclaiming of his 'Rosies,' "We have no idea how precious they are!"[3] *Mother and Child* shares many characteristics with the related works in the group, from the rough and rich brown paper to the sparing use of simple harmonies of pastel, balanced between the flesh tones and the bright blues of the dress and rich purple of her cap.

Throughout his career Whistler moved freely between media. By the time he embarked upon the series of drawings of Rose Pettigrew, he had devoted more than a decade to working seriously with the medium of pastel. In 1879 Whistler traveled to Venice to produce etchings of the storied city and left fourteen months later having achieved a major breakthrough with his pastel drawings of its picturesque alleyways and signature canals (fig. 1). As an artist who trained initially as a draftsman, then spent his early career learning to paint directly from nature, pastel offered a means of combining color and line.[4]

The critical attention garnered by the Venice pastels encouraged Whistler to pursue the medium more seriously. Upon returning to London, Whistler began to focus his efforts in pastel on the subject of studio models. Throughout the 1880s Whistler's pastels featured classically posed figures draped in delicate, flowing robes, as well as nudes lounging across sumptuously patterned fabrics. By the time he created *Mother and Child*, Whistler had honed his approach to such drawings, which relied upon several key stylistic principles readily apparent in this work. These include the large expanse of the unmarked paper, careful delineation of the figures and the drapery, and the subtle deployment of pastel to indicate form and balance the overall composition. Whistler used this deceptively straightforward formula to masterful effect, in an image that suggests as much as it describes, of the tender and loving relationship between the two figures and the deep-seated human emotion that bonds mothers and their children.

COREY PIPER

1. Margaret F. MacDonald, *James McNeill Whistler: Drawings, Pastels, and Watercolours, A Catalogue Raisonné* (New Haven, CT, and London: Yale University Press, 1995), 464.

2. Jill Berk Jiminez, *Dictionary of Artists' Models* (London: Taylor and Francis, 2013), 422.

3. James McNeill Whistler to Beatrice Whistler, June 11, 1891. *The Correspondence of James McNeill Whistler, 1855–1903,* edited by Margaret F. MacDonald, Patricia de Montfort, and Nigel Thorp; including "The Correspondence of Anna McNeill Whistler, 1855–1880," edited by Georgia Toutziari, http://www.whistler.arts.gla.ac.uk/correspondence.

4. Margaret F. MacDonald, *Whistler Pastels and Related Works in the Hunterian Art Gallery* (Glasgow: Hunterian Art Gallery, 1984), 11.

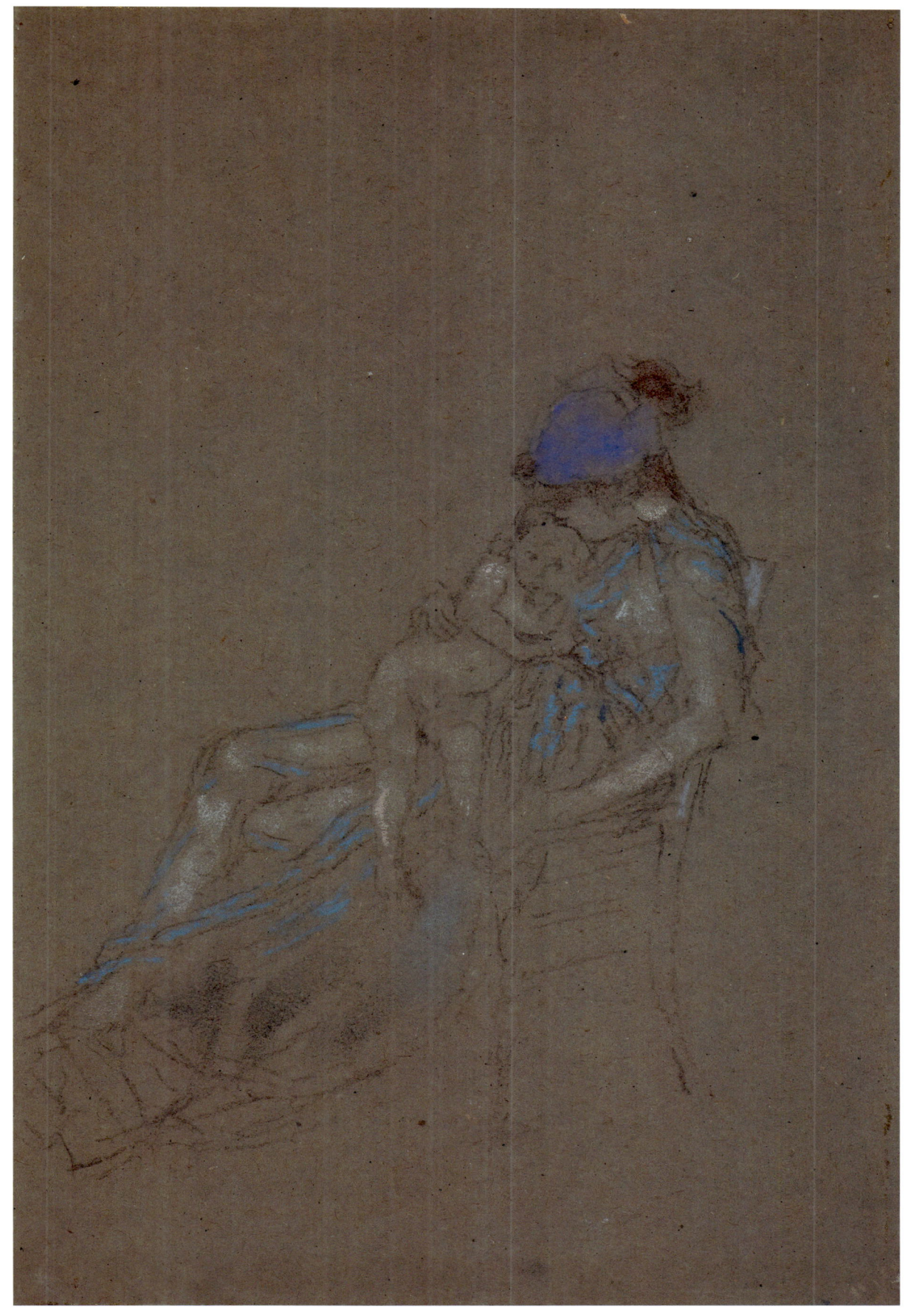

Mary Cassatt

AMERICAN, 1844–1926

Gathering Fruit, ca. 1893

Drypoint, soft ground etching, and aquatint printed in colors, on laid paper

16⅝ × 11¾ inches; sheet: 20 × 15½ inches

Museum purchase with funds given by the Macon and Joan Brock Collection of American Art, 2022.28

MARY CASSATT was the leading American Impressionist artist and one of the most innovative artists of her age. She associated closely with Edgar Degas and Camille Pissarro and produced a large body of work in painting, pastel, and print. Degas invited her to join the Impressionist group in 1877, and she went on to exhibit in four of the eight eponymous exhibitions they organized, the only American to do so. She was born in Pittsburgh in 1844, and after training at the Pennsylvania Academy of the Fine Arts in Philadelphia, her family's wealth allowed her to study art with the renowned academic painter Jean-Léon Gérôme in Paris.

Cassatt's intimate portrait painting of a little girl in a red cloak and prominent red beret shows a proud and determined girl boldly dressed and probably enjoying a visit to a park. Viewed from an adult's higher point of view, the child seems at once confident and vulnerable. The painting is a small sketch deliberately left unfinished, with a broad and indistinctly brushed-in green background space too expansive for a private garden.

Cassatt's body of work is an extraordinary exploration of the bond between children and their mothers, and the three works in the Brock collection are no exception. Her depictions of children are often about the rituals of their day, such as bathing, sleeping, mealtimes, or promenades like the one alluded to in the Brock painting. The delightful little girl is posed close to the artist; the ease and familiarity she expresses all suggest the intimacy of a close parental bond.[1]

The broken brushstrokes and partially finished canvas suggests a sketch for a larger work, but Cassatt's work here is a finished painting in keeping with impressionist technique. Her chief inspiration in producing virtuoso sketches was Edgar Degas, perhaps the artist with whom she was most closely associated artistically, and who used empty areas of canvas to great effect. The sketch remained with the artist until her death and passed from her estate into a private collection.

While painting is the medium the Impressionists are most immediately identified with, most of them were also printmakers who, like Cassatt, sought to translate the principles of Impressionism into the more popular and accessible but laborious medium of prints. Cassatt came to printmaking later in her career at the suggestion of Degas and also under the influence of American artist James McNeill Whistler, who was a leader in the etching revival of the late nineteenth century. As a result, Cassatt became one of the most ambitious and innovative printmakers of the late nineteenth century, experimenting with a wide range of novel techniques to produce the specific effects typical of her work in other media, such as soft, shimmering, painterly effects and the flattened shapes she admired in the Japanese woodcut prints so revered by the Impressionists.

The large color print *Gathering Fruit* was loosely excerpted from the center panel in Cassatt's immense fifty-eight by twelve feet, three-panel mural *Modern Woman*, painted for the south tympanum of the Gallery of Honor in the Women's Building at the 1893 World's Columbian Exposition in Chicago. No longer extant, the mural showcased the achievements and ambitions of women throughout history (fig. 1). Cassatt's evocative subject shows women picking fruit, a motif that extends to antiquity and alludes to the story of Adam and Eve in the Garden of Eden. She executed the immense painting in a glass-roofed studio constructed for the commission in Bachivillers, almost fifty miles northwest of Paris.

This copperplate intaglio print consists of work in drypoint, soft ground, and aquatint. In contrast to traditional acid-bath etching, these techniques correspond to the painterliness of impressionist technique, as well as the softness and atmospheric quality the artists sought in their paintings.[2] She refined this print through a process of an astonishing eleven states, most of which consist of only one or two impressions, except for the final one. Only twenty impressions of the eleventh and final state were documented by the great dealer of the Impressionists, Durand-Ruel, as having been produced.

This color print was not made through the traditional technique of carefully registered consecutive impressions

FIG. 1 Mary Cassatt, *Modern Woman*, 1893, reproduced for *Harper's Magazine*, 1902. Engraving, New York Public Library

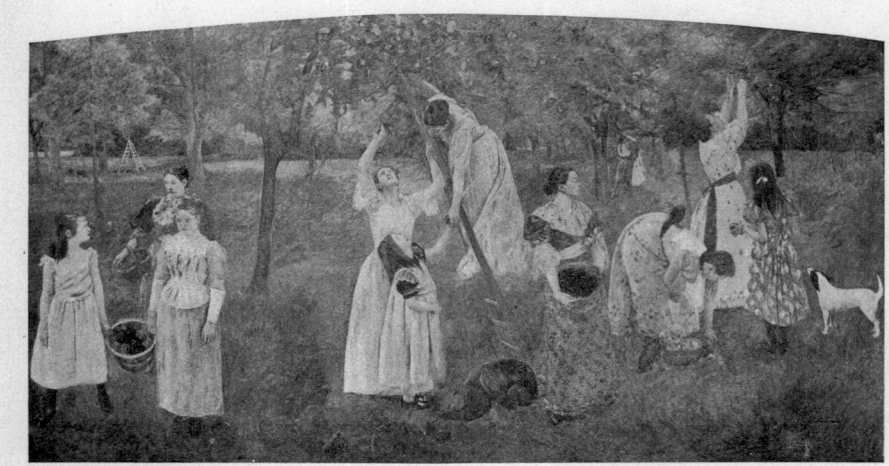

MODERN WOMAN (SECTION OF TYMPANUM). BY MARY CASSATT.

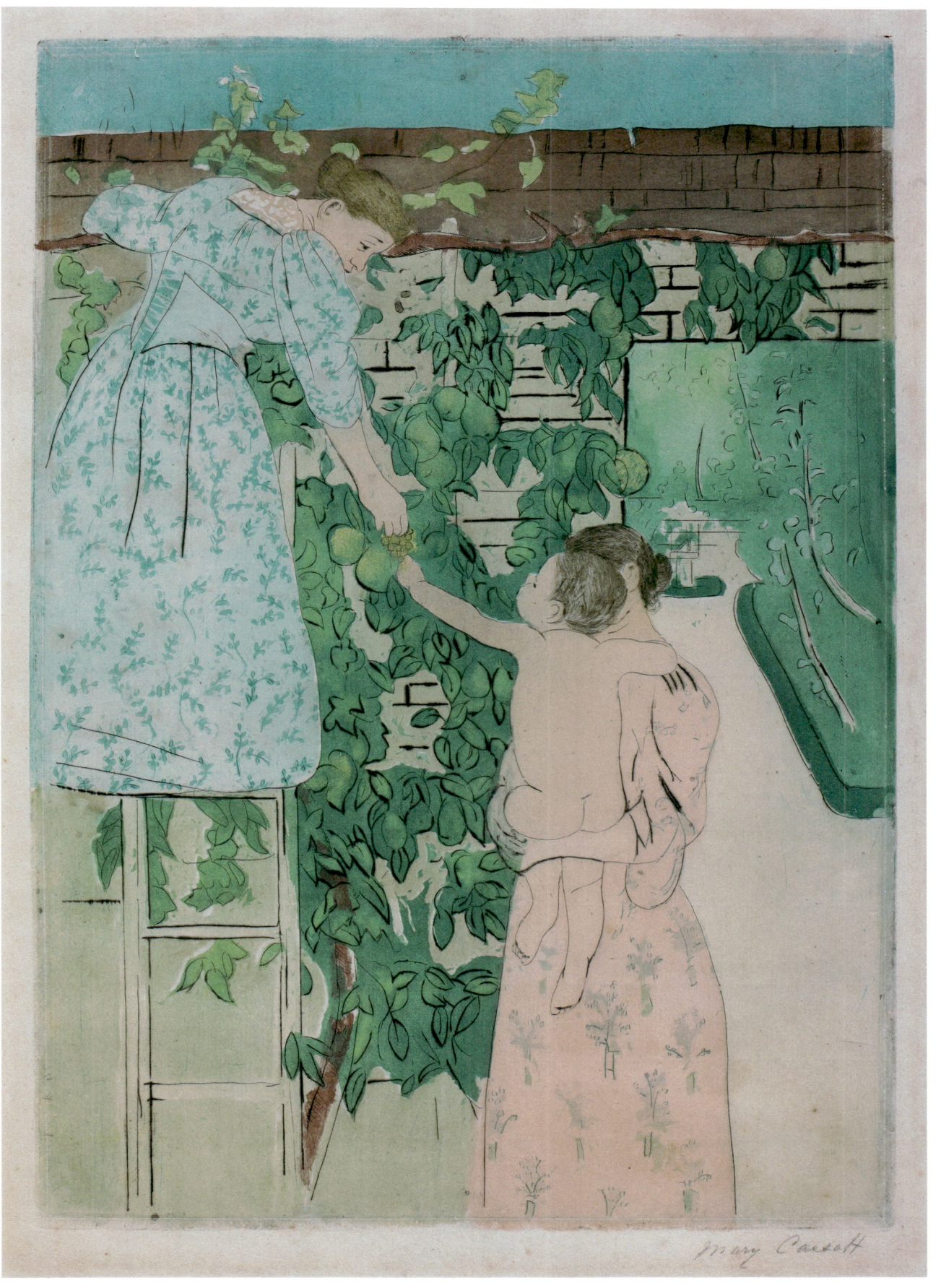

Mary Cassatt

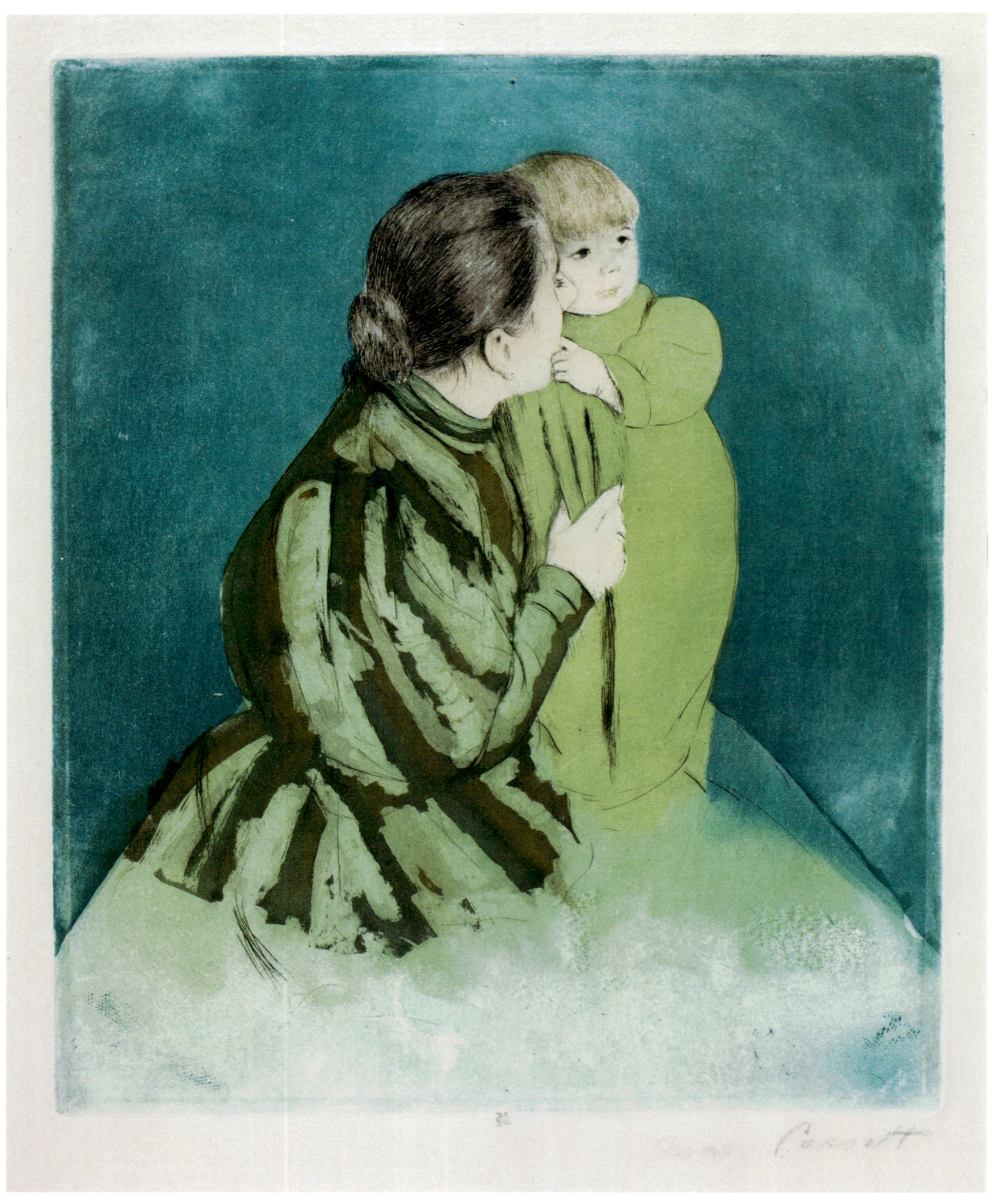

Peasant Mother and Child, ca. 1894
Drypoint and aquatint printed in colors, on laid paper
11¾ × 9½ inches; sheet: 12⅛ × 17¼ inches

Museum purchase with funds given by the Macon and Joan Brock Collection of American Art, 2022.27

The Lamp, 1890–91
Drypoint, soft ground etching, and aquatint printed in colors, on laid paper
12¾ × 9⅞ inches; sheet: 17 × 11⅞ inches

Museum purchase with funds given by the Macon and Joan Brock Collection of American Art, 2023.12

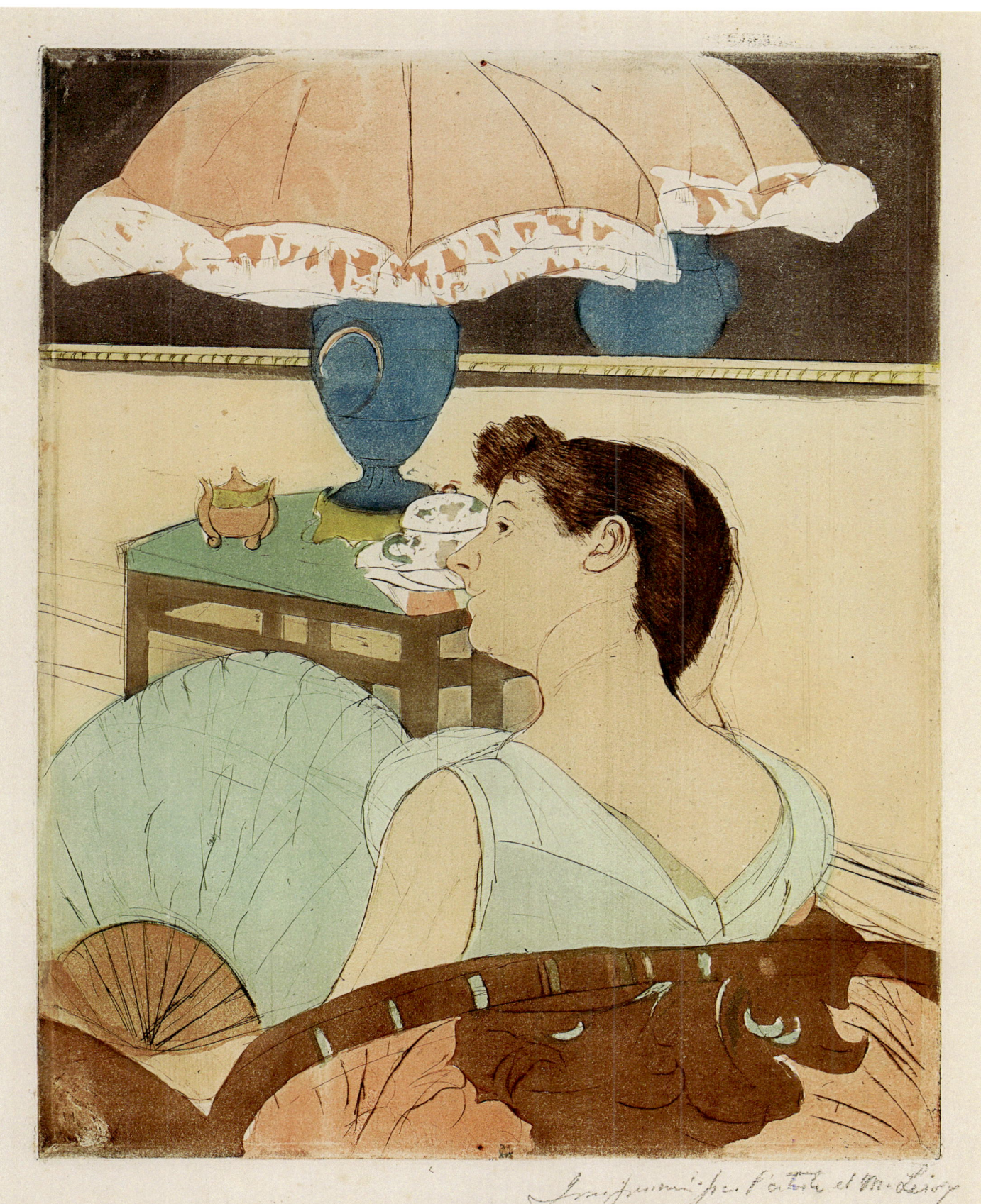

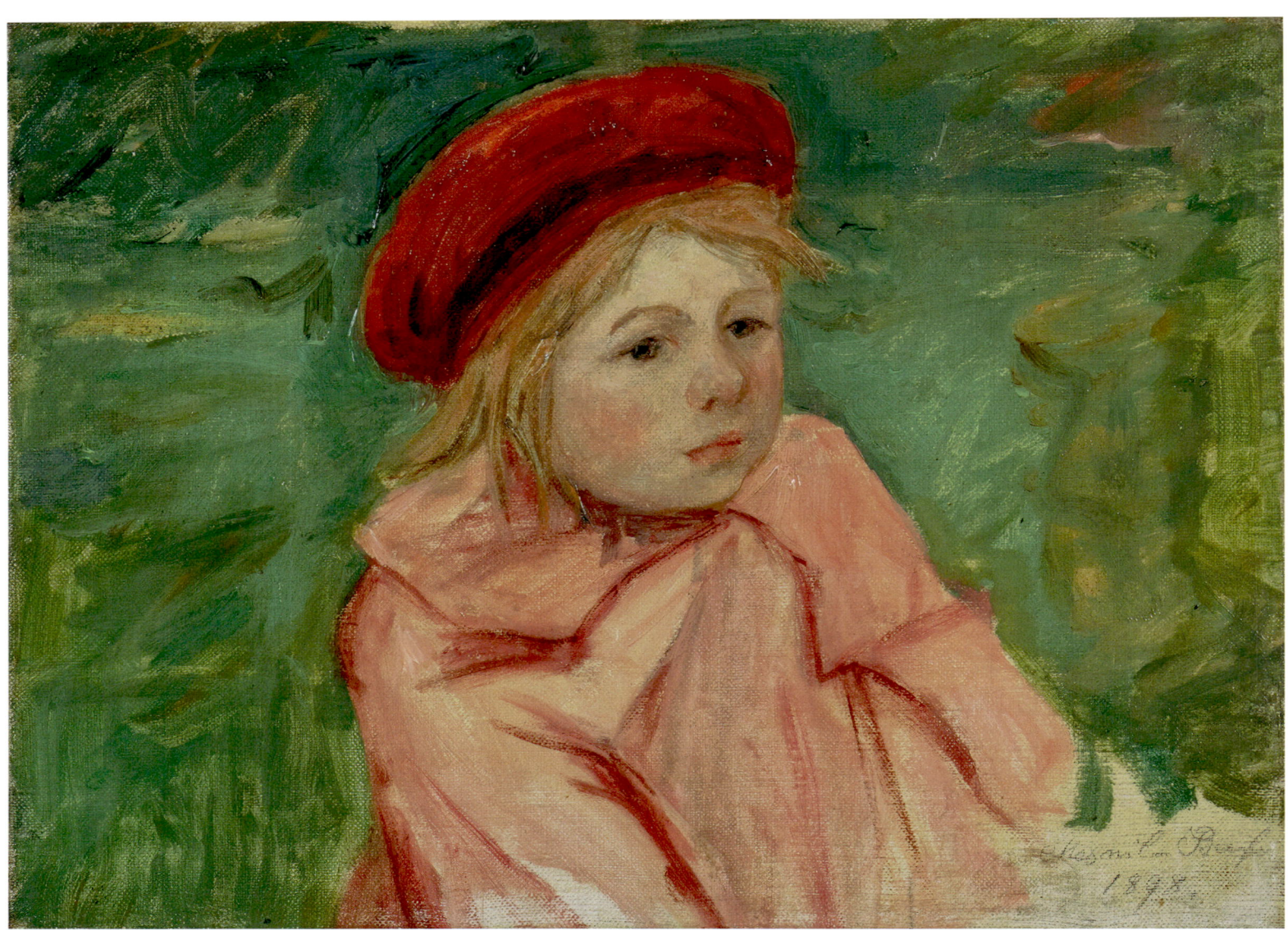

Little Girl in a Red Beret (Le béret rouge), 1898
Oil on canvas
9½ × 13 inches

from a series of separate plates, each inked with one single color. Rather, all the different colored inks were applied to only three plates in separate areas using a tool consisting of bundled cloth, nicknamed a *poupée* (doll) because of its shape. This achieved a more painterly effect and ensured each print was somewhat different from the others. This impression, for example, has a light green background at left and a strip of wall in light brown. Most of the others have a light tan background and darker strip of bricks.

The smaller copperplate print *Peasant Mother and Child* of the following year is produced in drypoint and aquatint techniques as well and is part of a larger edition of fifty prints. Like the other works by Cassatt in the Brock Collection, it deals with the lives of women and children. As with *Gathering Fruit* and many of her prints, it is loosely based on a work in other media, in this case a pastel sketch now in Belgrade and the finished version in pastel (now lost).[3] *Peasant Mother and Child* was accomplished with a variety of inking on a single plate in her usual, highly experimental technique. Cassatt gave this impression to her second cousin, Mrs. Thomas A. Scott, and it passed from Scott's descendants to the Anne and Gordon Getty Collection in 1996.

The Brock Collection boasts a superb range of Cassatt's most characteristic and ambitious works. The artist carved out a distinctly feminine space in the world of avant-garde art; she also encouraged Americans like the Havemeyers to collect Impressionist art. She thus contributed to Americans' acceptance of and interest in the leading modern movement in art.

LLOYD DEWITT

1. Judith A. Barter, "Mary Cassatt: Theme, Sources, and the Modern Woman," in *Mary Cassatt, Modern Woman* (Chicago: Art Institute of Chicago, 1998), 73.

2. Nancy Mowll Mathews and Barbara Stern Shapiro, *Mary Cassatt: The Color Prints* (Williamstown, MA: Williams College Museum of Art, 1989), 27.

3. Matthews and Shapiro, *Mary Cassatt*, 168.

Mary Fairchild MacMonnies

AMERICAN, 1858–1946

In the Garden, Giverny, ca. 1895

Oil on canvas

15 × 18 inches

Gift of the Macon and Joan Brock Collection of American Art, 2023.4.6

THE MACMONNIESES' HOME in Giverny served as a magnet for American painters who flocked to the village in Normandy, drawn by the presence of the famed but reclusive Impressionist Claude Monet and the pursuit of artistic nourishment found painting out of doors amidst the region's verdant gardens and landscapes. Mary Fairchild MacMonnies began frequenting Giverny during the summers starting around 1890, and in 1895 she established a more permanent residence there with her husband, the sculptor Frederick William MacMonnies, whom she had wed in 1888. The couple first rented a comparatively modest home known as Villa Bêsche and a few years later purchased a more palatial seventeenth-century former monastery where they would live until their divorce in 1909.

In 1885 as a young art student in St. Louis, Mary Fairchild earned a three-year scholarship to study abroad in France, an experience that would dramatically transform the shape of her career. She enrolled at the Académie Julian in Paris and within a year of her arrival had her first work accepted at the Salon. Subsequent years saw her exhibiting work at the Salon and the 1889 Exposition Universelle in Paris as well as back in the United States. These successes led to the prestigious commission to create a mural for the Woman's Building at the 1893 World's Columbian Exposition, a space designed to highlight the artistic accomplishments of women. MacMonnies's mural *Primitive Woman*, along with Mary Cassatt's *Modern Woman*, occupied the most prominent positions within the tympana towering above either end of the building's interior walls.[1] The major commission conferred stature upon MacMonnies, who was still relatively early in her career and largely unfamiliar to American audiences.

Buoyed by her success at the exposition, MacMonnies settled into an idyllic and artistically fruitful life in Giverny. By this time the artistic heart of the village centered less on the figure of Monet but instead had developed into an artists' colony, populated by numerous painters, overwhelmingly American, drawn to Giverny to explore the principles of Impressionism among like-minded practitioners. MacMonnies and her husband occupied the center of this American expatriate community in the village that included painters like Lilla Cabot Perry, Theodore Robinson, and Will Hicok Low (who MacMonnies would later marry following her divorce).

In the Garden likely dates from MacMonnies's earliest years in Giverny, possibly depicting the outdoor space at Villa Bêsche. A different model appears in the same setting in a related painting, *Woman in White under an Arbor*.[2] An earlier date of ca. 1890 has been suggested for that work, which could place the site at either the Hotel Baudy, a popular residence for American visitors where the MacMonnies stayed from 1890 to 1895, or even MacMonnies's Paris residence and studio. Through many years and two different homes in Giverny, the garden would remain a key subject for MacMonnies. Her paintings often featured family members, caregivers, and her immediate domestic circle engaged in simple leisure amidst brilliant light and lush plants. In such works her natural command of impressionist techniques and deep familiarity with her subjects combine to express a vision of contentment in which the artist's personal and artistic worlds are harmoniously intertwined.

COREY PIPER

1. Both murals are now presumed lost. See Carolyn Kinder Carr and Sally Webster, "Mary Cassatt and Mary Fairchild MacMonnies: The Search for Their 1893 Murals," *American Art* 8 (Winter 1994): 52–69.

2. See Musée de Vernon, *Portraits de femmes* (Rouen: Editions point de vues, 2016), 86–87. I wish to thank Kirstin Ringelberg for helping illuminate the connection between these two paintings and the early chronology of MacMonnies's residence in Giverny.

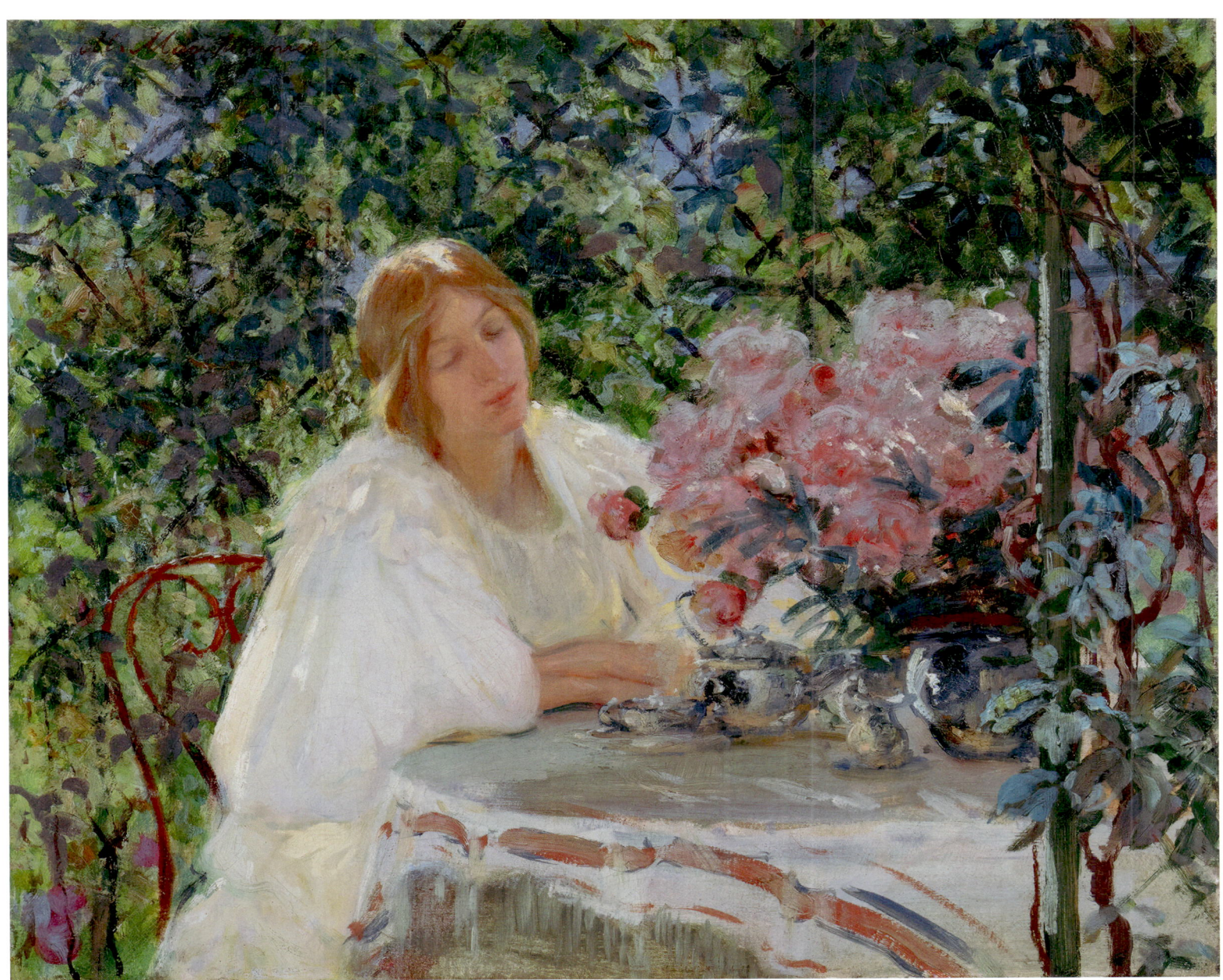

Irving Ramsay Wiles

AMERICAN, 1861–1948

Sunshine and Shadow, ca. 1895

Oil on panel

13½ × 16½ inches

Promised Gift of the Macon and Joan Brock Collection
of American Art

MEASURED IN TERMS of critical reputation and commercial success, Irving Ramsay Wiles occupied a position at the center of the American art world around the turn of the twentieth century. He was often grouped with his friends and contemporaries, like William Merritt Chase, James Carroll Beckwith, and John Singer Sargent, as a key exponent of a cosmopolitan style of painting that embraced an eclectic source of modern stylistic elements in service of an elegant and genteel subject matter, drawn from the polite contours of upper-class society. Though he would eventually develop into a leading society portraitist, he devoted considerable attention throughout his career to subjects from his immediate domestic and social sphere, like *Sunshine and Shadow* and *A Summer Day*. Dated nearly four decades apart, the two works depict his wife and daughter, respectively, in almost identical moments of leisure.

As the son of painter Lemuel Wiles, Irving Ramsay Wiles was encouraged in his artistic pursuits from a young age. He sought training at the Art Students League, where he first met Chase, a teacher who would remain a lifelong friend. At the urging of Chase and his other teacher Beckwith, Wiles traveled to France, where he eventually found a space in the atelier of the brash French painter Carolus-Duran, following in the footsteps of many American progressive artists, including Beckwith and Sargent. However, unlike many American artists, Wiles never seemed inclined to remain abroad. Instead he returned to the United States, where he assisted his father at the Silver Lake Art School and found steady employment as an illustrator for the leading periodicals of the day, including *Scribner's* and *Harper's Weekly*.

Wiles continued to develop his career as a painter, exhibiting work at the National Academy of Design, the Society of American Artists, the American Watercolor Society, and many other leading venues. In 1895 he acquired a small homestead at Peconic on Long Island and began a regular pattern of summers spent working out of doors and among the family's gardens. *Sunshine and Shadow*, dating from around this first summer at Peconic, likely depicts the artist's wife, Mary Lee, reading over the back of a bench.[1] The paintings that Wiles produced on Long Island offered the artist a forum to hone his stylistic approach in a deeply personal manner that eschewed narrative detail in favor of a harmonious aesthetic. The author Theodore Dreiser noted the merits of this approach in an 1898 review, writing of Wiles, "He would himself rather that his pictures attract the eye by a subtle suggestion of beauty than that they attracted attention because of a deed being enacted."[2] Wiles remained steadfastly committed to this path throughout his life. In *A Summer Day*, painted around 1932, the seated, dark-haired figure enjoying a leisurely moment outdoors is most likely his daughter Gladys.[3] Throughout his long career, Wiles rarely sought to expand the boundaries of modern painting but instead employed a modern pictorial language of his era to pursue a personal aesthetic vision with great dexterity and to delightful effect.

COREY PIPER

1. Barbara Novak, *The Thyssen-Bornemisza Collection: Nineteenth-Century American Painting* (London: Vendome Press, 1986), 294. The mountains in the distance do not appear to match the Long Island topography, suggesting that the work may have been created at an earlier date.

2. Theodore Dreiser, "Art Work of Irving R. Wiles," *Metropolitan Magazine* 7 (April 1898): 359.

3. Gladys has been identified as the young woman seated in *In the Studio* (American Academy and Institute of Arts and Letters) who appears nearly identical to the figure in *A Summer Day*. See Gary A. Reynolds, *Irving R. Wiles* (New York: National Academy of Design, 1988), pl. 59, 93.

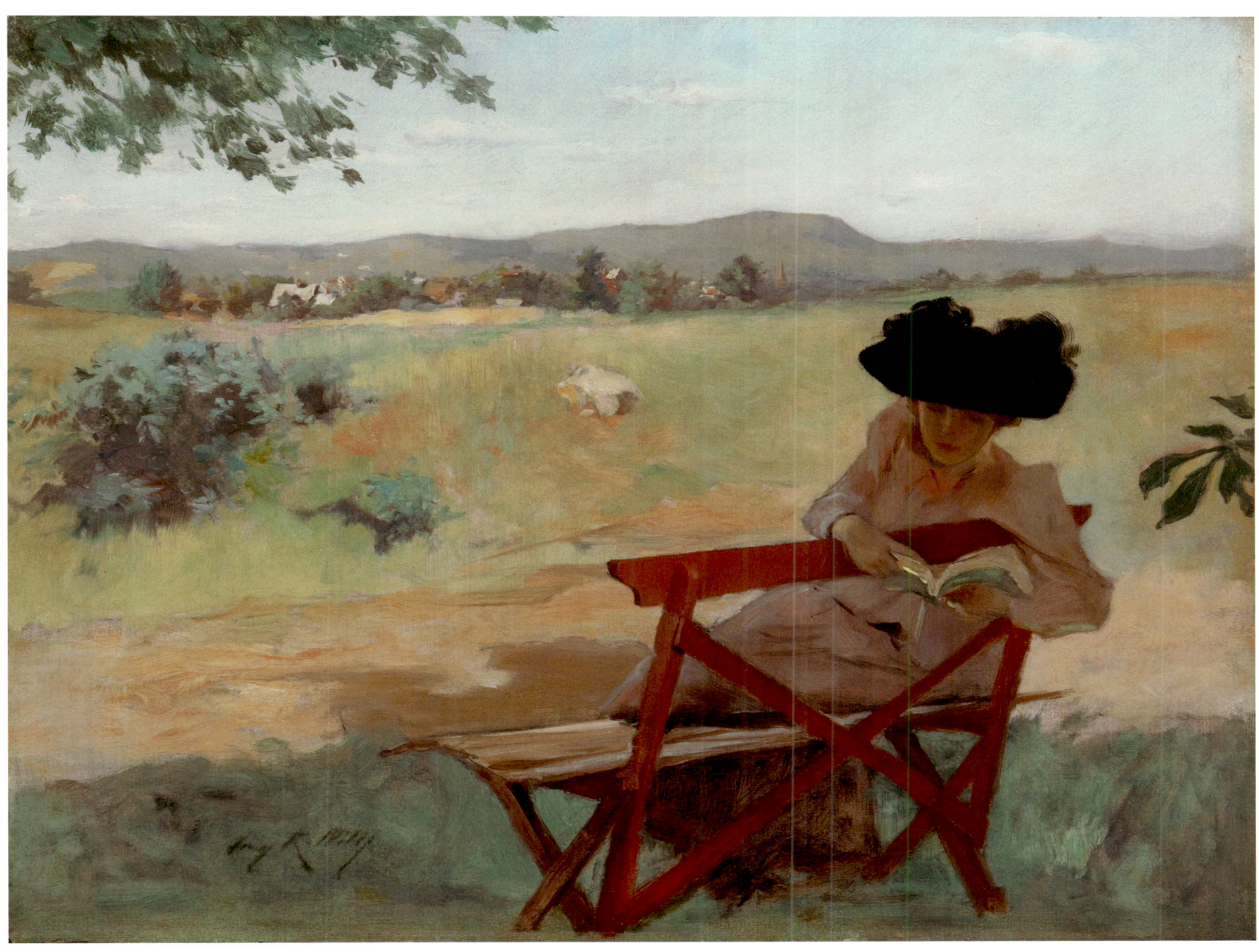

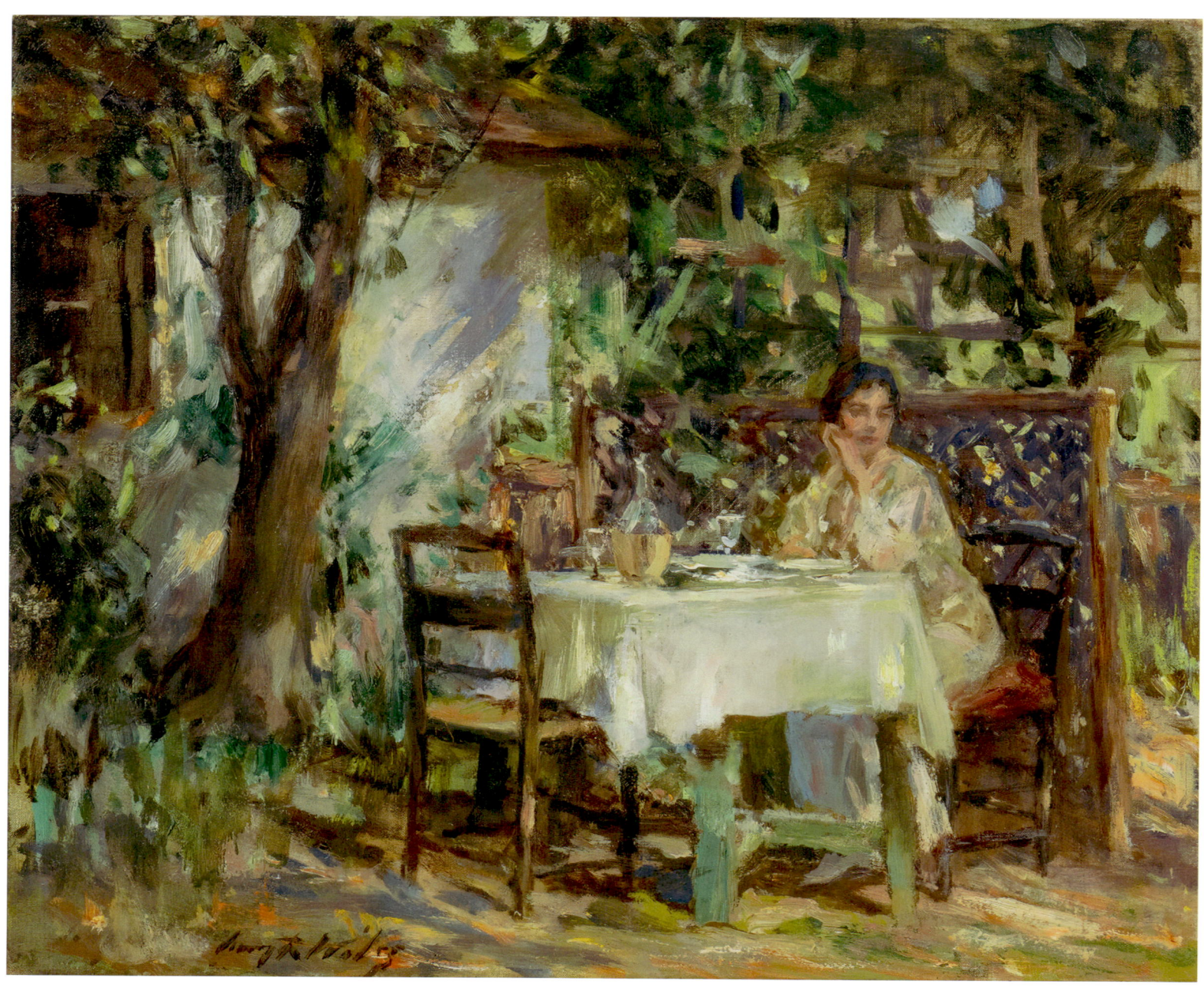

A Summer Day, ca. 1932
Oil on canvas
15 × 18 inches

Bouquet in a Blue Vase, ca. 1930s
Oil on canvas
18 × 15 inches

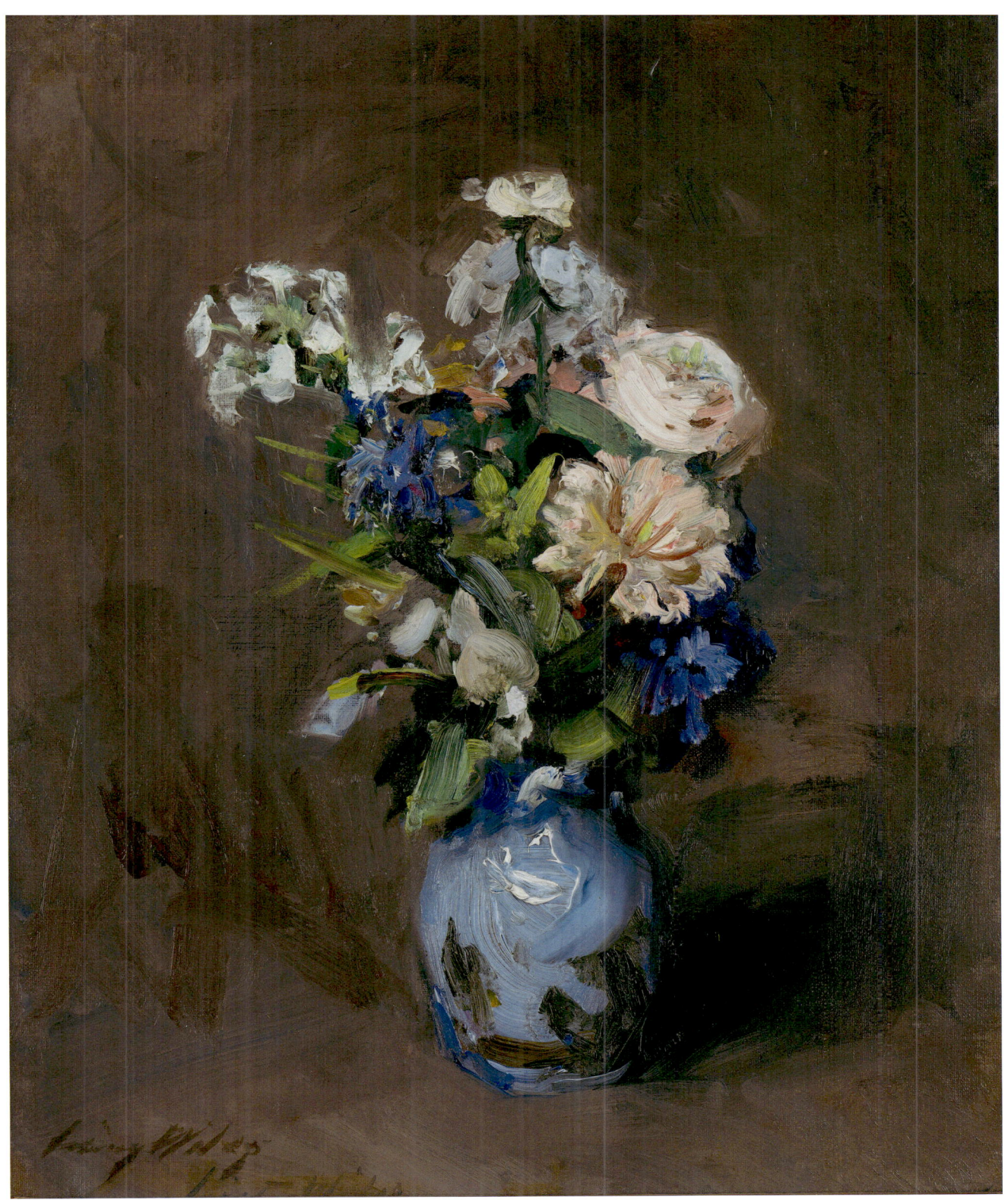

Helen Corson Hovenden

AMERICAN, 1846–1935

In the Gallery, 1901

Oil on canvas

36 × 20 inches

Promised Gift of the Macon and Joan Brock Collection
of American Art

WHEN AVANT-GARDE PRACTITIONERS of Impressionism were beginning to challenge the aesthetic norms of the art world in the United States, Helen Corson Hovenden adhered to naturalism and narrative art with works like *In the Gallery*. A young boy, who may be modeled after her son, has removed his hat and stands in awe of the artwork before him.[1] The gallery represented is most likely inspired by one of the many American annual exhibitions at which Hovenden had shown in cities like Philadelphia, New York, Boston, Chicago, and Washington, DC. Her home in Plymouth Meeting, Pennsylvania, is about twenty miles from Philadelphia, where she had her longest run exhibiting annually at the Pennsylvania Academy of the Fine Arts between 1877 and 1905. Hovenden highlights the boy's profile against the backdrop of a large rural landscape behind him. The wall he faces is hung in a "salon style" typical of turn-of-century galleries when paintings were commonly stacked close together, and some were "skied" high near the ceiling. The other pictures are suggestive of architectural scenes, portraits, and still lifes, but the painting that has captivated the attention of Hovenden's young subject is just out of view—inviting us to imagine what scene has him so mesmerized.

Hovenden was the daughter of Quaker abolitionists George and Martha Corson. George was a cofounder of the Plymouth Meeting Anti-Slavery movement. During the artist's youth and before the Civil War, the family homestead in Plymouth Meeting (known as Abolition Hall) was a significant stop on the Underground Railroad for enslaved African Americans seeking freedom. The Corsons must have supported Helen's artistic ambitions. She attended the Philadelphia School of Design for Women (now Moore College of Art and Design) and in 1875 traveled to Paris to study at the Académie Julian, which was popular with American students. She stayed in Paris for five years and exhibited at the Paris Salon an impressive three times. While there she met artist Thomas Hovenden during a trip to Brittany. They married in 1881 and moved into the Corson home, converting parts of it into a painting studio and room for photography. Helen was a talented photographer and aided her husband's rising career by creating study photographs for him to work from, documenting his paintings, and taking portraits of him as he painted.[2] Against the social atmosphere of Abolition Hall, where activists like William Lloyd Garrison and Lucretia Mott came to speak, the couple painted narrative genre and history scenes, some of which revealed their interest in African American subjects.[3] Tragically, Thomas was killed in 1895 when he accidentally stepped into the path of a passing train, leaving Helen widowed for the remainder of her life. Nevertheless, she continued to paint and was a member of the Plastic Club, one of the few clubs for women artists in Philadelphia. She became known locally for her portraits of family pets and floral still lifes. *In the Gallery* indicates Hovenden's consideration of art's power to move ordinary audiences outside of the professional art world—perhaps children were the critics she most aimed to impress.

JENNIFER STETTLER PARSONS

1. The boy resembles Thomas Hovenden, Jr., in photographs Helen took of the family about a decade earlier. He was about nineteen years old when this work was painted. See photographs in Anne Gregory Terhune, *Thomas Hovenden: His Life and Art* (Philadelphia: University of Pennsylvania Press, 2006), 173, 188.

2. Terhune, *Thomas Hovenden*, 102, 156, 157.

3. Thomas Hovenden's *Breaking Home Ties* (1890; Philadelphia Museum of Art) was voted the most popular painting at the 1893 World's Columbian Exposition in Chicago. It was modeled on the family's home, friends, and relatives, and some believe that Helen may have painted the family's dog into the composition. See Terhune, *Thomas Hovenden*, 156. For a comparison, see Helen's painting of the family dog in *Martha Hovenden and Her Dog* (1888; Woodmere Art Museum), https://woodmereartmuseum.org/explore-online/collection/martha-hovenden-and-her-dog (accessed October 2022). Related to abolitionism, a well-regarded work by Thomas Hovenden is *The Last Moments of John Brown* (1882–84; Metropolitan Museum of Art). One of the Hovendens' African American neighbors in Plymouth Meeting, Samuel Jones, became a favorite model. Both Thomas and Helen Corson Hovenden exhibited African American subjects at the National Academy of Design's 1881 exhibition; see Terhune, *Thomas Hovenden*, 102–5.

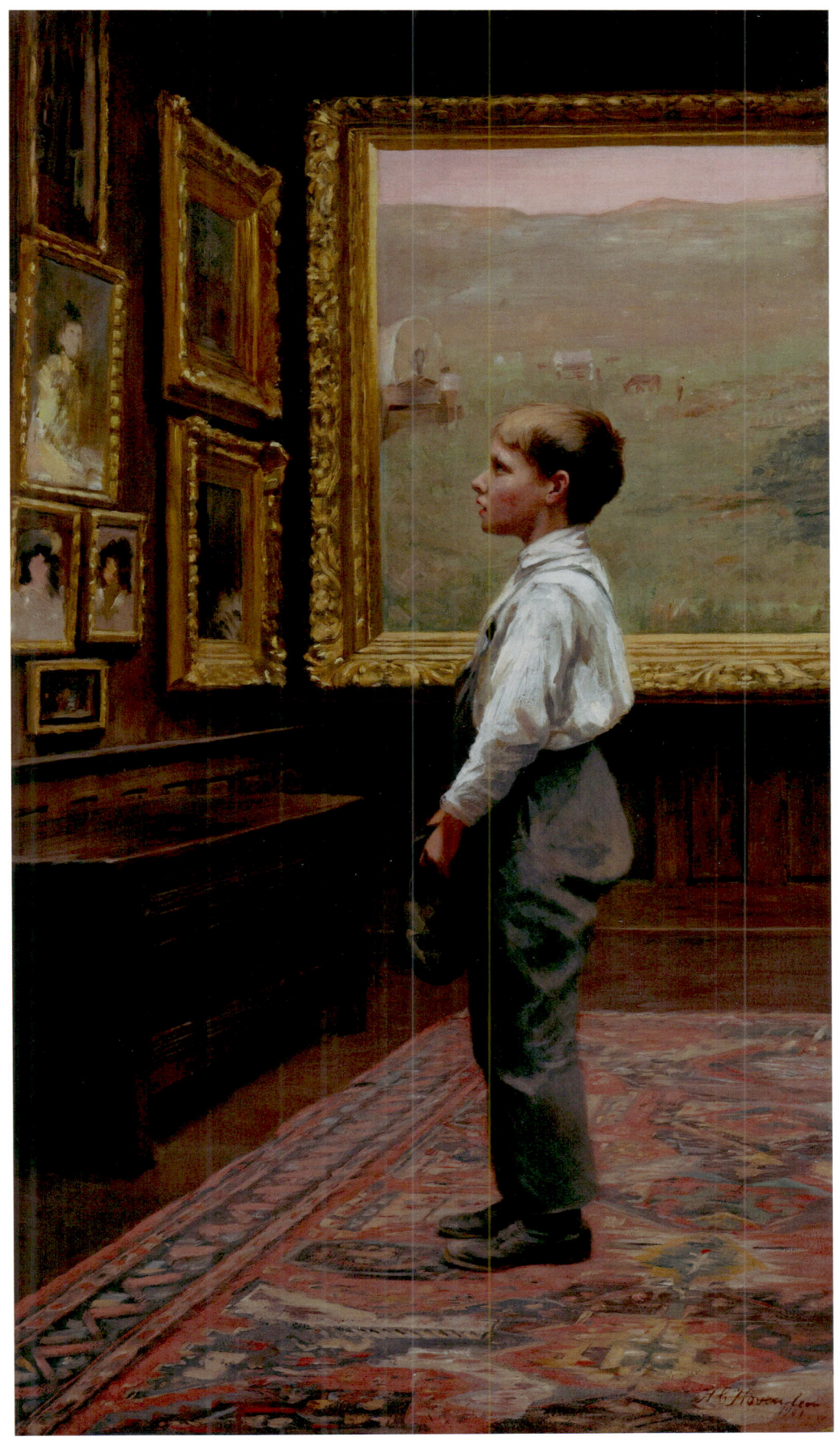

Alberta Binford McCloskey

AMERICAN, 1863–1911

Poppies, 1901

Oil on canvas

30 × 16 inches

Gift of the Macon and Joan Brock Collection
of American Art, 2023.4.11

DURING A CAREER that ranged back and forth across the North American continent and the Atlantic, Alberta Binford McCloskey mastered a style of still life painting that combined botanical realism with a sense of decorative flourish. Along with painters like Martin Johnson Heade, William Harnett, and Helen Searle, McCloskey fed a popular revival of the still life genre during the late nineteenth century. In *Poppies* McCloskey deployed a formula she had honed over nearly two decades to great effect. The ostentatious pink poppy blossoms are set against an austere, green studio backdrop and burst forth from spindly stems. The small Chinese enameled vase appears almost too precariously small to hold the entire arrangement but adds a hint of worldly eclecticism, a feature that McCloskey often incorporated into her paintings.[1] The vibrant pinks and reds of the petals are rendered in lush strokes of paint that convincingly convey both the brilliance and delicacy of the blossoms.

Alberta McCloskey began her career working in Denver, a city not then known as a center of artistic activity. There she met William McCloskey, a fellow painter who had trained at the Pennsylvania Academy of the Fine Arts, whom she would wed in 1883. The couple soon moved to Los Angeles, where they embarked on a fruitful artistic partnership that would take them across the globe and sustain both of their careers. The artists set up a studio in the burgeoning city and quickly attracted attention and commissions. Specializing in portraiture and still life painting, both William and Alberta exhibited their work within their semipublic home-studio-gallery space, and the two sometimes worked on canvases together. Alberta began to develop a specialty in still life, and in 1885 perhaps anticipating a move eastward, sent three still life works to the annual exhibition of the Pennsylvania Academy of the Fine Arts.[2] By the next year, the artists had established a residence in New York City, a prime location for a specialist in still life to pursue exposure and acclaim. While William developed the wrapped orange motif, for which he would eventually become best known, Alberta continued to pursue a wide range of floral subjects and compositional approaches. In New York the McCloskeys engaged in a sophisticated and bustling professional art world, exhibiting their paintings in their own private studio, as well as prominent local venues and likely worked with a number of commercial lithographers who sold fine art reproductions of their work.[3]

By 1898 the couple had separated, and Alberta settled in San Francisco, where she likely created *Poppies*. The species of flower depicted is the opium poppy, a variety possessing obvious natural beauty and aesthetic charm but also a contentious history. The flower was grown commercially in California until 1942, when congress outlawed the cultivation of the opium poppy. In this example McCloskey appears concerned primarily with the vivid character of the delicate blossoms, shown in various phases of bloom, from peak opening to the shedding of petals.

Following her move to San Francisco, poor health curtailed McCloskey's professional activities, and she died in 1911 in Jamaica, where she had traveled to convalesce.[4] This canvas likely stayed within the artist's daughter's possession, as it can be seen in a photograph of the family's roadside holiday retreat, which they operated in rural Oregon throughout the 1930s.[5]

COREY PIPER

1. McCloskey's still life paintings often featured Asian decorative arts, and this particular vase appears in at least one other painting, *Untitled (Yellow/ Pink Roses in a Chinese Vase)*, ca. 1901, oil on canvas, 14 × 10 inches, Bowers Museum, Santa Ana, California.

2. Peter Hastings Falk, *The Annual Exhibition Record of the Pennsylvania Academy of the Fine Arts* (Madison, CT: Soundview Press, 1989), 328.

3. Nancy Dustin Wall Moure, *Partners in Illusion: Alberta Binford and William J. McCloskey* (Santa Ana, CA: The Bowers Museum of Cultural Art, 1996), 25.

4. There is minimal, conflicting documentation of the artist's later years. She may have suffered from paralysis that prevented her from working. See Moure, *Partners in Illusion*, 43.

5. Illustrated in Moure, *Partners in Illusion*, 102, fig. 11.

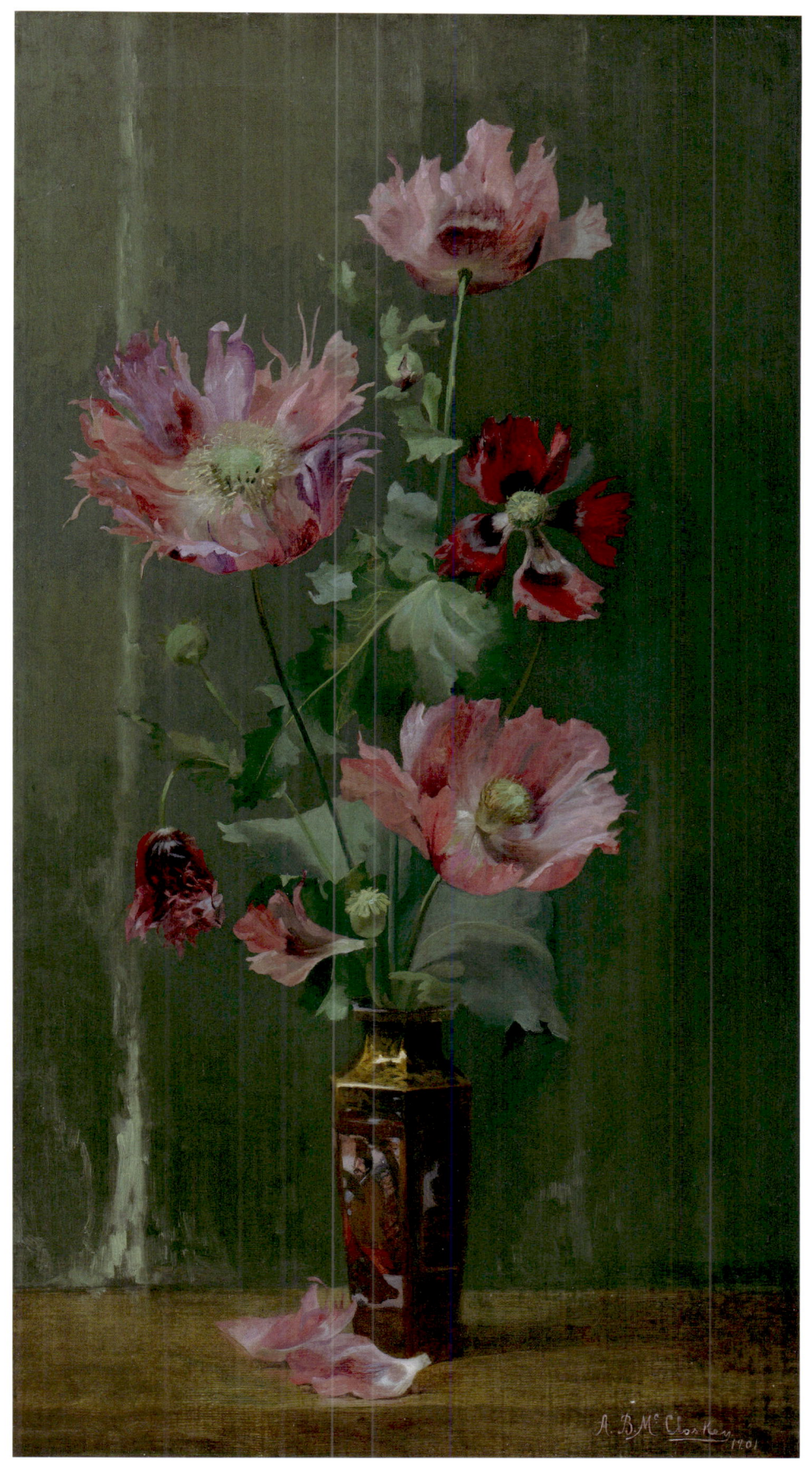

Alfred H. Maurer

AMERICAN, 1868–1932

Woman in Pink (Portrait of Roselle Fitzpatrick), 1902
Oil on canvas
16 × 12¾ inches

FEW ARTISTS MORE FULLY EMBODIED the drastic stylistic shifts that transformed American art in the early decades of the twentieth century than Alfred Maurer. Born into an artistic family, Maurer began his career in the nineteenth century, working for the lithography firm started by his father, Louis Maurer, who had made a career as one of the most prolific and successful artists working for Currier & Ives. Eager to develop his skills away from illustrative, commercial art, Maurer traveled to Paris in 1897 to pursue more formal training and professional opportunity as a painter. He enrolled briefly at the popular Académie Julian but soon left in favor of a wider-ranging and self-directed study amidst the city's rich and varied artistic circles. Positioned in France, where he would remain for most of the next two decades, Maurer engaged with a succession of avant-garde movements as he developed his own distinctive visual language and played a key role in ushering European Modernism to American shores.

Like many American artists who traveled to France, Maurer was drawn to the work of James McNeill Whistler, who around the turn of the century, near the very end of his career, was still widely considered the most celebrated and audacious of American painters working abroad. Whistler's example offered Maurer a forum to combine his rapidly developing facility with figure painting and an exploration of decorative interiors populated with eclectic art objects, all hallmarks of the Aesthetic Movement.

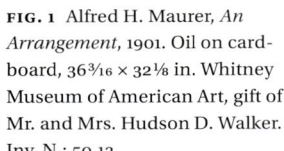

FIG. 1 Alfred H. Maurer, *An Arrangement*, 1901. Oil on cardboard, 36³⁄₁₆ × 32⅛ in. Whitney Museum of American Art, gift of Mr. and Mrs. Hudson D. Walker. Inv. N.: 50.13

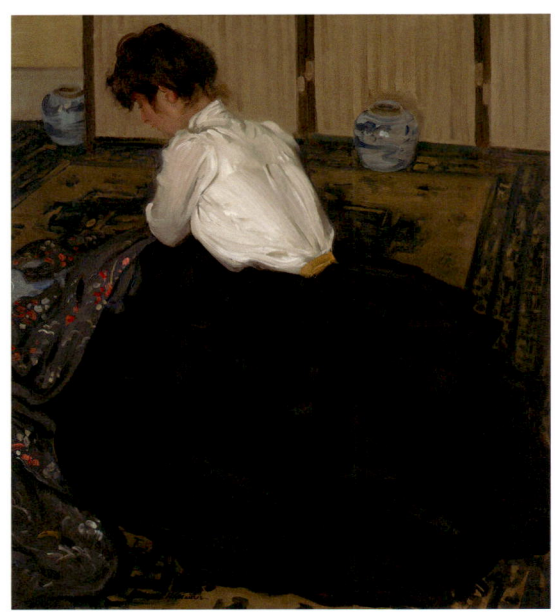

As a result Maurer quickly found success in Paris, exhibiting at the annual Salon and the American Art Association of Paris, an important nexus for American expatriate artists in France.

Buoyed by his successes abroad, Maurer returned to the United States for a year-long visit from 1901 to 1902, where he confirmed his reputation as a promising young painter steeped in the most up-to-date and cosmopolitan developments in European modern art. Critics hailed him as "a young man with serious ideals," and such judgments were seemingly confirmed by Maurer's accolades and awards at major exhibitions, including the Carnegie Institute's International Exhibition, where he was awarded a gold medal and a $1,500 prize for *An Arrangement* (fig. 1).[1] During his time in the United States, Maurer engaged an old friend, Roselle Fitzpatrick, to pose for several paintings, which included *Woman in Pink (Portrait of Roselle Fitzpatrick)*. Fitzpatrick's elegant garments, which render the painting's pleasing tonal harmonies and lend its Whistlerian title, were borrowed from Maurer and employed frequently by the artist in such studio concoctions.[2] The deceptively straightforward portrait encapsulates Maurer's command of the principles of Aestheticism.

Upon returning to France in 1902, Maurer remained dedicated to figure painting, continuing a preoccupation with the theme of women situated in elegant aesthetic interiors. *Seated Woman* depicts Jeanne Blazy, a model who worked frequently with Maurer and other American painters like Frederick Carl Frieseke and Frederick William MacMonnies. Blazy is perched almost precariously upon a bench, with the canvas's vertical composition and the viewer's perspective perched slightly above the sitter, accentuating the model's languid posture. Her rather somber dress is punctuated by an ostentatious red hat and fur stole, while decorative details like the Japanese fan attest to Maurer's wide-ranging aesthetic interests. At the same time, Blazy's direct address of the viewer, and the unconventional construction of the interior space, flattened toward the picture plane, signal new developments in Maurer's art. The flat white surface of the bottom of the hat box that Blazy holds in her left hand forms a void near the center of the canvas, defying academic conventions of perspective and form. Over the next decade, Maurer undertook a radical departure in his painting, working through progressive new pictorial theories derived from his study of Fauvism and Cubism. While such modernist works might seem a far departure from figurative paintings like these, the roots of Maurer's experimental spirit and eagerness to push his craft in new directions are detectable through each phase of his career in his readiness to absorb new influences and experiment with new modes of picture making.

COREY PIPER

1. David C. Preyer, "The New York Art World-II," *Brush and Pencil* 8 (May 1901): 94.

2. Stacey B. Epstein, *Alfred Maurer: At the Vanguard of Modernism* (Andover, MA: Addison Gallery of American Art, 2015), 36.

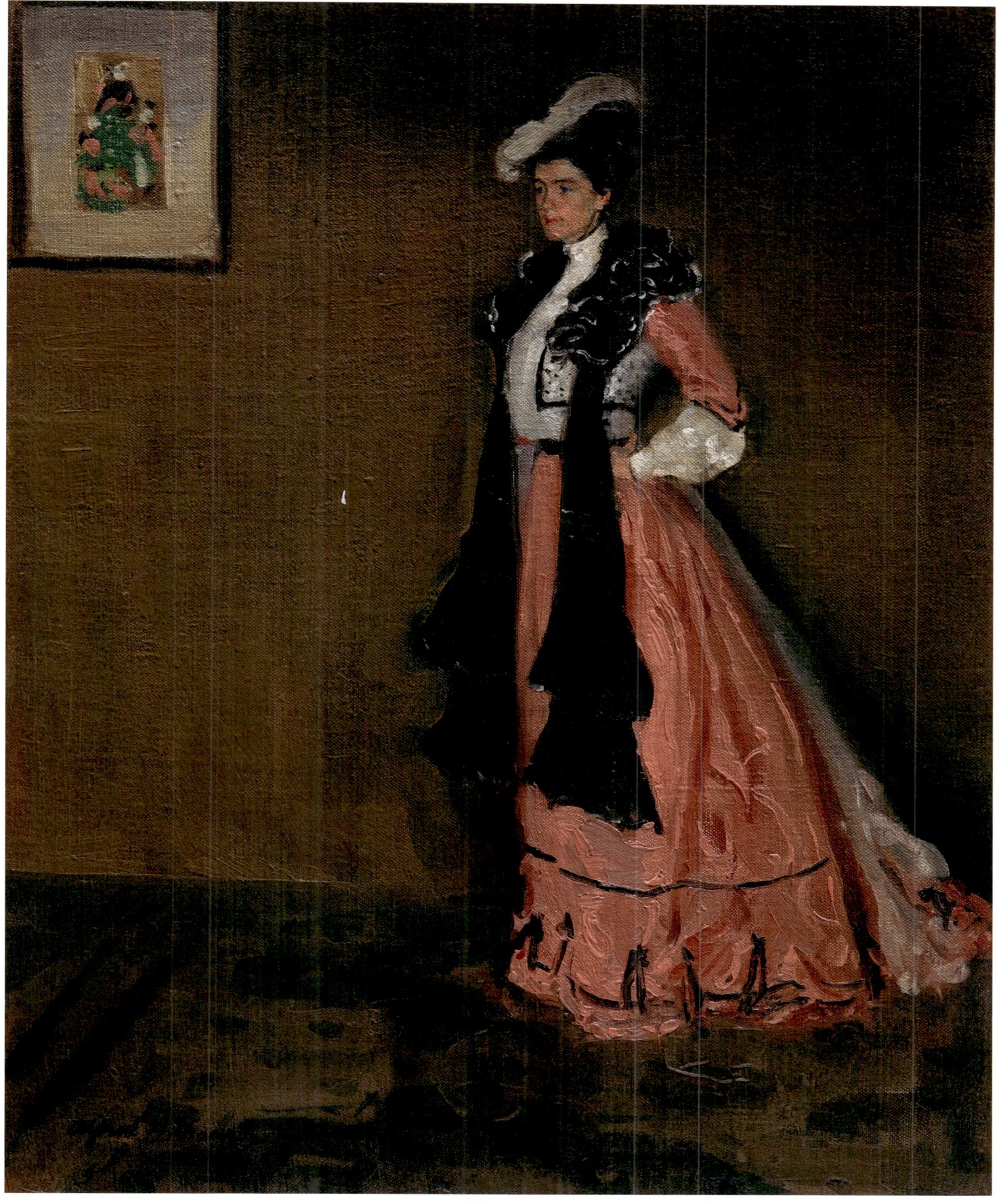

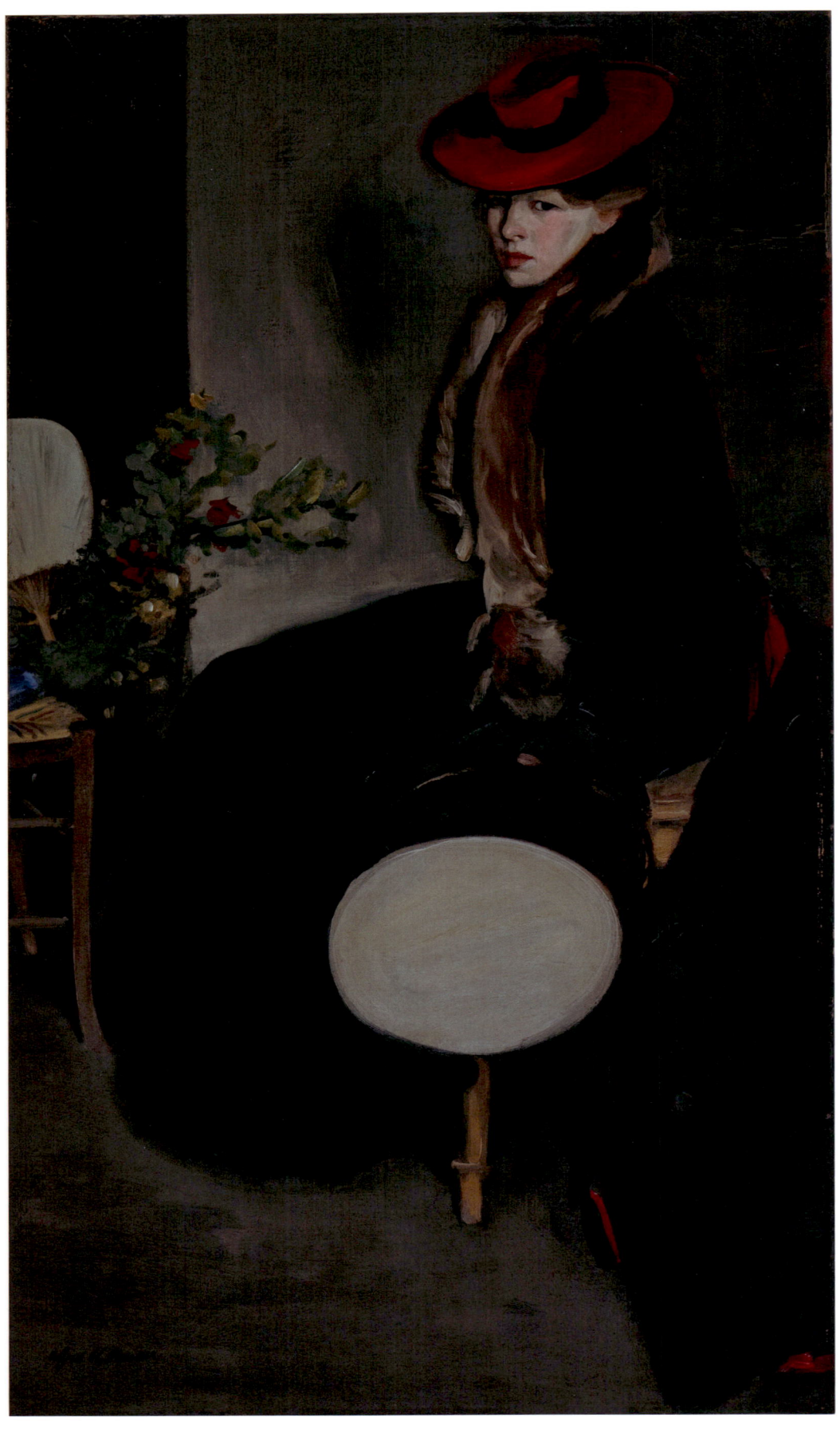

Seated Woman (Portrait of Jeanne Blazy), ca. 1902–4

Oil on canvas

32 × 17¾ inches

Promised Gift of the Macon and Joan Brock Collection
of American Art

John Singer Sargent

AMERICAN, 1856–1925

Spanish Convalescent, ca. 1903
Watercolor and pencil on paper
18 × 12 inches

Promised Gift of the Macon and Joan Brock Collection
of American Art

DURING HIS LIFETIME, John Singer Sargent was heralded as the "greatest contemporary portrait painter" of his era, celebrated on both sides of the Atlantic for capturing vivid likenesses of glamorous patrons with his bravura style.[1] Throughout his life he also painted landscapes and genre scenes in oil and watercolor, traveling widely in search of subjects and inspiration. Born in Florence, Italy, to American parents, he spent most of his life in Europe. Throughout a peripatetic childhood, his mother, an amateur artist, encouraged him to draw constantly, and he honed his precocious talent. He settled in Paris in 1874 and pursued artistic training there before moving to London for the rest of his life in the mid-1880s. Influenced by his mother's wanderlust, he would travel seasonally until his death. After 1890 he was occupied with mural painting, creating major works for the Boston Public Library and Museum of Fine Arts.[2] He traveled across Europe and into biblical lands, researching the art and architecture of the past for his murals and recording picturesque sights, scenery, and people with his signature fluidity and sprezzatura. These alluring works increasingly replaced portraiture in his oeuvre. After 1900 he worked in watercolor more frequently; the portable medium was well suited for travel, and its transparency was ideal for capturing brilliant effects of light that captivated him. His late watercolors are technically dazzling and arguably among the best ever made.

Sargent painted *Spanish Convalescent* at Santiago de Compostela during a three-month sojourn on the Iberian Peninsula in 1903.[3] He was enchanted by Spain and visited seven times between 1879 and 1913. Like many of his contemporaries, he was drawn there by the old masters—particularly Velázquez—at the Prado Museum in Madrid. He also reveled in the striking scenery, historical sites, sparkling southern light, and the congeniality of the Spaniards, whom he described as "the most amiable people in the world."[4] This informal portrait of an unidentified soldier belongs to a series of works that he made at the Hostal dos Reis Católicos at Santiago. The historic hostel was founded in 1492 by King Ferdinand and Queen Isabella as a resting spot for weary travelers who had completed the pilgrimage (the *camino*) to the tomb of St. James at the nearby cathedral. At the hostel Sargent observed soldiers from the garrison of Galicia convalescing in the courtyard beneath the renaissance loggia, which would become the setting for his watercolors.[5] *Spanish Convalescent* stands out among this series for its focus on a solitary figure. An unidentified soldier, shown at three-quarter length, leans casually against the base of a pillar. He crosses his arms and gazes directly toward the artist and viewer. In this informal portrait, Sargent conveys the patient's sense of weariness with pathos and sensitivity while delighting in the rendering of his shirt with broad washes of pale color and expressive strokes to describe its rumpled folds. Sargent defines the architectural space with loose passages of pigment and dark wet-on-wet washes to create shadow, displaying his remarkable ability to suggest detail and definition with minimal brushstrokes. Significantly, Sargent gifted this watercolor to a cherished friend and patron, Flora Wertheimer.[6]

In 1907, weary of the demands of portrait painting, Sargent formally declared that he would no longer accept commissions. Finally freed from the confines of the portrait studio, he traveled more often and for lengthier periods, often indulging in long summer holidays with artist friends and his extended family. In autumn 1909 he arrived at Corfu, a Greek island near the border of Albania, accompanied by his sister Emily and dear companions Eliza Wedgwood and husband and wife Wilfrid and Jane de Glehn. The coterie settled at the Villa Soteriotisa, a few miles north of the capital city. Jane described the glorious setting in a letter noting the views from the villa's garden terrace of "the bluest Ionian sea you ever saw & the Albanian mountains pink and dreamy blue." She added, "The island is a paradise. . . . We are all so happy here painting all day & bathing every day."[7] In his works Sargent focused on the lush foliage of the terraced gardens and olive groves surrounding the villa. He was particularly fascinated by the gnarled and curvilinear forms of the ancient trees.[8] Sargent used oil and watercolor with remarkable fluidity, exploiting saturated tones to create dynamic landscapes. Among the most vibrant pictures from the series, the oil *Olives at Corfu* conveys the tangled branches of the grove under sparkling sunlight. Sargent's exuberant brushwork includes swirling strokes and dynamic slashes, which verge on abstraction when viewed up close. At a distance, the density of the grove materializes against the brilliant blue hues of the sea and the distant pale mountains (as described by Jane). The apparent spontaneity of *Olives at Corfu* reflects Sargent's enthusiasm and delight as he painted for his own pleasure.

From 1908 until 1912, Sargent spent his annual holidays in the Alps. He was often accompanied by his sisters Emily and Violet and other members of the family, including Violet's six children. Though he never married or had children of his own, he adored these multigenerational trips, and family folklore—and photos—reveal that they were joyful, convivial gatherings. Sargent frequently enlisted his travel companions as models, depicting them

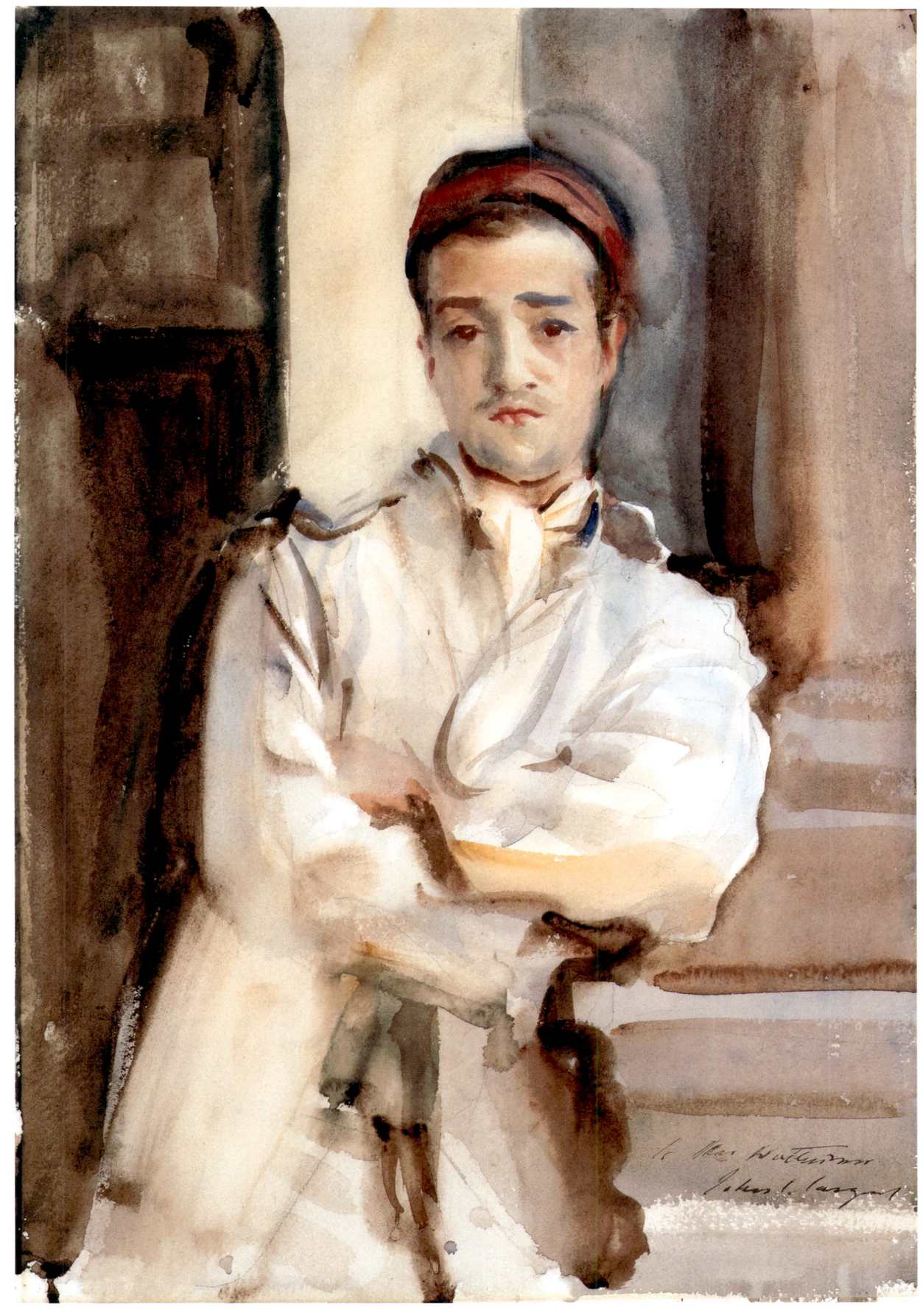

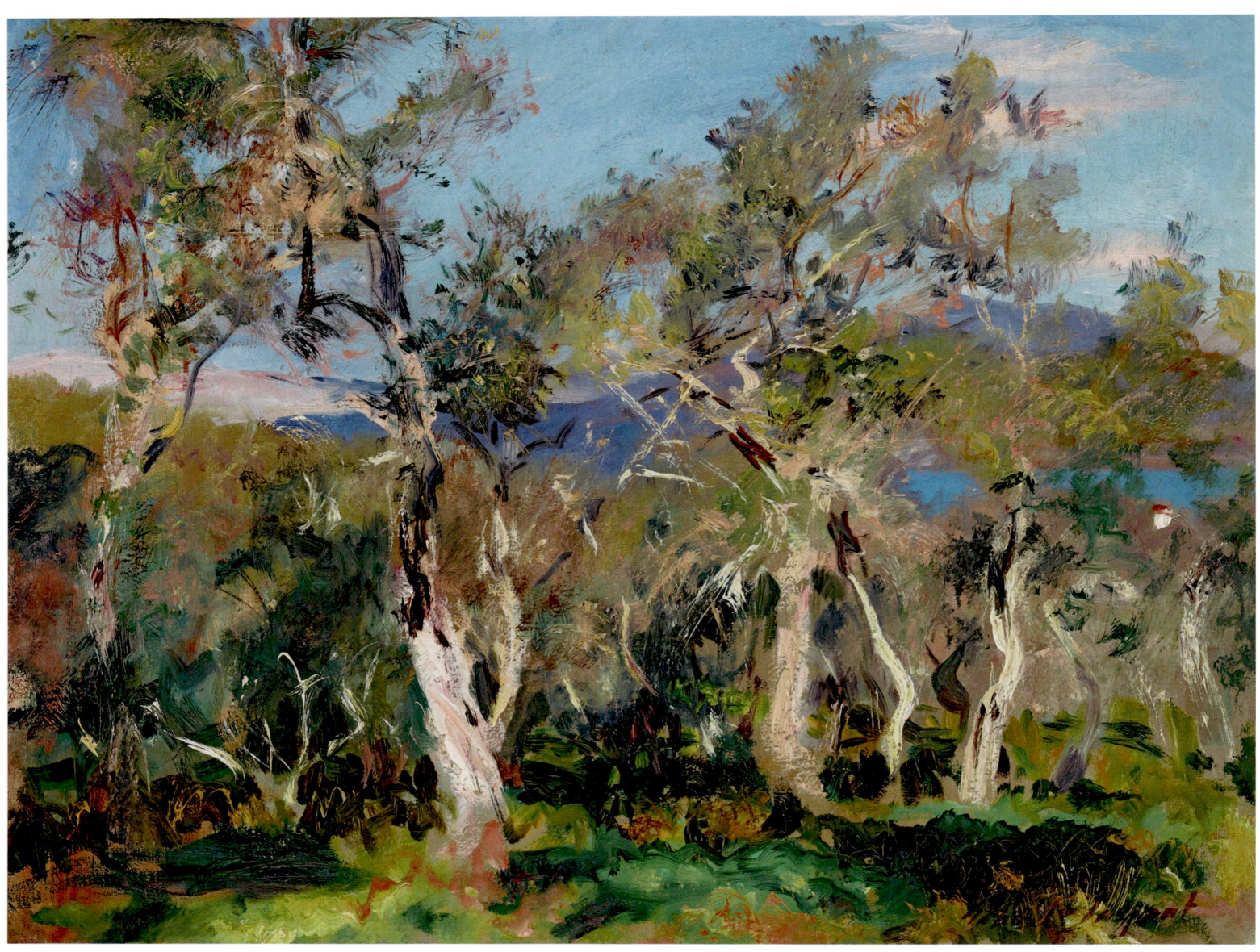

Olives at Corfu, 1909
Oil on canvas
22 × 28 inches

Gift of the Macon and Joan Brock Collection of American Art, 2023.4.1

outdoors, lounging in verdant alpine meadows or near mossy streams. He painted *Ladies in the Shade: Abriès* at the remote mountain village in the Dauphiné region in the French Alps. His beloved niece Rose-Marie Ormond, a favorite and frequent model, is shown seated against a tree trunk in a forest. (A second "lady," her companion, is rendered cursorily behind her at left.) Rose-Marie's flamboyant pink dress dominates the composition and seems to spill off the bottom edge of the paper. Broadly painted with pale washes, the ruffled flounces at her shoulders and skirt are defined by Sargent's calligraphic brushstrokes. Throughout his career Sargent delighted in painting lush textiles, especially in his portraits. On holiday and freed from the demands of patrons, he created a glorious watercolor, characteristic of his best works—with facility and seemingly effortless spontaneity—capturing the vibrancy of an era that would soon disappear as Europe entered the war in 1914.[9]

STEPHANIE L. HERDRICH

1. Charles H. Caffin, "John Singer Sargent: The Greatest Contemporary Portrait Painter," *World's Work* 7 (November 1903): 4099–116.

2. Sargent would also paint two mural panels for Widener Memorial Library at Harvard University (1920–24).

3. Sargent spent three months traveling through Spain and Portugal in 1903. While there he would paint at least thirty-five works (one oil and thirty-four watercolors). He would describe this trip as "delightful" to friend and patron Isabella Stewart Gardner. (Sargent to Isabella Stewart Gardner, August 8, 1903, quoted in Richard Ormond and Elaine Kilmurray, *John Singer Sargent: The Complete Paintings*, vol. 7 (New Haven, CT: Published for the Paul Mellon Centre for Studies in British Art by Yale University Press, 2012), 113.

4. Evan Charteris, *John Sargent* (New York: C. Scribner's Sons, 1927), 171.

5. Sarah Cash et al., *Sargent & Spain*, exh. cat. (Washington, DC: National Gallery of Art, 2022), 104. See also Ormond and Kilmurray, *John Singer Sargent*, 136ff (cats. 1266–1270).

6. Inscribed at lower right: *to Mrs Wertheimer/John S. Sargent*. Flora Wertheimer was the wife of art dealer Asher Wertheimer. Sargent painted a dozen portraits of various Wertheimer family members between 1898 and 1908.

7. Emmett family papers, quoted in Ormond and Kilmurray, *John Singer Sargent: The Complete Paintings*, vol. 8 (2014), 81. Sargent's trip to Corfu resulted in more than thirty oils and watercolors. His travel companions were also painters. The women were mostly accomplished amateurs, while Wilfrid de Glehn was a professional painter who exhibited his work regularly.

8. Sargent created a large-scale exhibition painting during the trip, *Albanian Olive Gatherers* (1903; City Art Gallery, Manchester).

9. Rose-Marie died in Paris in 1913 in the German bombardment of the church of Saint Gervais. Sargent was understandably devastated by the loss and kept this charming image of her until his death, when it was sold in his estate sale.

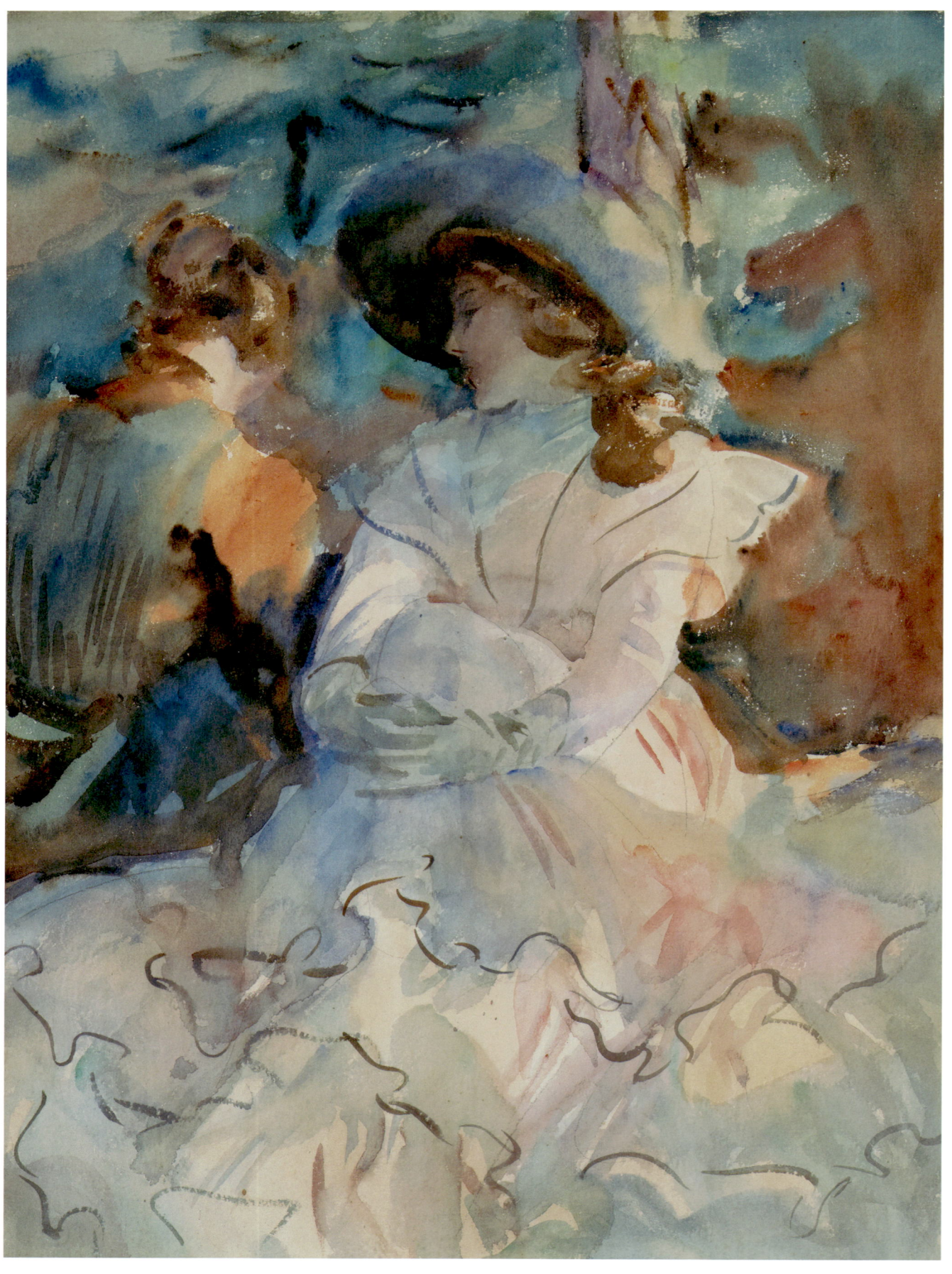

Ladies in the Shade: Abriès, 1912
Watercolor and pencil on paper
21 × 15¾ inches

Promised Gift of the Macon and Joan Brock Collection
of American Art

James Jebusa Shannon

BRITISH, 1862–1923

Portrait of a Young Woman, ca. 1889
Oil on canvas
18 × 14 inches

BORN IN UPSTATE NEW YORK, James Jebusa Shannon settled permanently in England as a young man, staking his place among the small but distinguished list of American painters, from Benjamin West to John Singer Sargent, who carved out lucrative and acclaimed careers within the British art establishment. Shannon first set out for London at the age of sixteen, where he enrolled in the South Kensington School of Art. As a young artist struggling to assert his professional identity, Shannon took a leading role in forming progressive art societies like the Chelsea Arts Club and the New English Art Club, which challenged the conservative values of institutions like the Royal Academy.

At the same time, Shannon sought to establish himself in a more traditional role as a portrait painter in the grand manner, an esteemed and rewarding position for artists who could attract major commissions. Shannon's professional breakthrough came in 1888 when he showed two large works, including a large full-length portrait entitled *Henry Virgne, Master of the Epping Forest Harriers* (now lost), at the exclusive Grosvenor Gallery and later at the 1889 Exposition Universelle in Paris. These prominent venues attracted the attention of patrons, most notably the aristocratic artist and aesthete Lady Violet Manners. Shannon's *Portrait of a Young Woman* dates from around the time that the artist was working to establish his portrait practice and demonstrates his efforts to hone his craft.[1] The portrait head of an unknown sitter, shown in strict profile, highlights Shannon's ability to blend painterly effects with an ennobling representation of the sitter's salient features, like the strong jawline and rosy cheeks seen here.

In relatively short order, Shannon's reputation as a high society portraitist soared in Britain and eventually in the United States. The artist exhibited among the British artists at the 1893 World's Columbian Exposition in Chicago, and his election to the Royal Academy in 1897 attracted the attention of numerous American critics, who were proud to point out his American lineage.[2] A seemingly inexhaustible supply of commissions from fashionable English nobles and brash American Gilded Age socialites followed on both sides of the Atlantic.

While portraiture sustained Shannon's income, he continued to explore genre themes, often featuring members of his own family, situated in fashionable interiors and engaged in intellectual or aesthetic pursuits. *The Sèvres Vase* features a young model, likely Shannon's daughter Kitty, seated at the table while delicately peeling grapes next to an ornate bronze and porcelain compote from which the painting takes its title. The varied decorative patterns, from the Japanese-inspired textile hanging off the girl's shoulders to the eighteenth-century French vessel, showcased the artist's wide-ranging aesthetic sensibilities and mastery of painterly effects. In such works Shannon encapsulated many of the aesthetic features that defined Edwardian upper-class taste, from the sensuousness of the female form to the intellectual discernment of the connoisseur.

COREY PIPER

1. See Barbara Dayer Gallati, *Seeking Beauty: Paintings by James Jebusa Shannon* (New York: Debra Force Fine Art, 2014), no. 3, 18.

2. Gallati, *Seeking Beauty*, 10.

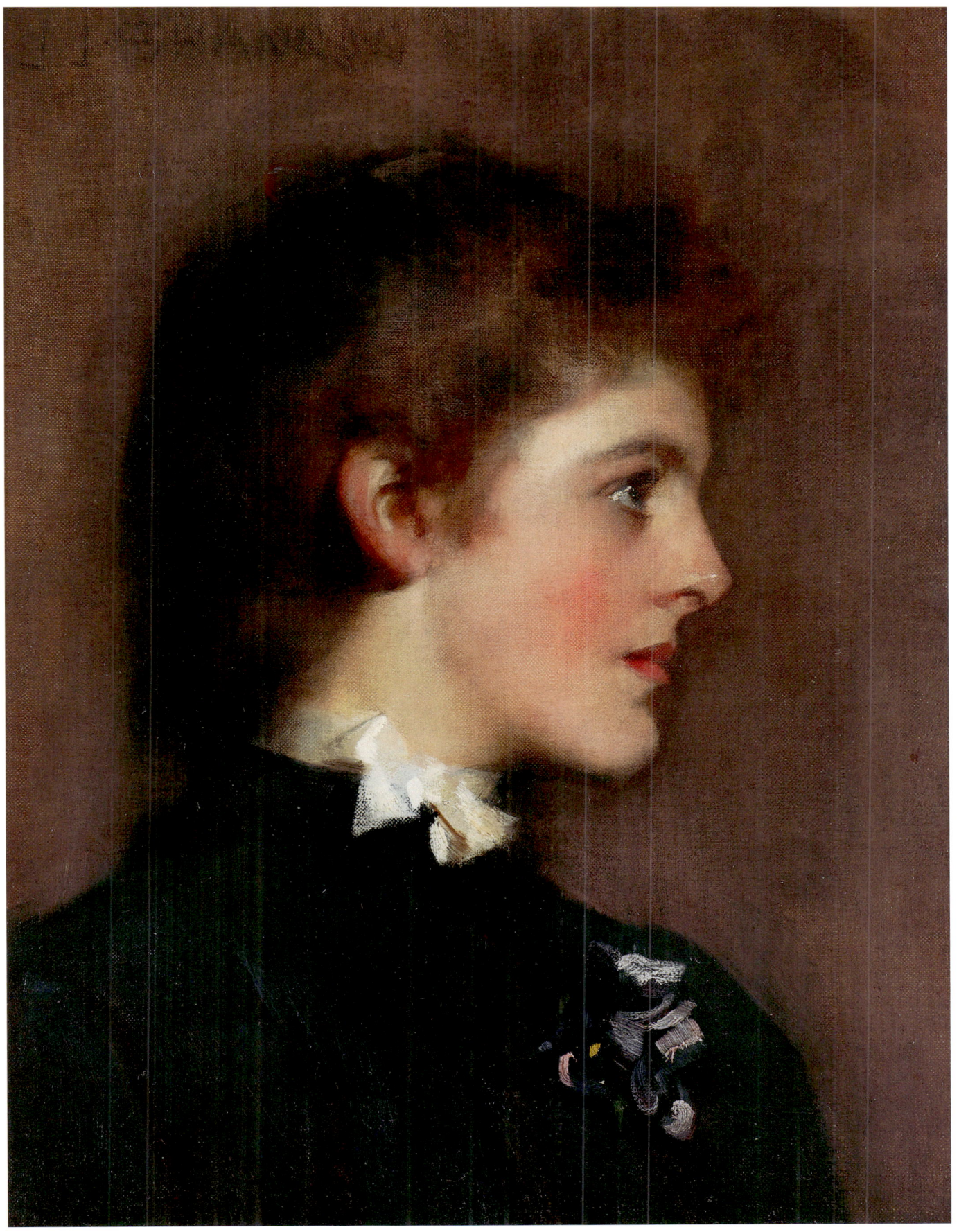

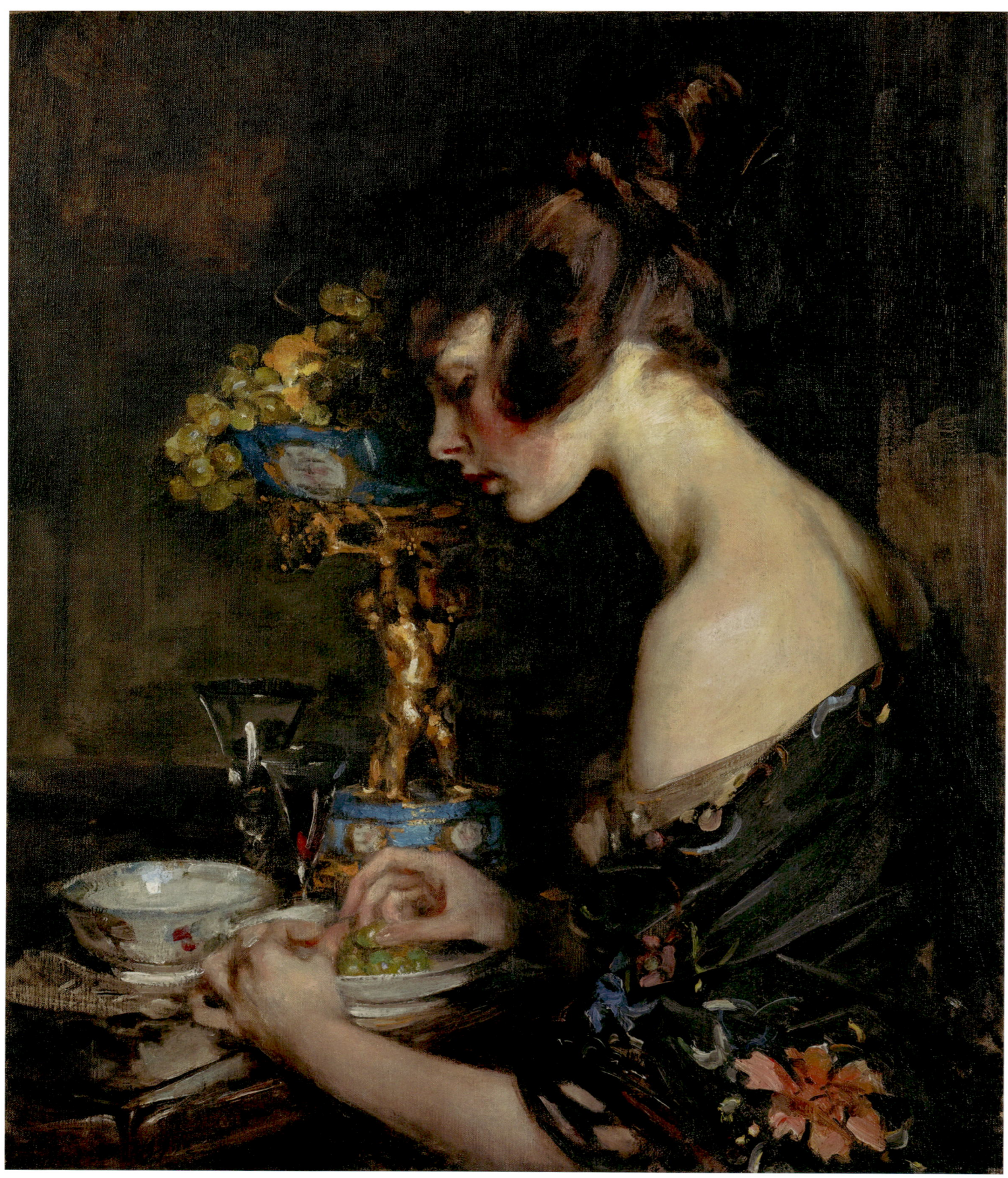

The Sèvres Vase, ca. 1910
Oil on canvas
30 × 25 inches

Promised Gift of the Macon and Joan Brock Collection
of American Art

John White Alexander

AMERICAN, 1856–1915

The Favorite Corner, ca. 1895–98

Oil on canvas

24 × 14 inches

Promised Gift of the Macon and Joan Brock Collection
of American Art

AT THE TURN OF THE CENTURY, John White Alexander was celebrated as a leading American figure painter. Influenced by time spent in the European art capitals of Munich and Paris, Alexander absorbed the aesthetics of German Symbolism and French fin-de-siècle Art Nouveau. While living in Paris in the 1890s, he found international acclaim for his depictions of graceful female figures in repose. Such works led the contemporary critic Christian Brinton to declare, "There should be scant hesitation in proclaiming John W. Alexander our foremost painter of women."[1]

The Favorite Corner illustrates Alexander's stated goal of producing "a subject and not a simple portrait," and his interest in painting a mood rather than a direct physical record would be the mark of his mature style.[2] A young woman is depicted reading a book while seated on an upholstered window seat. The closely studied scene deepens the focus on the model's face, encouraging the viewer to consider her interior life. (Alexander's preference for working indoors also draws out the interior qualities of his subjects.)[3] The flowing fabric of her dress harmonizes with the fabric of the cushion she sits upon, which suggests her sense of comfort and perhaps even alludes to the length of time she has spent already in her favorite spot, absorbed by the book she holds in her lap.

An articulation of Alexander's achievements as a figure painter, *The Favorite Corner* reflects the artist's stylistic and technical preferences. Contemporary critics noted his adoption of methods used by James McNeill Whistler, who painted in muted tones using a light hand applied to a coarsely woven canvas. This approach is evident here, with the weave of the canvas visible beneath lightly applied pigments. This coarse-grained fabric came to be called "Alexander" canvas.[4]

Although he was more interested in capturing the overall impression of a woman reading than in rendering a specific portrait of his sitter, Alexander did have a favorite model. From 1895 to 1900, he worked almost exclusively with Juliette Very, who also posed for Alexander's *Isabella and the Pot of Basil* (1897) and *Alethea* (1895), among others (fig. 1). Very captured the artist's imagination with her thick, black hair and distinctive profile.[5] She often appears in his canvases as a figure isolated in a small space, wearing voluminous dresses and absorbed by her thoughts. With her dark hair and fair skin, the woman represented in *The Favorite Corner* appears to be Very, strikingly attired and captured in a moment of repose.

The Favorite Corner also takes as its theme one of Alexander's preferred subjects: while images of women reading can be found throughout art history, appearing as early as the fourteenth century, Alexander did a great deal to make this theme his own.[6] The motif of the open book appears in many of his late works, often suggesting a state of dreamy reverie, and in Alexander's hands, this subject offers an opportunity to delve into the sitter's imagination.[7] Describing Alexander's female readers, thinkers, and dreamers, Brinton asserted, "In catching their favorite gestures and poses in depicting their precise allure and atmosphere, Mr. Alexander has added hitherto unpublished chapter to the social as well as the esthetic treasury of his country."[8]

LAUREN PALMOR

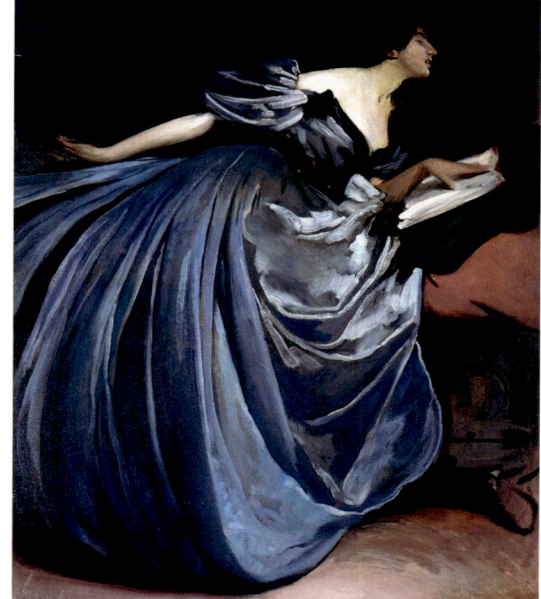

FIG. 1 John White Alexander, *Alethea*, 1895. Oil on canvas, 63½ × 52½ in. Private collection

1. Christian Brinton, "The Art of John W. Alexander," *Munsey's Magazine* 39 (September 1908): 744.

2. John White Alexander to Colonel Edward J. Allen, July 16, 1884, box 1, folder 37, John White Alexander Papers, Archives of American Art, Smithsonian Institution. Also see Mary Anne Goley, "John White Alexander's *Panel for Music Room*," *Bulletin of the Detroit Institute of Arts* 64, no. 4 (1989): 14.

3. Julie Anne Springer, "Art and the Feminine Muse: Women in Interiors by John White Alexander," *Woman's Art Journal* 6, no. 3 (Autumn 1985–Winter 1986): 3.

4. Alexander scholar Mary Anne Goley explains, "In generalizing the human figure, Alexander was able to simplify form. Paint is applied broadly to a loose-weave canvas without the nuances needed for finely modeled features." Goley, "John White Alexander's *Panel for Music Room*," 10.

5. Mary Anne Goley, "The Tribute of Isabella," *Apollo* 175, no. 594 (January 2012). Online, https://link.gale.com/apps/doc/A279261485/AONE?u=google scholar&sid=googleScholar&xid=935d4a77 (accessed September 22, 2022).

6. James Conlon, "Men Reading Women Reading: Interpreting Images of Women Readers," *Frontiers: A Journal of Women Studies* 26, no. 2 (2005): 37–58.

7. Springer, "Art and the Feminine Muse," 4.

8. Brinton, "The Art of John W. Alexander," 744.

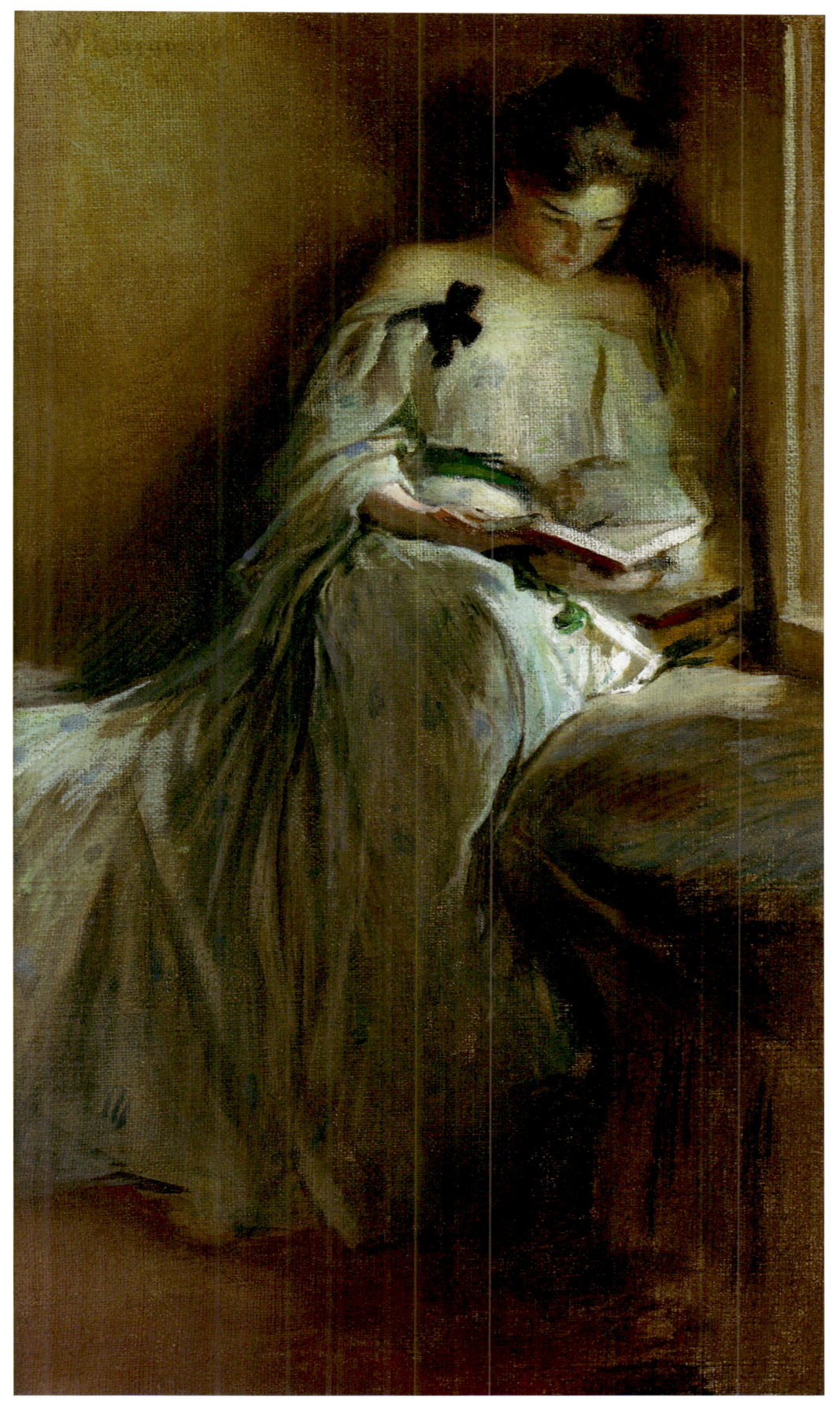

Thomas Wilmer Dewing

AMERICAN, 1851–1938

The Mask, 1902

Oil on panel

20 × 15¾ inches

Promised Gift of the Macon and Joan Brock Collection
of American Art

THOMAS WILMER DEWING used the female figure as the basis for calculated abstractions of form and color. The artist charted a course between two polarities found in international art at the time—psychological insight exemplified in the work of John Singer Sargent and the aestheticism of James McNeill Whistler. Both elements find expression in Dewing's oil *The Mask* and his pastel titled *In Pink No. 11*.

Born in Boston, Dewing spent his working life in New York City, where he found patrons among those connected with the railroads. For example, Charles Lang Freer, a boxcar builder from Detroit, bought *The Mask* for his business partner Frank J. Hecker.

The Mask depicted Dewing's new romantic interest, the Boston-born miniature painter Lucia Fairchild Fuller. She summered at the famed Cornish colony in New Hampshire, where the residents—Dewing among them—enjoyed a verdant setting far from the heat of the city. When he reviewed the 1902 exhibition of the Ten American Painters, critic Royal Cortissoz found "the woman in *The Mask* a frail phantom of delight, her russet hair and dress of indeterminant color . . . a variation on a certain key of color rather than a portrait. . . . It appears indefinably to the imagination as well as to the eye. It is thoughtful as well as sensuous."[1]

The mask itself is a centuries-old theme, one that signifies mystery, artifice, and hidden identity. In the painting, the sitter's profile echoes the shape of the exotic relic in her hand. It was the same prop, perhaps, that the Cornish players used when they put on a theatrical featuring Javanese masks for the visiting Freer, who was then circumnavigating the globe on his way to Asia.

The image also provided an interior view of the artist himself. The intense color of *The Mask* suggests that he was in an emotional state when he painted it. His heightened sentiments may have triggered the tense pose of the sitter, a figure suffused by the deep, palpitating color of a background drape. These disjunctions became singular Dewing hallmarks that he increasingly utilized as the twentieth century progressed.

In Pink, on the other hand, eschews the psychological features of *The Mask*. Drawn in 1910 it is diminutive, rendered in a size and palette inspired by Whistler's works in Freer's Detroit collection. Dewing emulated the expatriate's style, outlining his subject in black pastel with a line that barely indicates her legs, her long arms, and the placement of a handkerchief near her knee. The pastel's middle tones are provided by the brown paper background. Color seems to float independently over the piece as if wafted across it with the side of a crayon.

The pastel is one of several that Dewing drew that same year of a model seated on a Louis Seize bench with her body slightly turned to the viewer. The fallen shoulder strap of the sitter's peach-colored dress lends the work a sensuous quality, while the dapples on her shadowed face are characteristic of Dewing's drawings. When Anson Conger Goodyear purchased *In Pink*, it is possible that he obtained it from the artist's dealer Newman E. Montross. He went on to buy several other works on paper by Dewing. It is also likely that he knew Thomas Dewing himself, for in 1912 Goodyear and his wife purchased the Italianate villa in Cornish, known as High Court. It was previously owned by a legendary colony resident, Annie Lazarus, a close friend of the artist and his wife Maria.

In January 1909 Dewing began to number his pastels right below his signature. As the small drawings now appeared on exhibition along with his larger oils, he was concerned that they might get lost by a museum or a dealer. By numbering them he hoped to keep track of the works as they were "very difficult to identify . . . by any name," as he put it.[2] For reasons of safety, he also began to place the pastels in frames comprised of a simple, flat molding such as the one on *In Pink*. Each frame was gilded with a leaf that enhanced the tones in the pastel itself.

SUSAN A. HOBBS

1. Royal Cortissoz, "Art Exhibitions," *New York Daily Tribune*, April 2, 1902, 9.

2. Dewing to C. Powell Minnigerode, November 12, [1923], Corcoran Gallery of Art Archives, Special Collections Research, George Washington University Archives.

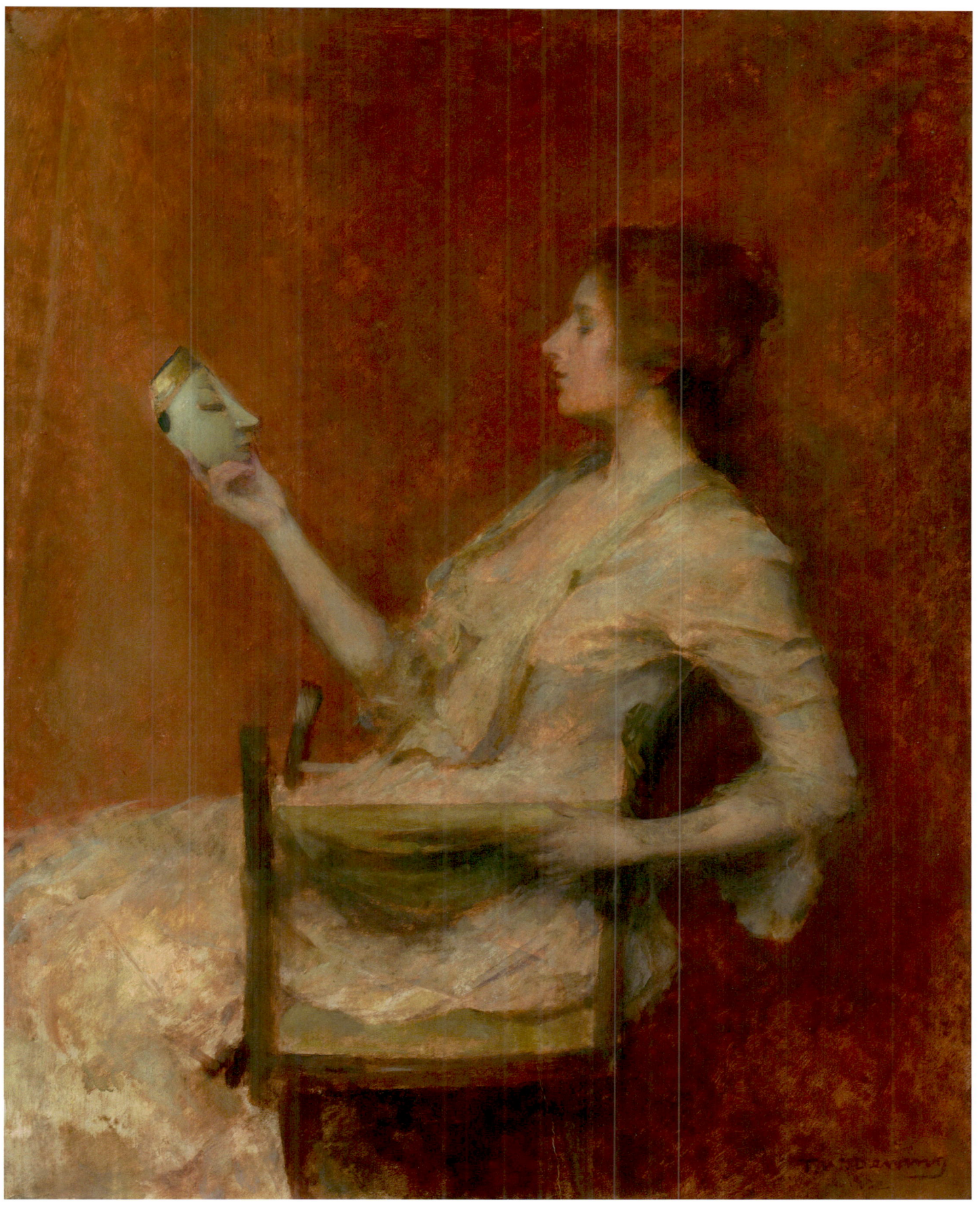

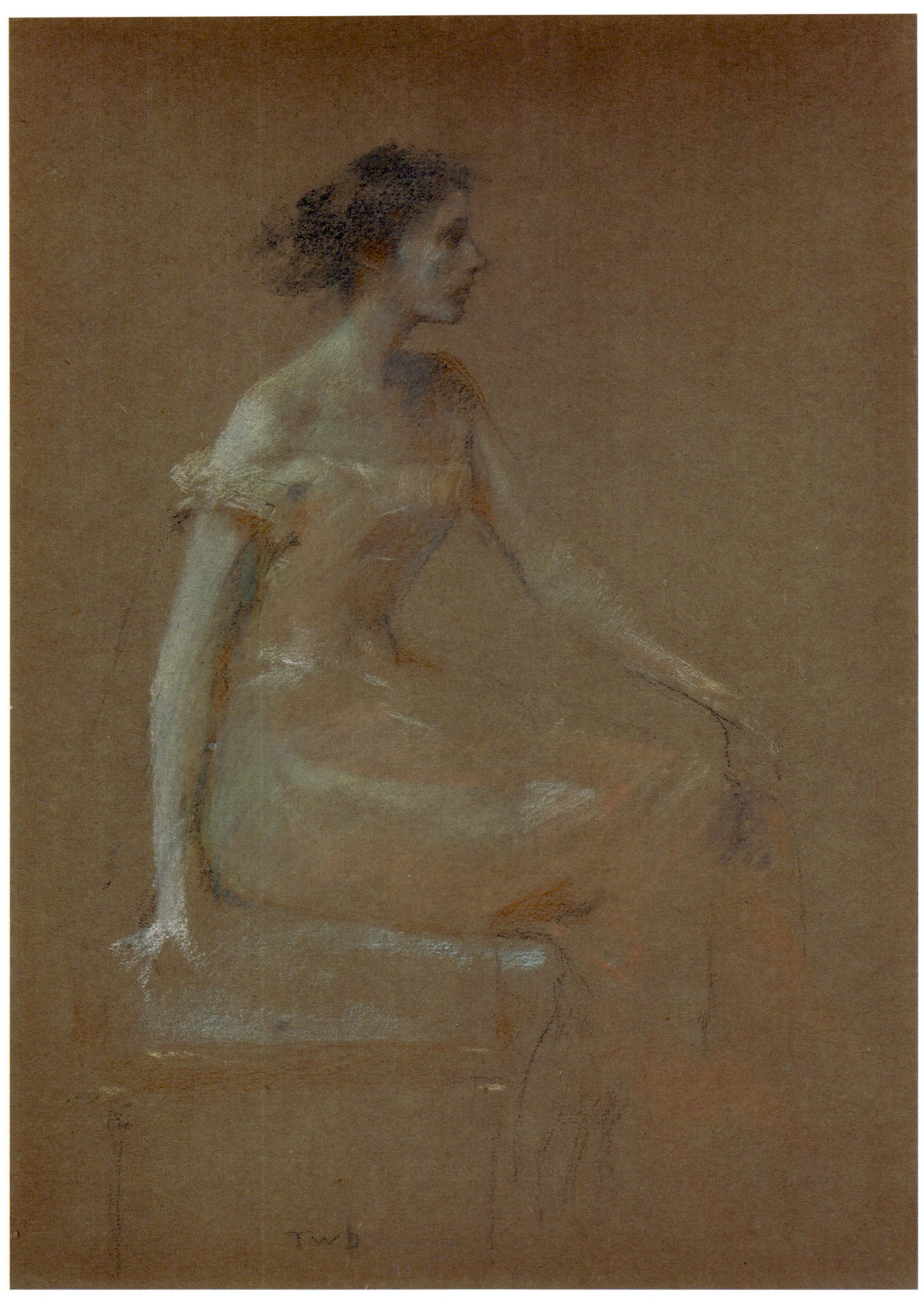

In Pink No. 11, 1910
Pastel, chalk, and graphite pencil on brown paper
10¼ × 7 inches

Promised Gift of the Macon and Joan Brock Collection
of American Art

Abbott Handerson Thayer

AMERICAN, 1849–1921

Profile of a Girl (Alice Rich), 1917

Oil on panel

24 × 18 inches

Promised Gift of the Macon and Joan Brock Collection of American Art

ABBOTT HANDERSON THAYER was born in Boston in 1849 and grew up in Keene, New Hampshire. After studying with Jean-Léon Gérôme in Paris, he returned to America and by the 1880s was one of the most admired painters of his generation. Thayer became a leading light in the artists' community of Dublin, New Hampshire, where he depicted local women who captured his imagination in a series of idealized works such as this one of Alice Rich. Thayer painted a head or a figure rather than an actual likeness, so the result was a work of art rather than a specific portrait. In rendering this sitter's face, for example, he combined his academic training with muted, modern colors such as green and mauve and was drawn to the introspective and psychological themes in art, which were coming into vogue at the turn of the twentieth century.

Thayer produced at least three known images of Alice Rich. The first was probably this one that the artist's wife termed a "Sketch of Alice Rich" in a letter she wrote to the artist's dealer, Robert Macbeth, when she was sorting through his studio shortly before Thayer's death in 1921. Later she termed it a "Head of a Young Girl." This work was followed by a "life size painting" in the same profile pose. Records show that the artist produced a frontal version of the sitter as well.[1]

This expressive painting of Alice Rich is an example of the artist's mature style that was known for its subdued palette and freely applied brushwork. Her plump cheeks and chiseled profile are firmly etched in the manner of the Italian Renaissance, a historical era that Thayer greatly admired. The sitter's youth and sweet insouciance, however, is the work's most striking feature. Her visage is fresh and appealing rather than merely exacting. As Thayer's friend and fellow artist Maria Oakey Dewing explained, "He aimed at . . . the idealization of the feminine head, with a beauty that was more of the spirit than of the flesh . . . his mind was fixed on one idea—the expression of a woman's face."[2]

Bits of red pigment under her eye serve to bring the girl's face forward. At the same time, the color appears throughout her rough-hewn garment—a mere swathe of fabric that the artist depicted in abstract strokes of heavy impasto. Thayer sometimes startled his colleagues by working a painting's surface with his hands or utilizing unorthodox means such as the application of a broom. The unusual striations along the lower part of this picture were likely created with a palette knife or another abrasive material.

SUSAN A. HOBBS

1. Emma Thayer to Robert Macbeth, July 20, 1920; January 16, 1921, Macbeth Papers, Archives of American Art; Clipping File, Library of Smithsonian Museum of American Art, June 1929, loose illus. from *New York American*; see also the catalogue *Abbott H. Thayer, Paintings–Drawings*, April 19–May 2, 1931, Macbeth Gallery, illus. Alice Rich, no. 23.

2. Quoted by Nelson C. White, *Abbott H. Thayer, Painter and Naturalist* (Hartford: Connecticut Printers, 1951), 213.

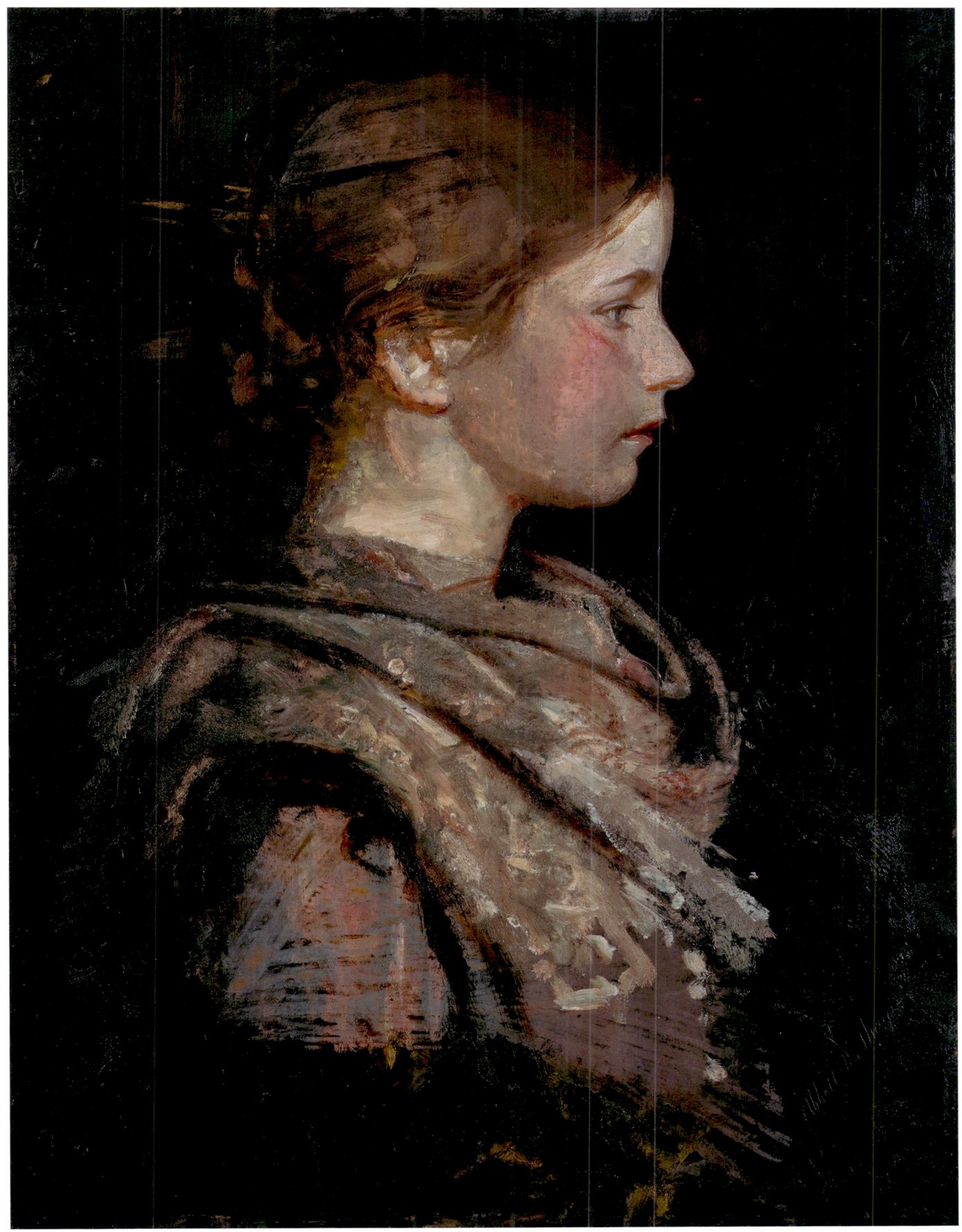

Frank Weston Benson

AMERICAN, 1862–1951

The Seamstress, 1913

Oil on canvas

36 × 26 inches

Promised Gift of the Macon and Joan Brock Collection of American Art

IN *THE SEAMSTRESS*, Boston School artist Frank Weston Benson uses impressionist techniques to bring modernist energy to the painted surface of this otherwise academic interior scene. Benson's daughter, Eleanor, sits by the light from a window in his St. Botolph Street studio, sewing a garment that cascades down her lap.[1] The artist uses the color red to draw our eye around the picture in a circular movement—from the textile she sews to the spool of thread on the table, to the flowering plant and rose-colored curtain, over to the framed still life and down to Eleanor's hair. Benson's distinctive, textured brushwork adds additional liveliness while at the same time harmonizing the scene's components into an environment of peaceful, domestic stability. The admiration for classical compositions and attention to qualities of light during this time were motivated in part by a revival of interest in the Dutch genre painter Johannes Vermeer.[2] In *The Seamstress*, Benson echoes Vermeer's compositional formula and similarly filters the light to delicately illuminate the interior and lend an angelic air to his female subject.

Born in Salem, Massachusetts, Benson was among the inaugural group of students to attend the School of the Museum of Fine Arts, Boston, along with several of the men who would later join him in forming the Ten American Painters, including Willard Metcalf, Robert Reid, Edmund C. Tarbell, and Edward Simmons.[3] Benson and Tarbell shared a Boston studio and formed a close friendship and similar representational styles. In 1889 Benson was hired by the Museum School to teach the antique class and then taught painting from 1893 until 1912, when he resigned over a policy conflict and instead became a visiting instructor. The Ten American Painters broke from the more conservative Society of American Artists in 1897 to acquire autonomy for their modern sensibility. During his affiliation with the Ten, Benson gained a reputation for sun-filled figure paintings of fashionable women by the seaside and at leisure in verdant landscapes. He and his family summered in North Haven, Maine, where Benson frequently painted his wife and four children and used photography as an aid to capture fleeting poses.[4]

The year that Benson created this painting was one of great change for the art world, when abstract artworks exhibited at the landmark Armory Show in New York City would oust the Impressionists from their vanguard status. However, when Benson exhibited *The Seamstress* in the Ten's seventeenth annual exhibition in 1914, it still appealed to a large audience who enjoyed idyllic scenes of leisure performed along traditional gender binaries. His work sold so promptly that dealers often wrote to Benson to request more pictures. In 1914 the *Boston Herald* noted Benson's critical and popular success and called him the "nation's most medaled painter."[5]

JENNIFER STETTLER PARSONS

1. The textile appears to be a similar studio prop worn by women in other interior scenes by Benson, like *Figure in a Room* (1912; New Britain Museum of American Art) and *The Open Window* (1917; National Gallery of Art, Washington, DC).

2. Faith Andrews Bedford, *Frank W. Benson: American Impressionist* (New York: Rizzoli, 1994), 10, 137. Benson's Boston School colleague Philip Leslie Hale championed Vermeer in these years by publishing the first monograph on the artist in the United States in 1913.

3. The other members of the Ten American Painters were Joseph DeCamp, Thomas Wilmer Dewing, Childe Hassam, John Henry Twachtman, and J. Alden Weir.

4. Bedford, *Frank W. Benson*, 109.

5. Quoted in the biography of Benson by Erica E. Hirshler, in Trevor Fairbrother et al., *The Bostonians: Painters of an Elegant Age, 1870–1930* (Boston: Museum of Fine Arts, Boston, 1986), 199.

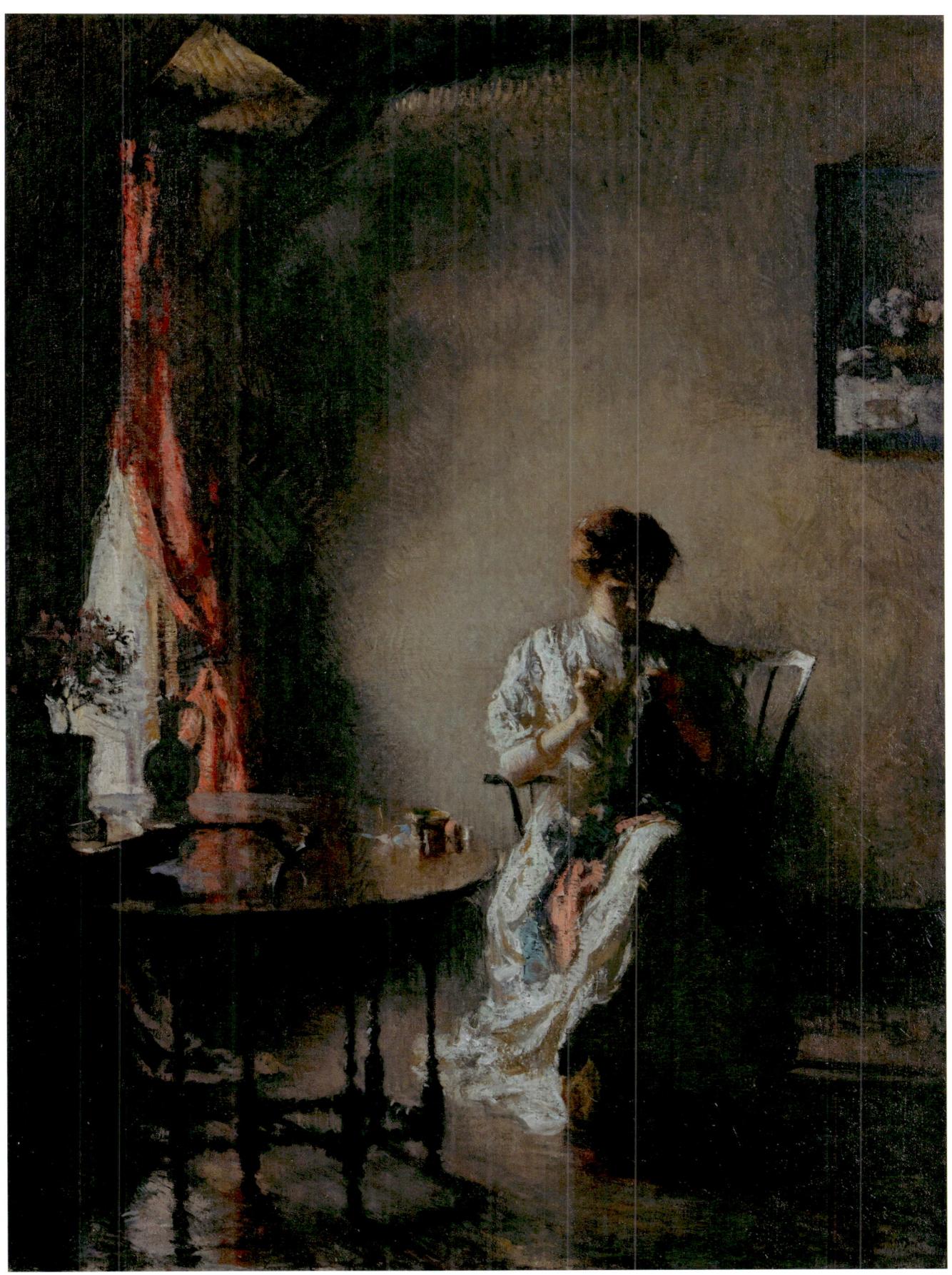

William McGregor Paxton

AMERICAN, 1869–1941

The Green Princess or *The Album*, ca. 1913

Oil on canvas

30 × 25 inches

Promised Gift of the Macon and Joan Brock Collection of American Art

STRIKING A PLEASING balance between elegant formality and quiet introspection, William McGregor Paxton's wife, Elizabeth Okie Paxton, served as the model for *The Green Princess* and in many of the interior and genre scenes he produced throughout his career. An artist herself, Elizabeth Okie married Paxton in 1899, and together they served as leading proponents of the Boston School of painting that developed during the first decades of the twentieth century. Trained in Paris at the Académie Julian and the more conventional École des Beaux-Arts, Paxton embraced art historical traditions but also incorporated modern painterly techniques. He especially admired the work of old master painters like Diego Velázquez and Johannes Vermeer. The seemingly narrow focus of Paxton's subject matter, largely composed of elegant women in well-furnished interiors, belies a complex approach to the optical properties of light, color, and space, and a deep interest in the psychological intensity of figures in their environment.

The Green Princess belongs to a series of works Paxton created around 1913 that reference the recent past. Elizabeth modeled for the painting in the parlor of the house that the Paxtons stayed in on Cape Cod during the summer of 1913. The distinctive patterns decorating the wall stood out for their associations with Victorian design of the late nineteenth century.[1] Elizabeth is shown delicately perusing an album of Gem tintypes, a technology that became popular after the Civil War as an affordable method of collecting multiple photographic portraits of friends and relations. The vibrant green dress and headpiece evoke the style of women's formal attire from the 1870s and was made specifically for Paxton's use as a studio prop.[2] The same costume is worn by a different model in Paxton's *1875*, created around the same time (fig. 1).

While Paxton often placed his female figures in copiously decorated interiors, in *The Green Princess* Elizabeth appears in strict profile, seated in an almost impossibly truncated register of space. The format recalls the style of

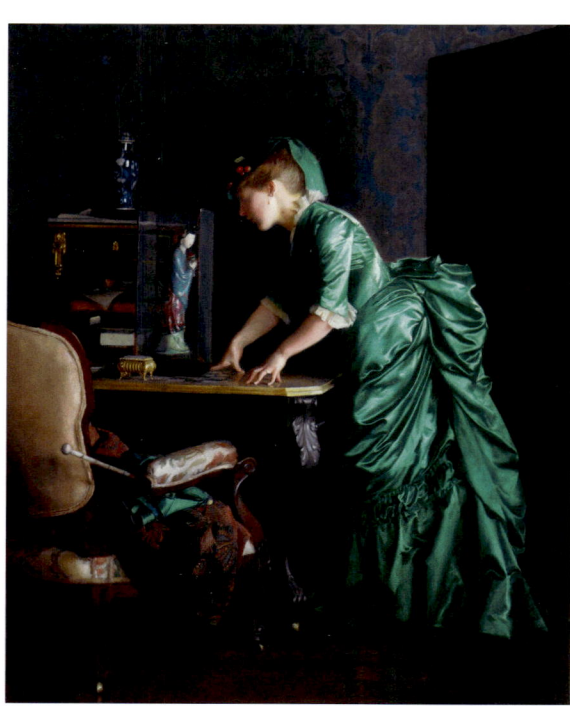

FIG. 1 William McGregor Paxton, *1875 (The Green Dress)*, 1914. Oil on canvas, 36 × 28 in. Private collection

Renaissance portraiture practiced in fifteenth-century Italy but also highlights the painting's most salient feature: the bold and shimmering green dress. When the painting was first exhibited, critics were understandably drawn to this feature, some to detrimental effect. A review in the *New York Times* called the shade "a dead and acid green, the kind that brings with it whiffs of aniline."[3] However, a year later, Paxton's *1875*, featuring the same green costume, won the award for best figure painting at the annual exhibition of the Pennsylvania Academy of the Fine Arts. When both *The Green Princess* and *1875* were shown together in Boston in 1916, they were praised for the "brilliant" and "attractive" hue of the distinctive green dress.[4] Despite Paxton's self-conscious and perhaps nostalgic evocation of the past in *The Green Princess*, by combining such a wide array of sources, from distant art history, Victorian fashion, and modern color theory, he achieved a vision that appears both strikingly modern and deceptively timeless.

COREY PIPER

1. Jessica Todd Smith, "Is Polite Society Polite?: The Genteel Tradition in the Figure Paintings of William McGregor Paxton (1869–1941)" (PhD diss., Yale University, 2001), 166.

2. Smith, "Is Polite Society Polite?" 167.

3. "Philadelphia Has Art Surprise," *New York Times*, February 8, 1914, 14.

4. "Boston," *American Art News* 14 (February 5, 1916): 5.

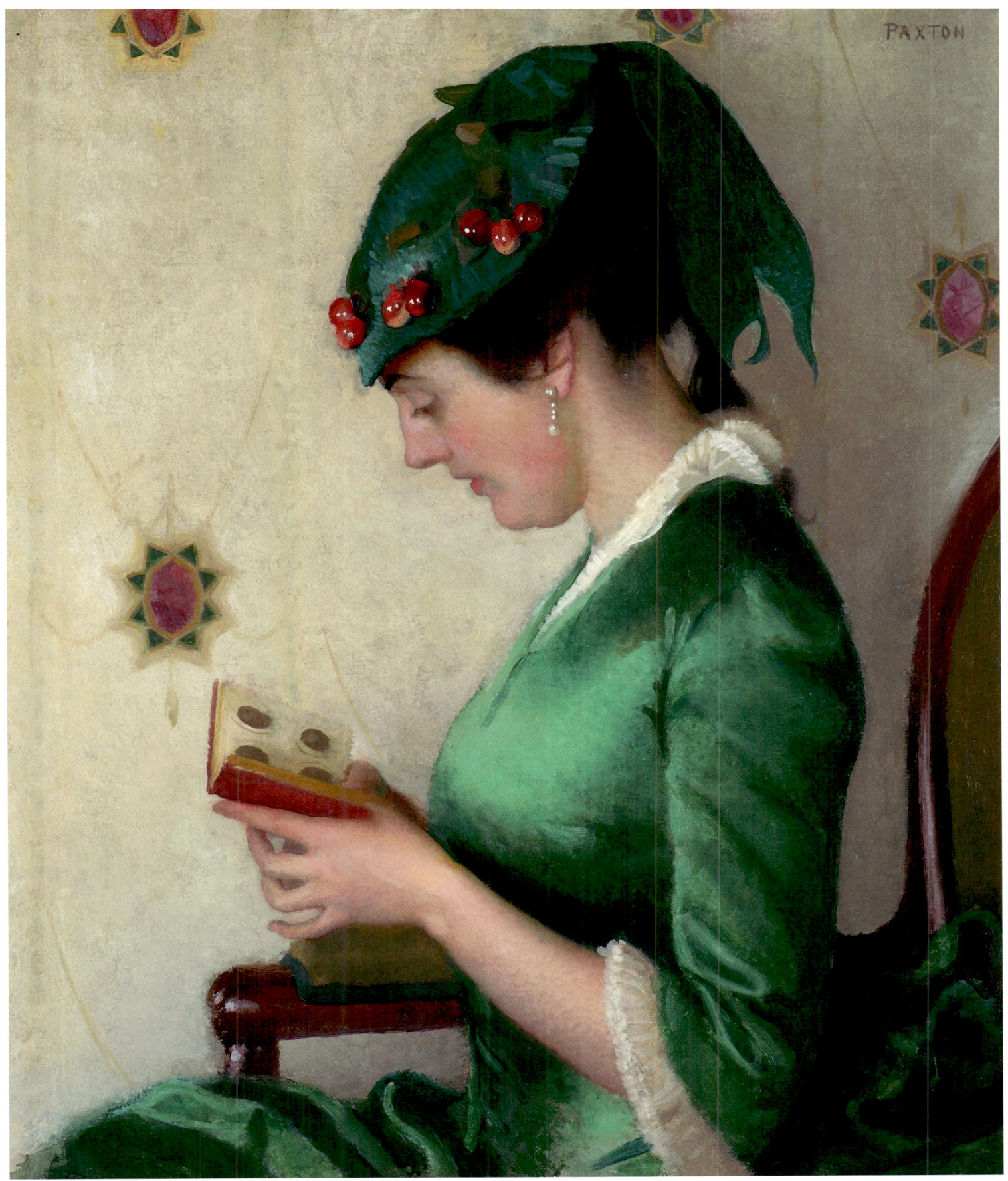

Dennis Miller Bunker

AMERICAN, 1861–1890

Yellow Rose, ca. 1885
Oil on panel
10½ × 13¾ inches

DENNIS MILLER BUNKER, who studied with William Merritt Chase in New York and then in Paris with Jean-Léon Gérôme, is widely regarded as the first artist in New England to engage the principles of French Impressionism—especially the expressive possibilities of light on variegated surfaces. He worked in France in 1884 but was back in the United States, teaching at the Cowles Art School in Boston, by 1885 and spent much of his life in the city. His works are rare—he died young, at the age of twenty-nine, and is known to have produced only about two hundred paintings. Among these works are several roses dating to the mid-1880s. *Yellow Rose* comes from the beginning of this period.

In this painting, the yellow rose and green leaves top the lip of a bottle, into which the plant's stem submerges. Dominating the space of the picture plane, the close-up view of the larger-than-life rose gives it a monumental sensibility that belies the composition's modest size. The illusion of the rose's proximity to the viewer appeals to the senses of sight, smell, and touch. The background morphs from light brown at left to muddy green at right and adds to the painting's visual power. Somewhat paradoxically, while we might well think of the rose's appearance as lifelike and realistic, the contrast with the background's negative space renders abstract the light-absorbent passages of yellow and green. "Unlike most still lifes, which evince a firm sense of three-dimensional materials," notes art historian and Bunker specialist Erica Hirshler, "Bunker's images seem ephemeral, the physicality of the blossoms contradicted by the indecipherable spaces they inhabit."[1] Based on the light-reflecting and -refracting bottle, we do know however that the work suggests painting sessions during daytime hours.

Bunker is probably best known for his stunning, vibrant landscapes and naturalistic, psychologically probing portraits. The 1880s floral still life paintings, while smaller in number, have a decidedly personal meaning and history. He often gave these smaller compositions to friends, sometimes inscribing the work to the recipient; this sort of gifting within elite social circles in Boston signals his participation in and acceptance within that environment.[2] He might have produced more of them but tended to paint "costly, out-of-season roses"; he complained, "It seems to cost as much to do flowers as to have models."[3] With the expressive, chiaroscuro modeling of the crisply painted plant forms, Bunker granted the flower the sort of vibrancy one might expect to find in a portrait depicting a human being's face. We therefore might consider Bunker's *Yellow Rose* a flower portrait.

LEO MAZOW

1. Erica E. Hirshler, "'From the School of Mud to the School of the Open Air': The Metamorphosis of Dennis Miller Bunker," in Hirshler et al., *Dennis Miller Bunker: An American Impressionist* (Boston: Museum of Fine Arts, Boston, 1994), 48. Hirshler notes that these flowers suggest the influence of fellow Boston artists John La Farge and Abbott Handerson Thayer; ibid.

2. David Park Curry, "Reconstructing Bunker," in Hirshler et al., *Dennis Miller Bunker*, 111.

3. Erica E. Hirshler, entry for *Yellow Roses*, in *Dennis Miller Bunker and His Circle* (Boston: Isabella Stewart Gardner Museum, 1995), 28.

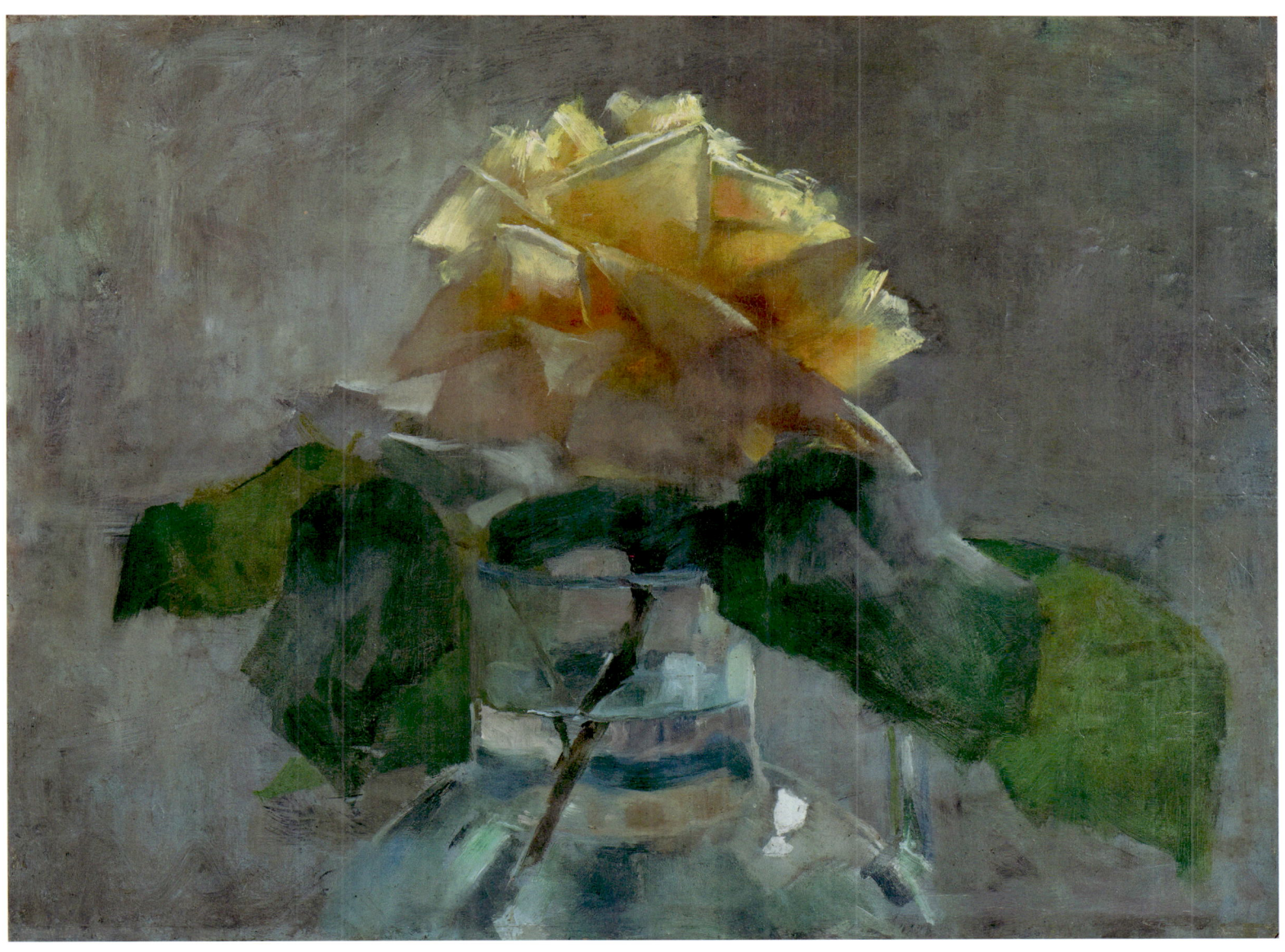

John Leslie Breck

AMERICAN, 1860–1899

Apple Trees in Bloom, ca. 1890–93

Oil on canvas

18¼ × 22 inches

Promised Gift of the Macon and Joan Brock Collection
of American Art

WITH *APPLE TREES IN BLOOM*, John Leslie Breck invites us to join him in an orchard among colorful grasses, lichen-covered boulders, and fragrant apple blossoms painted in thick impasto. Among American Impressionist painters, Breck is notable as one of the only American artists to develop a close relationship with Claude Monet at Giverny, about fifty miles outside of Paris. Breck arrived in Giverny in 1887, when Monet was already famous, and settled into what became a colony for American artists in and around the Hotel Baudy.[1] While Monet rarely accepted American painters into his milieu, Breck won enough favor to paint alongside him, became close with other members of the artist's family, and used Monet's impressionist painting style as a basis for his own.[2] This is evident in works like *Apple Trees in Bloom*, where Breck layers individual, unblended brushstrokes to suggest light and shadow rather than modeling three-dimensional form in the academic manner. In this way the impressionist style emphasizes the painted surface and the artist's hand in its creation. Further, Breck conveys a sense of direct encounter with the landscape by focusing the composition on one dramatic tree, whose blossom-covered branches dominate the canvas. Breck's abrupt cropping of the treetop reflects his lifelong interest in Japanese art and nature's temporality. Like a glimpse or memory, the picture encapsulates a fleeting moment in time, as the delicate blossoms will inevitably fall to the ground.

Breck painted the picture on a French canvas (stamped "Foinet"), but the boulders and rock wall in the background suggest the New England landscape rather than France.[3] The artist most likely purchased his materials during a trip abroad and painted this scene during a visit to Cape Ann, Massachusetts, in May 1893, when he rented a cottage in Annisquam. Located near Gloucester, Annisquam was a draw for artists before and after Breck, from William Morris Hunt in the 1870s to Edward Hopper in the early twentieth century.[4] He likely exhibited this painting in his first one-man show at the St. Botolph Club in Boston. Like Monet, Breck often painted in series, and there are seven known works of apple trees.[5] When three of them were exhibited at St. Botolph's in 1895, a reviewer commented that Breck's paintings "welcome to us the very spots until we seem almost to detect . . . the odor of the pink and spring blossoms."[6] Breck's talent for highlighting the ephemeral is poignant considering the legacy of his brief career, as his life was abruptly snuffed out by gas poisoning three weeks before his thirty-ninth birthday.

JENNIFER STETTLER PARSONS

1. In October 1887 the press reported, "Quite an American colony has gathered, I am told, at Givernay [*sic*] . . . the home of Claude Monet, including our Louis Ritter, W. L. Metcalf, Theodore Wendell [*sic*], John Breck, and Theodore Robinson of New York. A few pictures just received from these young men show that they have all got the blue-green color of Monet's Impressionism and 'got it bad.'" Greta, "Boston Art and Artists," *Art Amateur* 17 (October 17, 1887): 93. Jonathan Stuhlman et al., *John Leslie Breck: American Impressionist* (Charlotte, NC: The Mint Museum, 2021), 47.

2. A detailed account of what is known of Breck's relationship with Monet and his family is in Stuhlman, *John Leslie Breck*, 39–59.

3. For ideas in this paragraph, I am indebted to the expertise of Jonathan Stuhlman, Jeffrey R. Brown, and Royal W. Leith, who shared their knowledge about this work by email with Chrysler curator Corey Piper. See correspondence in Object File, Chrysler Museum of Art.

4. William Morris Hunt brought his class of female students to Annisquam in 1875, timed to arrive "in the season of apple blossoms." "The Early Art Colonies of Cape Ann: Annisquam," https://www.capeannmuseum .org/annisquam-art-colony/ (accessed November 2022). See also Rita and Elinor Teele, "Annisquam's Apple Trees," *Notes From the Firehouse*

(Annisquam Historical Society), https://static1.squarespace .com/static/5e35e50ee72e4563 b10feea7/t/5f99a08d167a3e3ec 5dd9128/1603903634676/AHS +2020+October+Notes+from +Firehouse+Annisquam%27s +Apple+Trees+reduced+pdf+% 281%29.pdf (accessed November 2022).

5. Email correspondence from Royal Leith to Jonathan Stuhlman, November 30, 2021. Object File, Chrysler Museum of Art. For a discussion of three of Breck's other apple tree paintings, see Stuhlman, *John Leslie Breck*, 89–92.

6. "Talk of the Day," *Boston Journal*, March 7, 1895, 8. Stuhlman, *John Leslie Breck*, 90. Breck often changed the titles of his paintings from one exhibition to the next, making it difficult to track exhibition history precisely. The number 40 on the back of this canvas corresponds to number 40 in the catalogue of Breck's memorial exhibition at the National Arts Club. Based on the title of the painting and others recorded in Breck's exhibition catalogues from the 1890s, scholar Jonathan Stuhlman believes that Breck may have exhibited this work in his first one-man exhibition at the St. Botolph Club (no. 41), in 1893 in the Chase's Gallery show (no. 13), and possibly in the 1895 St. Botolph Club exhibition (no. 23 or no. 27). Object File; and see exhibition history in Stuhlman, *John Leslie Breck*, 191–92.

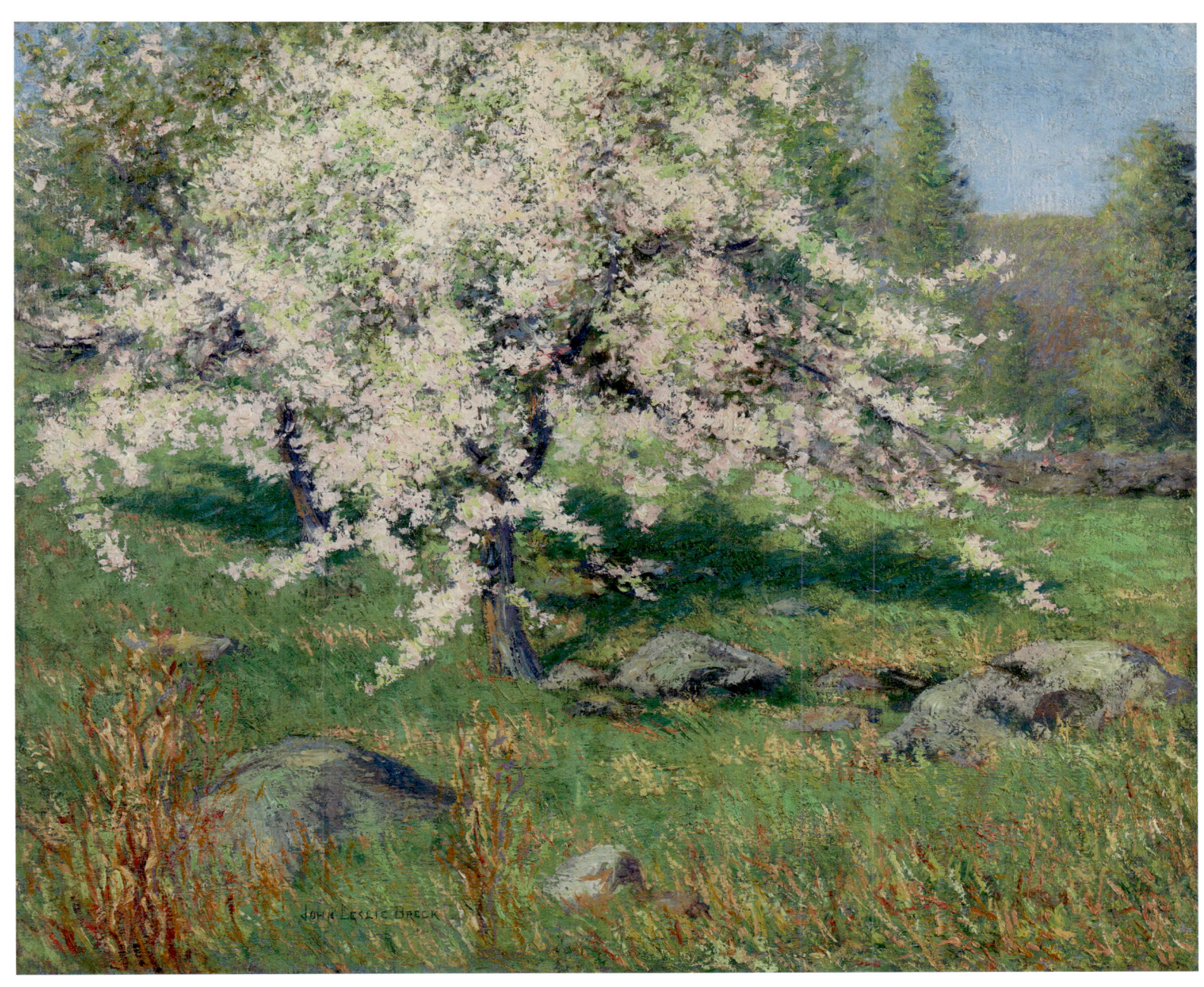

John Henry Twachtman

AMERICAN, 1853–1902

Spring, ca. 1898

Oil on canvas

30⅛ × 25 inches

Promised Gift of the Macon and Joan Brock Collection of American Art

IN THIS CONTEMPLATIVE LANDSCAPE, John Henry Twachtman combines his talent for abstract design with his faithfulness to nature and affection for family. *Spring* represents Twachtman's eldest daughter, Marjorie, in a flat-bottomed boat that meanders on Horseneck Brook, which ran through the artist's property in Greenwich, Connecticut.[1] His use of compositional asymmetry was one of the modernist hallmarks that animated the impressionist style, imparting a sense of dynamic encounter with nature. Still, Twachtman's use of calm, harmonious colors, paired with his brushy, layered paint application, communicates the atmosphere of bucolic sanctuary that he cherished about his Greenwich home. He chose the location not only for its easy commuting distance to New York City (where he taught at the Art Students League) and vicinity to Cos Cob (where he helped found an art colony at the Holley House) but for its rural quality.

Born in Cincinnati, Twachtman studied with renowned teacher Frank Duveneck and went with him to Munich, an art center that gained a reputation for producing students whose expressive brushwork melded old master techniques with contemporary energy. Through more training at Paris's Académie Julian and travels elsewhere in Europe, Twachtman linked up with like-minded American artists such as Willard Metcalf and J. Alden Weir, who were experimenting with impressionist methods. Reuniting back in New York, they found the contemporary art scene too conservative for their developing aesthetics. In 1897 they broke from the Society of American Artists to cofound the Ten American Painters, enabling them to exhibit their modern painting style without constraint.[2] The following year Twachtman exhibited *Spring* in the Ten's inaugural exhibition in New York. A reviewer commented in the press, "In an 'Early Spring' there is a queer anatomical construction of nature, for a boat on a stream seems to be running uphill, while the composition is uninteresting to a degree."[3] This response to the painting's pared-down subject and flattened sense of space reflects the initial bewilderment of some to the impressionist style. But for Twachtman (and other members of the Ten), his selective perspective and idiosyncratic paint handling captured more honestly his direct experience in nature. He often painted outdoors (*en plein air*) and even let the shining sun and rain meld with the oil paints on his canvas to achieve the desired texture.[4] Twachtman knew the landscape represented in *Spring* intimately and groomed the land to his visual preference by planting the willow trees seen along the water's edge. His daughter, drifting in the skiff, framed by the landscape, may be a metaphor for Twachtman's belief in the necessity of immersing oneself in nature. As he once described to Weir, "I feel more and more contented with the isolation of country life. . . . To be isolated is a fine thing and we are then nearer to nature."[5]

JENNIFER STETTLER PARSONS

1. Among Twachtman's many children, Marjorie can be identified by her long, blonde hair through comparisons with Twachtman's other paintings (such as *On the Terrace*, ca. 1890–1900; Smithsonian American Art Museum) and in photographs of the family (such as one by Gertrude Käsebier of Twachtman with his family on their front porch in Greenwich, ca. 1899; Mary Fanton Roberts papers, 1880–1956, Archives of American Art, Smithsonian Institution). For a thorough examination of Twachtman's Greenwich paintings and the modifications the artist made to his property, see Lisa N. Peters, *Life and Art: The Greenwich Paintings of John Henry Twachtman* (Cos Cob, CT: Greenwich Historical Society, 2021).

2. Other members of the Ten American Painters were Frank Weston Benson, Joseph DeCamp, Thomas Wilmer Dewing, Childe Hassam, Willard Metcalf, Robert Reid, Edward Simmons, Edmund C. Tarbell, and J. Alden Weir. Several years after Twachtman's death in 1902, his place was taken by William Merritt Chase.

3. "The Art World: Ten American Painters at the Durand-Ruel Gallery," *New-York Commercial Advertiser* (March 30, 1898), 7. Lisa N. Peters, *John Henry Twachtman Catalogue Raisonné* (Greenwich, CT: Greenwich Historical Society, 2021). Online, https://www.jhtwachtman.org/catalogue/entry.php?id=266 (accessed October 28, 2022).

4. The anecdote about sun and rain on Twachtman's canvases comes from a monograph written by one of his students, Eliot Clark. See Eliot Clark, *John Twachtman* (New York: privately printed, 1924), 58.

5. Twachtman to Weir, Greenwich, December 16, 1891, Weir Family Papers. Lisa N. Peters, *John Henry Twachtman: An American Impressionist* (High Museum of Art; New York: Hudson Hills Press, 1999), 111.

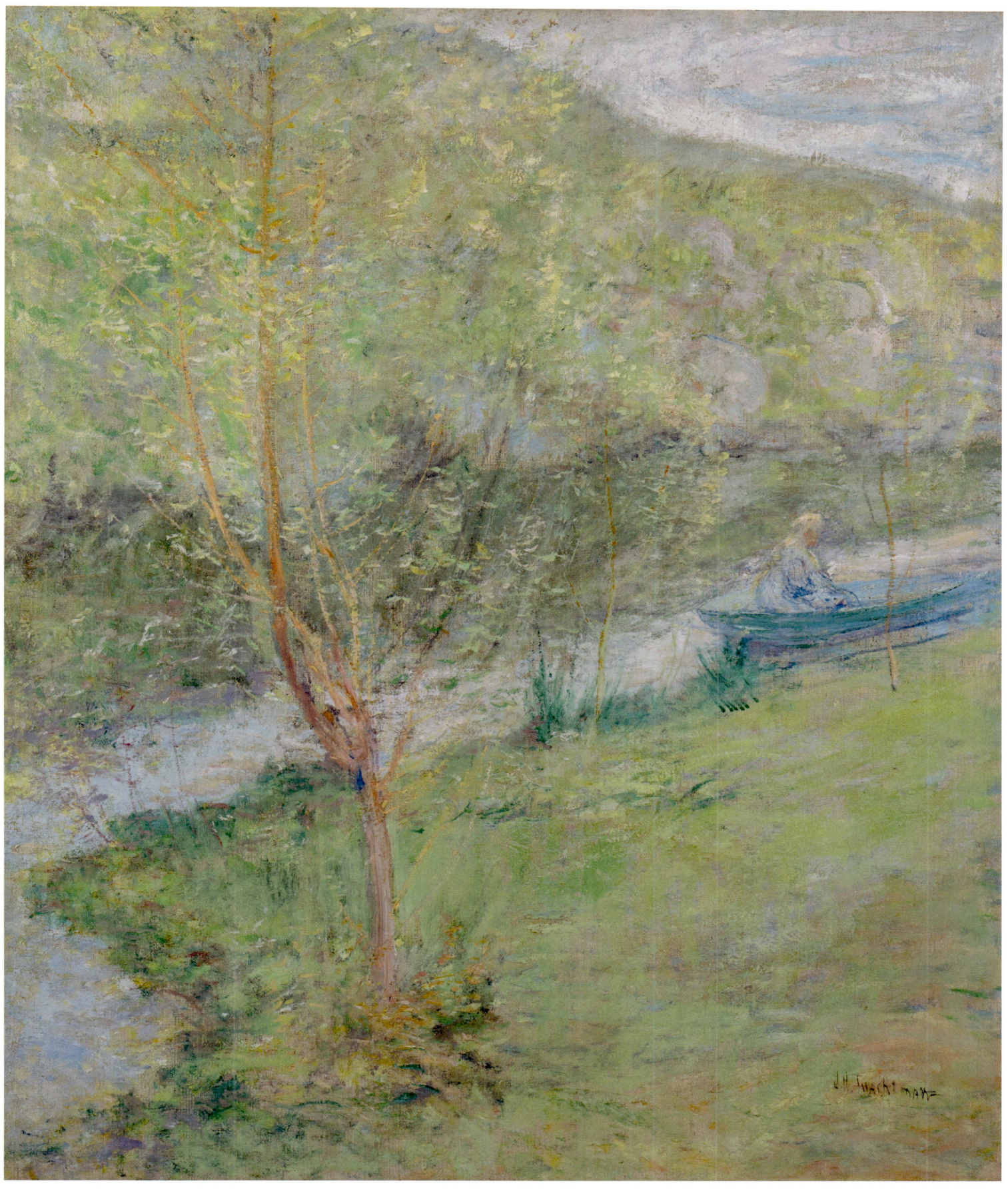

Childe Hassam

AMERICAN, 1859–1935

Snowstorm, Fifth Avenue, New York, 1907

Oil on canvas

16⅛ × 12 inches

Promised Gift of the Macon and Joan Brock Collection
of American Art

LEADING IMPRESSIONIST PAINTER Childe Hassam pioneered the modern representation of urban scene painting in the United States beginning in the late nineteenth century. In *Snowstorm, Fifth Avenue, New York*, he revisited a fond memory of his first winter in his new studio at the intersection of Fifth Avenue and Seventeenth Street, when he saw a messenger boy outside his window. Hassam had made a larger composition of an identical subject about fifteen years earlier called *Fifth Avenue in Winter*, with a similar messenger boy standing on the corner, set apart from the commotion of street traffic and other pedestrians (fig. 1).[1] The artist had recently returned from several years in Paris, where he was inspired by the French Impressionists to immerse himself in everyday urban life and create pictures that communicated the immediacy of his encounter with ordinary Parisian routines. Once back in New York, Hassam combined his interest in the city, its humanity, and atmospheric effects into paintings that found a ready market and catapulted him to popularity.

By 1907 he had moved up to 27 West Sixty-seventh Street but kept *Fifth Avenue in Winter* as a personal favorite and exhibited it on numerous occasions.[2] When he painted its progeny, *Snowstorm, Fifth Avenue, New York*, Hassam lowered his perspective to street level, centralizing the boy's experience in the blustery storm. Hassam's brushwork features a limited palette of appropriately cool colors and suggests the hazy veil of falling snow, which unifies the architecture, street vehicles, and figures into a snow globe–like environment. In contrast to the dark figure behind him who shields herself with an umbrella, the messenger boy is exposed and vulnerable to the elements. Snow has gathered on his cap, weighs on his shoulders, and sticks to his pants with each labored step. Hassam defers on details of the boy's face but suggests the discomfort of exposure to icy precipitation through strokes of bright, orangey-pink paint and red dots for eyes and nose. Hassam remarked, "There is nothing so interesting to me as people. I am never tired of observing them in every-day life, as they hurry through the streets on business or saunter down the promenade on pleasure. Humanity in motion is a continual study to me."[3] For Hassam, the messenger boy personifies the modern city.

Born in Dorchester, Massachusetts, outside of Boston, Hassam first trained as a watercolorist and illustrator for periodicals. After studying at the Boston Art Club and Cornell Institute, New York, he traveled to Europe in the 1880s and enrolled at the Académie Julian in Paris. Returning to the United States, Hassam settled in New York and shook the art world by resigning from the Society of American Artists to cofound the Ten American Painters, who exhibited together from 1898 to 1919.[4] During those years Hassam frequently left the city for the countryside, finding inspiration and respite in the art colonies of the northeast, including Old Lyme, Cos Cob, Newport, Portsmouth, Gloucester, and the Isles of Shoals. He continued to push the conventions of urban representation during the war years, when he made a series of approximately thirty paintings begun in 1914 known as the "flag pictures," when American flags were displayed along Fifth Avenue and other major thoroughfares in support of the Allied effort during World War I. The success of these paintings spurred critic Henry McBride to reflect on Hassam's long documentation of the metropolis, remarking that "Childe Hassam has been Fifth avenue's historian for years."[5]

JENNIFER STETTLER PARSONS

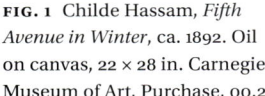

FIG. 1 Childe Hassam, *Fifth Avenue in Winter*, ca. 1892. Oil on canvas, 22 × 28 in. Carnegie Museum of Art, Purchase, 00.2

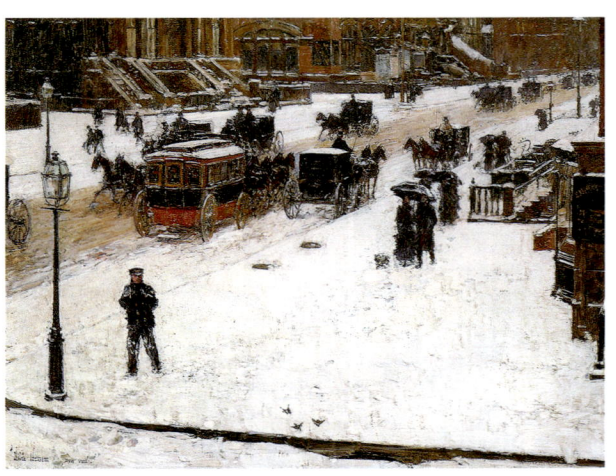

1. Other works portraying this subject are *Messenger Boy* (1903; Rhode Island School of Design Museum) and *Street Scene in Winter* (1901; formerly Metropolitan Museum of Art, deaccessioned February 1969, location unknown). H. Barbara Weinberg, *Childe Hassam: American Impressionist* (New Haven, CT, and London: Yale University Press, 2004), 211, 228n20.

2. Ulrich W. Hiesinger, *Childe Hassam: American Impressionist* (New York: Prestel-Verlag, 1994), 65.

3. A. E. Ives, "Talks with Artists: Mr. Childe Hassam on Painting Street Scenes," *Art Amateur* 27, no. 5 (October 1892): 116–17.

4. Members of the Ten American Painters were Frank Weston Benson, Joseph DeCamp, Thomas Wilmer Dewing, Childe Hassam, Willard Metcalf, Robert Reid, Edward Simmons, Edmund C. Tarbell, John Henry Twachtman, and J. Alden Weir.

5. Henry McBride, "Childe Hassam and the Americanization of Fifth Avenue," *New York Sun*, November 24, 1918, 10. Weinberg, *Childe Hassam*, 203.

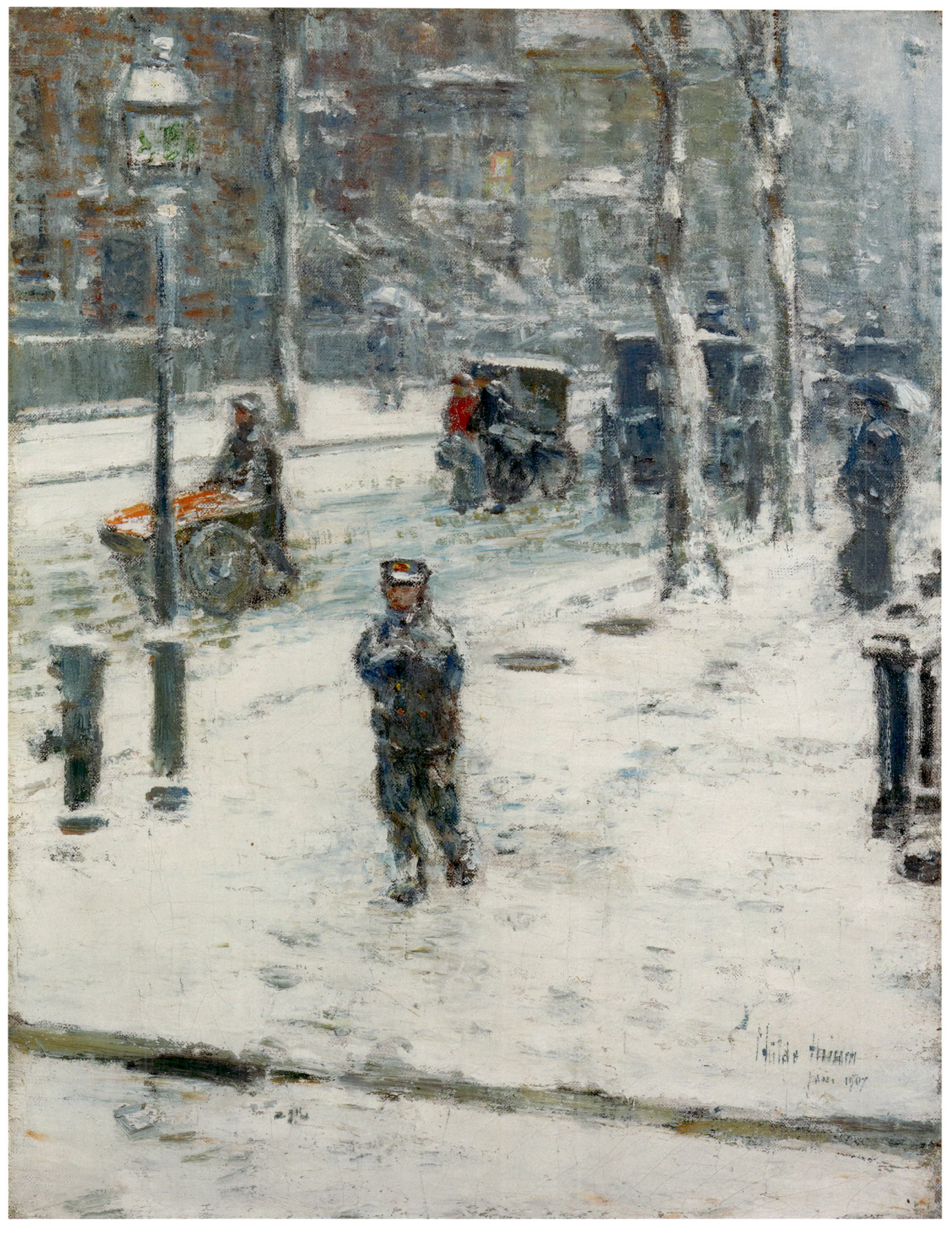

Karl Albert Buehr

AMERICAN, 1866–1952

Breakfast on the Green, ca. 1911–12
Oil on canvas
31½ × 39 inches

WITH ITS BRILLIANT PLAY of dappled light effects, high-keyed palette, and monumental treatment of middle-class leisure, *Breakfast on the Green* represents a high point of the American Impressionist movement that coalesced in Giverny, France, during the beginning of the twentieth century. The German-born Buehr followed a rich and varied path through his early life that eventually led him to the thriving American artist colony outside Paris. Buehr immigrated to Chicago as a young man and enrolled at the School of the Art Institute in 1888. However, he interrupted his studies to enlist in the army, serving in the Spanish-American War from 1898 to 1899. He followed his service with extensive travels throughout Europe, where he would spend the bulk of the next decade. Between 1900 and 1907, he studied at the Académie Julian in Paris, the Academy of Rome, and the London School of Art.

By 1908 Buehr had returned to France, eventually settling in Giverny, where he and his wife, the miniature painter Mary Guion Hess, connected with fellow Chicagoans Lawton S. Parker, Louis Ritman, and Frederick Frieseke and became fixtures of the expatriate American community. While the presence of Claude Monet in the vicinity had initially provided the impetus for the colony's foundation in the late nineteenth century, by the time Buehr arrived, few Americans had the pleasure of interacting with the French master and instead were drawn by the well-established network of Americans who had lived and worked there. Indeed, the Buehrs eventually settled in a home rented to them by Parker and, along with their children, formed rich social bonds with the other artists' families who summered and lived in Giverny.[1]

Beyond the amiable social scene, Buehr found a vibrant artistic atmosphere in Giverny that allowed him to expand his aesthetic approach to incorporate more modern pictorial elements borrowed from Impressionism and Japanese art and design. *Breakfast on the Green* showcases many of these attributes. Buehr employed high impasto and tactile brushwork to create a rich panoply of color and light, which suffuses the verdant waterside clearing surrounding the model. The flattened composition and disregard of perspectival space, along with the Japanese-inspired design of the parasol, echo the Giverny group's intense interest in *Japonisme*, which influenced a wide swath of European and American art and design around the turn of the twentieth century. Buehr sent the painting back to exhibitions in the United States, showing it at the Art Institute of Chicago, the Pennsylvania Academy of the Fine Arts, the Corcoran Gallery, and the Panama-Pacific International Exhibition, each time altering its title slightly. Critical reaction to the painting is unrecorded, but Buehr eventually returned to a long and successful career in the US, where he taught at the Art Institute of Chicago from 1914 to 1939.

COREY PIPER

1. William H. Gerdts, *Monet's Giverny: An Impressionist Colony* (New York: Abbeville Press, 1993), 195.

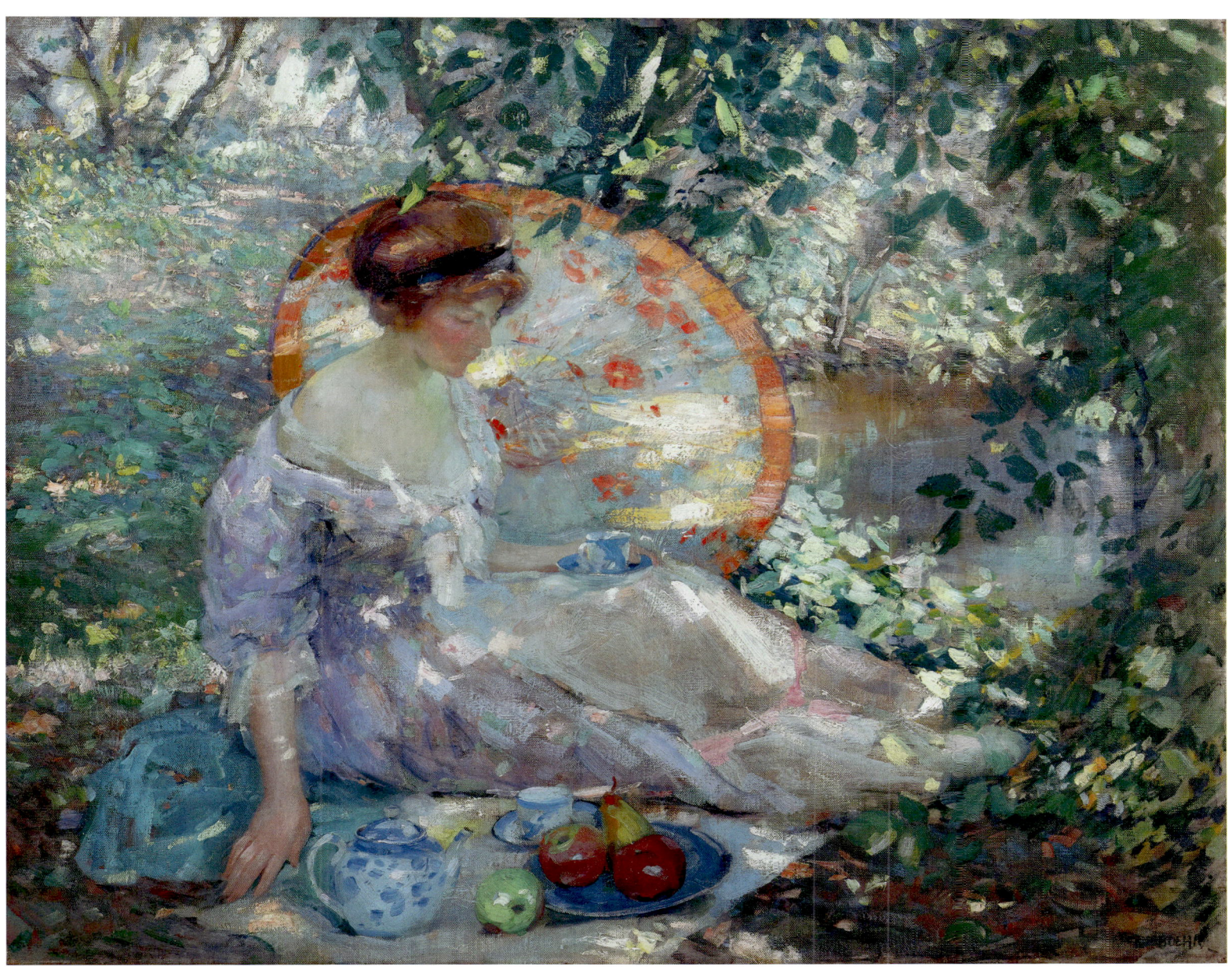

Frederick Carl Frieseke

AMERICAN, 1874–1939

Girl Sewing, ca. 1917
Oil on canvas
32 × 26¼ inches

MICHIGAN-BORN FRIESEKE ranks among the leading American Impressionists. His charming scenes of women and girls in dappled sunlight and cool shade, set in his garden and house at Giverny, France, were enormously popular with American collectors. He spent his entire career in France, moving there after growing up in Florida and studying at the Art Institute of Chicago and New York. He arrived in Paris in 1898 to study with Benjamin Constant and Jean-Paul Laurens at the Académie Julian and with James McNeill Whistler at the Académie Carmen.[1]

In 1905 Frieseke married American artist Sara O'Brien, who was also studying in Paris. Then, beginning in 1906, they started to divide their time between summers in Giverny and winters in Paris. Although they moved next door to Claude Monet in Giverny, Frieseke discounted the influence of Monet and the Impressionists, with the exception of Renoir, and at one point even referred to himself as self-taught. Although he served with an ambulance company in Neuilly during World War I, there is no hint in his work of the cataclysm unfolding in the trenches to the north.

Many of his works around 1917 feature the same green-blue palette we see in the Brock Collection's *Girl Sewing*, which suggests the coolness of the shade contrasted with the effects of brilliant, dappled sunlight and its indirect reflections. This mottled effect is accentuated by the broken stroke of his impressionist technique. Frieseke claimed to paint exactly what was in front of him, "to make a mirror of the canvas."[2] He was unambiguous about his obsession with the effect of variegated sunlight, and the great majority of his unfailingly charming works feature women and girls at work or in repose in gardens or at sunlit windows or in the boudoir.

The model in the Brock painting appears to be Albertine Louise Feron, daughter of a local tree nurseryman.[3] She was eighteen in 1917 and a friend of the family nurse, Alphonsine Tersinet. In this year she began to appear in many of Frieseke's works, including *Girl with Earrings*, where she wears the same lace cap as in the painting in the Brock Collection (fig. 1). *Girl Sewing* recalls the great images by Dutch masters that Frieseke would have seen on view in the Louvre, such as Vermeer's *Lacemaker*, as well as other works on this subject by Renoir (Art Institute of Chicago, private collection).

Frieseke stayed on in France because of its libertine environment, stating, "I am more free and there are not the Puritanical restrictions which prevail in America. . . . I can paint a nude in my garden or down by the fish pond and not be run out of town."[4] In 1923 he broke with the Salon and exhibited with a group of Americans in Paris, including Cecilia Beaux and John Singer Sargent. From 1920 until Frieseke's death in 1939, the family lived in Normandy. Unfortunately, he was unable to travel to see the extensive retrospective of his work staged at the Grand Central Art Galleries by Macbeth, his New York gallerist, in 1932.

LLOYD DEWITT

1. Nicholas Kilmer, "Frederick Carl Frieseke, a Biography," *Frederick Carl Frieseke: The Evolution of an American Impressionist* (Savannah, GA: Telfair Museum of Art, 2001), 13–18.

2. Allen S. Weller, *Frederick Frieseke* (New York: Hirsch & Adler Galleries, 1966), unpaginated.

3. *Albert Feron, pépiniériste et sa famille*, https://www.pbase.com/image/122195822 (accessed Oct 27, 2022).

4. Weller, *Frederick Frieseke*.

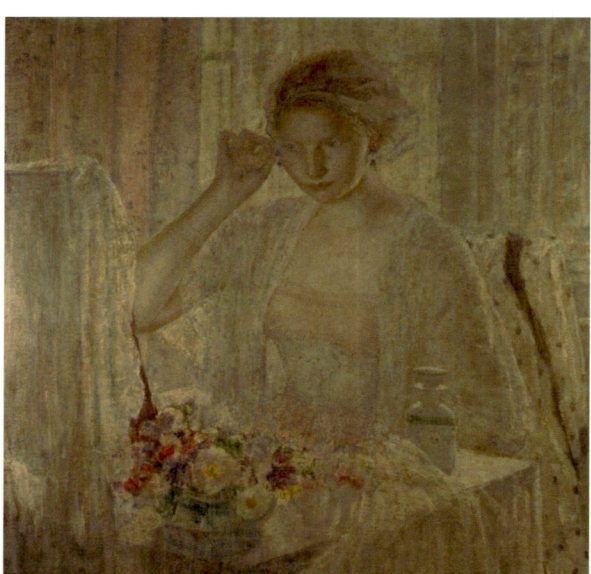

FIG. 1 Frederick Carl Frieseke, *Girl with Earrings*, 1917. Oil on canvas, 39½ × 39½ in. Krannert Art Museum, Urbana-Champaign, IL, 1924-5-1

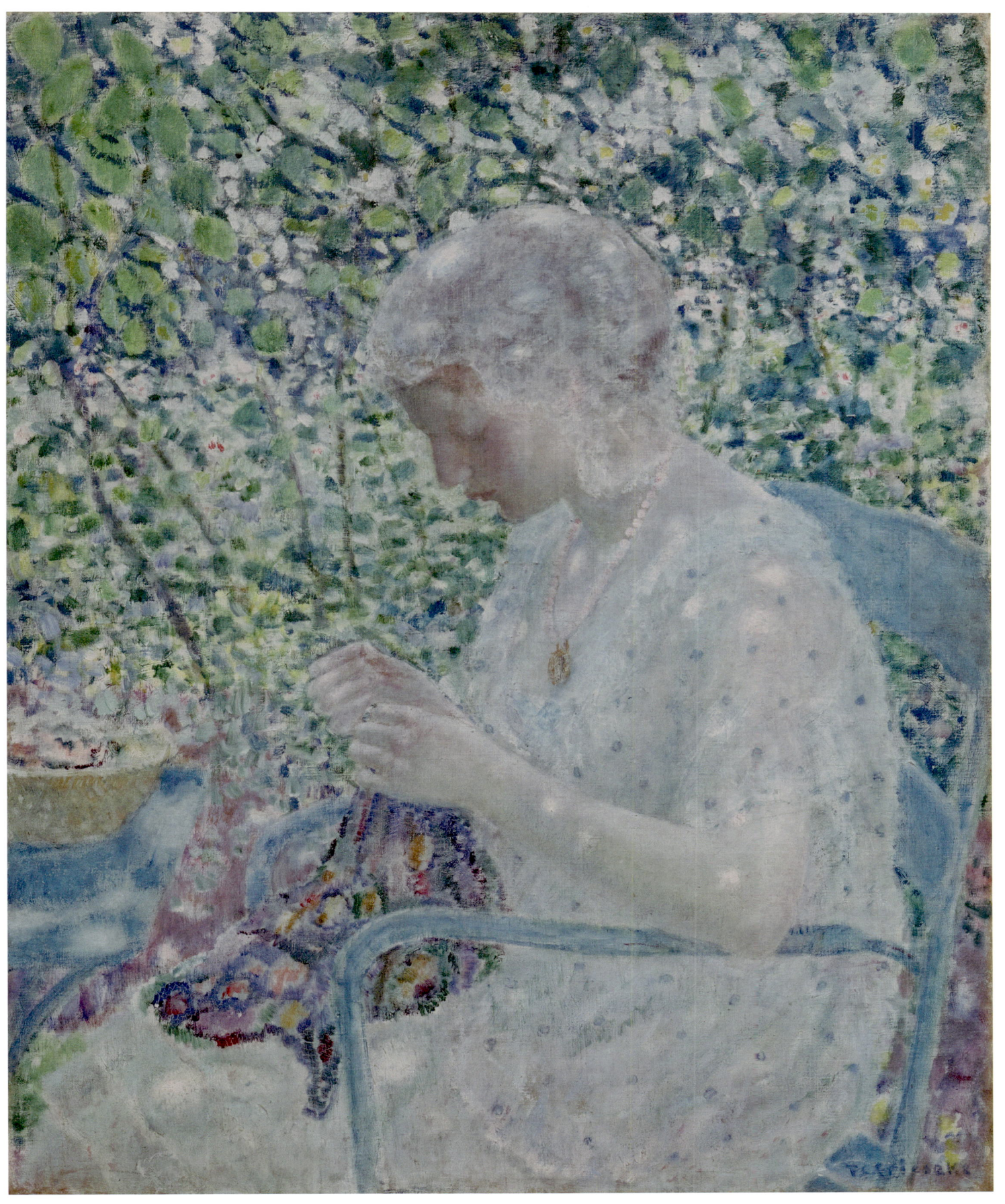

Willard LeRoy Metcalf

AMERICAN, 1858–1925

October Morning No. 1, 1910

Oil on canvas

21⅛ × 29 inches

Promised Gift of the Macon and Joan Brock Collection of American Art

TWO PAINTINGS in the Brock Collection by Willard Metcalf, *October Morning No. 1* and *The Village in Late Spring*, exemplify the dual subjects for which Metcalf is best known—the intimately observed landscape rendered *en plein air* and the transition of nature's seasons. These works, which were painted a decade apart, demonstrate Metcalf's stylistic maturation into Impressionism, while in his personal life they bookend the period of marriage to his second wife, Henriette McCrea. In the paintings Metcalf develops his idiosyncratic sense of space by layering broad bands of color and form across the canvas. Each register offers a revelation—the shimmer of moving water, minute human figures working the land, and glimpses of buildings among the foliage. Through these details the artist evokes a sensorial experience made possible not only by his practice of painting outdoors but by his attunement to the environment as an amateur naturalist.

By 1910, when Metcalf painted *October Morning No. 1*, he had experienced a high variability of disappointment and success, from a failed first marriage to professional acclaim in the art world to health problems and then new

love. Born in Lowell, Massachusetts, Metcalf was one of the inaugural students to attend the School of the Museum of Fine Arts, Boston. He worked as an illustrator to finance his travel to France, where he studied at the Académie Julian in Paris and went to the countryside to paint alongside other American artists at colonies like Grez-sur-Loing. By 1885 Metcalf was one of the first American artists in Giverny.[1] His understanding of the natural world so impressed Claude Monet that he arranged for Metcalf to tutor his son, Michel, and stepson, Jean-Pierre Hoschedé, in botany and ornithology.[2] A keen observer of nature, Metcalf also collected hundreds of bird eggs (including some at Giverny), moths, butterflies, and nests that he assembled into a naturalist's cabinet.[3] He traveled widely, including to England, Algiers, Tunisia, and Cuba, but it was to New England that Metcalf always returned and where he made paintings that earned him the title "Poet laureate of the New England hills."[4] *October Morning No. 1* and *The Village in Late Spring* prove the appropriateness of that designation.

In *October Morning* the eye's journey begins in the cold, blue river water before being drawn up by the warmth of the sun upon green grass and the shock of orange foliage against a pale blue sky. Metcalf's active, broken brushstrokes laid down on the canvas like threads in a tapestry coalesce into a harmonious rural idyll. This painting style, called Impressionism, was still popular in 1910 but was already being challenged by the next wave of Modernists interested in the urban scene and nonrepresentational abstraction. Metcalf had been at the forefront of the Impressionist movement in the United States when in 1897 he wrote the mission statement for the Ten American Painters, who collectively resigned from the more conservative Society of American Artists to show their vanguard paintings under optimal conditions.[5] Metcalf painted this view of the Hollenbeck River in Falls Village, northwestern Connecticut.[6] At the time he was courting his new love interest, Henriette, who would become his second wife in 1911. At the center of the painting, a white fence against a dirt road leads our eye between two figural groups—a man in an ox-pulled cart and a couple out walking together.

Metcalf painted a similar theme a decade later in *The Village in Late Spring*. From May to June 1920, the artist worked in Chester, Vermont, staying at the Fullerton Inn,[7] and made return trips over the next three years.[8] A related work, *The Village in Spring*, ca. 1923, shows the view of Chester Depot from the opposite side of the river, revealing that Metcalf traversed the landscape to

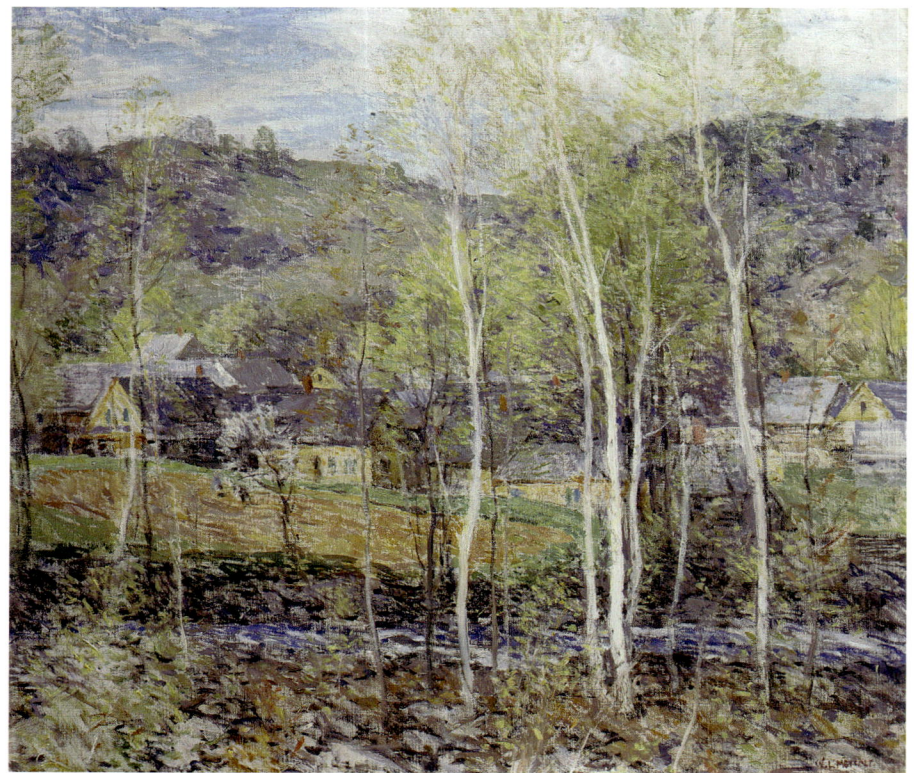

FIG. 1 Willard LeRoy Metcalf, *The Village in Spring*, ca. 1923. Oil on canvas, 28 × 31 in. Florence Griswold Museum, Gift of The Hartford Steam Boiler Inspection and Insurance Company, 2002.1.90

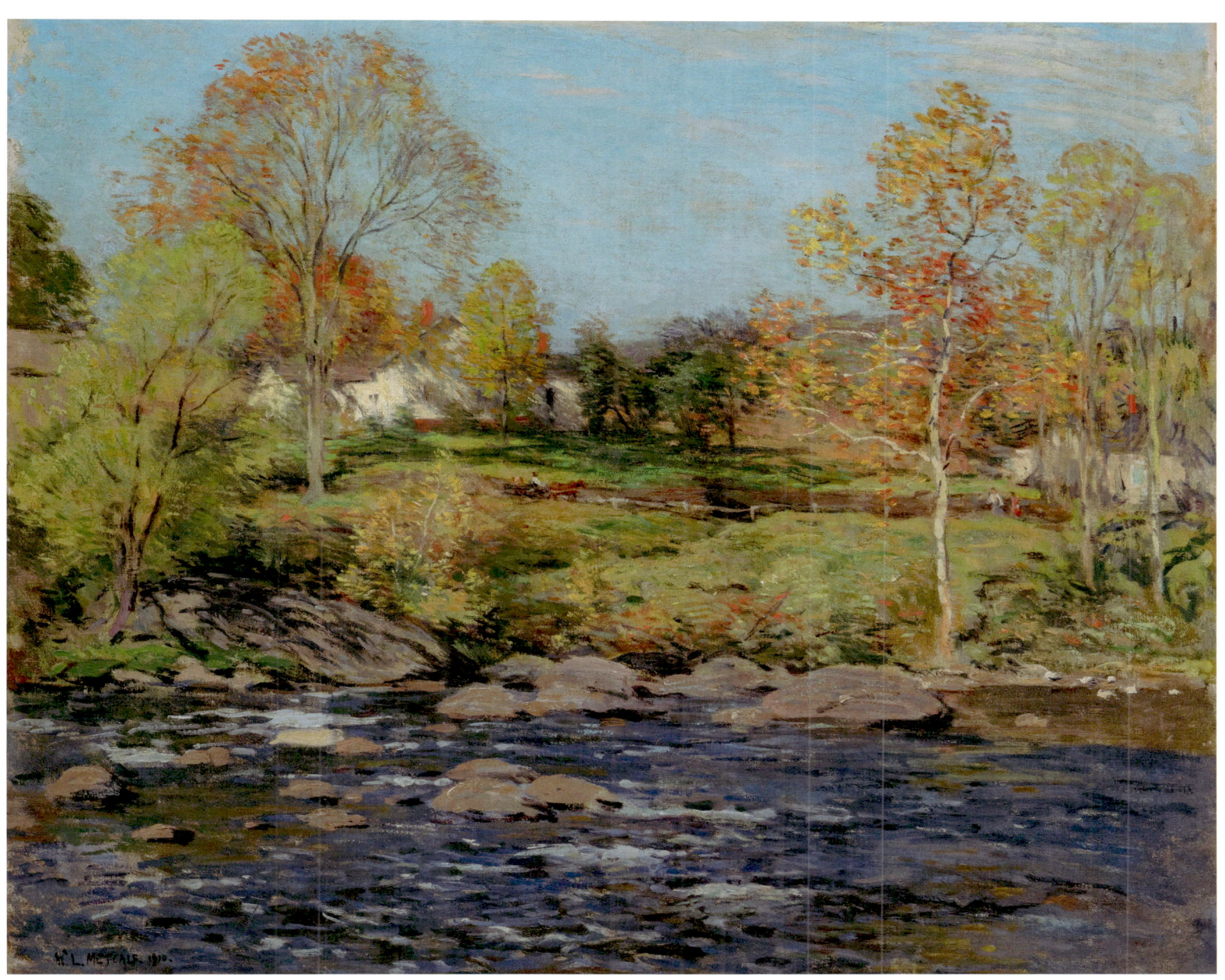

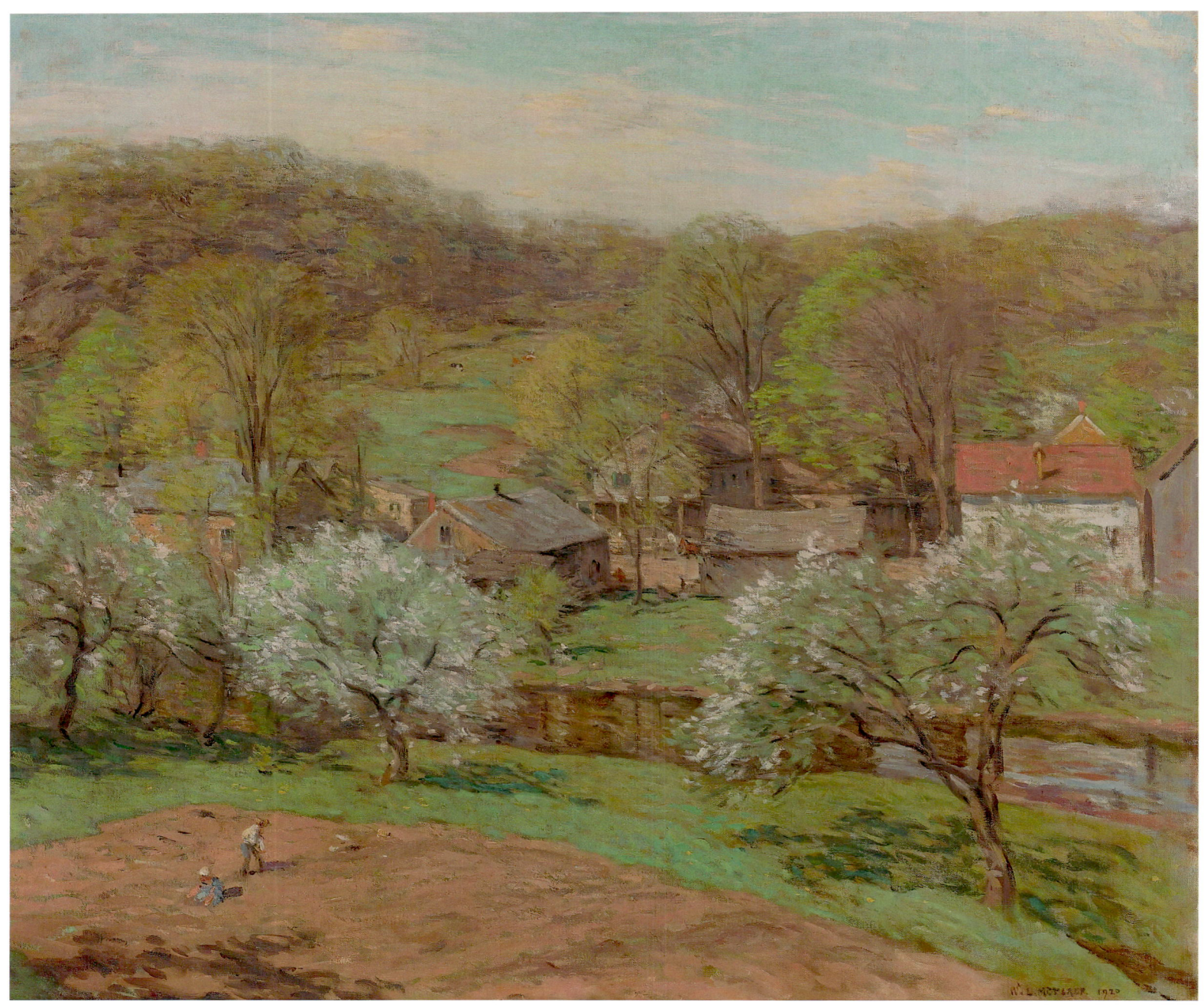

find varying perspectives (fig. 1). The Florence Griswold Museum's painting, done in a looser, more gestural style, shows the same plot of farmland viewed through a screen of tall trees. In the Brock Collection's *The Village in Late Spring*, Metcalf takes a bird's-eye view, with a clear perspective of the farmers tending the land and a glimpse of village life on the opposite side of the river. The flowering trees, as well as the grazing cattle near the high horizon, suggest the warming temperatures and the cycle of life tied to the seasons. A cycle would soon end for the artist in his family life as well, as Henriette asked Metcalf for a divorce in 1920. When faced with repeated poor health and personal hardship over his lifetime, Metcalf turned to nature for solace and renewal. The farmhands in *The Village in Late Spring* illustrate that connectedness. Though they are miniature figures within the rural panorama, Metcalf clearly depicts a man's feet planted firmly in the brown earth while a woman kneels with her hands in the soil. Like Metcalf's own painting practice, their cooperation with the landscape offers the possibility of new growth in the next season.

JENNIFER STETTLER PARSONS

1. This early date is known from the labeling on Metcalf's bird egg specimens, which he collected and stored in a twenty-eight-drawer cabinet. In drawer 1B (top drawer, right side) is a box that Metcalf labeled as a blackbird egg from Giverny, May 1885. Metcalf's second wife, Henriette, gifted the cabinet to the Florence Griswold Museum in Old Lyme, Connecticut, the site of the art colony that Metcalf participated in between 1905 and 1907, and where he collected additional natural specimens.

2. Bruce W. Chambers, *May Night: Willard Metcalf at Old Lyme* (Old Lyme, CT: Florence Griswold Museum, 2005), 19.

3. For more on Metcalf's naturalist cabinet, see Jennifer Stettler Parsons, *Flora/Fauna: The Naturalist Impulse in American Art* (Old Lyme, CT: Florence Griswold Museum, 2017); and Chambers, *May Night*.

4. In the catalogue essay that accompanied Metcalf's one-man exhibition at the Corcoran Gallery of Art in January 1925, Walter Jack Duncan called him the "poet laureate of these homely hills." (Metcalf passed away a couple of months later in March 1925.) Richard J. Boyle refined that moniker and

wrote, "'Poet laureate of the New England hills' would be even more accurate," in Richard J. Boyle and Elizabeth de Veer, *Sunlight and Shadow: The Life and Art of Willard L. Metcalf* (New York: Abbeville Press, 1987), 10.

5. Other members of the Ten American Painters were Frank Weston Benson, Joseph DeCamp, Thomas Wilmer Dewing, Childe Hassam, Robert Reid, Edward Simmons, Edmund C. Tarbell, John Henry Twachtman, and J. Alden Weir.

6. Another view that Metcalf painted of the region in spring of 1910 is *Blossoming Willows* (1910; Philadelphia Museum of Art).

7. Boyle and de Veer, *Sunlight and Shadow*, 270. In the decades since Metcalf resided there, the Fullerton Inn has changed owners and names several times, but in 2020 its original name was restored by the present owners. See https://www.fullertoninn.com/history (accessed November 1, 2022).

8. Boyle and de Veer, *Sunlight and Shadow*, 271; Object File for *The Village in Spring* (1923; Florence Griswold Museum, Old Lyme, CT).

Edgar Alwin Payne

AMERICAN, 1883–1947

Desert Skies, ca. 1917

Oil on canvas

28 × 34 inches

ONE OF THE MOST ADVENTUROUS of the historic California plein-air painters, Edgar Alwin Payne utilized the animated brushwork, vibrant palette, and shimmering light of Impressionism, but his powerful imagery was unique among artists of his generation. While most of his contemporaries favored a quieter, more idyllic representation of the natural landscape, Payne was devoted to subjects of rugged beauty, and his majestic, vital landscapes incorporated movement and dynamism. For him, it was important to express attributes that were "beyond vision." "The power is given to him to feel," he said, "the mystery and charm of fleeting clouds; the immensity and depth of blue skies and atmospheric distances; the grace and rhythm of living and expanding trees and other growths; the nobility, grandeur and strength of mighty peaks; the endless movement and vitality of the sea and its forms."[1]

Payne was born in Missouri and lived for a time in Chicago, studying very briefly at the School of the Art Institute of Chicago, though he considered himself self-taught. He met his future wife, artist Elsie Palmer, on his first trip to California in 1909. After encountering the West, he began to exploit the possibilities of California's sunshine, atmosphere, and terrain.

Payne's unending quest to convey the "unspeakably sublime" also led him to travel the world, and during his painting expeditions, he covered some 100,000 miles throughout the United States and Europe. He was among the first painters to capture the vigor of Southern California's Sierra Nevada, and his travels within the American Southwest resulted in equally magnificent depictions of the desert. In Europe, he rendered the towering peaks of the Alps and the colorful harbors of France and Italy.

Payne's fascination with the American Southwest began when he accepted an assignment from the Atchison, Topeka & Santa Fe Railway Company (commonly called the Santa Fe Railway) to paint the region's natural wonders. Provided with transportation by the railroad, he arrived in Gallup, New Mexico, with his wife and daughter in June 1916. The family set off by car, heading west to Ganado in Arizona and then to Canyon de Chelly. Thereafter, to take full advantage of the region's aesthetic opportunities, he rented a wagon to go from site to site. For the next four months, he sketched and painted the spectacular scenery, often adding human interest by incorporating Navajo riders into the terrain.

This early Southwestern trip resulted in an important but limited body of work, and it was not until 1930 that Payne would revisit the area regularly. He did so for the next fifteen years. In 1941 he shared what he had learned in his self-published *Composition of Outdoor Painting*, "a short and concise handbook on the essentials of outdoor painting for the practical student."[2] Diagnosed with cancer in 1946, his nomadic journeys came to an end, and he died the following year.

SCOTT A. SHIELDS

1. Edgar A. Payne, *Composition of Outdoor Painting* (Hollywood, CA: Seward, 1941); repr., 7th ed., ed. DeRu's Fine Arts, with addenda by Evelyn Payne Hatcher (Bellflower, CA: DeRu's Fine Arts, 2005), 28.

2. Payne, *Composition of Outdoor Painting*, vi.

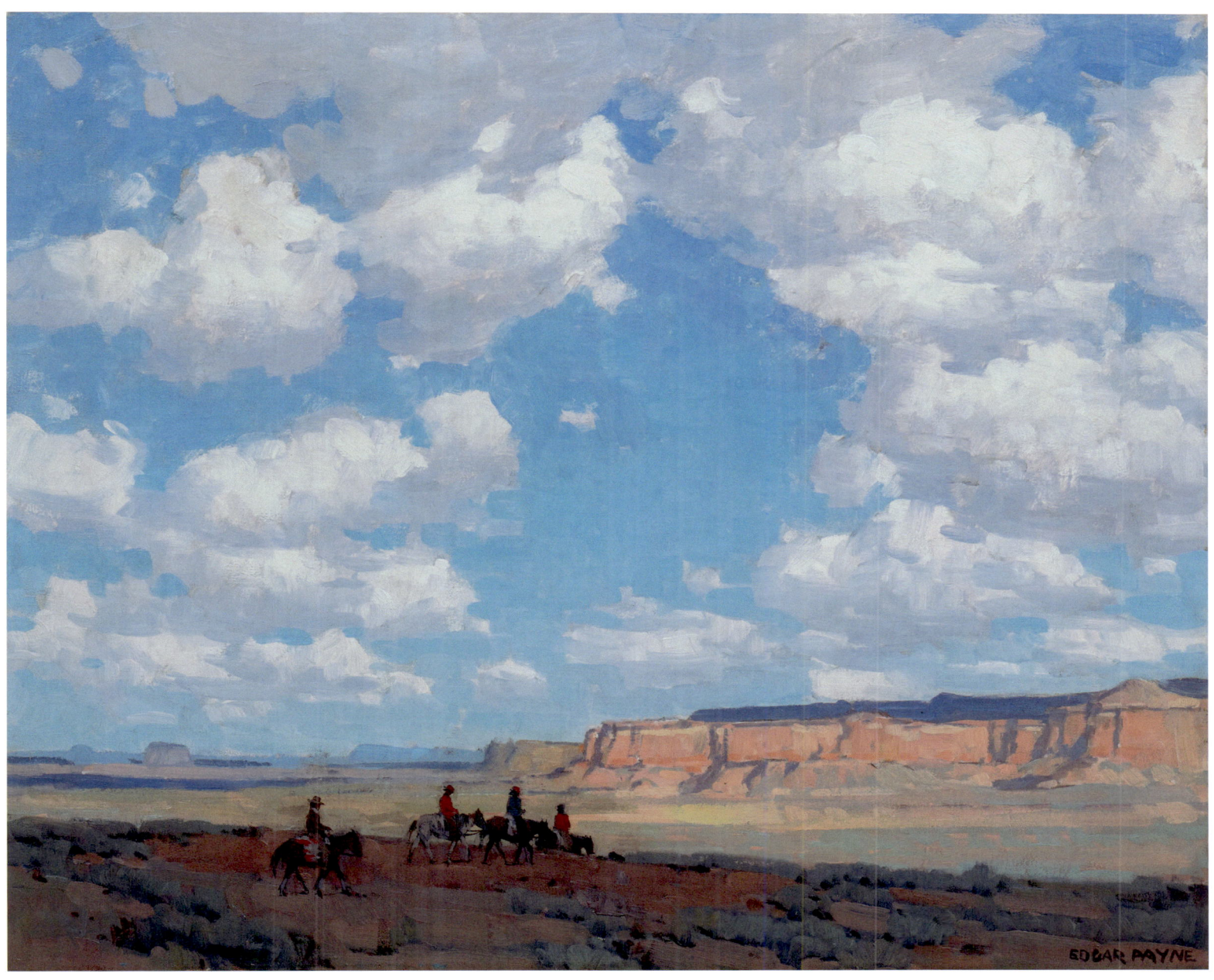

William Wendt

AMERICAN, 1865–1946

Mountain Willow, 1927
Oil on canvas
25 × 30 inches

ALTHOUGH WILLIAM WENDT'S earliest paintings emphasized the transient light and color of the Impressionists, his work became less lyrical over time, his canvases manifesting greater power, breadth, and patterning. Best known for his California landscapes, he found inspiration in the trees, hills, streams, and skies that he often painted on location. He had a deep reverence for California's nature and believed in its transcendental virtues. Some of his titles—such as *Where Nature's God Hath Wrought* and *Trees, They Are My Friends*—directly reference this. He therefore tended to avoid urban scenes, though he often included evidence of human habitation. Even then, however, it was a peaceful, often agrarian, coexistence between people and the land, with buildings, fences, and dirt roads adding interest to—but not overwhelming—California's natural beauty.

Wendt was born in the village of Bentzin in what is now northern Germany. He came to the United States as a teenager in 1880 and settled in Chicago, pursuing formal training with local artists and, starting in 1891, taking evening courses at the School of the Art Institute of Chicago. In 1894, his final year at the Institute, he made his first visit to California with artist George Gardner Symons, making additional trips there in subsequent years. He and Symons also went to England in 1898 and stayed several months in St. Ives, Cornwall, spending additional time in France and other European countries.

Wendt's talent matured rapidly, and he won a bronze medal at the Pan-American Exposition in Buffalo, New York, in 1901. He also took home a medal from the Louisiana Purchase Exposition of 1904 in St. Louis, this one a silver. Two years later he moved to Los Angeles with his wife, sculptor Julia Bracken Wendt, and became a member of the Painters' Club of Los Angeles. When it disbanded, he joined the new California Art Club, serving two terms as president. In 1912 he was elected an associate member of the National Academy of Design in New York.

The Wendts built a second home and studio in Laguna Beach in 1918, which by then had become an important art colony. William Wendt spent most of his time in Laguna, though Julia continued to reside in Los Angeles, where she taught. He became a member of the newly formed Laguna Beach Art Association and the Ten Painters' Club of California, the latter group organized in emulation of the East Coast's Ten American Painters. As in the east, the Ten Painters Club of California was composed largely of artists who pursued variations of Impressionism, the members exhibiting together at the Kanst Art Gallery in Los Angeles, the stable described as the "foremost painters of the West."[1] Among them, Wendt was one of the most respected, garnering him the unofficial title Dean of Southern California artists.

SCOTT A. SHIELDS

1. Antony Anderson, "Of Art and Artists," *Los Angeles Times*, August 10, 1919. The members included Maurice Braun, Benjamin C. Brown, Roi Clarkson Colman, Edgar Payne, Hanson Puthuff, Guy Rose, Jack Wilkinson Smith, Elmer Wachtel, Marion Kavanagh Wachtel, and Wendt.

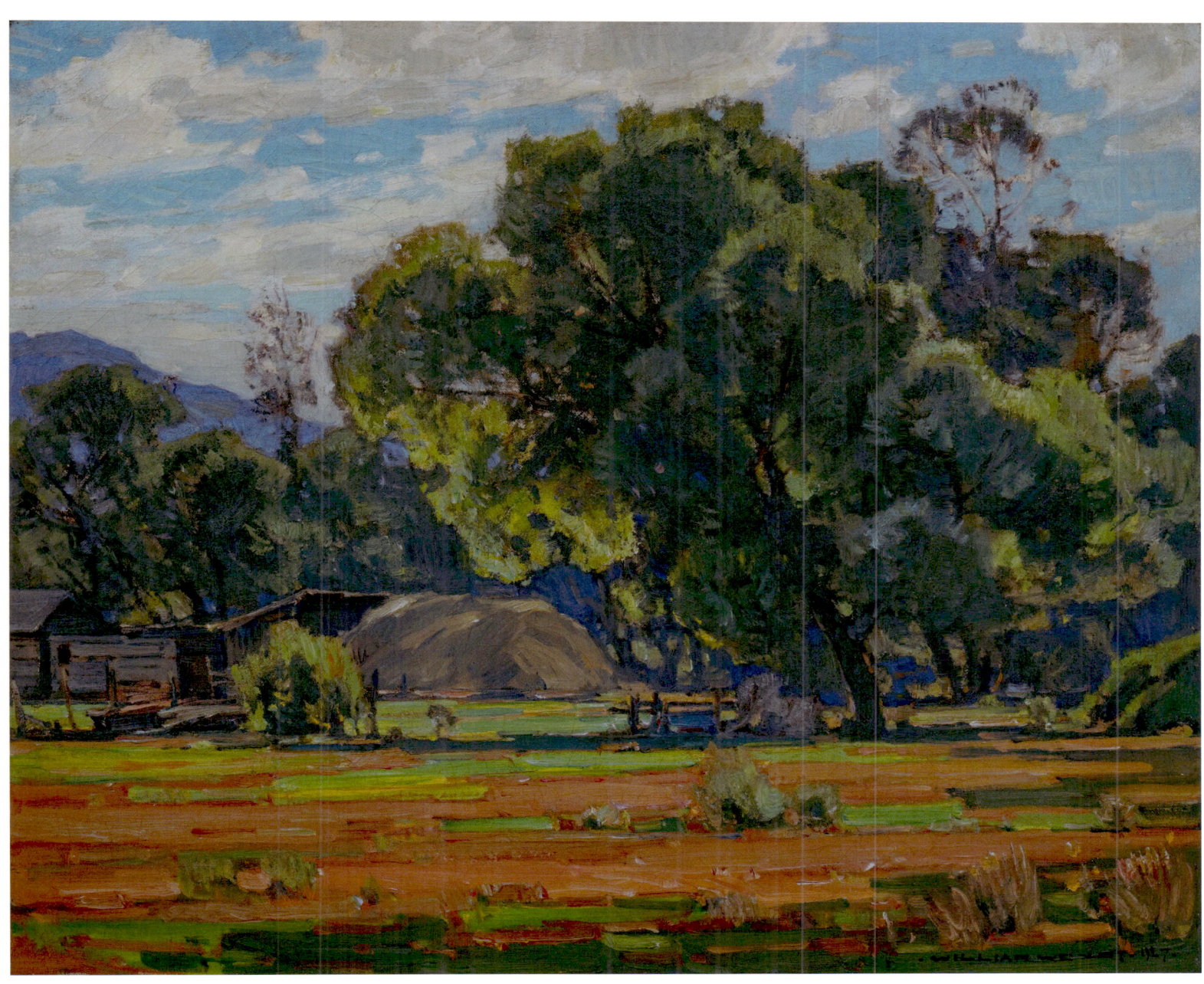

Granville Redmond

AMERICAN, 1871–1935

Lupine and Poppies
Oil on canvas
18 × 24 inches

GRANVILLE REDMOND produced paintings of California's diverse topography, vegetation, and color. These works represent both the northern and southern parts of the state and range from contemplative Tonalist paintings evoking a quiet calm to dramatic and colorful impressionist scenes, often with poppies.

Born in Philadelphia, Redmond contracted scarlet fever as a toddler, which left him permanently deaf. In 1879 his parents enrolled him as a boarding student at what is now the California School for the Deaf, then located in Berkeley (today in Fremont, California). He took art classes there, and his teachers, recognizing his talent, encouraged him to attend the California School of Design in San Francisco. In 1893, after completing his training in San Francisco, Redmond studied privately with Ernest Peixotto and then began attending the Académie Julian in Paris. While there he painted the surrounding countryside and forest of the Fontainebleau region, the Barbizon paintings he encountered influencing his own early landscapes.

Redmond returned to California in 1898 and settled in Los Angeles. A year later he married Carrie Ann Jean; the couple had three children. In California Redmond painted his immediate surroundings, as well as those in and around Laguna Beach and Santa Catalina Island. In 1908 he moved to Parkfield in Monterey County, where his bucolic landscapes often featured oaks. Trees continued to figure prominently in his paintings after he moved north to San Mateo County in 1910.

Wildflowers began to occupy Redmond's attention as well, and he became especially known for painting poppies. He often paired them with other wildflowers, most notably lupine, which was a perfect blue-purple complement to the poppy's orange-yellow hue. Earlier on, as in this painting, Redmond balanced color and quiet, the flowers enlivening an otherwise subtle expanse. Once Redmond fully gave in to Impressionism, however, he created scenes filled with colorful wildflowers and sparkling light throughout, limning most of these after he returned to Southern California in 1918. Despite the popularity of such subjects, Redmond himself remained personally inclined toward his more tonal—even nocturnal—productions. And yet, he confessed, "People will not buy them. They all seem to want poppies."[1]

Among Redmond's most ardent admirers was silent-film star Charlie Chaplin, who purchased several of Redmond's canvases and provided him with a workspace at Charlie Chaplin Studios in Los Angeles. He also cast him in several minor movie roles. Chaplin wrote of his friend's art:

Something puzzles me about Redmond's pictures. There's such a wonderful joyousness about them all. Look at the gladness in that sky, the riot of color in those flowers. Sometimes I think that the silence in which he lives has developed in him some sense, some great capacity for happiness in which we others are lacking. He paints solitude as no one else can convey it, and yet, by some strange paradox, his solitude is never loneliness. It's some sort of communion with Nature, I suppose.[2]

Redmond lived in Los Angeles for the rest of his life, painting there and in Laguna Beach and Catalina Island. At age sixty-four, he died of a heart ailment at Hollywood Hospital.

SCOTT A. SHIELDS

1. Granville Redmond, quoted in Arthur Millier, "Our Artists in Person, No. 24—Granville Redmond," *Los Angeles Times*, March 22, 1931.

2. Charlie Chaplin, quoted in A. V. Ballin, "Granville Redmond, Artist," *Silent Worker* 38 (November 1925): 89.

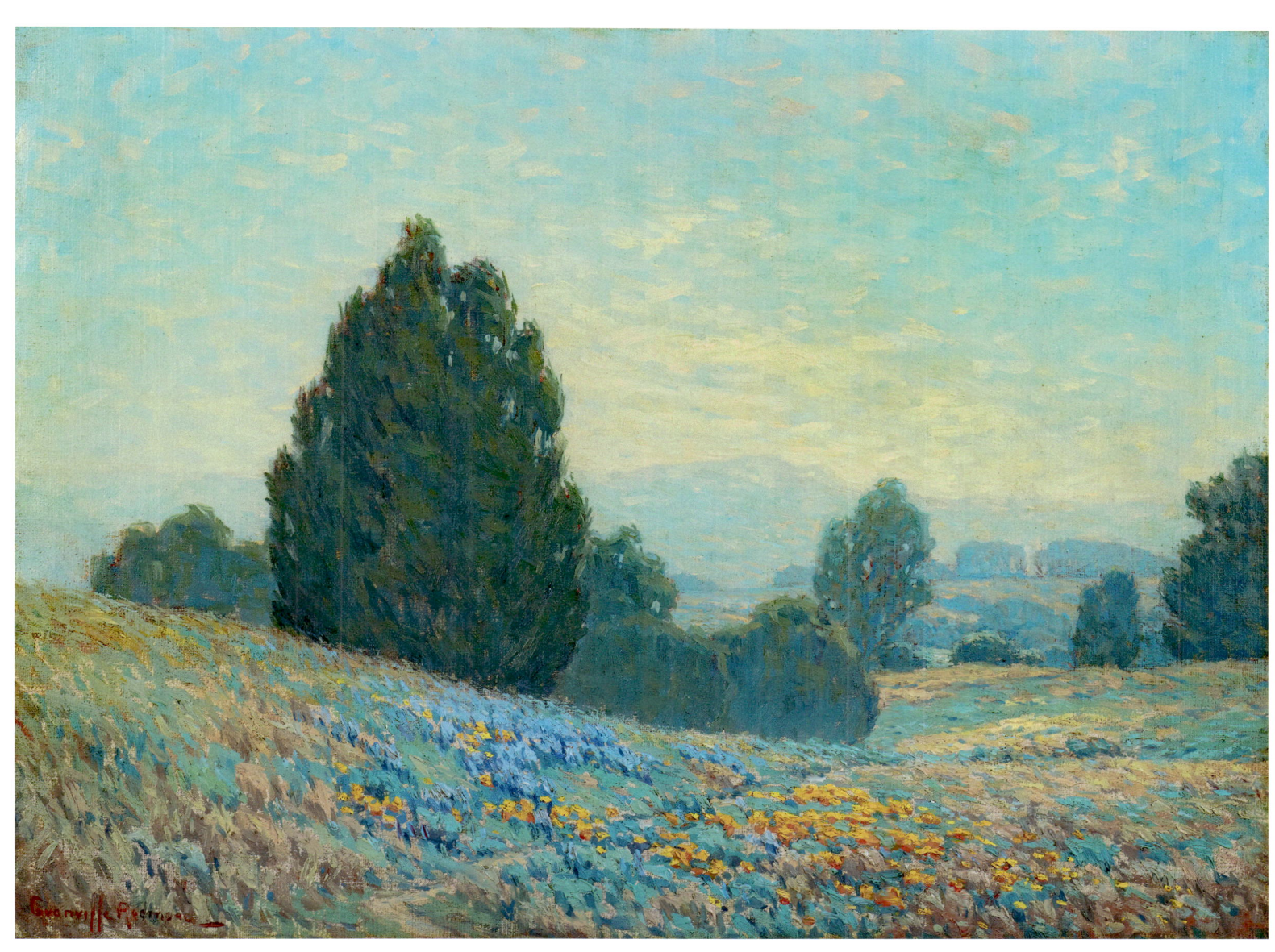

Carl Oscar Borg

AMERICAN, 1879–1947

Watching the Race
Oil on canvas
30 × 30 inches

THREE PUEBLOAN MEN sit astride their mounts on the slope of a hill overlooking a horse race. Above them, repetitive vertical strokes of tinted blue applied thinly over warm underpainting evoke the glow of a Southwest sky. Created with the confident and "skilful [*sic*] manipulation" of artist Carl Oscar Borg's "full and sure brush" in hues of sage, cerulean, and terra-cotta, the forms of the riders and their mounts visually command the foreground.[1] With their backs to us, the men direct our attention to the race in the "haze haunted distance" of the desert beyond.[2]

Born in Sweden to an impoverished farming family, Borg spent his young adult years painting houses, theater sets, and ships, finding passage on a number of these to France, England, and ultimately the United States. There he hopped around the East Coast before sailing to California, where he would spend the majority of his life, with extended time in New York City, Central America, Continental Europe, Sweden, and North Africa. Supported in California by a community of creatives and collectors, many associated with the circle of journalist Charles Lummis, Borg established a successful career as an artist and worked as an art director for numerous Hollywood films. In 1916 noted patron Phoebe Hearst funded Borg to paint Hopi and Navajo communities, whom she referred to as the "twilight gods" of the Southwest.[3] The belief that Indigenous peoples were living through the metaphorical sunset of an idealized pre-modern era—a cliché that had circulated for nearly a century—continued to motivate artists and anthropologists to document native cultures. Articulating that his purpose was to "try and preserve some of their customs and religious life in a permanent form," Borg aligned himself with this mission.[4] Making annual trips to Arizona and New Mexico between 1916 and 1932, he produced a significant body of work in oil, gouache, watercolor, woodblock, and drypoint that he exhibited nationally and internationally.

In *Watching the Race*, Borg demonstrates a commanding technique in oil that harnesses its expressive possibilities while referencing the mosaiclike brushstrokes and vibrant transparency of his preferred medium, opaque watercolor.[5] Borg's artistic contemporary Olaf Wieghorst wrote that he, like Wieghorst, was "a stickler for authentic details."[6] Although Borg provides enough features to facilitate cultural identification in *Watching the Race*, his gestural and dynamic technique renders these elements secondary to a more immediate sense of first-person reportage and an effective (and often affective) expression of the American Southwest. In the words of one period critic, "His ground is solid, his skies are vast, he gets the spirit of the place, permits himself no cheap passages."[7] Another aptly noted that his "canvases are harmonies rather than contrasts,"[8] thereby highlighting Borg's finessed color acumen while also alluding to the peripatetic artist's own experience of the desert as a place "Holy, sequestered, apart," where "the soul of the world / Speaks to my own."[9]

JR (JENNIFER R.) HENNEMAN

1. Jessie A. Selkinghaus, "The Art of Carl Oscar Borg," *American Magazine of Art* 18, no. 3 (March 1927): 144.

2. From Borg's poem "On the Desert Horizon," published in Helen Laird, *Carl Oscar Borg and the Magic Region: Artist of the American West* (Salt Lake City: Gibbs M. Smith/Peregrine Smith Books, 1986), 80.

3. Helen Laird, "Carl Oscar Borg" in *Swedish-American Historical Quarterly* 37 (1986): 86.

4. Selkinghaus, "The Art of Carl Oscar Borg," 147.

5. According to one reviewer, Borg preferred opaque watercolor because it "strikes a happy medium of transparency and strength," while oil paint seemed too heavy and watercolor too delicate to articulate "the brooding force of the Unknown" in the "wild country" of the Southwest. See Selkinghaus, "The Art of Carl Oscar Borg," 147.

6. Olaf Wieghorst, "Forward" in Helen Laird, *Carl Oscar Borg and the Magic Region*, xi.

7. Arthur Millier, "Two Pairs of Painters and Some Singles Offer Shows," in *Los Angeles Times*, September 17, 1933. Carl Oscar Borg scrapbook 1: The Los Angeles years, 1903–1935, Archives of American Art, Smithsonian Institution.

8. Fred Hogue, "'Who's Who' of California Landscape Painters Given," *Los Angeles Times*, August 26, 1934. Carl Oscar Borg scrapbook 1: The Los Angeles years, 1903–1935, Archives of American Art, Smithsonian Institution.

9. From Borg's poem "On the Desert Horizon," published in Laird, *Carl Oscar Borg and the Magic Region*, 80.

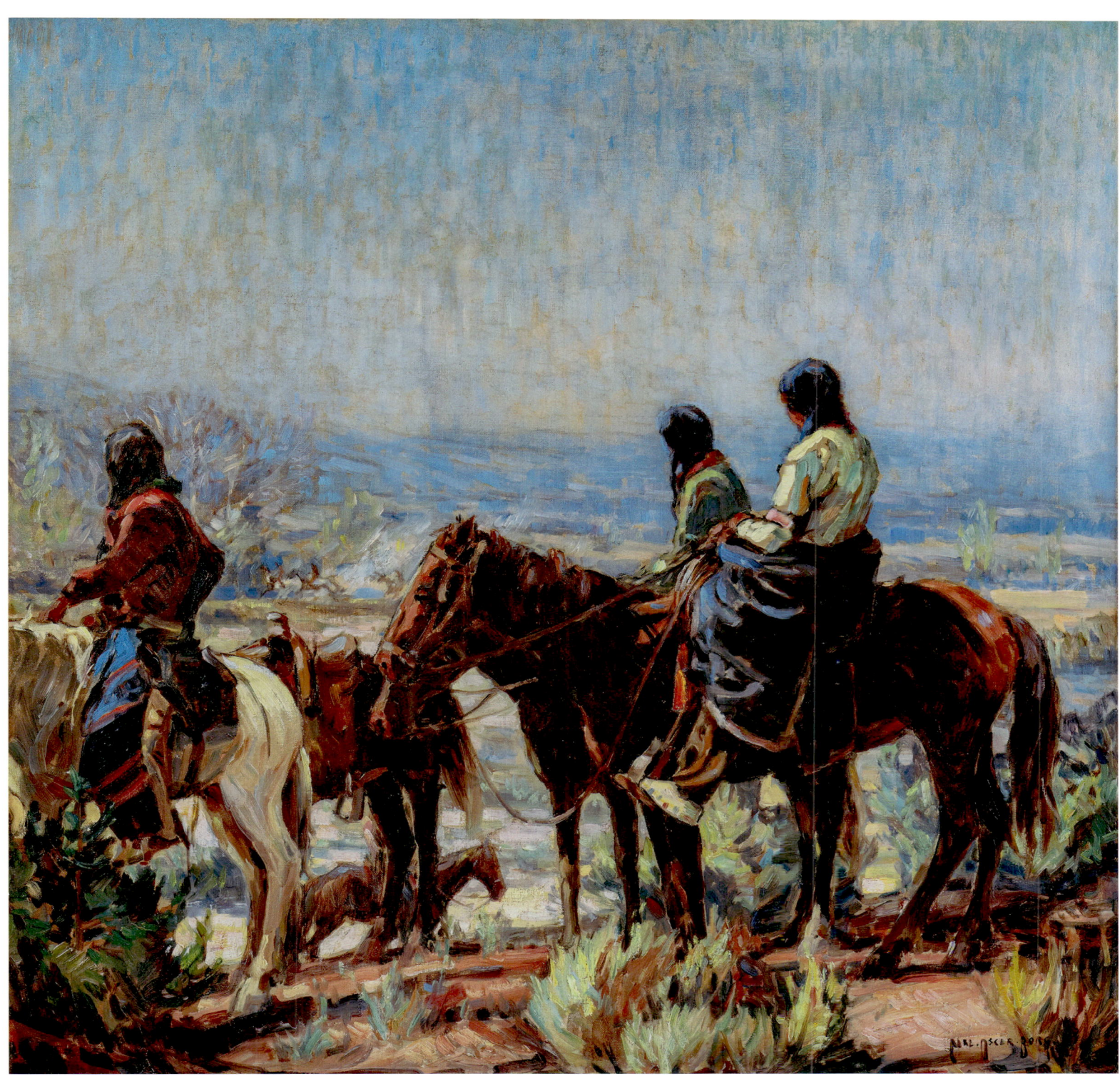

George Bellows
AMERICAN, 1882–1925

Upper Broadway, 1907

Oil on board

11½ × 15½ inches

Promised Gift of the Macon and Joan Brock Collection
of American Art

ASHCAN SCHOOL ARTIST George Bellows was one of the most innovative chroniclers of New York City in the early twentieth century. As he once explained, "It seems to me that an artist must be a spectator of life; a reverential, enthusiastic, emotional spectator. . . . There are only three things demanded of a painter: to see things, to feel them and to dope them out for the public."[1] *Upper Broadway* encapsulates Bellows's ability to translate the city's energy and dynamic temporality, as he viewed it from a window on a rainy summer day. Three years earlier, in 1904, Bellows had dropped out of Ohio State University to play semipro baseball and pursue his career as an artist. He left his hometown of Columbus and moved to New York, where he quickly fell under the influence of Robert Henri at the New York School of Art. Henri advocated that artists explore the city as a "sketch hunter" in search of a new, individually felt realism that should be translated into paintings where every element and brushstroke was "constructive of an idea, expressive of an emotion."[2] Bellows heeded that advice in *Upper Broadway*, where he lays down swaths of paint with his palette knife and adds suggestive color and detail with his paintbrush to communicate the confluence of rain, sun, and wind on urban architecture and street surfaces. A streetcar moves down the center of the canvas, which appears bifurcated by dark, tonalist colors on one side of the painting, and bright, light blue, watery reflections on the other side.[3] Several figures have exited the car and make their way to the sidewalk. Bellows's facility is shown through his rendering of the pedestrians in just a few deft strokes of pure black paint—one holds an umbrella and takes a large stride to avoid a puddle.

Before his life was cut short at the age of forty-two by a ruptured appendix and peritonitis, Bellows produced an incredible range of subjects, from portraits, sporting scenes of boxing matches, tennis, and polo, to landscapes highlighting urban construction and shipbuilding, and a variety of figural groups. He often worked in series, sometimes returning to a subject several years later, but always reinterpreting it and rarely repeating himself.[4] Bellows made a second painting of *Upper Broadway* in 1910, though it is radically different from the first version.[5] Through comparison with the 1910 composition, we can better understand the geography of Broadway, where the perspective looks south from the west side of the street, rather than east, yet it lacks the expressive urgency captured in the earlier picture.[6] When Bellows made *Upper Broadway* in 1907, he had only been painting for about two years, but that same year he began showing in nearly every annual exhibition at the National Academy of Design, the Pennsylvania Academy of the Fine Arts, the Carnegie Institute, and the Art Institute of Chicago.[7] Over his career he also won virtually every major award that could be attained by an American artist.[8] Despite his meteoric rise in the art world, Bellows remained closely connected with his family, and made visits home to Columbus with some frequency. He likely gifted *Upper Broadway* to his future sister-in-law, Lillian Story Griffin, during the 1907 Christmas holiday in Columbus.[9] Griffin lived in Manhattan and would have understood firsthand the urban vitality Bellows sought to convey. Later, Griffin was active in the Woman Suffrage Party in New York City, a cause also important to George and Emma Story Bellows, who participated in demonstrations for women's rights.

JENNIFER STETTLER PARSONS

1. George Bellows, quoted in "The Big Idea: George Bellows Talks About Patriotism for Beauty," *Touchstone* I (July 1917): 270–75.

2. Robert Henri, *The Art Spirit* (1st ed., 1923; Cambridge, MA: Basic Books ed., 2007), 13, 17.

3. The composition's stark contrast of light blue and dark color seems to foreshadow works like *Noon* (1908; private collection, Washington, DC) and *Blue Morning* (1909; National Gallery of Art, Washington, DC).

4. Charles Brock, *George Bellows* (Washington, DC: National Gallery of Art, 2012), 23–24.

5. For an illustration, see *George Bellows' Catalogue Raisonné*. Compiled and organized by Glenn C. Peck, http://hvallison .com (accessed November 2022).

6. The author thanks Glenn C. Peck, Bellows scholar and organizer of the *George Bellows' Catalogue Raisonné*, for sharing information and his interpretation of the *Upper Broadway* paintings. Email correspondence, November 2022, Object File, Chrysler Museum of Art.

7. Brock, *George Bellows*, 304.

8. Brock, *George Bellows*, 7, and see Chronology, 304–9.

9. I thank Glenn C. Peck for suggesting this chronology and sharing with me the page from Bellows's record book, which notes that he also painted *Portrait of George Bellows, Sr.* on "Xmas 1907." Record Book A, p. 42, see Object File, Chrysler Museum.

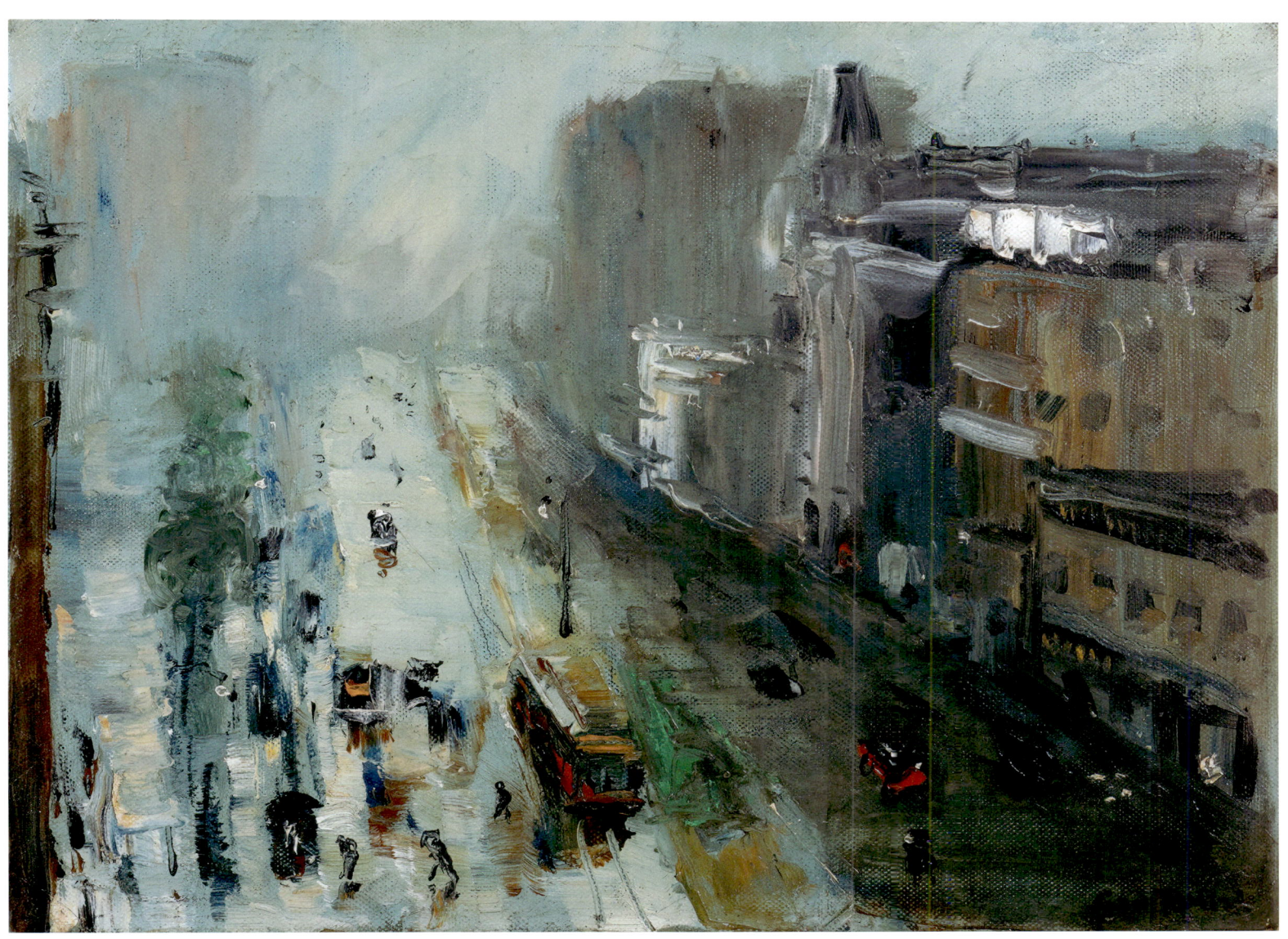

William James Glackens

AMERICAN, 1870–1938

Wickford Harbor, Rhode Island, 1909
Oil on canvas
26 × 32 inches

THE PAINTER AND ILLUSTRATOR William Glackens graduated from Central High School in Philadelphia, where Albert C. Barnes was one of his classmates. Glackens would later become the primary advisor for Barnes's famed collection of Impressionist and Post-Impressionist paintings. Based on his early work as an illustrator, and selected paintings around 1900 and shortly thereafter, Glackens has often been grouped with the Ashcan artists, such as Everett Shinn, John Sloan, and Robert Henri (an important early influence), who embraced social realist themes and vernacular subject matter, often in urban settings. He was one of the artists that Henri included in the 1908 exhibition called The Eight at New York's Macbeth Gallery, which protested the exclusionary practices and anti-progressive stances of the long-standing National Academy of Design.

As paintings such as *Wickford Harbor* demonstrate, however, Glackens was equally informed by tenets of French Impressionism. Through his work for Barnes, the artist became especially influenced by the French Impressionist Pierre Auguste Renoir. In the years following the notorious exhibition of The Eight, Glackens's style became "increasingly brightly colored and richly textured," with a newfound painterly energy, and he presented such works in the equally groundbreaking Independents Exhibition of 1910.[1] Glackens had left behind many of the Manet- and Goya-like dark tones that had characterized his Ashcan work. The critic and fellow painter Guy Pène du Bois in 1914 noted that Glackens was now "feasting on color."[2] Likewise important for his new vigorous style were the broken brushstrokes, cropping of form (to suggest a changing moment of time), and fleeting use of light and other atmospheric effects. These are precisely the stylistic characteristics found in his painting *Wickford Harbor, Rhode Island*, painted when he summered at this site in 1909.[3] The tableau, portraying an inlet on the west side of Narragansett Bay, may harken to the brushwork and out-of-doors subjects of French Impressionism, but its simplification of form and boldly applied passages of paint render the work an innovative melding of slightly older, traditional styles and up-to-date modernist experimentation.

Glackens divided his composition into four zones: the cloud-streaked skies; the narrow, foreshortened scrap of land on which are seen houses and trees; the bright blue waters traversed by small sailboats and, notably, the steam-powered paddleboat emerging at right with a flag on its bow; and the triangularly shaped, grassy shore, with a brown building at left balancing the paddleboat. American waterfront resorts such as Wickford Harbor were extremely popular in the 1910s, and the four areas of the painting unite to suggest a bustling resort town that would be, for an artist like Glackens, as ideal for seasonal living as it was for artistic subject matter.[4] With his loose painterly approach, Glackens modeled the foreground grass and middle-ground water with thick brushwork, which, in turn, suggests his keen attention to wind, light, and the natural environment. The sailboat and other crafts contribute to the evocation of a landscape of leisure and recreation. The subject matter indeed harkens to French Impressionism, but it also marks a continuation of the artist's long-standing interest in bustling, populated landscapes.

LEO MAZOW

1. Carol Troyen, "'Wonderful Color Palpitating about Us': William Glackens and the Independents Exhibition of 1910," in *The World of William Glackens*, vol. 2 (Fort Lauderdale, FL: Sansom Foundation, Inc., 2017), 228, quotation from 224.

2. Guy Pène du Bois, "William Glackens, Normal Man: The Best Eyes in American Art," *Arts and Decoration* 4, no. 8 (1914): 406; quoted in Troyen, "'Wonderful Color Palpitating about Us,'" 240.

3. Valerie Ann Leeds, *William Glackens: American Impressionist* (New York: Gerald Peters Gallery, 2003), 99.

4. Patricia Raub, "'Discover Beautiful Rhode Island': State Promotion of Tourism from 1927–2015," *Rhode Island History* 75 (Winter/Spring 2017): 7.

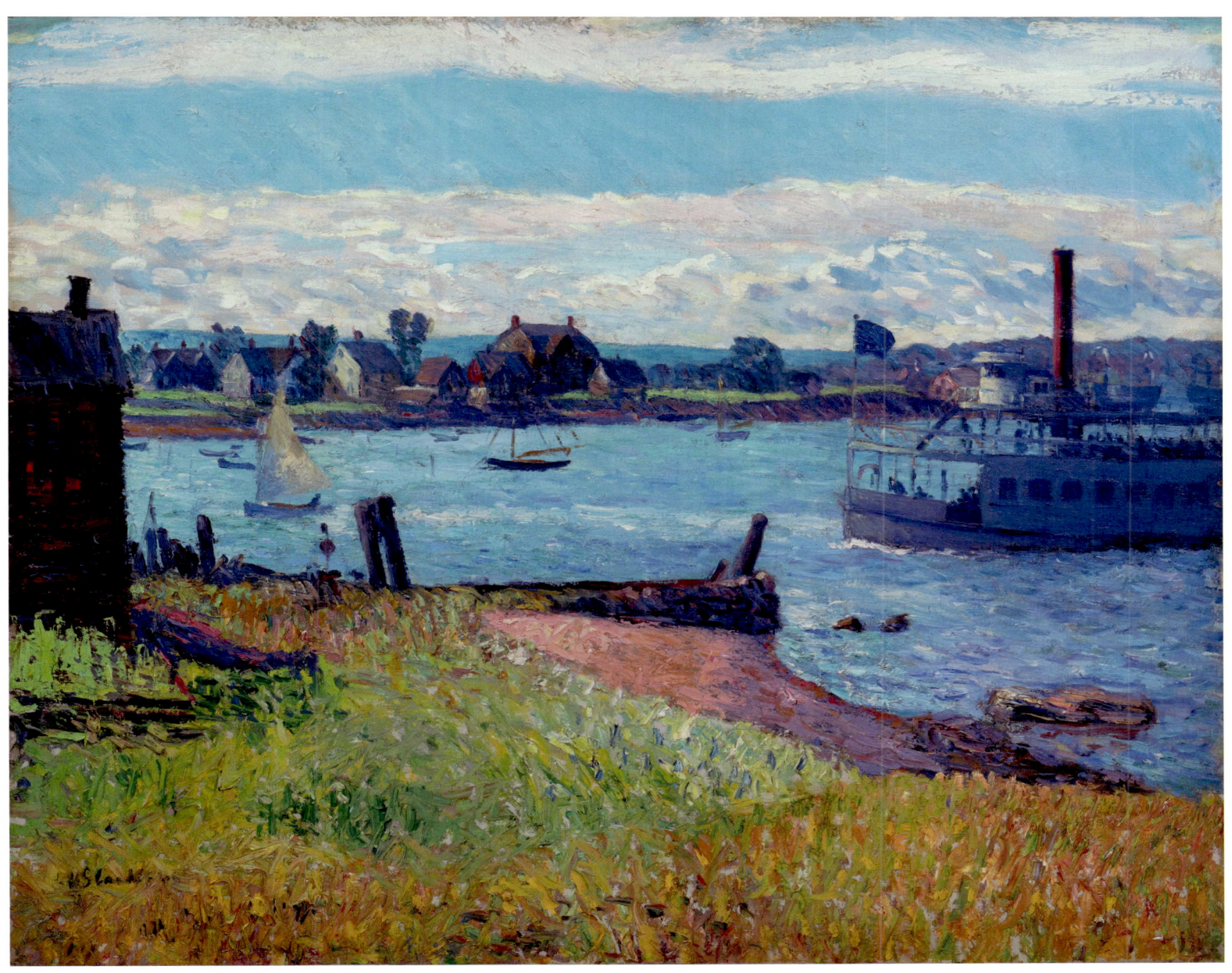

Ernest Lawson

AMERICAN, 1873–1939

Squatter's Huts, Harlem River, ca. 1914
Oil on canvas
17 × 21 inches

WHEN ERNEST LAWSON EXHIBITED *Squatter's Huts, Harlem River* in a two-person show at the Art Institute of Chicago in 1917, a reviewer described the display as "some very modern-to-the-minute landscapes."[1] Indeed, during his thirty-eight years living in New York, Lawson was at the forefront of the modern art world through his participation in such avant-garde exhibitions as The Eight at the Macbeth Gallery in 1908, the 1910 Exhibition of Independent Artists, and the landmark Armory Show in 1913. Modernist proponent Albert Eugene Gallatin, who owned *Squatter's Huts, Harlem River* in the early twentieth century, likewise described Lawson as an "innovator . . . genius . . . he has always gone straight to nature for his inspiration and painted his picture in a sane and sincere manner."[2] Audiences appreciated Lawson's use of color, his impasto paint application, and his particular construction of space that straddled Impressionism, Realism, and Abstraction.

Born in Halifax, Nova Scotia, Lawson moved to the United States at age fifteen and studied art at the Kansas City Art Institute. In 1889 he went to Mexico City to work as an engineering draftsman and took classes at the San Carlos Art Academy. He arrived in New York in 1891 and enrolled at the Art Students League, where he met John Henry Twachtman. Both Twachtman and J. Alden Weir, with whom he painted at Cos Cob, Connecticut, would have a significant influence on Lawson's adaptation of Impressionism. After further study at the Académie Julian in Paris and travels elsewhere, Lawson settled with his wife and two daughters in the Washington Heights neighborhood of New York in 1898. From there he was drawn to paint scenes of upper Manhattan near the Hudson and Harlem Rivers, at the border of urban development.[3]

In *Squatter's Huts, Harlem River*, Lawson focuses the composition on a small group of ramshackle houses ensconced within a winter landscape. Lawson's thickly layered, broken brushwork adds to the dilapidated quality of the structures, which seem to grow out of and be supported by the hilly landscape and rickety fencing that surrounds it. The setting may appear rural without its identifying title, which in combination and through comparison with other works painted around the same period, reveal it as the semi-urban area of Spuyten Duyvil, across the Harlem River from the Inwood section of the Bronx, a place on the social and geographic fringes of New York City in the early twentieth century. Lawson had begun to paint the area serially during different times of day and seasons, a common impressionist practice. Other works showing alternative perspectives of the area include *Harlem River, Winter* (1910; Chrysler Museum of Art), *Spuyten Duyvil* (ca. 1912–14; private collection), and *Upper Harlem River* (ca. 1915; Amon Carter Museum of American Art).[4] As scholar Ross Barrett has shown, contemporaries recognized Lawson's paintings of squatter shanties as symbolic of a nostalgia for humans' relationship with the land. While squatters were considered a nuisance to land developers in the late nineteenth century, they began to take on new meaning for the public when Lawson painted their communities. As Barrett explains, "Increasingly, the figure became a cultural screen for the projection of local anxieties over the perceived costs of urbanization and especially the loss of historical and natural spaces."[5] Within the context of impending land speculation and development at the urban frontier, a lone yellow light emanating from the top window of the tall, white house in *Squatter's Huts, Harlem River* alludes to the unseen inhabitant with an uncertain future.

JENNIFER STETTLER PARSONS

1. The joint exhibition was *Paintings by Hayley Lever and Ernest Lawson*, March 3–April 2, 1917. Evelyn Marie Stuart, "Exhibitions at the Chicago Galleries," *Fine Arts Journal* 35, no. 4 (April 1917): 302.

2. Albert Eugene Gallatin, "Ernest Lawson," *International Studio* 59 (July 1916): 14.

3. As Ross Barrett detailed, Lawson and his family moved downtown in 1906 to 450 West Twenty-Third Street, but he continued to travel to the northern end of Manhattan to seek out his subjects. For a thorough examination and contextualization of these works, see Barrett, "Speculations in Paint: Ernest Lawson and the Urbanization of New York," *Winterthur Portfolio* 42, no. 1 (Spring 2008): 1–26. For more on his methods of transportation and process after his 1906 move downtown, see Barrett, 4.

4. For an illustration of *Spuyten Duyvil*, see Barrett, "Speculations in Paint," 16.

5. Barrett, "Speculations in Paint," 19.

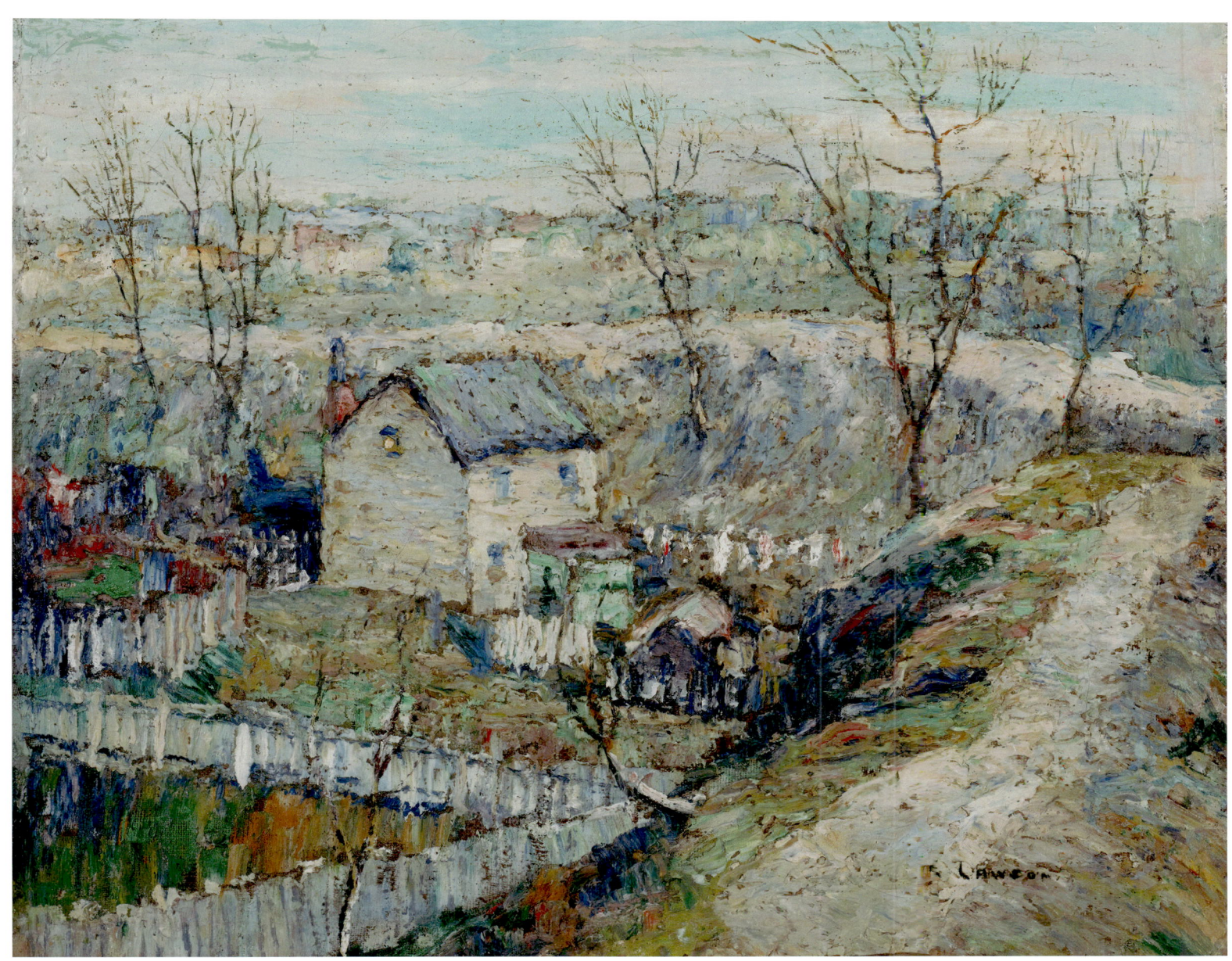

George Benjamin Luks

AMERICAN, 1867–1933

Poverty Hump, Maine, ca. 1922

Oil on canvas

25 × 30 inches

Gift of the Macon and Joan Brock Collection of American Art, 2021.25

GEORGE LUKS ROSE TO PROMINENCE as a member of the Ashcan School, a group of independent artists who cast off the hierarchy and stylistic formality of American art institutions like the National Academy of Design. Like fellow Ashcan artists William James Glackens, Everett Shinn, and John Sloan, Luks began his career as a newspaper illustrator in Philadelphia and then New York. Though he gained formal artistic training at the Pennsylvania Academy of the Fine Arts and European academies, the graphic style that he honed as an illustrator of urban life would carry forward into the paintings he created in the early twentieth century. The wild and rugged seaside setting of *Poverty Hump, Maine* might initially seem far removed from Luks and his fellow artists' interest in chronicling the bustling pace and social dynamism of cities. However, Luks maintained a lifelong interest in subjects drawn from nature, exploring its high-stakes drama in a style both frank and forceful.

In 1908 Luks participated in the groundbreaking exhibition of The Eight held at New York's Macbeth Gallery. The show, which featured Ashcan artists and other forward-thinking painters like Maurice Prendergast and Arthur B. Davies, signaled a startling new direction in American art that emphasized blunt realism and independence from academic styles of painting. Luks in particular was heralded during this period for works like *Hester Street* (1905; Brooklyn Museum), which depicted New York's urban landscape and the people who populated the fast-paced, heterogeneous city. In figural artworks like the Chrysler's *The Wedding Cake* (ca. 1910), Luks married a straightforward and unflinching approach to his subjects, often drawn from the city's immigrant and working-class communities, with a rich, painterly style that avoided sentimentality or condescension while acknowledging his subjects' inherent dignity (fig. 1).

In 1919 Luks undertook a fishing trip to Nova Scotia that bolstered his interest in landscape and wilderness subjects. He followed this with a journey to Maine in 1922, where he spent the summer working in and around Cape Elizabeth on the Atlantic coast just south of Portland.[1] Luks completed around fifteen canvases that summer, one of which was likely *Poverty Hump*. A rocky outcropping, perhaps a fishing outpost, dominates the composition. Battered by waves, several small huts and a signal tower sit atop the craggy shore. In the foreground, two figures struggle with a boat and gear amidst the swirling waters and brooding skies. The high-keyed colors evident in the rusty orange of the rocks and blue-greens of the sea reflect Luks's brightened palette as he moved into the 1920s and away from the bluntness of his urban subjects.

Later in the fall of 1922, Luks's Maine scenes were exhibited to great acclaim back in New York. Many critics found the hardscrabble figures and seaside dramas as a natural corollary to his earlier work. As one author summarized, "He likes nature where it is most natural, not in green, becattled pastures but on the coast of Maine where gaunt rocks challenge the powerful surf."[2] *Poverty Hump, Maine* perfectly embodies this spirit of the vigor of nature. Indeed, in the broad and assured brushstrokes and plainly articulated natural forms of *Poverty Hump*, Luks conveys a captivating vision of an essential and enduring interplay between humans and their environment.

COREY PIPER

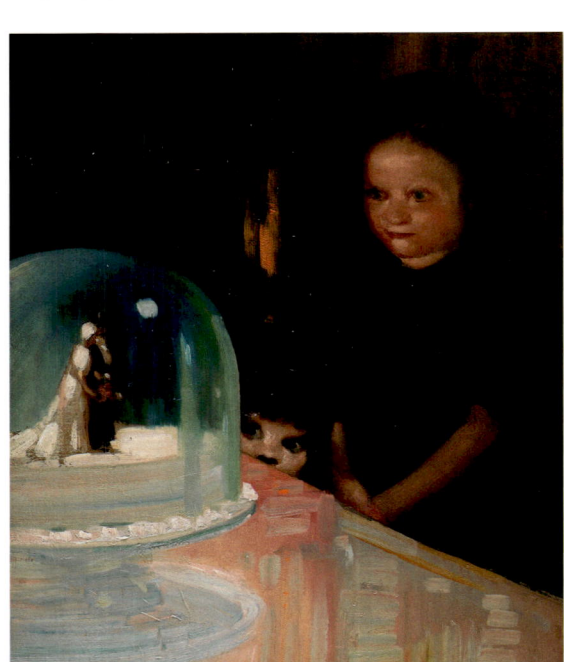

FIG. 1 George Benjamin Luks, *The Wedding Cake*, ca. 1910. Oil on canvas, 30 × 25 in. Chrysler Museum of Art, Gift of Walter P. Chrysler, Jr., 71.678

1. See Carl Little, "Henri, Bellows, and Luks: The Ashcan School in Maine," *Island Journal* 37 (2021). Online, https://www.islandjournal.com/art/henri-bellows-and-luks-the-ashcan-school-in-maine/ (accessed July 7, 2022).

2. Elizabeth Luther Cary, "George Luks," *American Magazine of Art* 14, no. 2 (February 1923): 76.

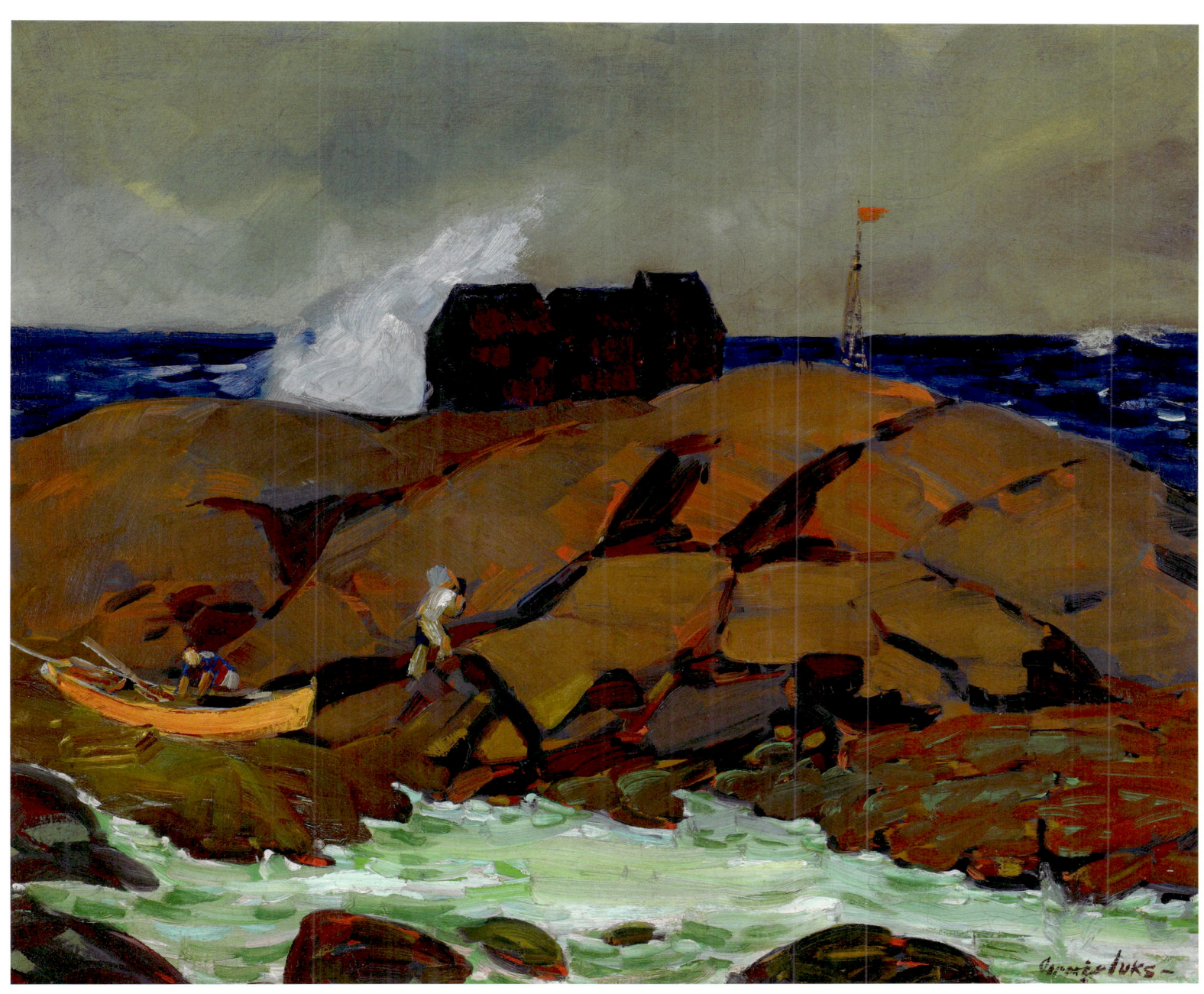

Max Weber

AMERICAN, 1881–1961

Two Female Figures, ca. 1908

Oil on board

27 × 24 inches

Gift of the Macon and Joan Brock Collection of American Art, 2023.4.7

MAX WEBER WAS BORN in present-day Poland and immigrated to the United States with his family in 1891. He attended Pratt Institute, where he studied under Arthur Wesley Dow. After teaching in public schools for a couple of years, Weber then traveled to Paris in 1905 to continue his studies. He stayed in Paris for nearly five years, becoming a close member in the circle of American writer and expat Gertrude Stein. Weber befriended Pablo Picasso, Henri Rousseau, and Henri Matisse, regularly spending time in the studio of Matisse, who became an informal tutor to him. Returning to New York in 1909, Weber continued painting and networking. He had a solo exhibition at Alfred Stieglitz's 291 Gallery in 1911, where Weber is credited with introducing Cubism to American audiences. The show received much press attention, although the reviews were overwhelmingly negative.[1]

Two Female Figures was painted during Weber's stint in Paris and shows the influence of his avant-garde acquaintances. Two nude women are depicted bathing outdoors under a fruiting tree. One bends down to fill a bowl with water, while the other stands holding on to a branch. Behind the women is a small pond from which they fill their bowls. Weber used bright colors, with the ground ablaze in purple, red, and orange, suggesting a field of wildflowers. Hazy blue mountains in the background meet a yellow sky. The figures and landscape are clearly delineated with black lines, contributing to the pictorial flatness of the scene, and it is reminiscent of Matisse's own paintings in its use of line and Fauvist color.

In the 1920s Weber's style shifted to a more expressionistic style, and later he painted scenes portraying Jewish life as recollections from his childhood in Europe. While Weber made a living teaching and lecturing, he did not get wide esteem until after his death. Indeed, in 1911, one reviewer wrote, "A future generation may call this Art but the present writer cannot conscientiously give it that term."[2] Critics were not yet ready to embrace what Weber brought to the field, but that perspective, as time showed, has evolved. Holger Cahill, national director of the Works Progress Administration, wrote in 1930 that Weber had lived the history of modern art in America.[3] Weber can be appreciated for his engagement with various avant-gardes, charting the path for modern art in the United States, which would witness the transition of art centers from Paris to New York.

CHELSEA PIERCE

1. The retrospective catalogue published in 1930 includes excerpts from the most excoriating reviews of Weber's work; see *Max Weber, Retrospective Exhibition, 1907–1930* (New York: The Museum of Modern Art, 1930), 14.

2. *American Art News* (January 1911), in *Max Weber*, 14.

3. Holger Cahill, *Max Weber* (New York: The Downtown Gallery, 1930).

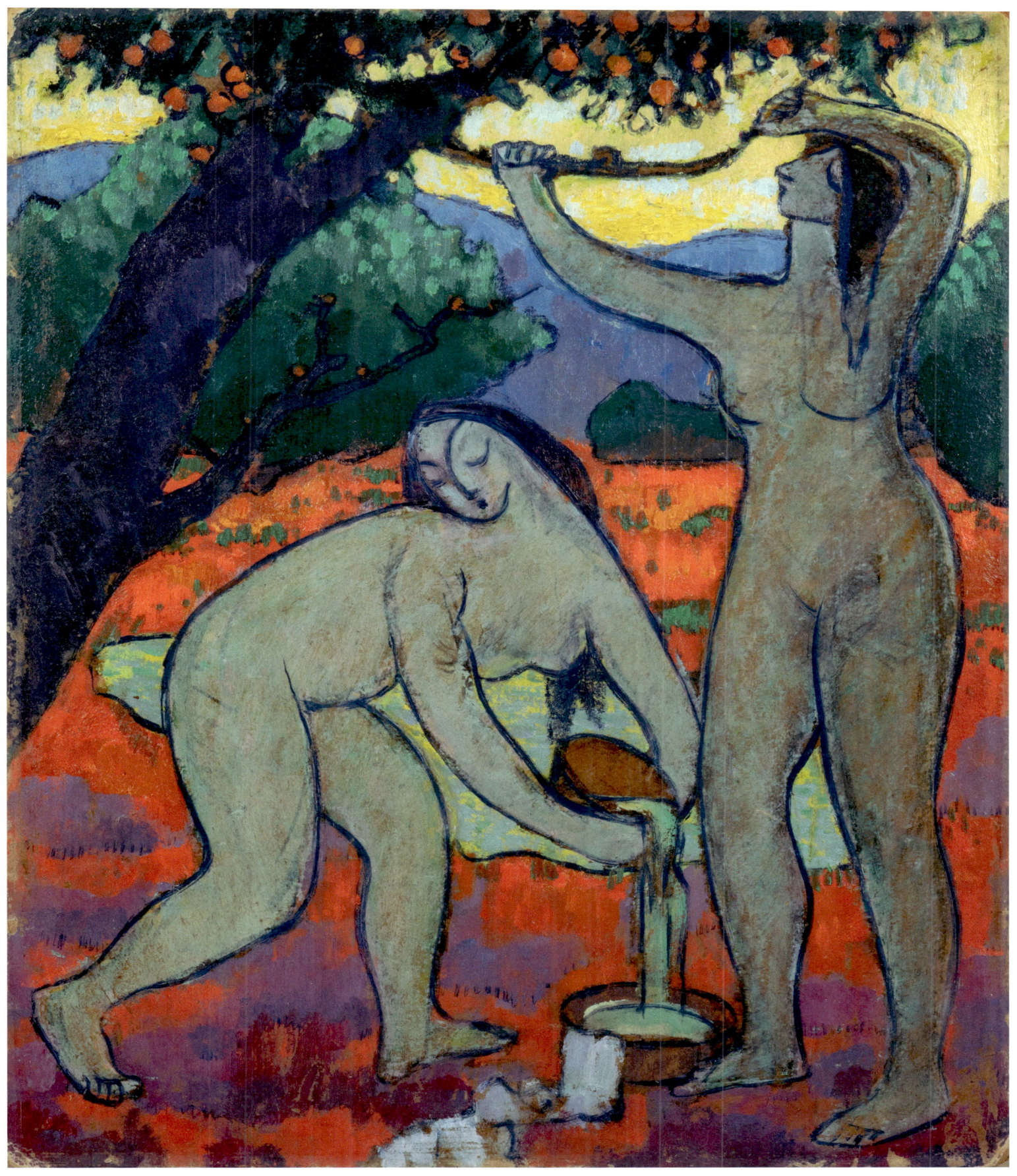

Charles Ephraim Burchfield
AMERICAN, 1893–1967

Hot Morning, 1915
Watercolor, gouache, and pencil on cream wove paper
9 × 11⅞ inches

Promised Gift of the Macon and Joan Brock Collection of American Art

CHARLES EPHRAIM BURCHFIELD is best known for his fantastical landscapes painted almost exclusively with watercolors. Unlike his contemporaries, Burchfield rarely made oil paintings. According to the artist, "My preference for watercolor is a natural one. [In oil] I have to stop and think about how I am going to apply the paint to canvas. To me, the medium of watercolor was more pliable, quick."[1] His ability with the medium is evidenced in *Hot Morning*, an early work likely made near his home in Ohio. The trees and flowers are thinly painted with transparent washes, allowing the pencil sketches to show through. After this preparatory step, he then applied brush to paper, working from light to dark. Dappled, abbreviated brushstrokes convey the daylight. One can imagine the artist rapidly applying dabs of red and blue pigment to create the rows of flowers. The towering shade tree at the right is more densely painted, with layers of blue and green creating opacity. Burchfield emphasized the warmth of a summer morning by painting the negative space or spaces between forms a radiant orange.

Burchfield's daily journal entries document his intensely emotional responses to the natural world. Views through windows or in the backyard offered ample opportunity to study weather patterns, flowers, birds, and insect life. His feelings of awe and rapture often resulted in synesthesia, or when one sense comes through as another. One particular journal entry from the summer of 1915 resonates beautifully with *Hot Morning*:

> *A hot sultry morning—crimson sun on rising above the emerald earth, gleaming thru a leaf dotted tree—walk to Villa—all trees spatterd [sic] with tiny green leaves. A wonderful feeling of whirling in the air—Buckeyes cast a shade—the filmy screen of leaves seems only a transitory veil that has been thrown over the trees—Blackbirds—I do not know what must become of me—while fired with the lofty enthusiasm of a picture I am painting all at once I am overcome with violent fearful desires.*[2]

Burchfield was born in 1893 in Ashtabula Harbor, Ohio. After high school he studied at the Cleveland School of Art from 1912 to 1916 with noted regional artists Henry G. Keller, Frank N. Wilcox, and William J. Eastman. In 1921 Burchfield moved to Buffalo, New York, to work for M. H. Birge and Sons, a prominent wallpaper company, becoming the chief designer in 1927. In 1929 Burchfield resigned from his day job to paint full time, and Frank K. M. Rehn Galleries in New York became his dealer. The following year the Museum of Modern Art's exhibition *Charles Burchfield:*

Early Watercolors 1916–1918 offered the artist major national recognition and effectively launched his career. In 1936 *Life* magazine declared Burchfield one of America's ten greatest painters. In the 1940s and 50s, he returned to ideas and works from decades prior and literally reworked and added on to his earlier compositions. Today the Burchfield Penney Art Center in Buffalo holds the largest collection of his work as well as his journals, letters, and other archival materials.

ERIN MONROE

1. Quoted in Patricia D. Hamm and Nancy Weekly, "Beyond Imagery: An Overview of Charles Burchfield's Materials and Techniques," *Watercolor* 3 (Spring 1997): 116–28, 118.

2. Charles E. Burchfield, Journals, vol. 25, August 24, 1915, https://burchfieldpenney.org/about/news/article:07-24-2013-5-30am-charles-e-burchfield-em-journals-em-vol-25-august-24-1915/ (accessed October 22, 2022).

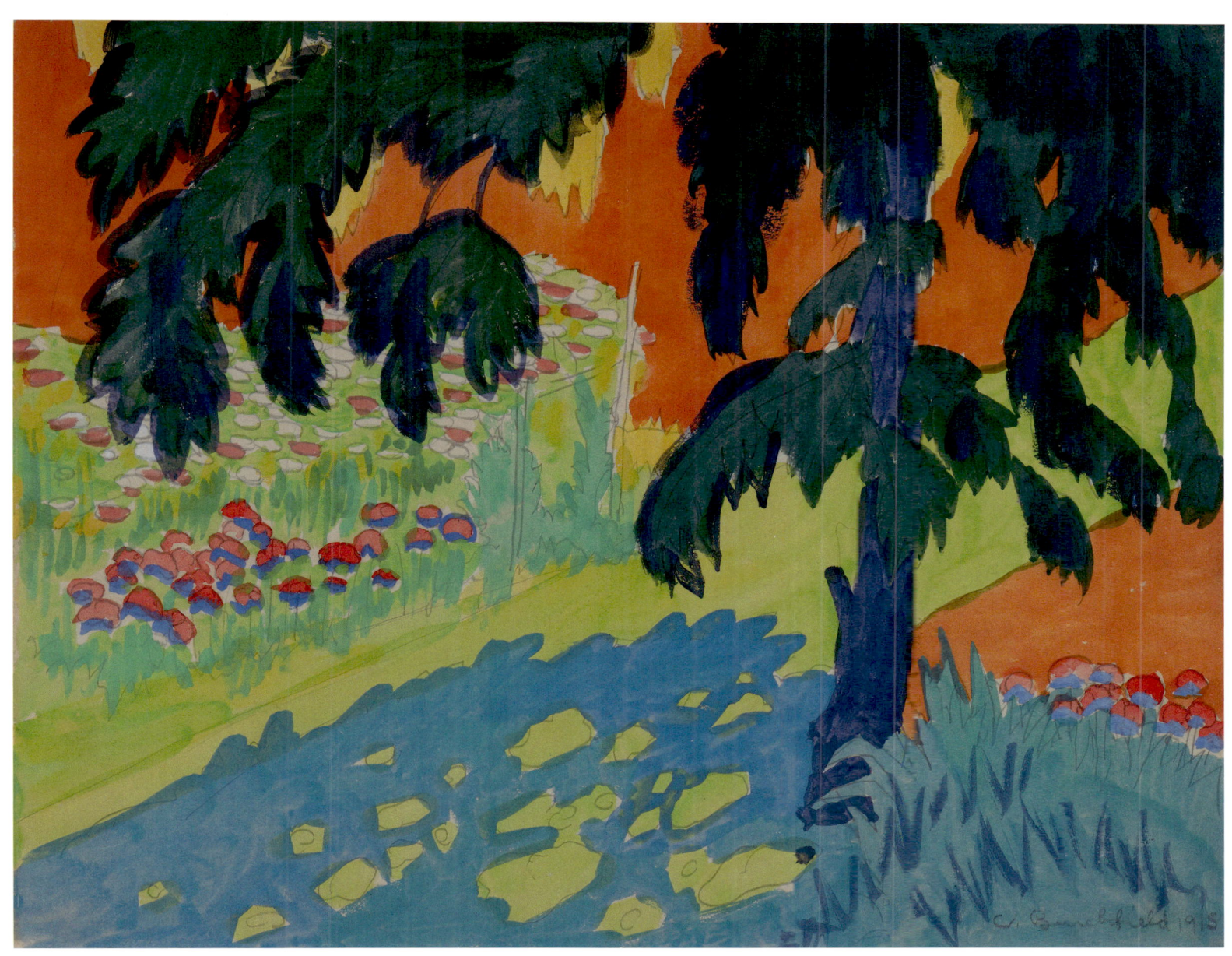

Arthur B. Davies

AMERICAN, 1862–1928

Nymphs Rejoicing, ca. 1920–28

Oil on panel

21½ × 30 inches

Promised Gift of the Macon and Joan Brock Collection
of American Art

ARTHUR BOWEN DAVIES was born in Utica, New York, and from an early age, showed promise as an artist. His parents recognized their son's artistic talents and enlisted a local painter, Dwight Williams, as an art instructor. In 1878 the Davies family moved to Chicago, allowing the aspiring artist to study at the Chicago Academy of Design. Davies would later go on to study at the Art Institute of Chicago and the Art Students League in New York.[1]

Following his extensive training, in 1894 Davies exhibited five paintings at the recently established Macbeth Gallery in New York City. Founded by William Macbeth, the gallery was among the first in the city to focus primarily on American art. The 1894 showing, coupled with William Macbeth's support, generated interest in Davies's work and paved the way for his first one-man show at Macbeth Gallery in 1896. Davies continued to make a name for himself by exhibiting at Pratt Institute (1897), winning a silver medal for painting at the Pan-American Exposition (1901), advising on the collections of wealthy art patrons such as Lillie Bliss and John D. Rockefeller, Jr., and exhibiting with The Eight at Macbeth Gallery (1908).[2] This later exhibition featured the works of Davies alongside the other seven members: Robert Henri, John Sloan, William Glackens, George Luks, Ernest Lawson, Maurice Prendergast, and Everett Shinn. Rather than a shared artistic style, the group formed through their distaste for the restrictive exhibiting policies of the National Academy of Design. Prendergast's and Lawson's Impressionism along with Davies's romanticism offered a sharp contrast to the realistic paintings of urban life that featured prominently among the other five members. Despite a mixed critical response, the group proved successful in their protest against academic style, marking a clear break from the authority of the National Academy.[3]

A staunch supporter of Modernist art, Davies played a key role in organizing the 1913 Armory Show, which introduced European modern art to an American audience. Davies's contributions to the exhibit also helped plant a foothold for European modern art among American art collectors and within the country's leading art institutions. Lillie Bliss, who later played a crucial role in founding the Museum of Modern Art, purchased twenty works during the run of the exhibition, while the Metropolitan Museum of Art purchased its first oil painting by Cézanne.[4]

Although Davies supported modern art and experimented with Cubism, sculpture, and printmaking, he primarily created paintings of idyllic scenes that usually featured women (nude or clothed) in nature. His work has often been described as dreamlike, which is unsurprising considering Davies's habit of jotting his dreams down on paper and placing them around his studio as references.[5] In *Nymphs Rejoicing*, Davies transports viewers into a dream in which several women, or "nymphs," gather with their arms held up in a dance. The women are surrounded by tall, vivid green, yellow, and orange trees that defy gravity by touching the sky. The rejoicing of the nymphs under the yellow warmth of a setting or rising sun evokes equal parts awe and mystery. Although Davies invites the viewer into this hazy dreamscape, the dream's narrative and meaning remain ambiguous, allowing each of us to make it our own.

TASHAE SMITH

1. Royal Cortissoz, *Arthur B. Davies* (New York: Whitney Museum of American Art, 1931), 14.

2. *Arthur B. Davies: A Chronological Retrospective, March 11–April 15, 1975* (New York: M. Knoedler & Co., 1975), 45–46.

3. Brooks Wright, *The Artist and the Unicorn: The Lives of Arthur B. Davies (1862–1928)* (New York: The Historical Society of Rockland County, 1978), 48–51.

4. Bennard B. Perlman, *The Lives, Loves, and Art of Arthur B. Davies* (Albany: State University of New York Press, 1998), xx, 223.

5. Wright, *The Artist and the Unicorn*, 114. Brooks Wright provides an example of Davies's jottings. This particular one shows a woman with children and the following notes:

> Three little girls and mother
>   with violin
> Children at sunset
> Boy with oxen
> Boy with bow and arrow
> Children and
> and and
> Lioness Lion

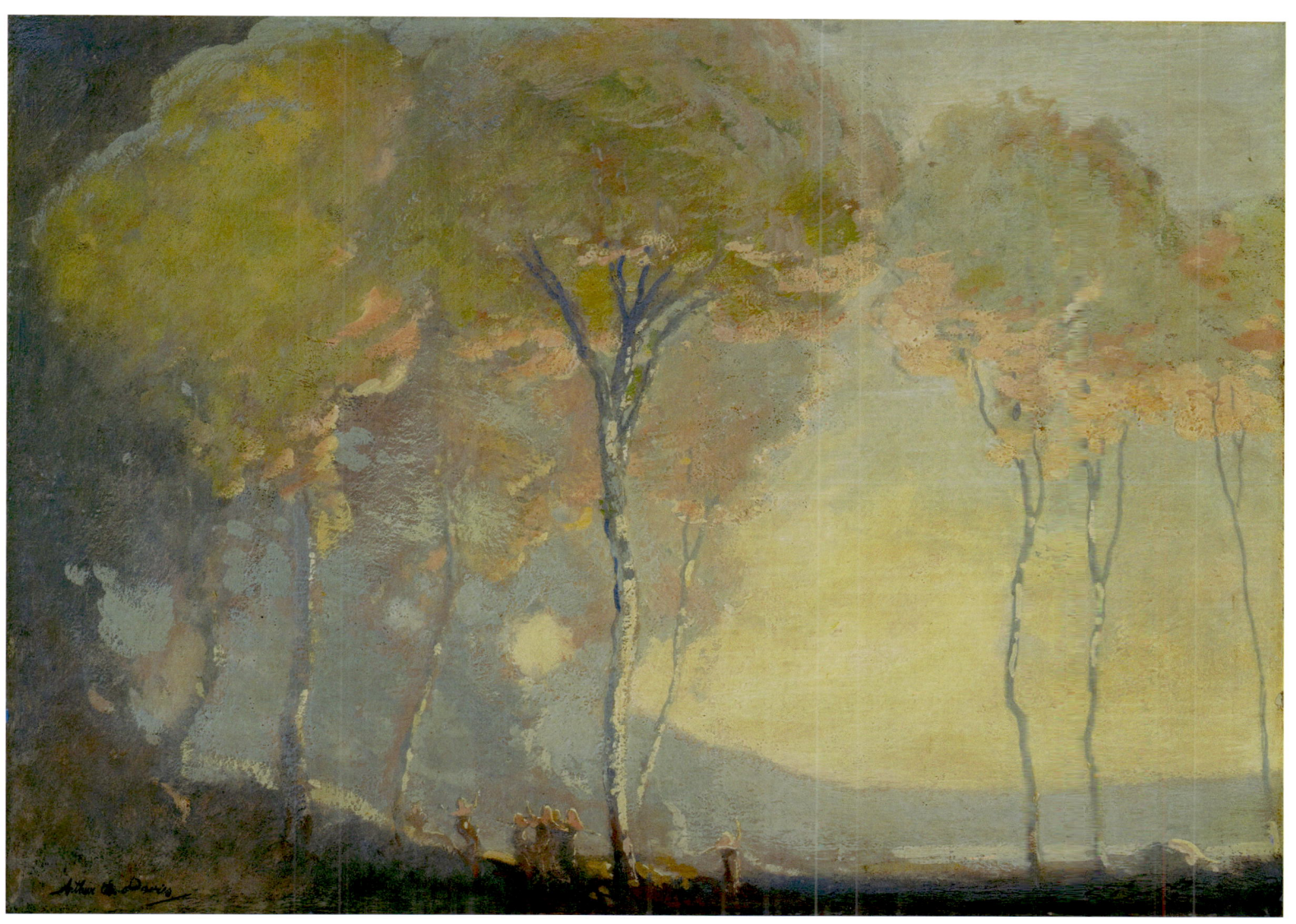

Marsden Hartley

AMERICAN, 1877–1943

Volupté, 1919

Oil on canvas

24 × 20 inches

Promised Gift of the Macon and Joan Brock Collection of American Art

BORN IN MAINE, Marsden Hartley began his studies at the Cleveland School of Art after his family relocated to Ohio in 1893. While there he was introduced to the work of the Barbizon School and Impressionist artists. His talent was evident to his mentors, who arranged a five-year scholarship for him to attend William Merritt Chase's School of Art in New York City. In 1909 Hartley was introduced to Alfred Stieglitz, who hosted a solo exhibition at his 291 Gallery. The show featured thirty-three landscapes of Maine created between 1902 and 1909, effectively launching Hartley's career.

Hartley's lifestyle was nomadic, never settling in one place for too long. In 1912 Stieglitz and painter Arthur B. Davies helped support Hartley's trip to Europe, where he stopped first in Paris and then Berlin. These travels were influential to the artist's development, as he could study Impressionism in Paris and Expressionism in Berlin. At the outbreak of World War I, Hartley painted an abstract series of war motifs inspired by the display of military pageantry he witnessed. Forced to return to the United States in 1915 due to the escalating conflict across Europe, Hartley landed first in New York, traveled around the Northeast and to Bermuda, and went on to New Mexico, arriving in Taos in 1918.[1]

In New Mexico, Hartley painted dramatic scenes of the landscape. There he also painted *Volupté*, continuing the study of voluminous forms seen across his still life and landscape paintings. *Volupté* features a tabletop draped heavily with cloth and a blue vase holding greenery and pink lily flowers. While previous still lifes were more tonally muted, recalling the palette of Cézanne, *Volupté* bursts with colors seen in the New Mexico landscape paintings of this period. The bright blue, red, and green evoke the work of Matisse that Hartley would have viewed during his time in Europe. The title might also be an homage to Matisse's painting *Luxe, Calme et Volupté* (1904; Musée d'Orsay, Paris). Hartley often painted from memory, and it seems his associations with travels past influenced this particular scene.

In 1921 Hartley returned to Europe and then back to the United States, Nova Scotia, and Mexico. He also visited Maine, where he made another painting series of the landscape, which, along with the war series, would come to be known as his greatest works. While his time in New Mexico is often overlooked, one cannot deny the pivotal aspect of Hartley's travels in the development of his colorful, voluminous aesthetic.

CHELSEA PIERCE

1. Gail R. Scott, "On the Ground and Into the Subject: Marsden Hartley in New Mexico, 1918–1919," in *Marsden Hartley: New Mexico, 1918–1920, An American Discovering America* (New York: Alexandre Gallery, 2003), unpaginated.

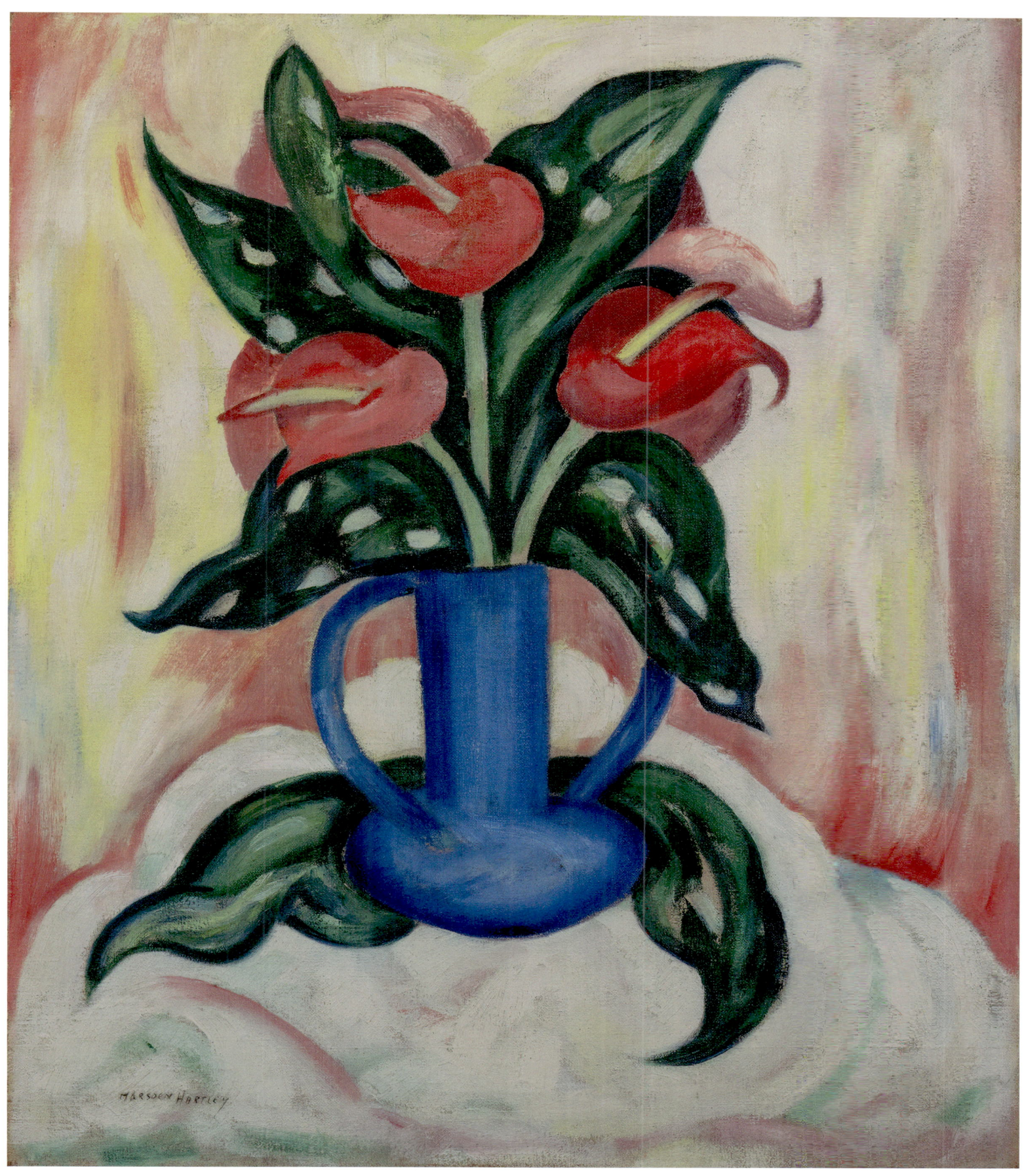

Preston Dickinson

AMERICAN, 1889–1930

Still Life No. 1, ca. 1924

Oil on canvas

24 × 20 inches

Promised Gift of the Macon and Joan Brock Collection
of American Art

PRESTON DICKINSON was known for his modernist landscapes and still life paintings in a style later termed Precisionist. In works such as *Still Life No. 1*, Dickinson employed unexpected viewpoints and emphasized geometric shapes and angles, helping to establish the hallmarks of the aesthetic. Throughout the still life series, he experimented with the texture, color, and volume of tabletop arrangements.[1]

Dickinson's objects are elegant and neat; the plums and pepper nestled inside a blue and white compote appear pristine, everlasting. The cool blue and green tones are complemented by the accent of bright orange, which draws the eye to the center of the composition. His use of color, combined with the patterning of the Art Deco–inspired curtains and faceted handle of the knife, add a sense of movement to this otherwise "still" setting. The forward tilt of the table also guides the viewer's eye dynamically across the composition. In a *New York Times* review of Dickinson's second solo exhibition in 1924, one critic noted, possibly in reference to this painting, "The lines of the [still life] are thrust and pulled into a more architectural relation . . . into a soaring, emotional irregularity expressing the cadences of life."[2]

Born into a working-class family in New York City, Dickinson left high school after his father's death in 1900 to help support his mother and his sister. Aided by financial assistance, he later attended the Art Students League from 1906 to 1910, where he studied with William Merritt Chase and Ernest Lawson. From 1910 to 1914, he studied in Paris, gaining exposure to art forms that influenced his mature style, most notably Japanese prints, Cubism, and Futurism. The discovery of pioneering European artists such as Picasso and Cézanne propelled Dickinson's art into new directions. With the outbreak of World War I, Dickinson returned to New York in 1914. He became closely aligned with other artists working in the modernist idiom, many of whom were represented by Charles Daniel, owner of the Daniel Gallery. Daniel was among the most active supporters of the Precisionist painters in the 1920s. Despite artistic successes, Dickinson was plagued by economic and personal problems. He moved to northeastern Spain with his companion and fellow artist Oronzo Gasparo in the summer of 1930 in search of an inexpensive place to live and paint. They envisioned producing paintings to be sold in either New York or Paris, but the impact of the Great Depression took its toll. The Daniel Gallery struggled (and ultimately closed), and in 1930 Dickinson died of pneumonia at age forty-one.

ERIN MONROE

1. For a generous introduction to Dickinson's life and work, including his still lifes, see Ruth Cloudman, *Preston Dickinson 1889–1930* (Lincoln, NE: Sheldon Memorial Art Gallery, 1979), 28, illus. fig. 7, 29.

2. "The World of Art: Art in the House and in the Galleries," *New York Times*, July 20, 1924, SM12.

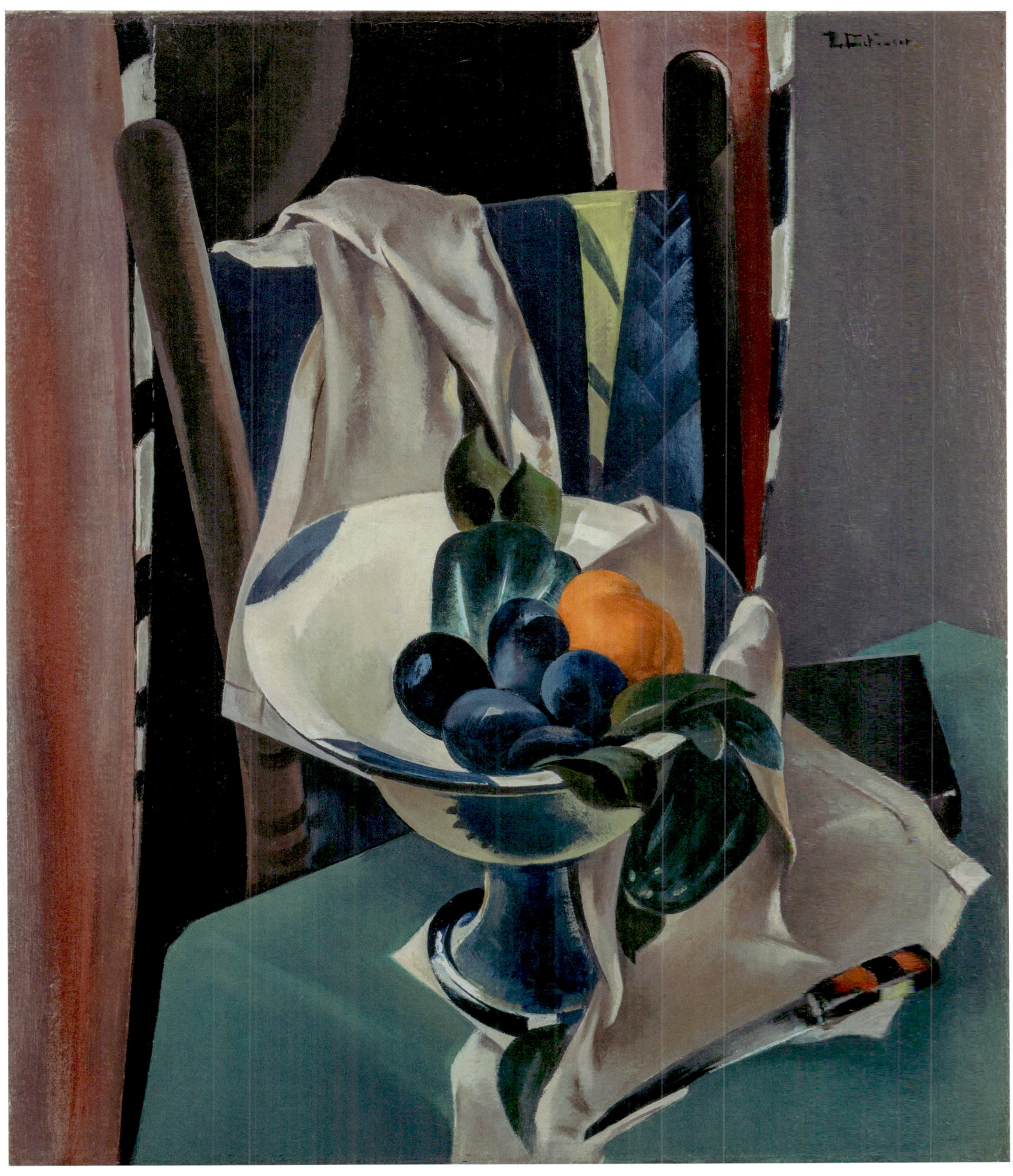

Charles Sheeler
AMERICAN, 1883–1965

Yellow Tulip, Blue Iris, 1925

Oil on canvas

24 × 18⅛ inches

Promised Gift of the Macon and Joan Brock Collection of American Art

CHARLES SHEELER WAS BORN in Philadelphia in 1883 to working-class parents; his father operated the Clyde Steamship Company line that traveled between Philadelphia and Norfolk. Sheeler first attended the School of Industrial Art before enrolling at the Pennsylvania Academy of the Fine Arts, where he studied under William Merritt Chase and graduated in 1906. Sheeler began working out of a studio in Philadelphia shared with Morton Schamberg. Both Pennsylvania Academy graduates were photographers as well as painters and soon became enmeshed in the local art scene, with Sheeler often writing art reviews for the local newspaper. However, Schamberg was stricken with pneumonia and died in 1918. Sheeler, devastated by the loss of his closest friend, was convinced by his professional acquaintance Alfred Stieglitz to move to New York City.

While in New York, Sheeler mixed with avant-garde artists associated with Stieglitz and worked toward shedding his academic style. In 1921 he collaborated with photographer Paul Strand on the short film *Manhatta* that navigated urban life through its various infrastructures, ranging from skyscrapers and bridges to ferries and trains. This project could be seen as the spark of Sheeler's interest in technology, later realized in his paintings that portrayed industrialization in precise, stark form. This movement was coined "Precisionism" and included Sheeler, Charles Demuth, and Preston Dickinson, among others.

Sheeler often worked as a commercial photographer for magazines like *Vanity Fair* but also photographed fine art for the Whitney Museum of American Art. The mechanics of photography were soon incorporated into his painting process and style.[1] This relationship between painting and photography can be seen in *Yellow Tulip, Blue Iris*, featuring a black oenochoe Etruscan vase filled with tulips and irises on an octagonal table set with a pitcher and apple.[2] Sheeler carefully laid the scene and could return to it over time, using photographic floodlights to cast even and consistent lighting. The objects depicted appear in serialized nature across Sheeler's photographic works and paintings, where he rearranged various elements in different settings. Although the still life exudes much of Sheeler's Precisionist details with the reduction of elements to basic shapes and forms, one can still see the influence of Chase in the background of *Yellow Tulip, Blue Iris*, with color and gesture pronounced in its impressionistic rendering.

CHELSEA PIERCE

1. Carol Troyen and Erica Hirshler, *Charles Sheeler: Paintings and Drawings* (Boston: The Museum of Fine Arts, Boston, 1987).

2. William Henning makes note of the oenochoe vase in Sheeler's collection, as the object was atypical of his main interest in American Shaker furniture and craft. The catalogue offers insight into the objects and furniture that Sheeler owned; see *Charles Sheeler: American Interiors* (New Haven, CT: Yale University Press, 1987), 30.

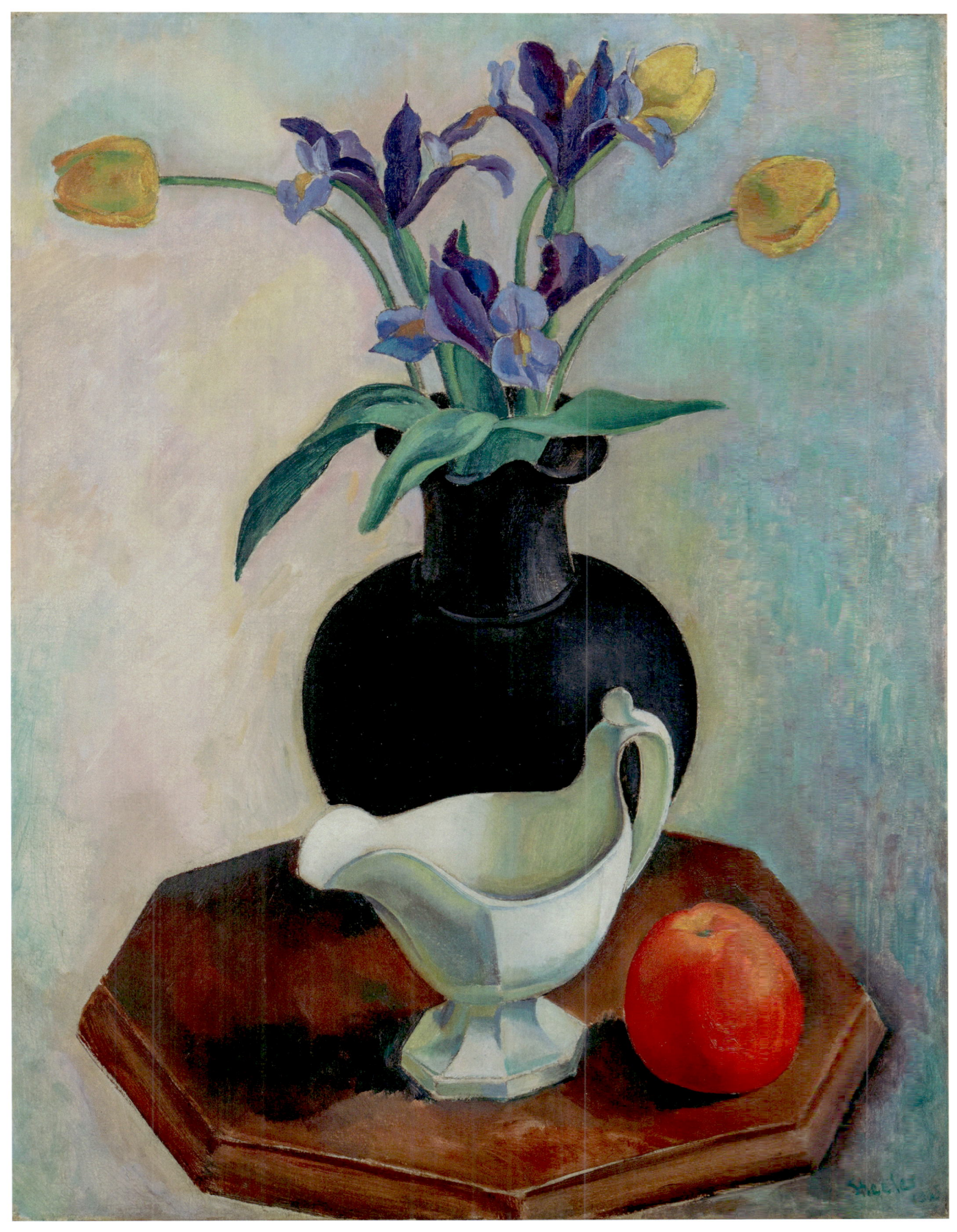

Leon Kroll

AMERICAN, 1884–1974

Poetry Reading, Maine, 1918
Oil on canvas
45¾ × 52 inches

LEON KROLL STUDIED with the American Impressionist artist John Henry Twachtman at the Art Students League in New York and continued his artistic education at the Académie Julian in Paris in 1918–19. He would eventually teach at the National Academy of Design in New York, the Maryland Institute of Art, and the Art Institute of Chicago. Earlier Kroll had spent part of the summers of 1913 and 1914 with the artist George Bellows and his wife Emma on Monhegan Island, Maine. He may have picked up from Bellows an interest in lush atmospheric effects in glades populated by friends and family. In 1918, this time working in Deer Isle, Maine, he produced such a canvas—*Poetry Reading, Maine*. The work depicts a standing man reading, a woman on a hammock, a boy on the ground, and a woman knitting, all framed by boughs, branches, and sun-streaked foliage through which five additional figures are visible.

The standing figure is the Modernist composer Leo Ornstein, whom Kroll had invited to join him in Maine—they occupied adjacent studios.[1] With his head bent down toward the small book, he reads poetry to the three attentively listening individuals, including the woman, whose recumbent form presents a horizontal contrasting with the man's verticality. The resulting, approximately 90-degree

angle intersection of his form with hers may harken to artist Jay Hambridge's then-famous theory of "dynamic symmetry," which advised that art should recreate right-angle relationships found in nature, and which Kroll encountered shortly before painting *Poetry Reading, Maine*.[2] By the time Ornstein posed for this painting, he had already found fame with an early biography, Frederick Martens's *Leo Ornstein: The Man, His Ideas, His Work*, appearing in 1918.[3] Kroll's painting grants to Ornstein a degree of gravitas and intellectual absorption that one would also find in his works as a composer.

Kroll depicted Ornstein in another 1918 painting, this time seated at a piano and engrossed in his playing and perhaps composing (fig. 1). Modern historians have noted that the latter shows the composer "in mystic communion with his music."[4] With the foreground figures engrossed in the recitation of the poetry, *Poetry Reading, Maine* suggests a literary version of the sort of intimacy one might otherwise have when listening to music. Somewhat paradoxically, the Cézanne-inspired modeling of branches and greenery both partitions and unites the painting's disparate parts. The foliage functions as a screen through which to see more, much like the plant forms in Kroll's 1920 painting *Still Life in the Studio Window, New York City*, which similarly beckon our gaze into the background. In the later painting, however, the leaves act like the window behind it, opening upon a view of the city. The canvas renders abstract and universal an otherwise specific urban topography marked by windows, chimneys, and variously shaped roofs, all topped by a partly cloudy sky. Although best known as a figure painter, Kroll found early fame for his still lifes, including a special mention for his work in this genre in the *New York Times* in 1918.[5]

In *Still Life in the Studio Window*, the ascending Easter lily plant emerges from the bunch of bananas, apples, and pears in a bowl, with an additional green pear at lower left, all of which sit on a panel reflecting the light from outside. The leaves maintain a visual clarity in contrast to the more loosely painted city backdrop. At both left and right, brightly colored drapes with floral motifs bracket the vista onto the city, acting as a frame within the framed painting. More than still life or landscape, Kroll was most interested in the expressive possibilities of the human form, yet "ubiquitous fruit still life inclusion[s]" are found in Kroll's works in other genres, such as his domestic interiors and nude subjects.[6] So expressively modeled in light and shade are the fruits in the bowl that they possess the sort of chiaroscuro with which an artist might compose a human face or torso. Careful to capture the black streaks on the almost

FIG. 1 Leon Kroll, *Leo Ornstein at the Piano*, 1918. Oil on canvas, 34 1/16 × 40 1/8 in. Art Institute of Chicago, Friends of American Art Collection, 1919.874

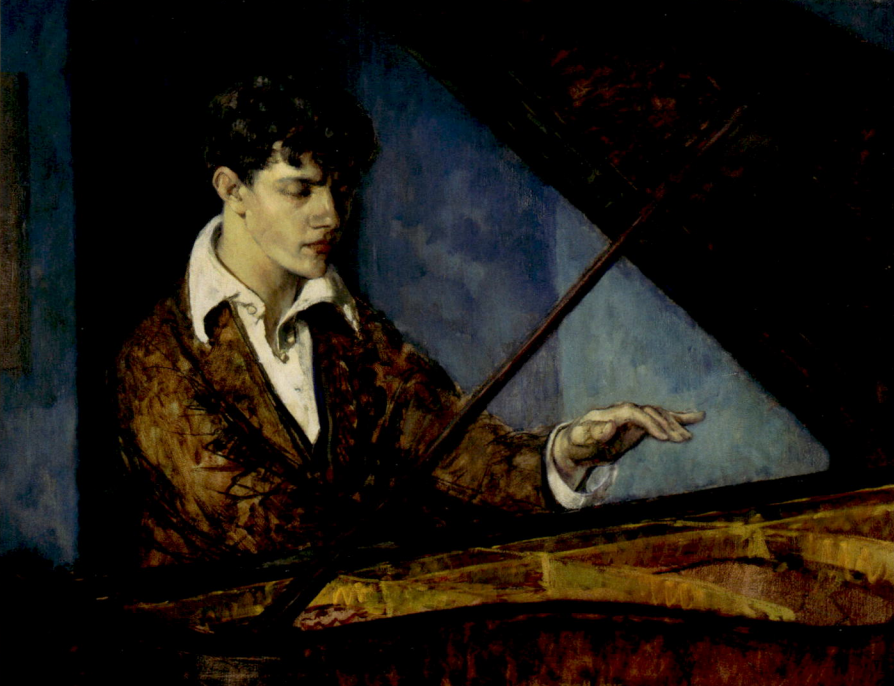

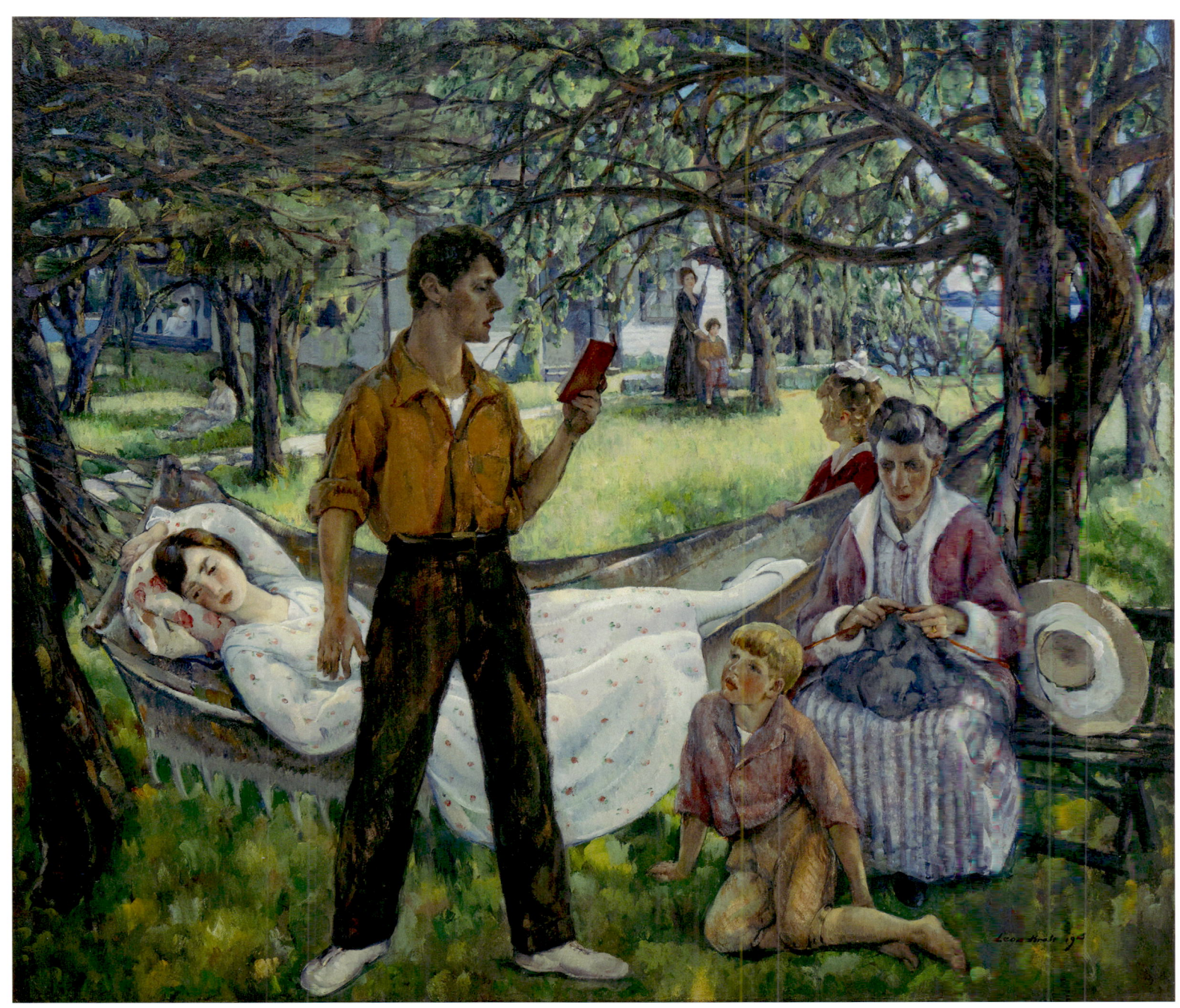

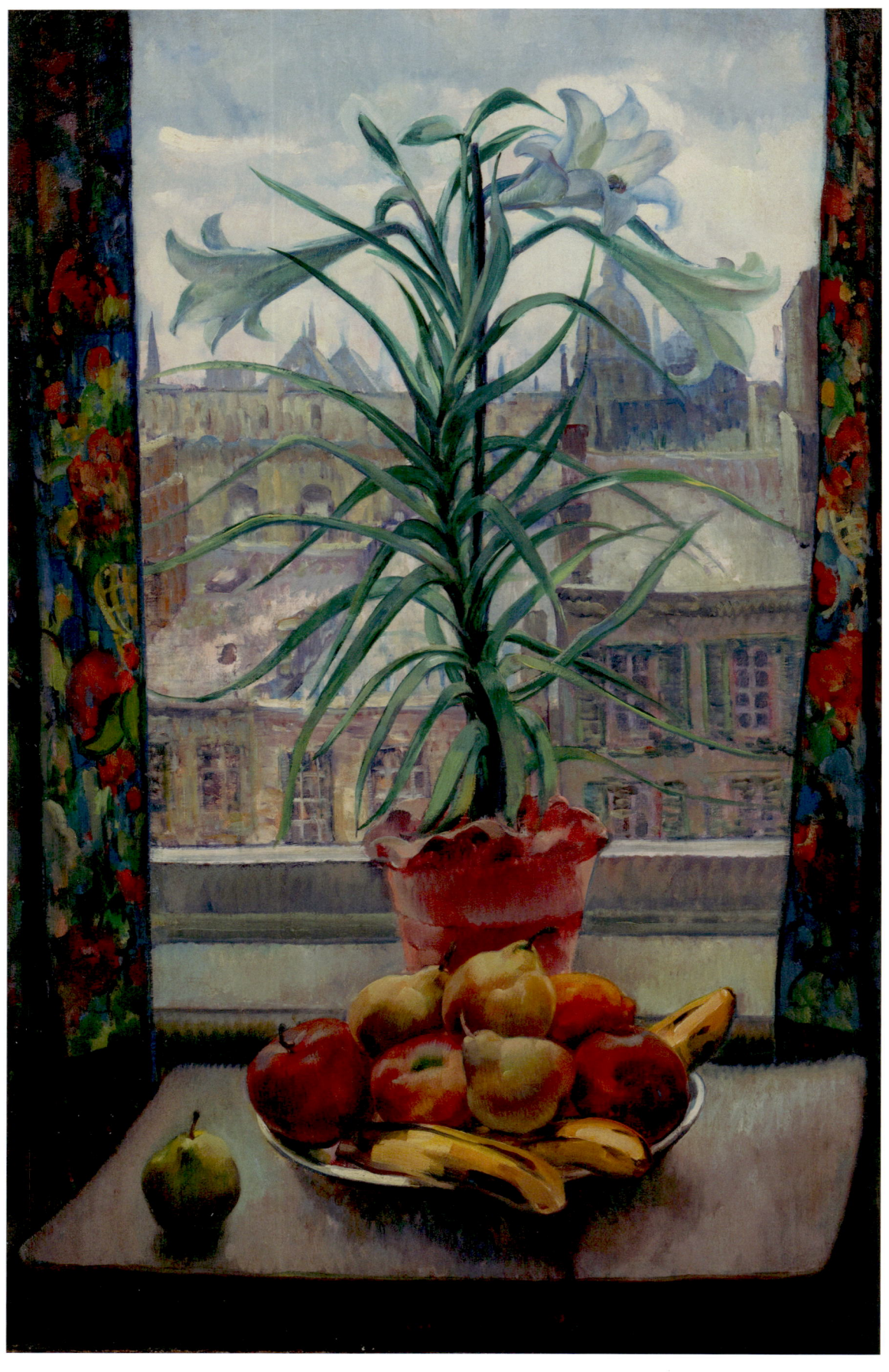

Still Life in the Studio Window, New York City, 1920
Oil on canvas
40 × 25 inches

too-ripe bananas, Kroll suggests the freshness and vivacity of the fruits. The naturalism of the fruit is rivaled by the thin leaves and flowers, carefully painted to offer a sense of growth, as if in the act of becoming—not unlike the city itself. Lilies typically connote purity, royalty, and summertime, but here they facilitate a back-and-forth of inside and outside, joining the window ledge itself as a visual impasse between urban landscape and cozy domestic interior.

LEO MAZOW

1. Special thanks to Corey Piper for sharing with me the Chrysler Museum of Art's wall label text for *Poetry Reading, Maine*, from which selected information comes. Nancy Hale and Fredson Bowers, ed. *Leon Kroll: A Spoken Memoir* (Charlottesville: University Press of Virginia, 1983), 43.

2. Kenneth Norton Davis, *The Life and Work of Leon Kroll with a Catalogue of his Nudes* (PhD diss.. The Ohio State University, 1953), 63–64.

3. https://www.nlkenarchive.org/artist/view/leo-ornstein (accessed September 2, 2022).

4. Michael Broyles and Denise Von Glahn, *Leo Ornstein: Modernist Dilemmas, Personal Dilemmas* (Bloomington: Indiana University Press, 2007), 98.

5. "Art Notes: Recent Paintings by Leon Kroll and Ernest Lawson," *New York Times*, January 31, 1915, 8.

6. See Davis, *The Life and Work of Leon Kroll*, 204, 209; quote from 209.

Guy Pène du Bois

AMERICAN, 1884–1958

Protectrice, 1921
Oil on panel
25 × 20 inches

GUY PÈNE DU BOIS WAS BORN in New York to a family of French creatives. His father, William Pène du Bois, a Louisiana Creole by heritage, was a writer and illustrator. His mother, Yvonne, was a painter. Pène du Bois was encouraged from a young age to pursue arts, attending the New York School of Art and studying first under William Merritt Chase and later with Robert Henri. In 1905 Pène du Bois traveled to Paris with his father and attended the Académie Colarossi. He took cues from artists such as Edgar Degas and Henri de Toulouse-Lautrec, who painted from daily life. Like Toulouse-Lautrec, Pène du Bois stationed himself in cafés to capture various social interactions. The father and son's time in Paris was cut short when Pène du Bois Senior fell ill, and the pair embarked on a ship to return to the United States; unfortunately, William died before they arrived home.

Back in America, Pène du Bois continued painting subjects in a stylized realism. He was included in the 1913 Armory Show, where six of his works were exhibited. His subject matter often depicted the bourgeoisie with which he spent ample time; he was close to Gertrude Vanderbilt Whitney, who collected his work, and was neighbor to novelist F. Scott Fitzgerald for a brief time in Connecticut.[1] After his father's death, he struggled to support himself, relying on patronages and contributing art reviews for commission.

In 1924 Pène du Bois was able to return to Paris and continue his aesthetic pursuits. *Bus Top (On Top of the Bus)* (1924) was possibly painted during this time. The scene features two women on the rooftop deck of a city bus. The ambiguous background shaded in tones of blue does not reveal any specific location. The two women wear cloche hats of styles typical in the 1920s. *Protectrice* (1921) has a similar cerulean background with two fashionably dressed women standing against a wall at what appears to be a riverfront. The hazy outline of buildings in the distance and slight marks of white to depict dim lights reveal more of the urban environment. One woman in a red coat leans against the wall, while her companion stands self-possessed with a hand at her hip. Like the pair of women on the bus rooftop, Pène du Bois shows members of the upper social echelons, evident through fashionable clothing and aspects of leisure.

Pène du Bois stayed in Paris for six years, returning to the United States in 1930. He taught at the Art Students League in New York. As a writer, Pène du Bois also produced monographs on fellow artists such as William Glackens, Edward Hopper, and John Sloan. He worked for the Works Progress Administration from 1936 to 1943, creating murals for various post offices in Upstate New York and the Northeast. Many of these murals still exist today, such as his scenes of horse races in the post office at Saratoga Springs, New York.

CHELSEA PIERCE

1. Jack Flam, "Guy Pène Du Bois," *American Heritage* 40, no. 1 (February 1989). Online, https://www.americanheritage.com/guy-pene-du-bois.

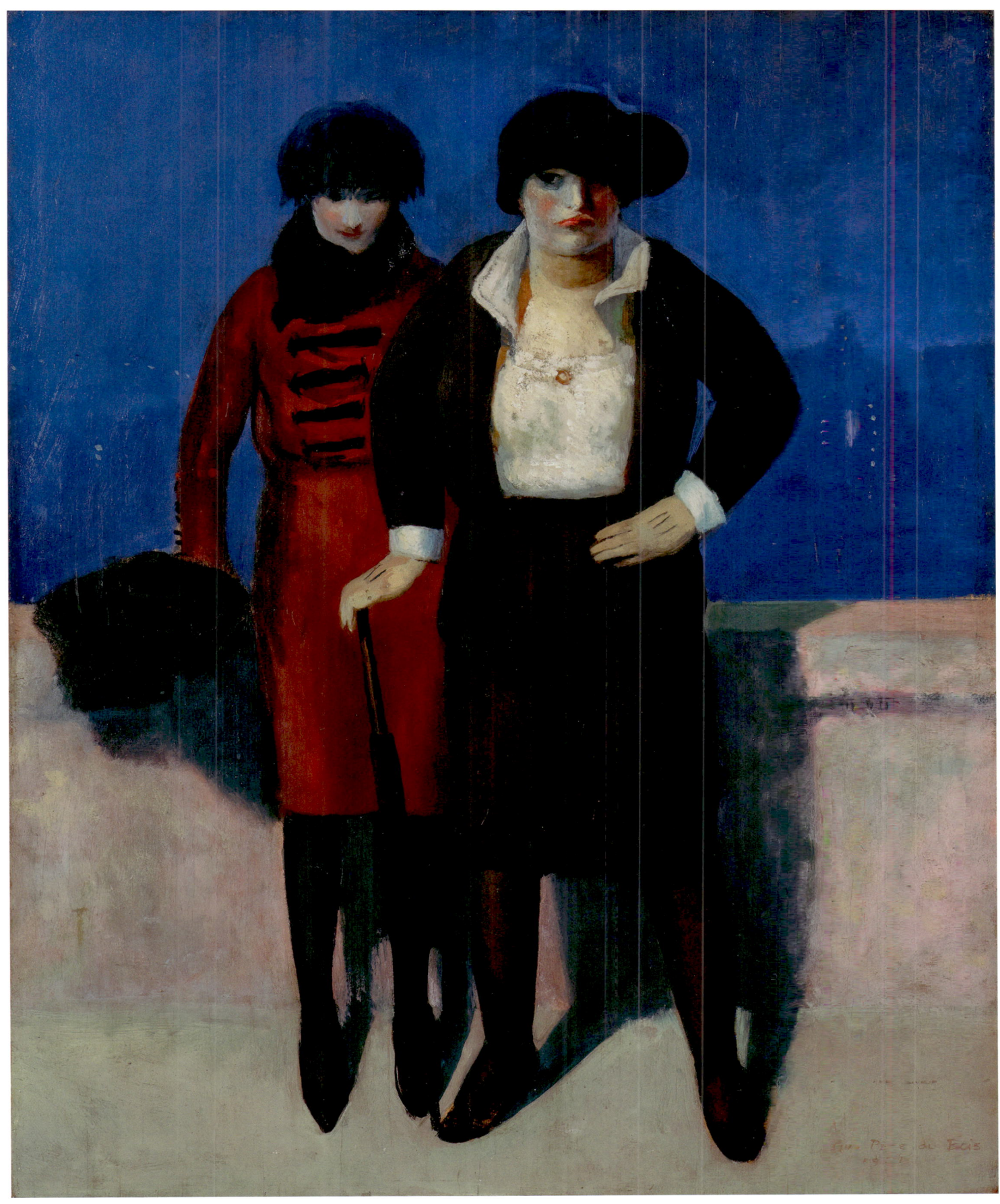

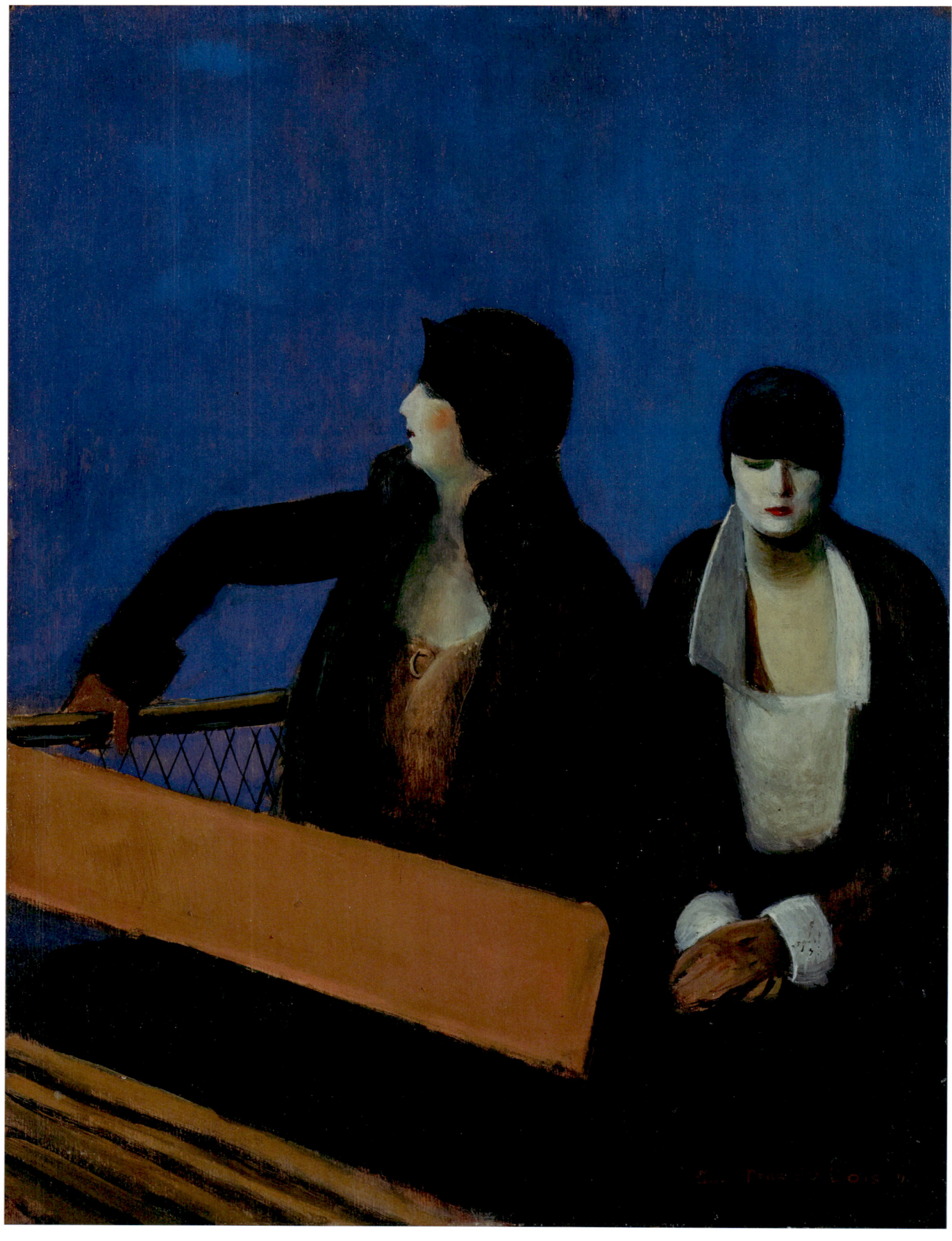

Bus Top (On Top of the Bus), 1–24
Oil on panel
20 × 15 inches

John Whorf

AMERICAN, 1903–1959

Siesta, ca. 1925

Watercolor on paper

15 × 20¾ inches

Gift of the Macon and Joan Brock Collection of American Art, 2023.4.5

FROM A YOUNG AGE, Whorf showed an interest in and aptitude for art. At his father's encouragement, he studied at the St. Botolph Studio and the School of the Museum of Fine Arts in Boston as early as fourteen. However, Whorf quickly tired of the strictures of academic training and wished to study independently. He fled Boston for Provincetown, Massachusetts, in 1917 at a time when many creatives were assembling in what was coined "P-Town." Whorf attended Charles Hawthorne's Cape Cod School of Painting (which opened in 1899) and made friends with fellow artist George Elmer Browne. Suffering a fall from an ill-fated stunt, Whorf was nearly bedbound for a year and henceforth had to use a cane. When he recovered, he traveled to Europe in the 1920s and developed a liking for watercolor.

Once he returned to the United States, Whorf's first solo exhibition at Boston's Grace Horne Gallery in 1924 was positively reviewed. All of his watercolors were sold and, reportedly, John Singer Sargent had purchased a work for himself.[1] At the Philadelphia Watercolor Club's 1929 exhibition, one reviewer wrote of his work that Whorf "with ecstasy of color casts a spell on the beholder, opens gates into enchanted worlds."[2] Certainly *Siesta* offers such a glimpse into a dreamlike scene painted in lush colors with mystic light evoking a scene from Shakespeare's *A Midsummer Night's Dream*. The watercolor portrays a sylvan setting with three women set up for an afternoon outdoors. Two of the ladies sit in folding chairs around a linen-laid table. The third woman lays idly in the grass, seemingly dozing as the work's title suggests. Despite the gestural brushstrokes, Whorf meticulously made out the features of each woman's outfit, demonstrating his mastery over the medium.

Whorf and his family continued to spend summers in Provincetown and rented a cottage from the family of painter Frederick Judd Waugh. This acquaintance with Waugh later influenced Whorf's seascapes. While Whorf remained well known for his watercolors, oil paintings such as *Southern Cruiser* were also in high demand. Years later, Boston gallerist Robert C. Vose, Jr., recounted the history of his family's art gallery and described how contemporary exhibitions often left the gallery "in the red" with few exceptions, one being Whorf, whose paintings and watercolors would consistently sell out.[3] *Southern Cruiser* is a night scene featuring a ship battling turbulent seas. Four figures can be seen on deck, one illuminated by the light from the open cabin door. The ship's mast emerges from the darkness and points toward the dim moonlight, portending that this crew would soon find safety. While many regarded Whorf as an artistic heir of Sargent, the seascape's title of "nocturne" suggests that Whorf also found an affinity with the work of James Abbott McNeill Whistler.

CHELSEA PIERCE

1. "John Whorf," Granary Gallery artist page: https://granary gallery.com/artist-biography .php?artistId=196786&artist =John+Whorf.

2. Thornton Oakley, "The Philadelphia Water Color Club and its Twenty-Sixth Annual Exhibition," *American Magazine of Art* 20, no. 1 (1929): 22–28.

3. Robert C. Vose and Robert F. Brown, "Boston's Vose Galleries: A Family Affair," *Archives of American Art Journal* 21, no. 1 (1981): 8–20.

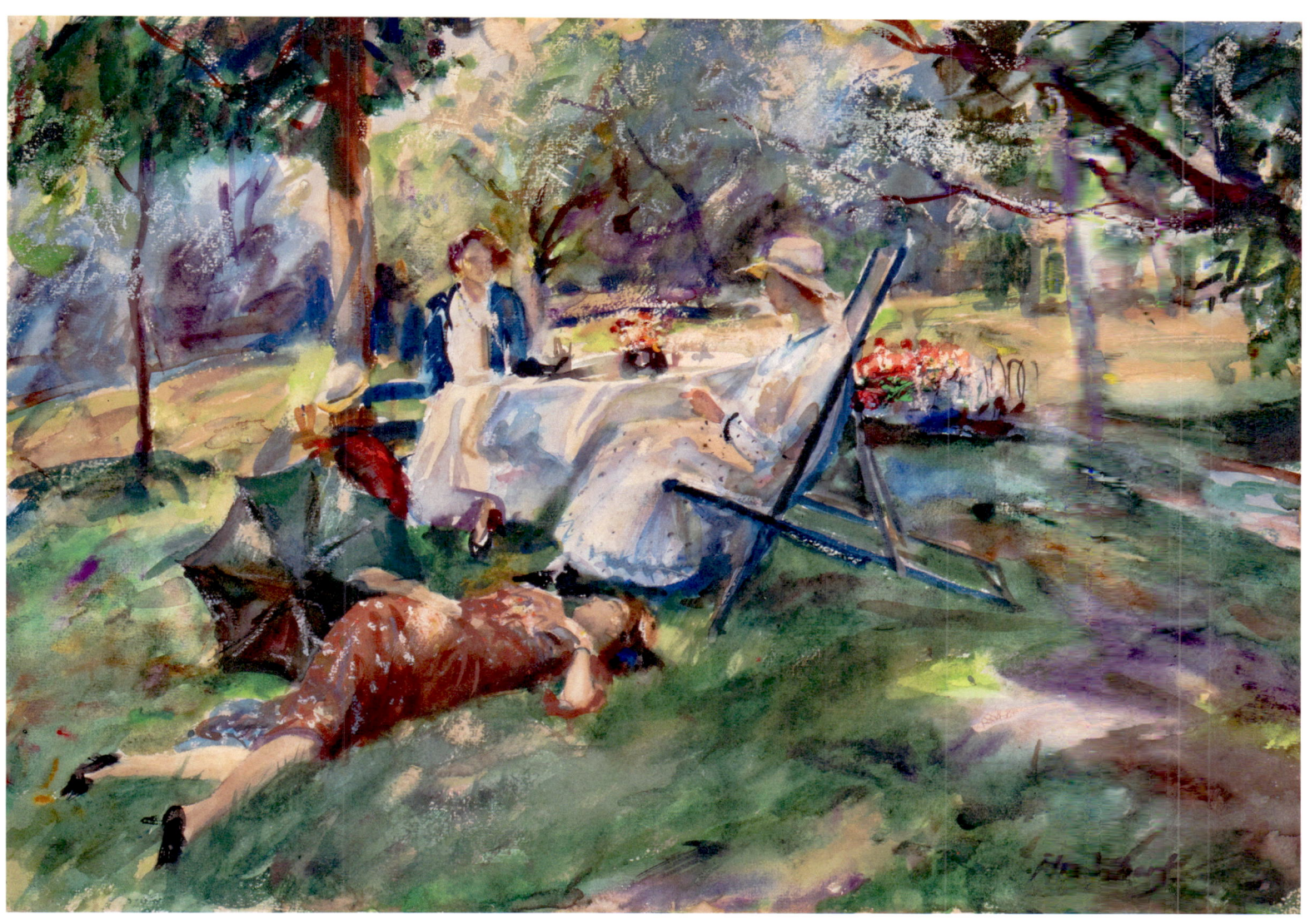

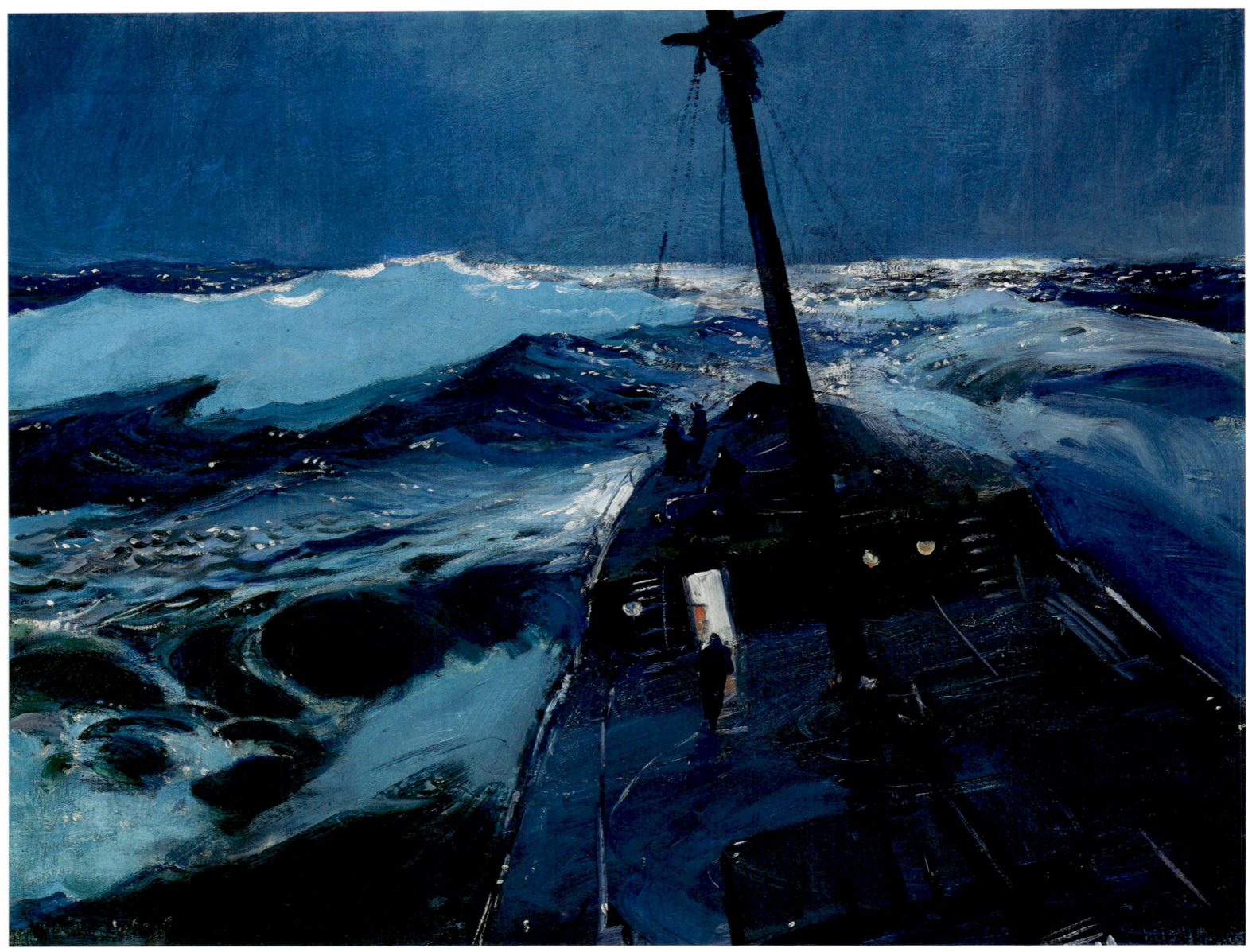

Southern Cruiser (Maritime Nocturne with Ship in Rough Water), ca. 1930
Oil on canvas
28 × 36 inches

Promised Gift of the Macon and Joan Brock Collection of American Art

Rockwell Kent

AMERICAN, 1882–1971

Sledging, ca. 1932–35
Oil on canvas, mounted on plywood
40 × 60 inches

AS BOTH A PAINTER AND POLYMATH, Rockwell Kent possessed a pioneering spirit. Kent operated at the vanguard of Modernist painting in the early twentieth century, while also mastering other vocations as a printmaker, traveler, author, and champion of progressive political causes. He traveled widely throughout his life, often drawn to geographic and climatic extremes in the northern and southern latitudes. His evocative depictions of the harsh but enchanting landscapes in places like Newfoundland, Alaska, and Greenland stand as some of his most enduring and impactful works. *Sledging*, created upon the artist's second or third sojourn in Greenland, presents a monumental and seemingly inhospitable landscape. Receding into the distance, a dogsled team carves a path dotted with dozens of snowy paw prints onward through the snow, their simple and effective adaptations in travel aiding daily life at the extremes of human habitation.

Kent began his career training in architecture at Columbia University but never escaped the lure of painting. Throughout his student years in New York, he spent summers painting with William Merritt Chase at his school at Shinnecock Hills on Long Island and later worked as an assistant in the New Hampshire studio of Abbott Thayer. In 1905 Kent moved to Monhegan, Maine, where he would spend the next several years enthralled by the elemental collision of the sea and rocky shore. His stark paintings of Monhegan landscapes and village views earned critical praise in New York and spurred the artist to embark on a pattern of travel, seeking ever more extreme geographies, that carried into the next decade. In 1914 Kent moved with his family to Newfoundland, and in 1918 he undertook a voyage to Alaska. Accompanied by his son, he settled in a simple cabin along Resurrection Bay, south of Anchorage. Kent found Alaska's isolation and otherworldliness inspiring, but before long he was again tempted to journey, this time southward to Tierra del Fuego.

By 1929, when Kent accepted an invitation to join a sailing crew on a journey to Greenland, he had grown into a seasoned adventurer. After surviving a harrowing shipwreck, he settled in Greenland for the summer, growing enchanted with the landscape and people he encountered there. He followed this journey with two subsequent stays in Greenland in 1931 and 1934. *Sledging* resulted from Kent's experiences on these later stays, during which he produced many landscapes as well as studies of the Indigenous people he came to know there. The imposing mountains of Greenland served as a dramatic backdrop for many of Kent's compositions, framing the vast frozen expanse. Kent later attributed his love of Greenland to its "icy mountains."[1] In works like *Sledging*, their rocky forms, interspersed with ice, reflecting the ever-present sun, offered a potent subject for exploring the extremes of creation. The sublime beauty of the scene, and the steadfastness of the human and animal team at center, attests to Kent's immersive understanding of the distinctive character of the landscape and its singular hold upon him.

COREY PIPER

1. Rockwell Kent and Paul Cummings, "An Interview with Rockwell Kent Conducted by Paul Cummings at Ausable Forks, New York, February 26–27, 1969," *Archives of American Art Journal* 12 (January 1972): 17.

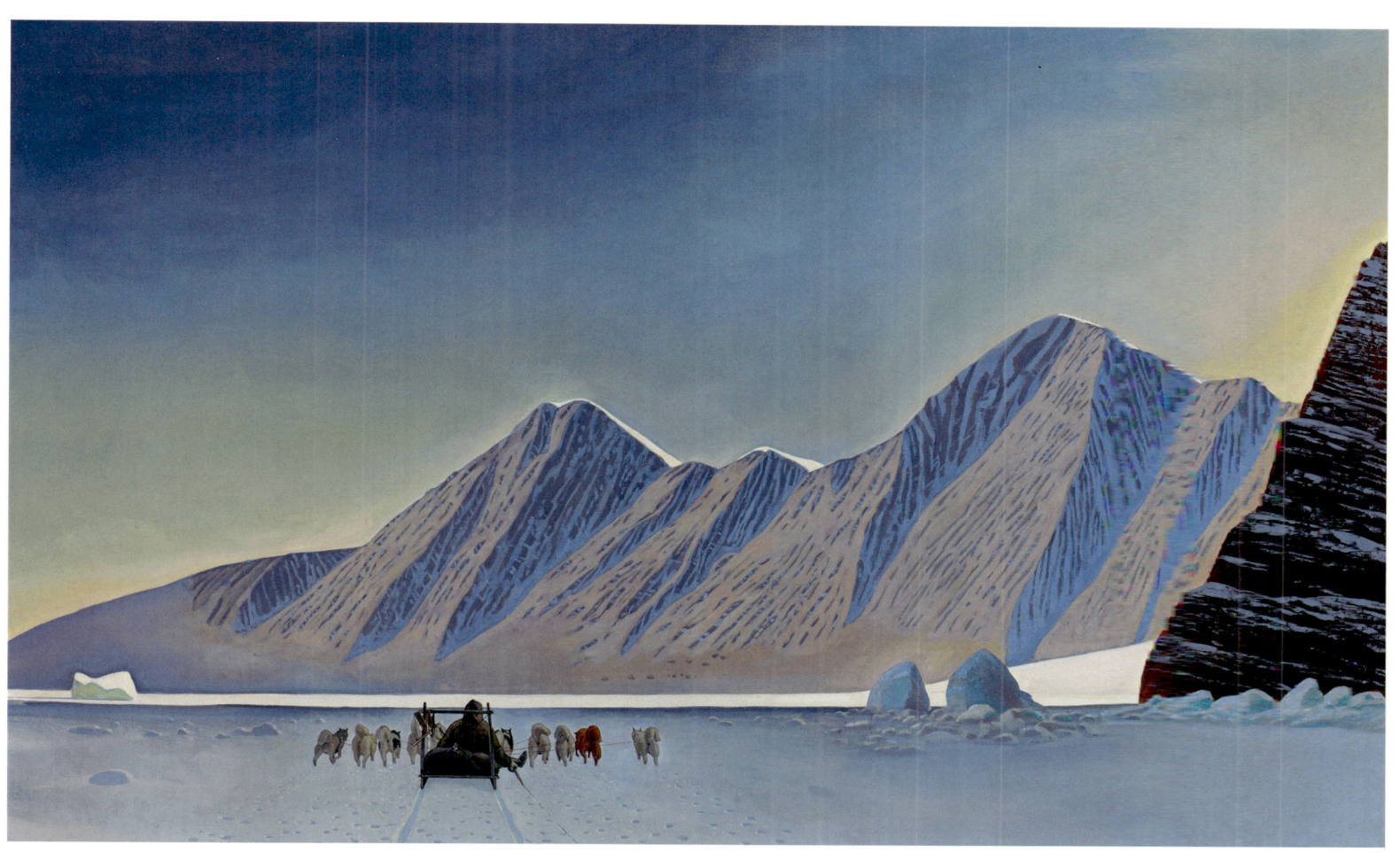

Jane Peterson

AMERICAN, 1876–1965

Petunias, ca. 1932

Oil on canvas

30 × 24 inches

Promised Gift of the Macon and Joan Brock Collection of American Art

"I paint flowers because they are my friends and I love them."

—Jane Peterson[1]

THROUGHOUT HER CAREER, Jane Peterson was celebrated for her vibrant and expressive take on American Impressionism. Although her subjects were wide-ranging, including harbor scenes, urban views, and exotic images of foreign shores, she is often most closely identified with her floral still lifes—a subject that dominated her oeuvre after 1925.

Flowers appealed to Peterson for a variety of reasons. Primarily, as she explained, "the reason I paint flowers is because of all things in the world, I think flowers the most beautiful."[2] Peterson was also encouraged to focus on this subject when, in 1925, she married retired lawyer Bernard Philipp. Her new husband preferred that she paint floral still lifes, which were then considered an appropriate artistic subject for a refined society woman. Peterson complied, dedicating herself to painting "portraits" of subjects found in her gardens at Rocky Hill, the couple's summer estate in Ipswich, Massachusetts. Peterson's garden offered countless opportunities for studying flowers, and she handpicked blossoms based on her interest in their shape, color, and texture. She would arrange her chosen subjects in a vase she selected to provide visual balance to the overall display before taking her brush to the canvas.

Petunias presents a striking example of Peterson's achievements as a flower painter. Featuring an overflowing bouquet of purple, white, pink, lavender, and red petunias, Peterson's arrangement is attractively set in a purple Arts and Crafts vase, perhaps a piece of American art pottery, encircled with molded points connecting to ridges down the body. The shape of the ridges recalls the partially fused, velvety petals of the flowers, while the color of the vessel echoes that of the darkest petunia placed at the top of the bouquet, crowning the composition. Set against a sky-blue ground, this flower portrait is a poetic celebration of the various shades, sizes, and shapes of petunia blossoms. In Peterson's words, this arrangement demonstrates the distinctive ways that petunias "scintillate the prismatic hues of the rainbow."[3]

In 1946 Peterson published *Flower Painting*, a how-to book that offered guidance to artists interested in painting floral still lifes and replicating the types of visual effects featured in *Petunias*. The book includes recommendations for selecting flowers and foliage, choosing a vase, creating balance, designing backgrounds, and arranging flowers for still life painting and for the home.

Peterson's booklet opens with a poem by Nanette Bayne entitled "Jane's Flowers (A Tribute to Jane Peterson)," an ode to that artist's achievements in floral still life:

Jane's flowers, ever fair, forever new,
And sparkling with the dew that fills our eyes;
Starched lilies, orchids, blooms of fairy hue
Hail matchless zinnias under saffron skies.

Frail bits of splendor strewn along the earth,
Soft fragments of the sunset's afterglow –
We called you flowers in a flash of mirth,
Sweet whispers of God's kingdom here below.[4]

LAUREN PALMOR

1. Jane Peterson, *Flower Painting* (New York: Art Books for All, 1946), unpaginated.

2. Jane Peterson, "Why I Paint Flowers," *Garden Magazine* 36, no. 1 (September 1922): 31.

3. Peterson, "Why I Paint Flowers," 31.

4. Nanette Bayne, "Jane's Flowers (A Tribute to Jane Peterson)," frontispiece for Peterson, *Flower Painting*.

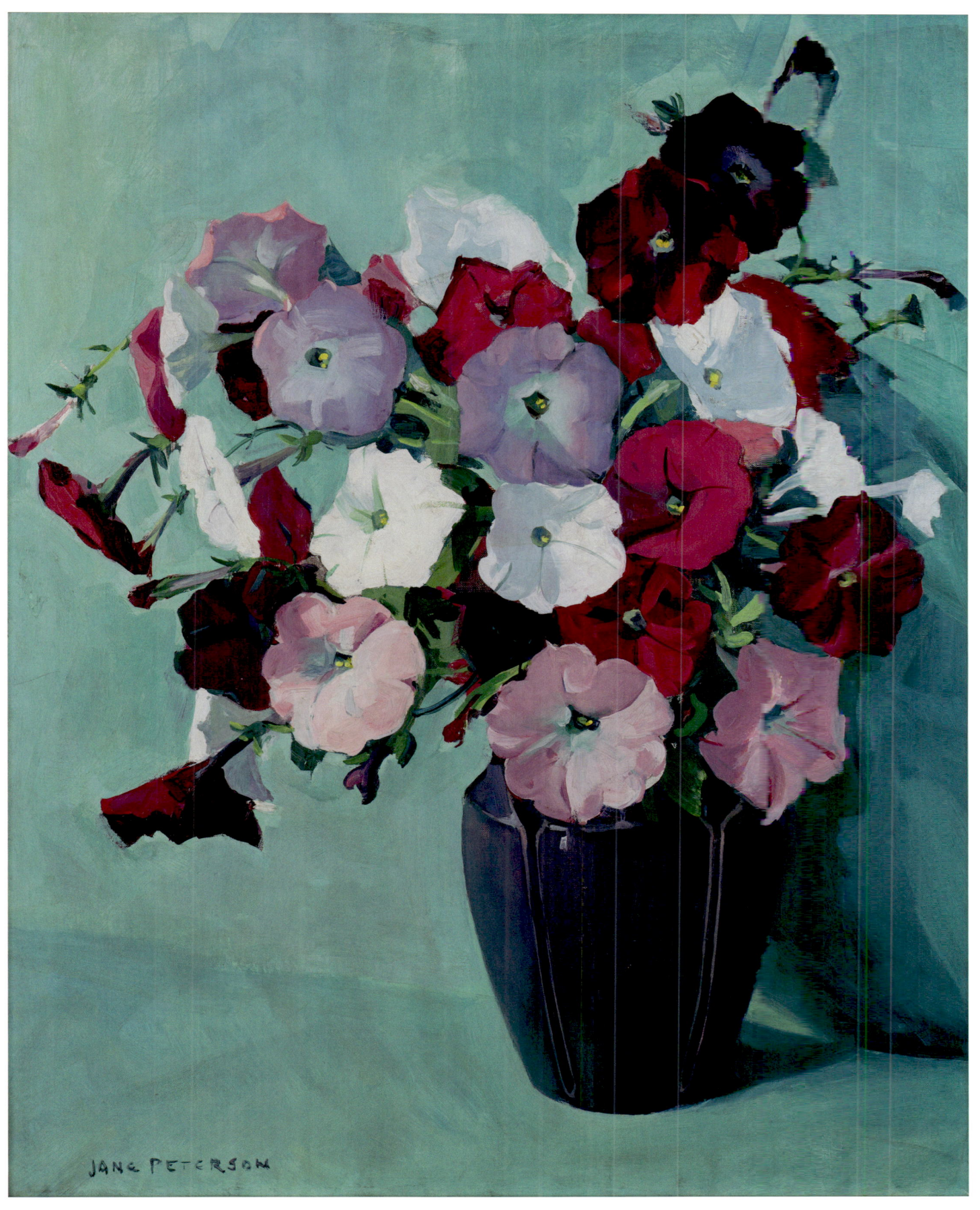

JANE PETERSON

Thomas Hart Benton

AMERICAN, 1889–1975

Still Life with Flowers and Fruit, 1948
Oil and tempera on panel
29½ × 16¼ inches

IN THE 1930S Missouri-born Thomas Hart Benton found enormous fame and occasional controversy for four large-scale, public mural projects. He also produced myriad easel paintings and several dozen lithographs that were aggressively marketed by the firm Associated American Artists, which only propelled his level of renown further. Finding his subject matter in regional and national history and politics, Benton emphasized the leisure and labors of what he perceived as ordinary Americans in identifiably American settings. However, with the onset of World War II and the increasing appeal of European Modernism, Benton's brand of so-called Regionalism—this label usually grouped him with the painter-printmakers Grant Wood and John Steuart Curry—lost favor in the 1940s. Regionalism's representational aesthetic waned as audiences clamored for Abstraction.

Benton's embrace of historical subjects persisted, but he increasingly applied his rich, painterly swirls and dynamic modeling to the natural world. *Still Life with Flowers and Fruit* marks Benton's renewal of interest not only in flora and still life but also in the explorations of form that he had first undertaken as a student, when he sought to interpret American histories and landscapes alike through a modernist, often cubist idiom. Benton had been fired from his teaching position at the Kansas City Art Institute in 1941, but his still life works offered a clinic in natural history illustration and the expressive properties of surfaces.[1] During these later years, he would also produce decorative panels of fish, ocean waves, and other dynamic forms.

Two pears in a Revere-style bowl top two additional, unidentified fruit and lead the eye to a decanter holding red, pink, and yellow zinnias, as well as leaves and other plant life in various states of green and brown. Benton had a keen understanding of plant life; a friend from later in his life has reminisced that "he could name all the flowers."[2] A colonial revival–style silver saltshaker joins the compact composition in accentuating the vertical thrust of the painting's format. The vase itself suggests classical Georgian styles; the ripeness and youth of the fruit, that is, contrast with the purposefully aged aesthetic of the decorative ware. The flattened, white tabletop appears tilted forward in defiance of the laws of linear perspective, yielding the illusion that the lemon, green pepper, and red fabric at lower left could somehow fall out of the picture plane. Equally dramatic is the distinction of flowers and foliage with the teal, almost-turquoise color comprising the background.[3] This painting demonstrates Benton's ability to enliven and animate the time-honored genre of still life.

LEO MAZOW

1. Benton's firing, due to his homophobic comments, from the Kansas City Art Institute is well chronicled, but especially helpful is Justin Wolff, *Thomas Hart Benton: A Life* (New York: Farrar, Straus and Giroux, 2012), 272–75.

2. John Callison, interview with author, Kansas City, July 26, 2006.

3. I wish to acknowledge the input of Dan Linder and Susie Rawles on the matter of, respectively, the flowers and decorative arts in this painting.

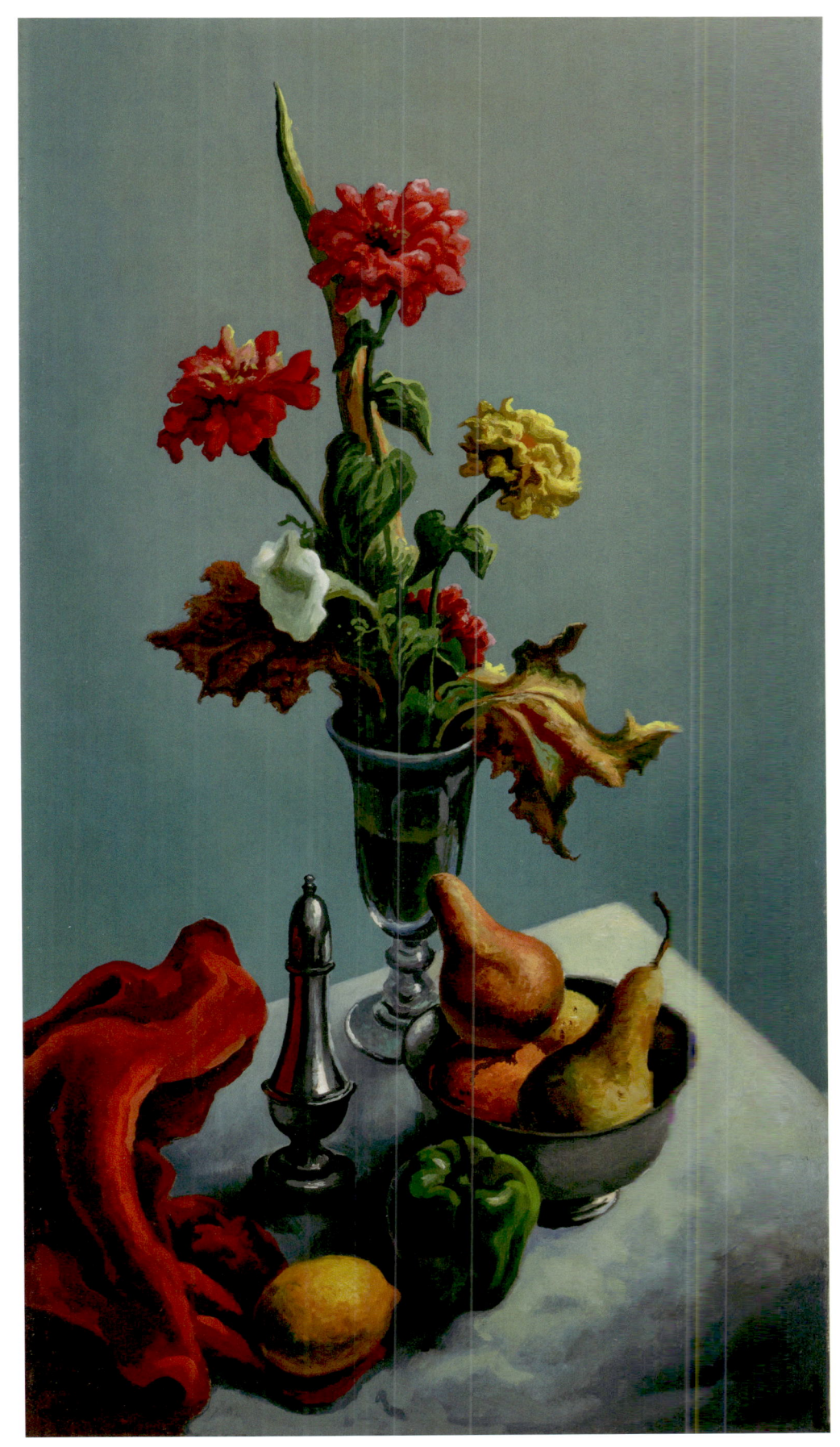

Reginald Marsh

AMERICAN, 1898–1954

On Fifth, 1939
Tempera on panel
18½ × 12½ inches

IN THIS PAINTING, two fashionably dressed women sporting stylish hats stand on the sidewalk before a gray and brown building. The figure at right wears a pink outfit, and the woman at left wears a gray skirt and a black top. They are flanked by a male mannequin in a display window and a Bonwit Teller sign. The signage and the painting's title suggest that they are on Fifth Avenue near Fifty-Sixth Street—the midtown Manhattan flagship location of this famous department store (fig. 1). The position of their arms and legs joins their facial expressions to suggest a moment in time, a reaction or sensibility that will change quickly. The loose application of the tempera medium upon the panel contributes to the dynamism of the picture, yielding the sensation of figures in motion—and perhaps coming to a momentary stop.

On Fifth is a signature work by a member of the so-called Fourteenth School group of artists (ca. 1920–1950) who found social realist subject matter in the hordes of individuals populating the stores, buses, banks, trains, restaurants, and other public sites around Union Square and Fourteenth Street in lower Manhattan and, as this painting shows, further uptown. The primary artists of this group were Isabel Bishop, Reginald Marsh, Kenneth Hayes Miller, and Raphael Soyer. Their work depicts Black and white, and rich and poor subjects alike, with special attention, as Marsh's *On Fifth* demonstrates, to the New Woman, the quintessential shopper-worker-provocateur of 1920s–1940s America.[1] In this painting, the women's purses indeed suggest their role as consumers.

The allusion to Bonwit Teller provides much of the meaning in *On Fifth*. Beginning in 1923 and continuing well into the World War II years, the store set out to make its premises into something like an art museum. Under the public relations direction of Estelle Hamburger, its advertisements and display windows sought to merge commerce and culture, art and advertising. Surely in response to the ever-present New Woman model, a 1934 Bonwit Teller publicity campaign illuminated the "woman's angle," and by 1938 the company would name a woman—Mary Lewis—as a vice president. Merging a sense of artistic appeal with the promise of "fashionable self-presentation," the company empowered women as consumers in these years.[2] In *On Fifth*, Marsh took notice of what we might call the Bonwit Teller promise—the artful embrace of style that comes from just being associated with the store. In a group of photographs taken the year after the painting's completion, Marsh depicted women before the store's windows, continuing his investigation into the intersection of womanhood, fashion, and consumerism.

LEO MAZOW

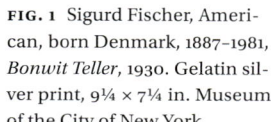

FIG. 1 Sigurd Fischer, American, born Denmark, 1887–1981, *Bonwit Teller*, 1930. Gelatin silver print, 9¼ × 7¼ in. Museum of the City of New York

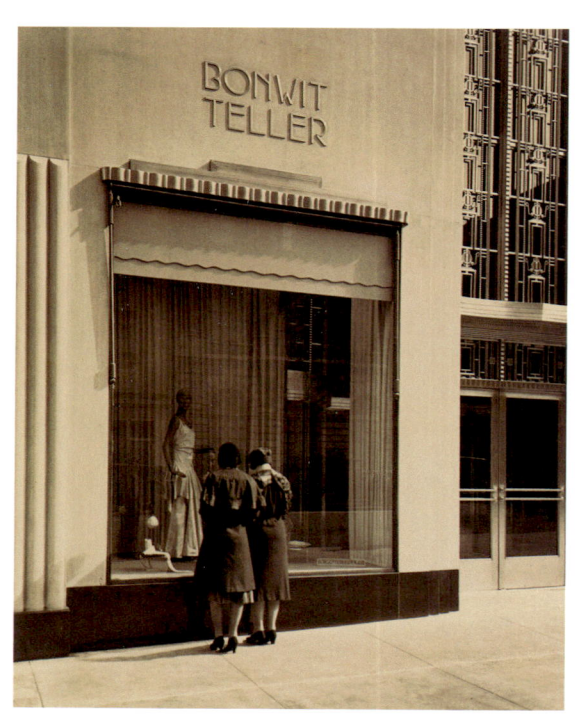

1. See Ellen Wiley Todd, *The "New Woman" Revised: Painting and Gender Politics on Fourteenth Street* (Berkeley: University of California Press, 1993).

2. Marie Clifford, "Working with Fashion: The Role of Art, Taste, and Consumerism in Women's Professional Culture, 1920–1940," *American Studies* 44 (Spring/Summer 2003): esp. 59, 71; quotations on 71 and 79.

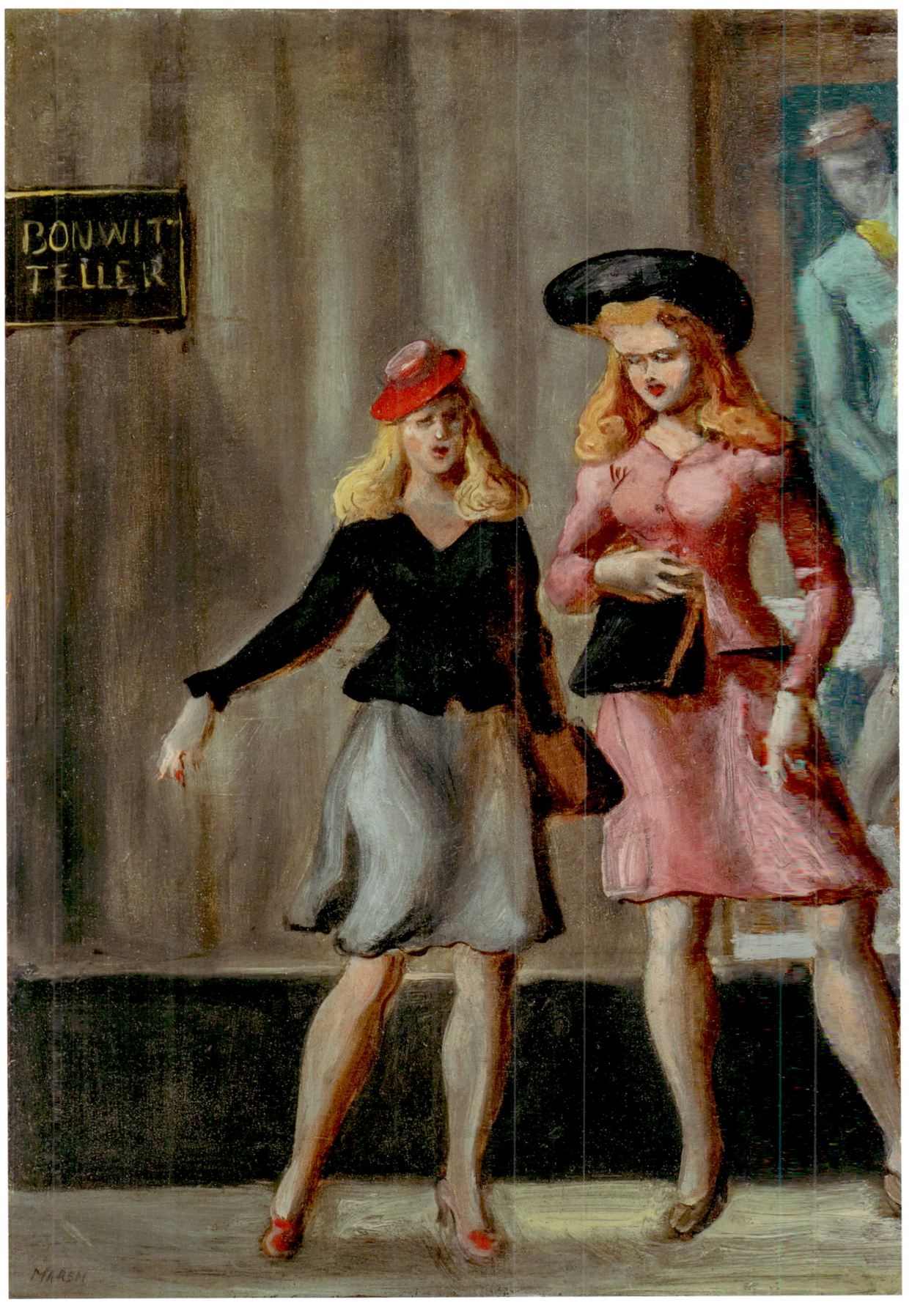

Hovsep Pushman

AMERICAN, 1877–1966

In Silent Challenge, 1941
Oil on panel
25¾ × 23⅛ inches

ARMENIAN-BORN HOVSEP PUSHMAN began to study at the Constantinople School of Art at age eleven. Regarded as a prodigy, he was the youngest student ever accepted. He came to the United States at seventeen, began teaching art in Chicago, and maintained success throughout his career. In 1916 the Art Institute of Chicago presented twenty-one portrait paintings by Pushman, with the show receiving rave reviews. The subjects came from across the globe—a Nubian princess, a "Hillsman of Kurdistan"—and also allegorical figures such as a female Narcissus. These portraits, with their bold, jewel-like colors, were noted by one critic to exude "a universal symbolism or language of color."[1] At this same time, Pushman developed an interest in Eastern cultures, particularly Chinese mysticism, that would come to dominate his mature work.

He spent some years in Paris, where he studied at the Académie Julian under Adolphe Déchenaud, Jules-Joseph Lefebvre, and Tony Robert-Fleury. Pushman exhibited at the Salon des Artistes Français and won medals for his painting in 1914 and 1921. After first settling in California, where he opened a studio and helped to form the Laguna Beach Art Association, Pushman returned to Paris for two years before relocating permanently to New York City. His success continued in New York with one solo exhibition at the Grand Central Art Galleries in 1932, selling on the first day all of the sixteen paintings included.

Later in his career, Pushman refined his syncretic style, continuing to focus on allegory but through the still life genre. As a collector of Asian art, he compiled his objects into scenic tableaus painted in his highly detailed style. Pushman often repeated motifs, using the same figurines in different variations, such as one polychrome wood figure of a portly Chinese sage that appears in the paintings *In Silent Challenge* and *The War God* (ca. 1940). The title for *In Silent Challenge* refers to the central seated figurine's obdurate posture, with hands on his hips, gazing at a small black jar before him. In the background is a Chinese painting of a saddled horse adorned with Imperial caparison, a commonly used backdrop for Pushman's still lifes. The figure's intent stare at the object before him could be tied to broader Eastern philosophy, perhaps reflecting a Buddhist kōan or a Confucian legend. The viewer is tasked with putting the different narrative elements together, a practice noted to be shared with French genre painter Jean-Baptiste-Siméon Chardin.[2] Both moralizing and emotionally charging, Pushman remains an underappreciated yet significant figure in American art.

CHELSEA PIERCE

1. Evelyn Marie Stuart, "The Dawn of a Colorist," *Fine Arts Journal* 34, no. 2 (1916): 79–84.

2. Lawrence J. Cantor, "Hovsep Pushman, 1877–1966: The Armenian Spirit Glorified in Art," *America's Distinguished Artists* series, Traditional Fine Arts Organization, 2010, https://www.tfaoi.org/newsm1/n1m664.htm.

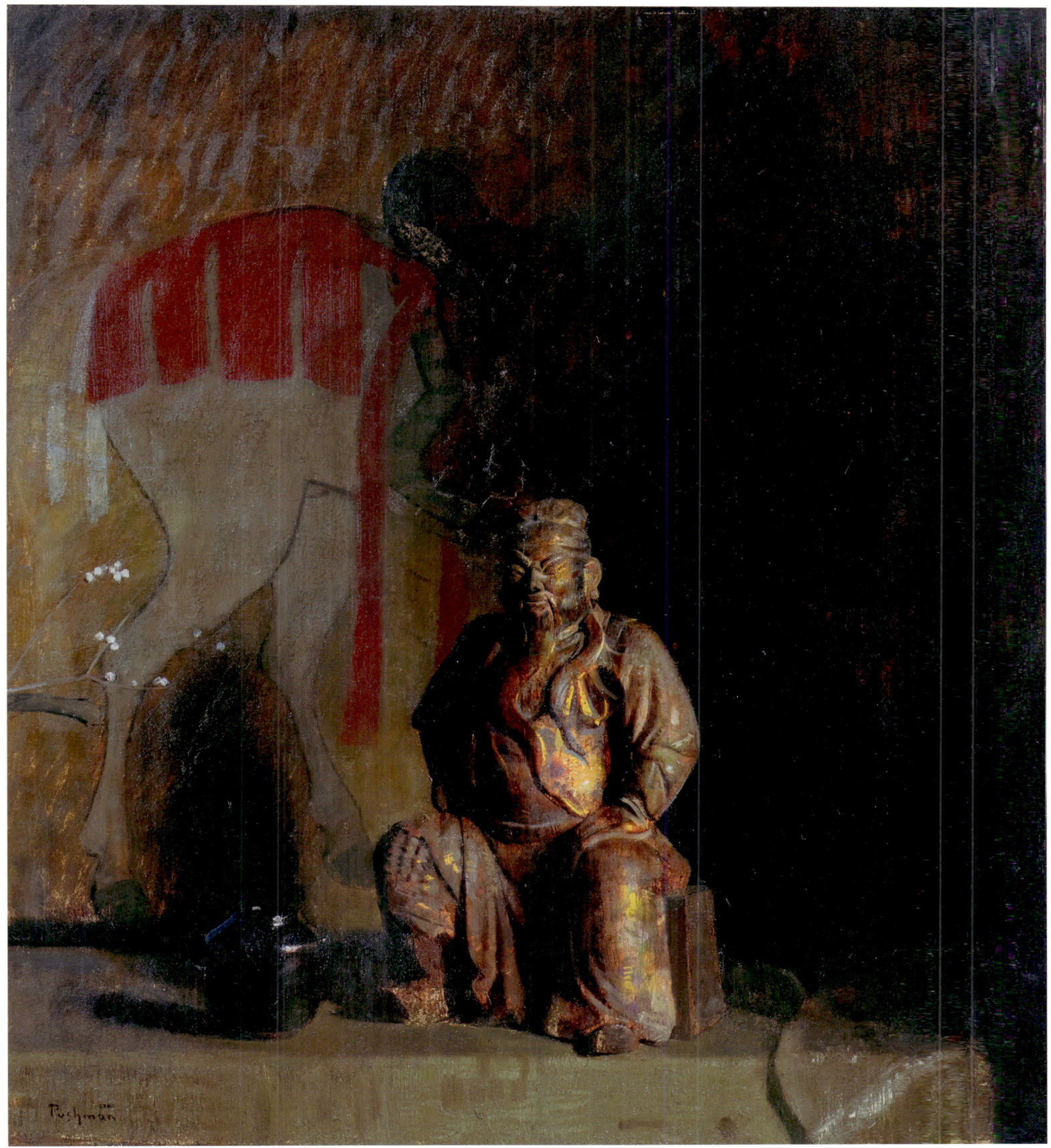

William Baziotes

AMERICAN, 1912–1963

Figures in a Landscape (Pierrot II), 1948

Oil on canvas

20 × 24 inches

Gift of the Macon and Joan Brock Collection of American Art, 2023.4.8

BAZIOTES'S FANTASTICAL FIGURES of the late 1940s, ranging from the bizarre to amusing, defined his breakthrough period. Though playful in their appearance, these paintings featuring simplified shapes often belied nuanced or outright mysterious meanings.

Figures in a Landscape (Pierrot II) visually conjures an enigmatic, dreamlike world. The inspiration for the cycloptic figures in this painting and other works from the same period reveal the range of Baziotes's artistic interests and sources, from prehistoric forms to mythology to the motif of the target.[1] *Figures in a Landscape* appears closely related to *Pierrot* (1947; National Gallery of Art, Washington, DC), and the title *Pierrot II* was later appended to this work.[2] Although one scholar cautioned, "Baziotes was well known to apply a name [to his work] for no other reason than whimsy," the imagery is suggestive of the pantomime character from the seventeenth-century *commedia dell'arte* or Italian performance troupe.[3] Typically dressed in a loose, white costume wearing white face makeup, the character evolved over centuries into a fixture of popular culture as the trope of a clown, loner, or melancholic sufferer (fig. 1). In *Pierrot II*, the lopsided body is painted an electric green rather than white. This silly figure emerges from a deep-blue background; the verdant palette suggests an aquatic or botanical world. With the title in mind, the strange, chair-like form to the left may allude to a stage prop or interior setting. Baziotes's works are open ended as to their meanings. Is the misshapen, childlike figure the innocent foppish Pierrot or, because of its unstable body and strange setting, a mystical visitor from another world?

The son of Greek parents, William Baziotes grew up in Reading, Pennsylvania. From 1931 to 1933, while working at a local glass company, he attended evening sketch classes, where he met the local poet Byron Vazakas. Vazakas nurtured the young artist's interest in poetry by introducing him to the work of Charles Baudelaire and the French Symbolists. Their preference for the illogical or intuitive over the rational and expected had a significant impact on Baziotes's work as well as on his fellow emerging modern artists. In 1933 Baziotes moved to New York and enrolled in the National Academy of Design. From 1936 to 1941, the Works Progress Administration (WPA) Federal Art Project employed him first as an art teacher and then in the easel division, where he met the Surrealist émigrés who fled Europe during the war who had a major influence on his artistic development. He experimented with automatic drawing, a Surrealist technique that gave free rein to unconscious imagery, and was similarly fascinated by a stream-of-consciousness approach to his art. Baziotes later founded the short-lived Subjects of the Artist School, aimed at promoting avant-garde art and Abstract Expressionism, with David Hare, Robert Motherwell, and Mark Rothko. From 1952 until his death, Baziotes taught at the Brooklyn Museum Art School, New York University, and Hunter College.

ERIN MONROE

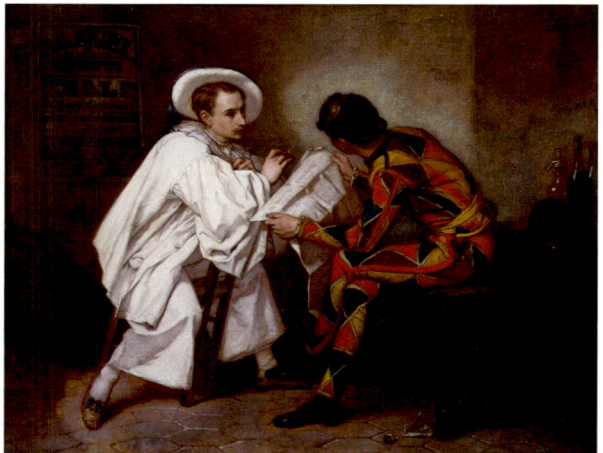

FIG. 1 Thomas Couture, French, 1816–1879, *Pierrot the Politician*, 1857. Oil on canvas, 44½ × 57½ in. Chrysler Museum of Art, Gift of Walter P. Chrysler, Jr., dedicated by the Trustees to Thomas G. Johnson, Jr., in gratitude for his long and distinguished service to the Chrysler, June 2005, 71.2064

1. Barbara Cavaliere, "William Baziotes: The Subtlety of Life for the Artist," in *William Baziotes: A Retrospective Exhibition* (Newport Beach, CA: Newport Harbor Art Museum, 1978), 45.

2. When the Brock Collection acquired the work from Thomas Colville Fine Art, the canvas was assigned this title based on the visual similarity to the work at the National Gallery of Art. The Baziotes expert Michael Preble noted the stylistic comparison between the two. Preble also suggested Baziotes's interest in clowns dated to earlier in his career, as evidenced by "a more literal version in *Untitled, Clown and Apple*, 1940, illustrated in the Guggenheim Venice Collection catalogue, page 60." See also *Untitled (Circus Clowns)*, ca. 1935, sold Christie's Online Sale #2013825, February 25–March 11, 2021, Lot 79.

3. Email with Michael Preble, editor of the *William Baziotes Catalogue Raisonné*, November 2022. My thanks to Michael for sharing insights regarding stylistic comparisons with other works by Baziotes. He noted, "The broad, almost frantic brushstrokes of *Pierrot II* do indeed mimic those of *Pierrot*, NGA. Interestingly, this stroke is more associated with earlier work, particularly those of the early 1940s in his alliance with cubistic elements. That technique hung around until about 1952 when *The Flesh Eaters* [Met Museum] began his next turn. I think *Night Form*, 1947, from Washington University, St. Louis, deserves a moment's attention; *Cyclops* from AIC; and *Mirror Figure*, 1948 [present location unknown], illustrated in the Guggenheim Memorial show catalogue, 1965."

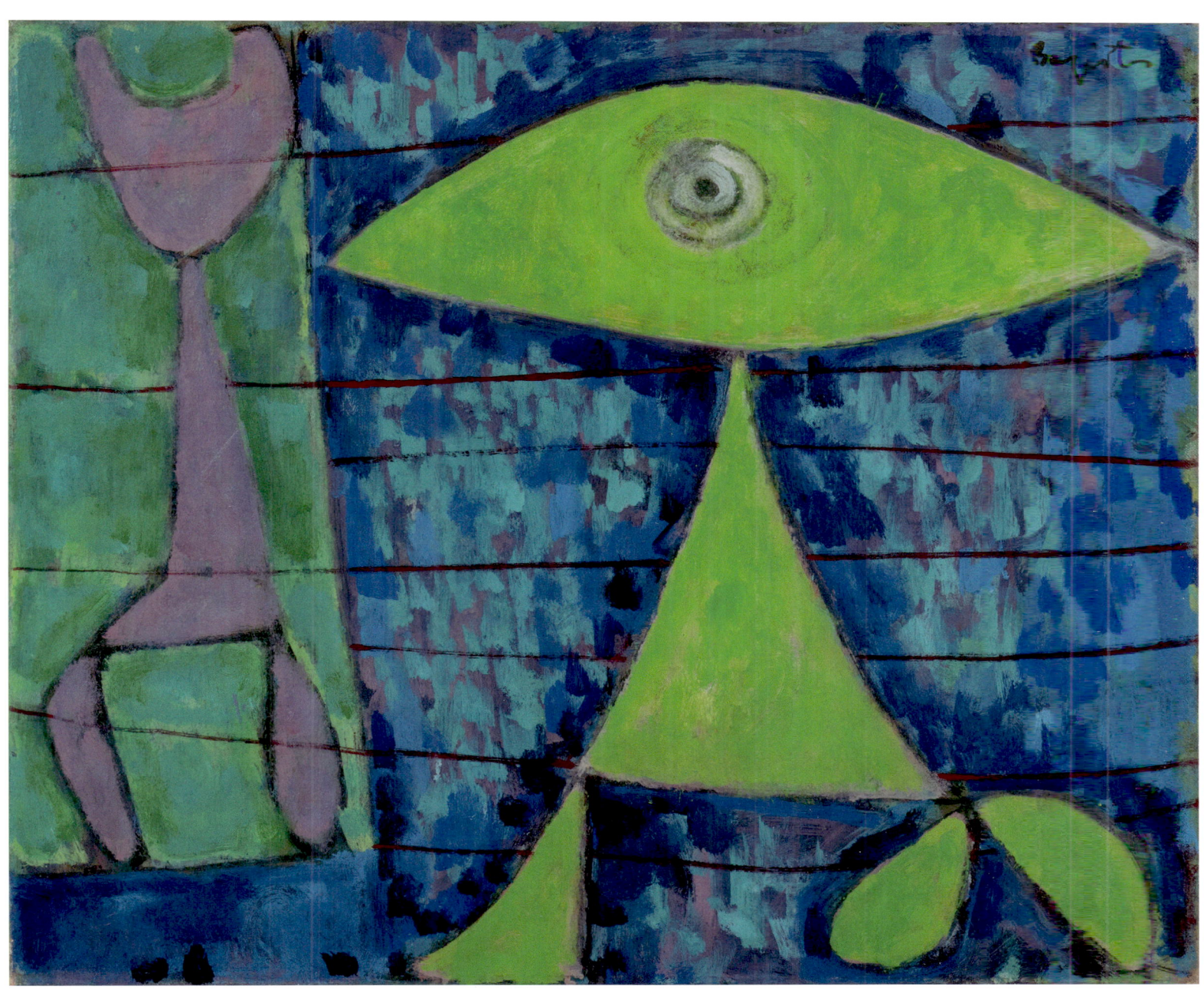

Sally Michel Avery

AMERICAN, 1902–2003

Autumn, 1956

Oil on canvas

42 × 24 inches

Gift of the Macon and Joan Brock Collection of American Art, 2023.4.9

SALLY MICHEL AVERY'S ART is often discussed in relation to that of her husband, fellow artist Milton Avery. For forty years Milton and Sally were inseparable, and their artistic visions evolved side by side. Recent scholarship, however, has recognized a mutual influence and no longer considers Sally's work to be solely derivative of Milton's.[1] Their respective painting styles have parallels, but each remains unique.

Born in Brooklyn in 1902, Sally knew she wanted to be an artist from an early age. She began freelance work after high school, creating fashion illustrations for Macy's Department Store. She later attended the Art Students League in Manhattan and then met Milton Avery one summer in Gloucester. Her dedication mirrored his daily routine, rising early and sketching all day. At the time Milton was painting impressionist works and living with his family in Connecticut. He soon followed Sally to New York, and they married in 1926. In 1932 they welcomed their daughter, March. In the 1930s Sally helped support Milton's career and the Avery family by completing freelance illustrations for *The New York Times,* various children's books, and other publications.

By the 1940s Milton became established as a modern artist, and soon after that Sally was able to devote more time to her own career. The family enjoyed annual road trips and excursions outside New York City. This included several summer stays at artist retreats such as Yaddo in Saratoga Springs, New York, and the MacDowell Colony in Peterborough, New Hampshire. Sally's shift from commercial to fine artist in the 1950s may have been facilitated and even encouraged by these experiences.[2] *Autumn* may have been inspired by the changing New Hampshire landscape viewed during their time at the MacDowell Colony in 1956. Her eye-popping color choices combine tones of yellow and peach alongside teals and blues. The expressionistic palette lends her work an emotional force.[3] Using the positive and negative spaces flattened and modernized her landscapes. As in *Autumn,* she achieves a unified composition where the leaves and foliage inhabit in a single plane, like a patchwork quilt or stained-glass window.

Following Milton's passing in 1965, Sally continued to champion his legacy but also blossomed as an artist. She worked for another twenty-five years, creating fresh, colorful paintings. As the contributions of women artists are increasingly recognized, she is receiving her due for helping to rethink and refresh Realist painting in the second half of the twentieth century. She died in 2003 at the age of one hundred.

ERIN MONROE

1. See Deedee Wigmore, *Sally Michel: Reshaping Realism, 1950–1985* (D. Wigmore Fine Art, Inc., March 2–May 18, 2022); and Roberta Smith, "A Singular American Painter and His Perennially Disregarded Wife," *New York Times*, May 12, 2022, C12.

2. Kenneth E. Silver, "On the Road with Milton, Sally, and March," *Summer with the Averys: Milton, Sally, March* (Greenwich, CT: Bruce Museum, 2019).

3. Smith, "A Singular American Painter and His Perennially Disregarded Wife."

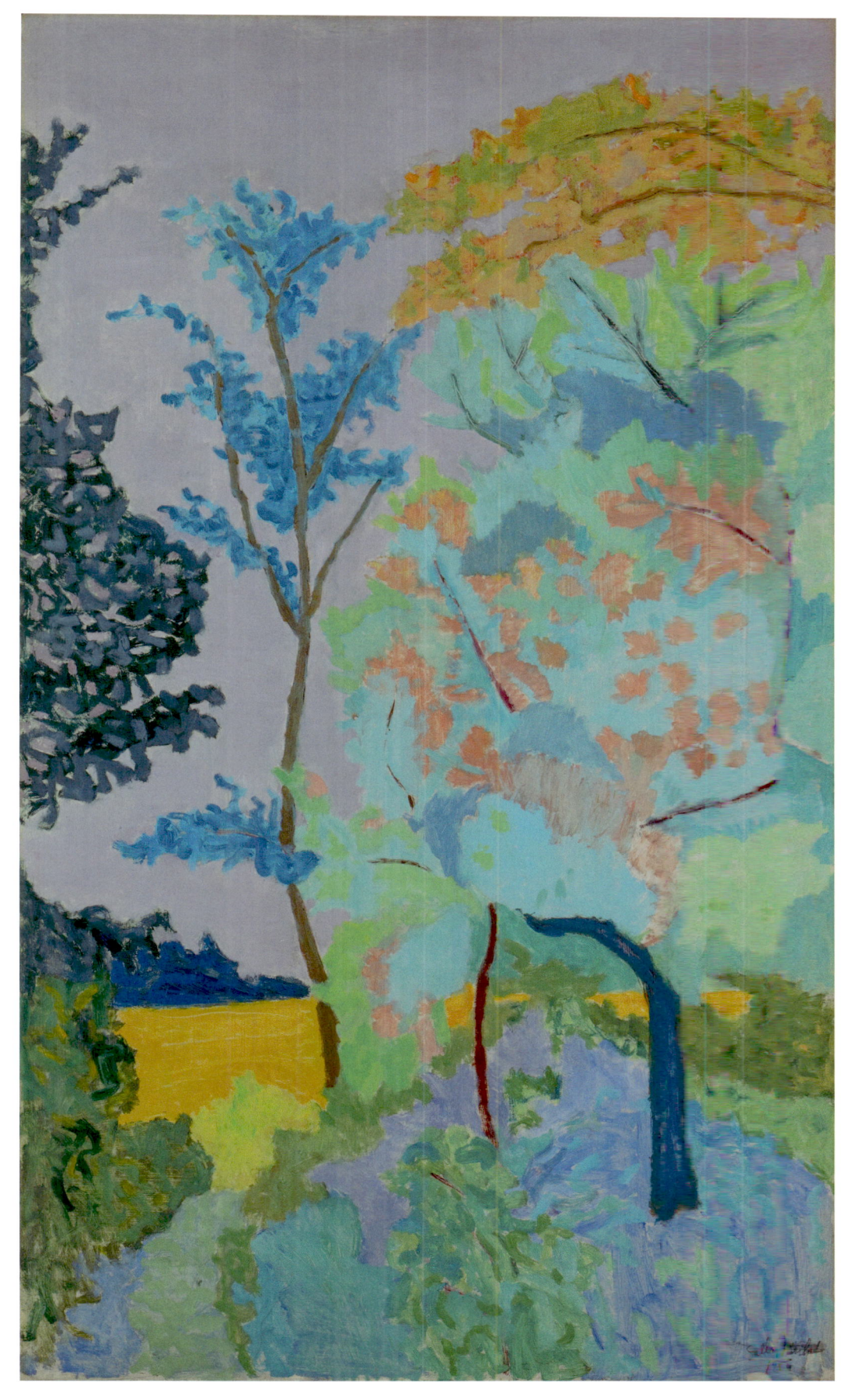

Milton Avery
AMERICAN, 1885–1965

Dancing Trees, 1953
Oil on canvas
32 × 48 inches

FROM HIS IMPRESSIONISTIC LANDSCAPES to late large-scale abstractions, Milton Avery's art reflected the dramatic evolution of modern painting by midcentury. Avery never affiliated with any one group, instead forging his own unique path throughout a forty-year career. As one scholar noted, "Avery does not fit neatly into any formal account of American painting. . . . [T]here was always a sense that [his] work stood slightly apart from current tendencies or movements."[1]

Milton Avery was born in 1885 in Altmar, New York, to a working-class family that later settled near Hartford, Connecticut. At age twenty he enrolled in the Connecticut League of Art Students. For another two decades, he continued taking art classes in the city while working full time in various local factories. In 1924 he met Sally Michel, a fellow artist, in Gloucester, Massachusetts. They married in 1926 and then moved to New York City, welcoming their daughter March in 1932. Sally continued to support the family as a freelance illustrator while Milton found his artistic footing throughout the 1930s. As a result, they lived frugally and spent many nights at home, hosting a lively mix of art-world friends at their apartment. The two made weekly visits to museums and evening drawing classes, further shaping Avery's development. In the mid-1940s, he secured representation by the Paul Rosenberg Gallery and received critical acclaim for his distinctive compositional style. He earned the designation as a "colorist" for his unique and expressive use of the palette and interlocking forms of solid color, reminiscent of jigsaw puzzles.

The Averys called New York City home and made annual summer trips throughout New England and along the Eastern Seaboard, searching for inspiration outside the built environment. Their destinations included Cape Cod, New Hampshire, Upstate New York, and Vermont. Canvases such as *Dancing Trees* evidence Avery's enduring interest in landscape painting throughout his career. Throughout the 1950s his experiments with color and shallow, flattened spaces lent his work a modern feel. As he employed "non-associative" or expressionistic colors—also described as poetic—his trees appeared blue, and grasses became pink.[2] His longtime friend and fellow artist Mark Rothko once proclaimed, "Poetry penetrated every pore of the canvas to the very last touch of his brush."[3] Invoking the painting's title, the wiggly, slender trees lend the scene a joyful mood. *Dancing Trees* also reveals Avery's evolution from his earliest impressionistic landscapes to more distilled representations of nature rendered with solid masses. Wide bands of yellow and pink bracket the central line of overlapping green and blue trees. Avery's

experiments with texture are also on display here. He scratched crosshatched white lines into the wet paint surface to convey texture in the tree foliage.

Pared-down works such as *Sea Gull* reveal a greater degree of abstraction in Avery's approach to figurative portraits and paintings of animals from the 1950s. He radically simplified his subjects, subtracting details and leaving only the essential elements on the canvas. The seabird's body is beautifully silhouetted against a black abyss, unifying color—or in this case, white—and form. The horizontal bands at the top and bottom allude to sky and sand (or a sea wall?), maintaining a subtle connection to reality. As one critic noted, "Avery is able to deal with subject matter in such a way that the subject slips in and out of recognition, yet is never completely lost, teetering precariously on the edge of interpretation."[4] Avery also achieved smoother areas of color by applying pigment with a rag, giving his canvases a greater flatness. The spare qualities of this painting presaged the large-scale, Rothko-esque geometric abstractions Avery created several years later.

Avery's unique ability to balance a traditional approach with innovation, confidence with reserve, earned him a distinctive place in modern art. As the reticent artist famously stated, "Why talk when you can paint?" His paintings champion the understated beauty of the world around us. By relying on the expressiveness of painting, he created a poetic body of work that continues to inspire fellow artists and art audiences today.

ERIN MONROE

1. Edith Devaney, "Milton Avery: 'Poetic-Inventor,'" in *Milton Avery* (London: Royal Academy of Arts, 2021), 22.

2. Devaney, "Milton Avery," 28.

3. Mark Rothko, "Tribute to Milton Avery, 1965," Milton Avery papers, 1926–1982, bulk 1950–1982. Archives of American Art, Smithsonian Institution.

4. Thomas H. Garver, "Los Angeles: Milton Avery, U.C. Irvine," *Artforum* 9 (April 1971).

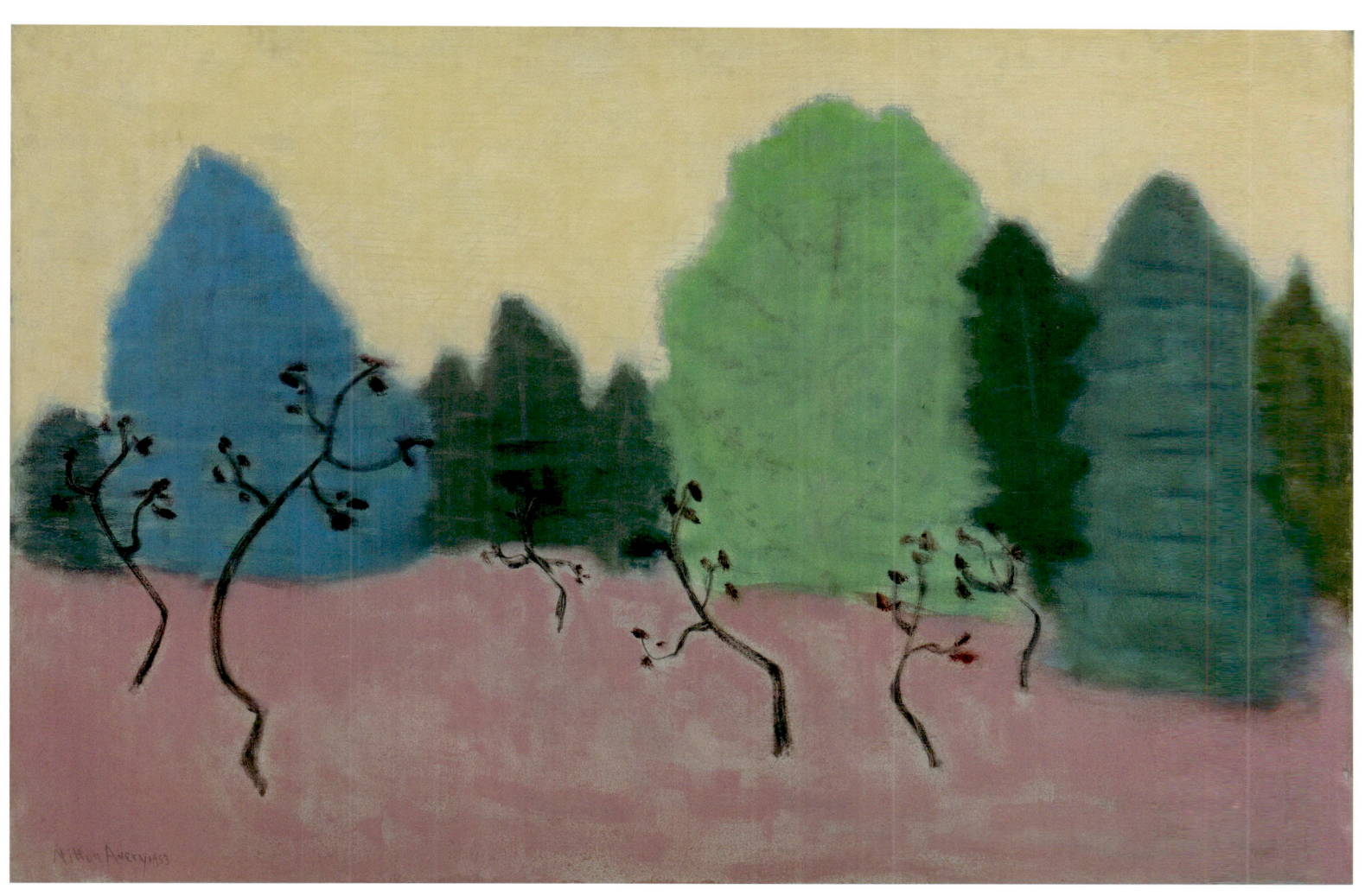

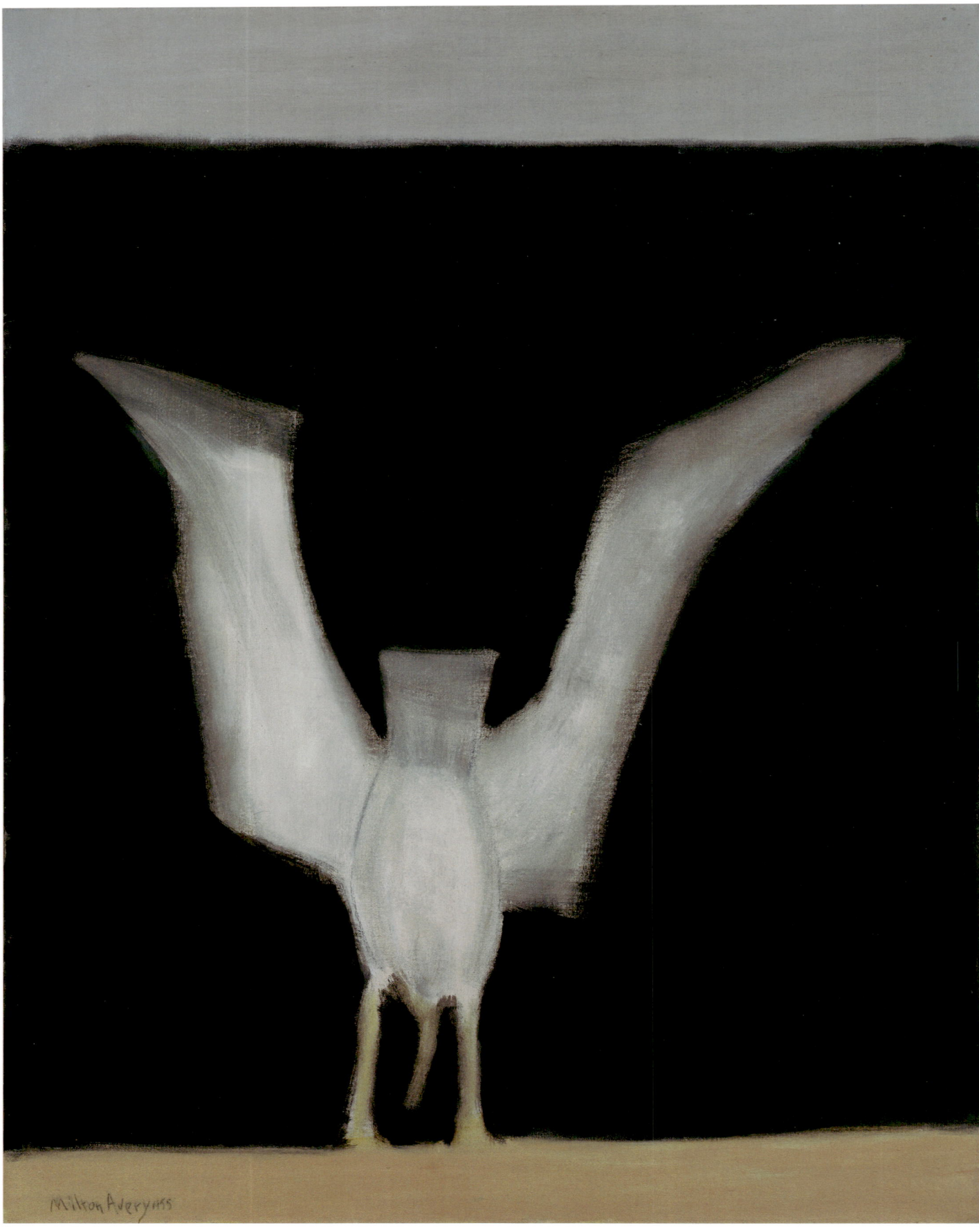

Sea Gull, 1955
Oil on canvas
38 × 26 inches

Promised Gift of the Macon and Joan Brock Collection
of American Art

Fairfield Porter

AMERICAN, 1907–1975

Still Life with White Boats, 1968

Oil on canvas

20 × 20 inches

FAIRFIELD PORTER WAS A REALIST painter working during the peak of the Abstract Expressionist movement in the United States. The art critic Clement Greenberg warned him off painting representative pictures, yet this only further encouraged Porter to continue the pursuit of his own style.[1] Despite resisting the dominant mode of Abstraction, Porter had a successful career as a painter and art critic. Porter's father was an architect and art lover who instilled his passion for Italian Baroque paintings and classical architecture in his son. Born in the suburbs of Chicago in 1907, Porter studied art history at Harvard under Arthur Pope, receiving his degree in 1928 and immediately enrolling in the Art Students League in New York as a drawing student. He visited Italy, where he met the imitable art historian Bernard Berenson and together visited galleries looking at old master paintings. However, it was an exhibition of Jean-Édouard Vuillard and Pierre Bonnard that Porter saw in Chicago in 1938 that would leave a lasting impression on the artist.

Porter met the young poet Anne Channing in New York City, and the two were married in 1932. The couple stayed in New York for a couple of years before moving to Winnetka, Illinois, and then to Peekskill, New York. It was upstate where Porter met Willem de Kooning and Elaine Fried (later de Kooning), forging a lifelong friendship. The Porters made the final move in 1949 to Southampton, New York, to be connected to the city and the beach, a proximity that allowed for frequent meetings with the poet and artist circles at the Cedar Tavern in Manhattan, a famous haunt for creatives in the 1950s and 60s. Through de Kooning, Porter was introduced to John Bernard Myers, who ran the Tibor de Nagy Gallery and held a solo show for Porter in 1951. That same year Elaine de Kooning introduced him to the editor at *ArtNews*, where Porter began writing art reviews. In his critical writing, Porter's breadth of knowledge, garnered from his formal study of art, was presented through the filter of an artist's eye. Porter later wrote reviews for *The Nation* until 1961, when he turned his full attention to painting.

In his youth Porter spent summers at a house on Great Spruce Head Island off the coast of Maine, designed and built by his architect father. Porter inherited the property and continued visits with his own family. It is from the porch of this waterfront home that he painted *Still Life with White Boats* (fig. 1). The painting features the breakfast table in the screened porch room that looks out to the rugged Maine landscape. On the table lays a pitcher and a plate bearing red fruit. In the scene beyond the house depicted through the panes of the window, Porter captured the white sailboats in the harbor. While this room at Porter's Great Spruce Head house appears in several of the artist's paintings, the composition of *Still Life with White Boats* is exceptional. One reviewer commented on the painting's details as well as "the Matisse-like aspect of brilliant exteriors seen through a window flanked by a still-life study."[2] Porter's mastery of light is seen in the reflection of the table's surface exuding the realism that he pursued for himself and that would inspire a younger generation of Realists.

CHELSEA PIERCE

FIG. 1 The porch at Fairfield Porter's Great Spruce Head Island home, black-and-white photograph, Fairfield Porter papers, Archives of American Art, Smithsonian Institution, Washington, DC

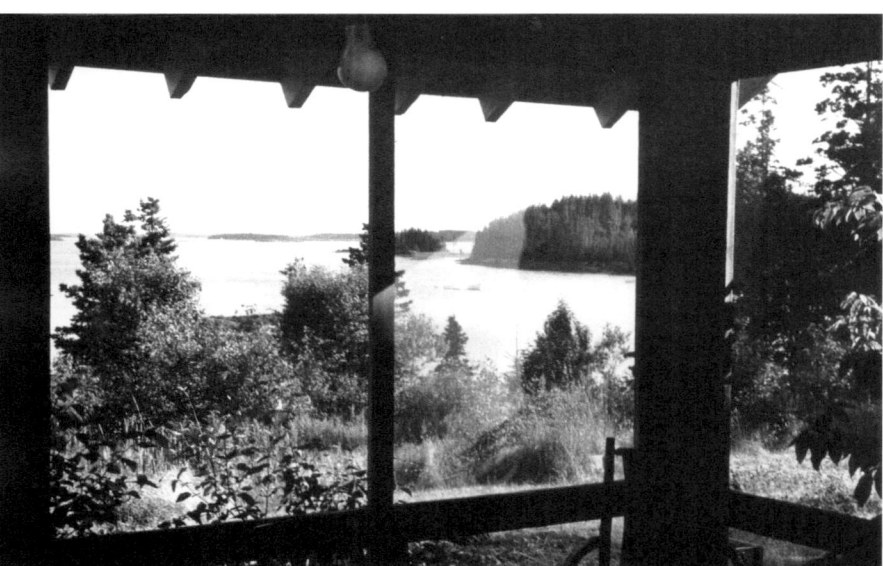

1. Rackstraw Downes, "Fairfield Porter: The Painter as Critic," *Art Journal* 37, no. 4 (1978): 306–12. Downes writes that Porter recounted Greenberg's feedback with, "If that's what he says, I think I will do just exactly what he says I can't do! . . . I might have become an abstract painter except for that."

2. Jud Yalkut, "Figuration/Abstraction: Fairfield Porter/Willem de Kooning," *Dialogue: Arts in the Midwest* 18, no. 6 (November/December 1995): 20.

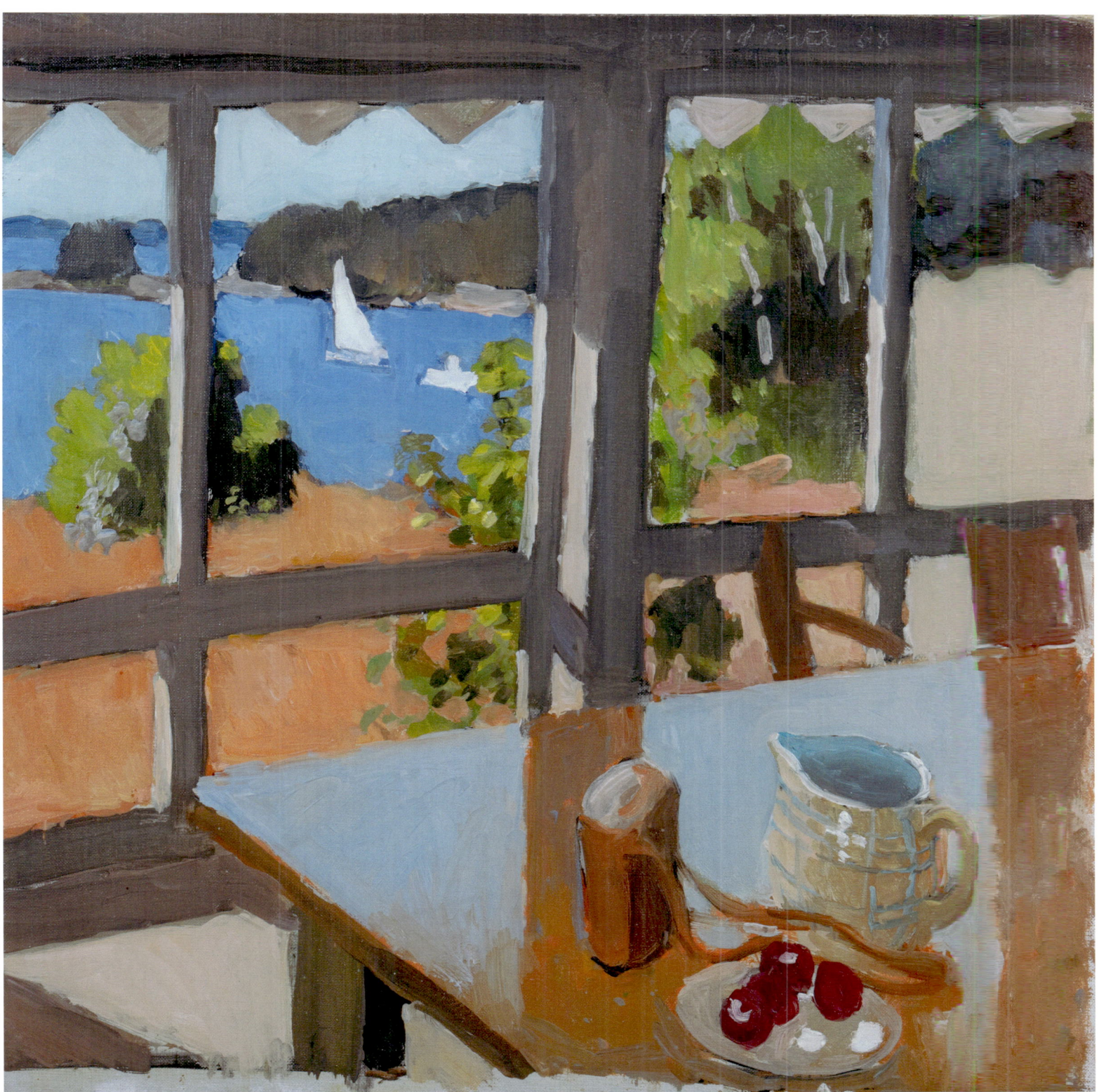

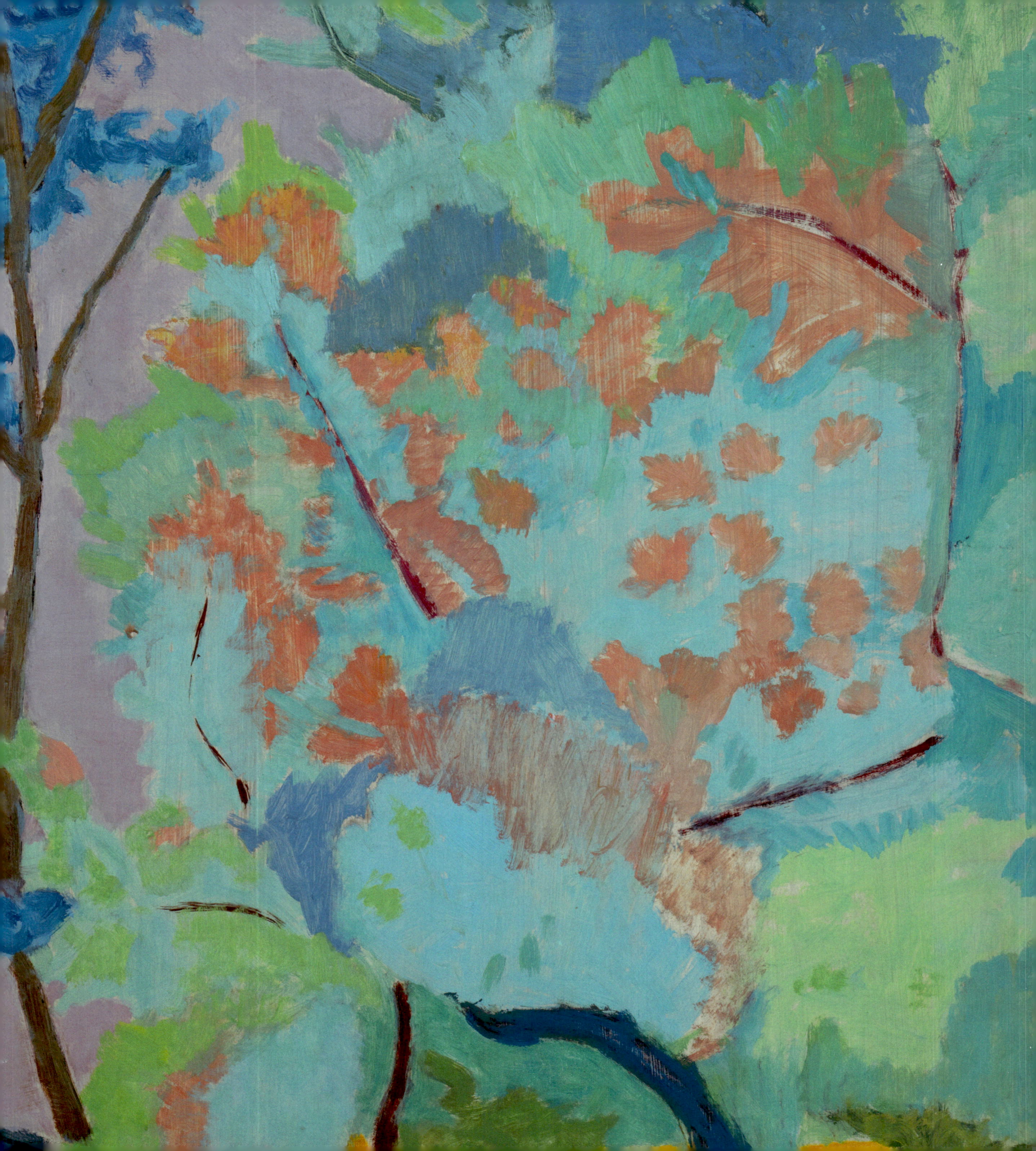

Checklist

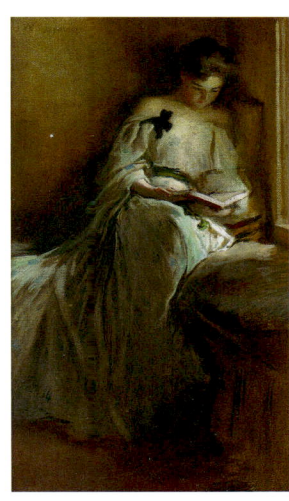

John White Alexander
American, 1856–1915
The Favorite Corner, ca. 1895–98
Oil on canvas
24 × 14 inches
Promised Gift of the Macon and Joan Brock
Collection of American Art

PROVENANCE
Mrs. John White Alexander
Gift to the Mint Museum of Art, Charlotte,
North Carolina
Christie's, *Important American Paintings,
Drawings, and Sculpture*, December 3,
1997, lot 28
Private collection, 1997–2015
The Macon and Joan Brock Collection of
American Art, 2015

EXHIBITION HISTORY
*American Paintings from Southern
Collections*, Columbia Museum of Art
and Science, Columbia, South Carolina,
July–August 1982.

PUBLICATION HISTORY
[Possibly] *Catalogue of Paintings: John
White Alexander* (Pittsburgh, PA: Depart-
ment of Fine Arts, Carnegie Institute,
1916), p. 59 [as *Girl Reading* owned by
Mrs. John White Alexander].

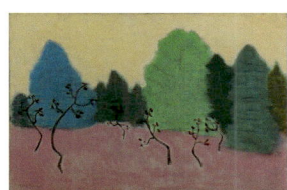

Milton Avery
American, 1885–1965
Dancing Trees, 1953
Oil on canvas
32 × 48 inches

PROVENANCE
Donald Morris Gallery Birmingham,
Michigan
Private collection, 1979
Sotheby's, New York, May 21, 2014, lot 27
The Macon and Joan Brock Collection of
American Art, 2014

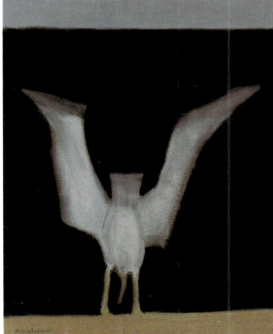

Sea Gull, 1955
Oil on canvas
38 × 26 inches
Promised Gift of the Macon and Joan Brock
Collection of American Art

PROVENANCE
Donald Morris Gallery Bloomfield Hills,
Michigan
Mr. and Mrs. Clifford West, Bloomfield
Hills, Michigan, by 1962
Maurice and Margo Cohen, New York,
by 1982
Private collection, Greenwich, Connecti-
cut, 2006
The Macon and Joan Brock Collection of
American Art, 2015

EXHIBITION HISTORY
Milton Avery, Whitney Museum of
American Art, New York, September 16–
December 5, 1982, no. 172.

PUBLICATION HISTORY
Hilton Kramer, *Milton Avery: Paintings
1930–1960* (New York: Thomas Yose of,
1962), no. 37, illus. [as *Sea Gull*].
Barbara Haskell, *Milton Avery* (New York:
Whitney Museum of American Art
in assoc. with Harper & Row, 1982),
not illus.

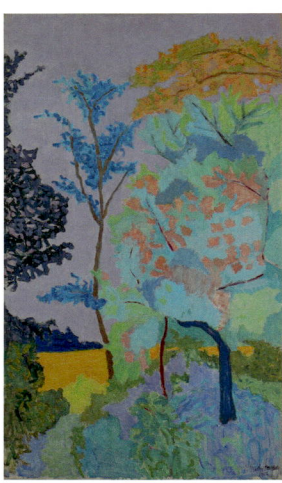

Sally Michel Avery
American, 1902–2003
Autumn, 1956
Oil on canvas
42 × 24 inches
Gift of the Macon and Joan Brock Collection of American Art, 2023.4.9

PROVENANCE
Milton and Sally Avery Arts Foundation
D. Wigmore Fine Art, Inc.
The Macon and Joan Brock Collection of American Art, 2015

EXHIBITION HISTORY
Sally Michel: Rhythms of Light and Color, D. Wigmore Fine Art, New York, November 16, 2015–January 13, 2016.

PUBLICATION HISTORY
Tom Wolf, *Sally Michel: Rhythms of Light and Color* (New York: D. Wigmore Fine Art, 2015), p. 25.

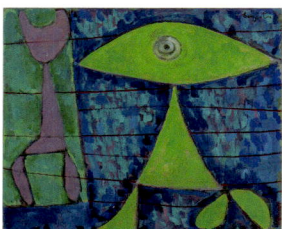

William Baziotes
American, 1912–1963
Figures in a Landscape (Pierrot II), 1948
Oil on canvas
20 × 24 inches
Gift of the Macon and Joan Brock Collection of American Art, 2023.4.8

PROVENANCE
Kootz Gallery, New York
Private collection, New Jersey (acquired from the above)
Thence by descent to the former owner
Sotheby's, New York, November 17, 2021, lot 151
Thomas Colville Fine Art
The Macon and Joan Brock Collection of American Art, 2022

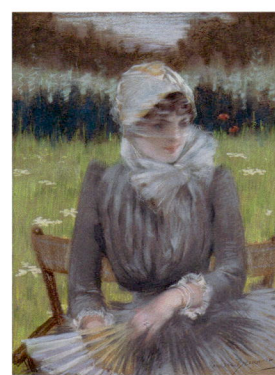

James Carroll Beckwith
American, 1852–1917
The Grey Gown, 1882
Pastel on paper
32 × 24½ inches
Promised Gift of the Macon and Joan Brock Collection of American Art

PROVENANCE
The artist
H. Wunderlich & Co., until 1890
J. M. Lichtenauer, 1890
American Art Galleries, 1913
Dr. George C. F. Williams, Hartford, Connecticut
The Macon and Joan Brock Collection of American Art, 2013

EXHIBITION HISTORY:
Fourth Exhibition of the Society of Painters in Pastel, H. Wunderlich & Co., New York, May 1–24, 1890, no. 14.
Collection of an Amateur: American and European Pictures Collected by the Late J. M. Lichtenauer, Esq., American Art Galleries, New York, February 22–27, 1913, no. 147.

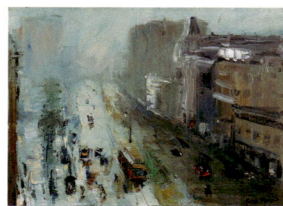

George Bellows
American, 1882–1925
Upper Broadway, 1907
Oil on board
11½ × 15½ inches
Promised Gift of the Macon and Joan Brock Collection of American Art

PROVENANCE
Gift to Mrs. Lillian Story Griffin
H. V. Allison & Co., New York
Katherine Hepburn
Sotheby's, New York, May 19, 2004, lot 110
Berry-Hill Galleries, New York
Private collection
The Macon and Joan Brock Collection of American Art, 2012

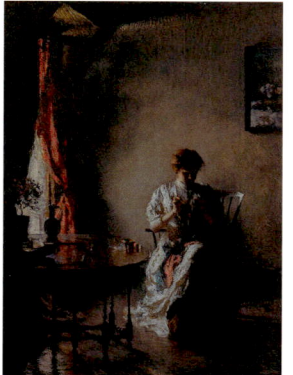

Frank Weston Benson
American, 1862–1951
The Seamstress, 1913
Oil on canvas
36 × 26 inches
Promised Gift of the Macon and Joan Brock Collection of American Art

PROVENANCE
Mr. and Mrs. Sabin Woolworth Colton II, Philadelphia, ca. 1920s
By descent to Rosalind Colton Hoge
Christie's, *American Art*, May 22, 2013, lot 125
The Macon and Joan Brock Collection of American Art, 2013

EXHIBITION HISTORY

Buffalo Fine Arts Academy, Buffalo, New York, 1913.

The Inaugural Exhibition, Memorial Art Gallery, University of Rochester, Rochester, New York, October 8–29, 1913, no. 7.

Special Exhibit, Museum of Fine Arts, Boston, 1914.

The Ten American Painters, 17th Annual Exhibition, The Montross Gallery, New York, 1914, no. 1.

One Hundred and Tenth Annual Exhibition, Pennsylvania Academy of the Fine Arts, Philadelphia, February 7–March 28, 1915, no. 378.

Special Loan Exhibition of Paintings by Frank W. Benson and the Late Edmund C. Tarbell, Museum of Fine Arts, Boston, November 16–December 15, 1938.

PUBLICATION HISTORY

The Inaugural Exhibition (Rochester, NY: The Memorial Art Gallery, 1913), pp. 14, 46, no. 7, illus.

F. A. Bedford, *Frank W. Benson: American Impressionist* (New York: Rizzoli, 1994), p. 47.

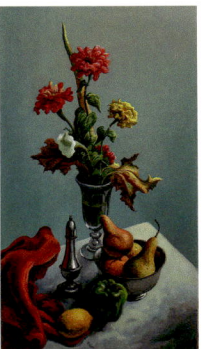

Thomas Hart Benton

American, 1889–1975
Still Life with Flowers and Fruit, 1948
Oil and tempera on panel
29½ × 16¼ inches

PROVENANCE

From the artist to private collection, Kansas City

By descent to private collection, Maryland

Private collection, Ohio

The Macon and Joan Brock Collection of American Art, 2007

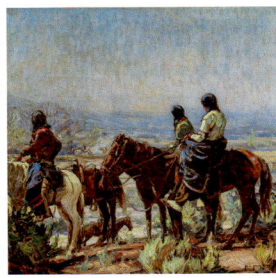

Carl Oscar Borg

American, 1879–1947
Watching the Race
Oil on canvas
30 × 30 inches

PROVENANCE

Maxwell Gallery, San Francisco

Mable Corbett Moore, 1975

Sotheby's, New York, May 24, 2000, lot 158

Private collection

Sotheby's, New York, December 3, 2008, lot 122

The Macon and Joan Brock Collection of American Art, 2008

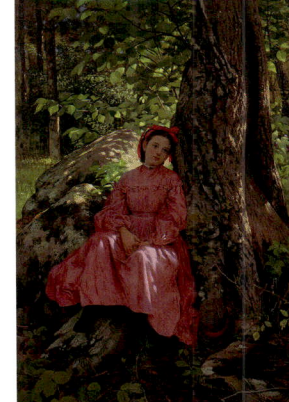

John Leslie Breck

American, 1860–1899
Apple Trees in Bloom, ca. 1892–93
Oil on canvas
18¼ × 22 inches
Promised Gift of the Macon and Joan Brock Collection of American Art

PROVENANCE

Margaret Breck

Private collection, Massachusetts

Woodside Antique and Estate Auction, Farmville, North Carolina, 2010

Thomas Colville Fine Art

The Macon and Joan Brock Collection of American Art, 2010

EXHIBITION HISTORY

[Possibly] *J. L. Breck Memorial Exhibition*, National Arts Club, New York, February 24–March 10, 1900, no. 4.

Building a Legacy: Chrysler Collects for the Future, Chrysler Museum of Art, Norfolk, Virginia, November 13, 2021–March 5, 2022.

John George Brown

American, 1831–1913
Resting in the Woods (Girl Under a Tree), 1866
Oil on canvas
18 × 12¼ inches
Promised Gift of the Macon and Joan Brock Collection of American Art

PROVENANCE

Hermann Warner Williams, Washington, DC, late 1930s

George P. Guerry, New York

Mr. and Mrs. Ferdinand H. Davis, New York

Lee B. Anderson, New York

Robert Mann, Miami

Hirschl & Adler Galleries, New York, 1973

Jo Ann and Julian Ganz, Jr., 1973

Sotheby's, *American Paintings, Drawings & Sculpture*, December 3, 2003, lot 4

The Macon and Joan Brock Collection of American Art, 2008

EXHIBITION HISTORY

[Probably] *Forty-Second Annual Exhibition*, National Academy of Design, New York, 1867, no. 552.

The American Vision, Paintings 1825–1875, M. Knoedler & Co., Hirschl & Adler Galleries, Paul Rosenberg and Co., New York, October–November 1968, no. 65, illus.

The Good Life, An Exhibition of American Genre Painting, Museum of Fine Arts, St. Petersburg, Florida; Loch Haven Art Center, Orlando, Florida, September–November 1971, no. 6, p. 40, illus.

18th and 19th Century Paintings from Private Collections, Whitney Museum of American Art, New York, June–September 1972, no. 7.

American Paintings, Watercolors and Drawings from the Collection of Jo Ann and Julian Ganz, Jr., Santa Barbara Museum of Art, Santa Barbara, California, June–July 1973, no. 12, illus.

Tradition and Innovation, American Paintings 1860–1970, Meredith Long & Company, Houston, January 1974, no. 3, p. 15, illus.

A Century and a Half of American Art, National Academy of Design, New York, October–November 1975, pp. 37–38, illus.

An American Perspective: Nineteenth-Century Art from the Collection of Jo Ann and Julian Ganz, Jr., National Gallery of Art, Washington, DC; Amon Carter Museum, Fort Worth, Texas; Los Angeles County Museum of Art, October 1981–September 1982, p. 117, illus. in color p. 56.

Country Paths and City Sidewalks: The Art of J. G. Brown, George Walter Vincent Smith Art Museum, Springfield, Massachusetts, March–December 1989, no. 34, illus. in color p. 43.

American ABC: Childhood in 19th-Century America, Iris and B. Gerald Cantor Center for Visual Arts, Stanford University, Stanford, California, February–May, 2006, no. 9.

Our Community Collects: From Durer to Warhol and Beyond, Chrysler Museum of Art, Norfolk, Virginia, September 21–December 31, 2011.

PUBLICATION HISTORY

Donelson Hoopes, "The Jo Ann and Julian Ganz, Jr., Collection," *American Art Review* (September–October 1973): 52, illus.

Linda Ayres, "An American Perspective: Nineteenth-Century Art from the Collection of Jo Ann and Julian Ganz, Jr.," *The Magazine Antiques* (January 1982), p. 266, illus. in color pl. XIII.

Claire Perry, *Young America: Childhood in Nineteenth-Century Art and Culture* (New Haven, CT: Yale University Press, 2006), illus. in color p. 39.

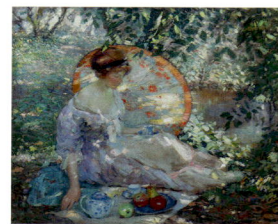

Karl Albert Buehr
American, 1866–1952
Breakfast on the Green, ca. 1911–12
Oil on canvas
31½ × 39 inches

PROVENANCE
Rogers Park Women's Club, Chicago
Mongerson-Wunderlich Gallery, Chicago, 1970s
Private collection, 1990
Hirschl & Adler Galleries
The Macon and Joan Brock Collection of American Art, 2011

EXHIBITION HISTORY
107th Annual Exhibition, Pennsylvania Academy of the Fine Arts, Philadelphia, 1912, no. 63 [as *The Lunch*].

25th Annual Exhibition of American Paintings and Sculpture, Art Institute of Chicago, 1912, no. 25 [as *Breakfast on the Green*].

Fourth Exhibition of Oil Paintings by Contemporary American Artists, Corcoran Gallery of Art, Washington, DC, 1912–13, no. 181 [as *Un Déjeuner sur L'Herbe*].

Panama-Pacific International Exposition, San Francisco, 1915, no. 4089 [as *Luncheon Outdoors*].

The Giverny Luminists: Frieseke, Miller, and Their Circle, Berry-Hill Galleries, New York, 1995–96 [as *Le Déjeuner sur L'Herbe*].

Fort Wayne Collects II, Fort Wayne Museum of Art, Fort Wayne, Indiana, 1997.

PUBLICATION HISTORY
William H. Gerdts, *Monet's Giverny: An Impressionist Colony* (New York: Abbeville Press, 1993), pp. 194–95, pl. 163.

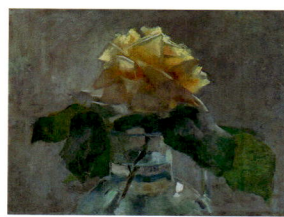

Dennis Miller Bunker
American, 1861–1890
Yellow Rose, ca. 1885
Oil on panel
10½ × 13¾ inches

PROVENANCE
The Macon and Joan Brock Collection of American Art, 2015

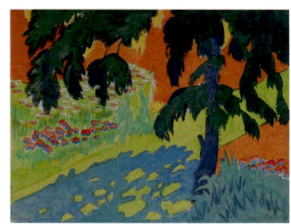

Charles Ephraim Burchfield
American, 1893–1967
Hot Morning, 1915
Watercolor, gouache, and pencil on cream
 wove paper
9 × 11⅞ inches
Promised Gift of the Macon and Joan Brock
 Collection of American Art

PROVENANCE
Possibly held by Kennedy Galleries,
 New York
Thomas Colville Fine Art
The Macon and Joan Brock Collection of
 American Art, 2015

EXHIBITION HISTORY
Watercolor: An American Medium, Chrys-
 ler Museum of Art, Norfolk, Virginia,
 February 21–June 23, 2019.

PUBLICATION HISTORY
Slide 368 in Charles E. Burchfield Foundation's slides of the artist's estate.

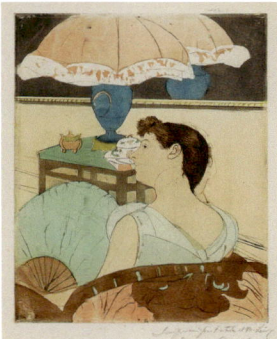

Mary Cassatt
American, 1844–192
The Lamp, 1890–91
Drypoint, soft ground etching, and aquatint
 printed in colors, on laid paper
12¾ × 9⅞ inches; sheet: 17 × 11⅞ inches
Museum purchase with funds given by
 the Macon and Joan Brock Collection of
 American Art, 2023.12

PROVENANCE
Christie's, New York, November 6, 1995, lot 28
Wolf Family Collection, No. 1112 (acquired
 from the above)
Sotheby's, New York, April 20, 2023, lot 460

PUBLICATION HISTORY
Adelyn Dohme Breeskin, *Mary Cassatt: A
 Catalogue Raisonné of the Graphic Work*
 (Washington, DC: Smithsonian Institution
 Press, 1979), no. 144, p. 141.
Nancy Mowll Mathews and Barbara Stern
 Shapiro, *Mary Cassatt: The Color Prints*
 (Williamstown, MA: Williams College
 Museum of Art, 1989), no. 6, pp. 111–13.

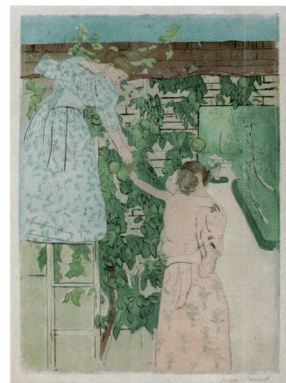

Gathering Fruit, ca. 1893
Drypoint, soft ground etching, and aquatint printed in colors, on laid paper
16⅝ × 11¾ inches; sheet: 20 × 13½ inches
Museum purchase with funds given by
 the Macon and Joan Brock Collection of
 American Art, 2022.28

PROVENANCE
Private collection, Chicago
Heritage Auctions, Dallas, November 5,
 2022, lot 67094

EXHIBITION HISTORY
Art Institute of Chicago, n.d.

PUBLICATION HISTORY
Nancy Mowll Mathews and Barbara Stern
 Shapiro, *Mary Cassatt: The Color Prints*
 (Williamstown, MA: Williams College
 Museum of Art, 1989), no. 5, pp. 157–58.

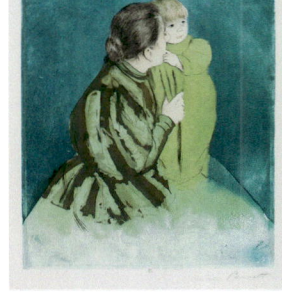

Peasant Mother and Child, ca. 1894
Drypoint and aquatint printed in colors, on
 laid paper
11¾ × 9½ inches; sheet: 19⅛ × 17⅛ inches
Museum purchase with funds given by
 the Macon and Joan Brock Collection of
 American Art, 2022.27

PROVENANCE
Gift from the artist to her second cousin,
 Mrs. Thomas A. Scott
Thence by descent to Edgar Scott, her
 grandson
Property from the Collection of Edgar and
 Helen Hope Montgomery Scott, Christie's, New York, April 29, 1996, lot 84
Ann and Gordon Getty
Christie's, New York, October 21, 2022,
 lot 173

PUBLICATION HISTORY
Adelyn Dohme Breeskin, *Mary Cassatt: A
 Catalogue Raisonné of the Graphic Work*
 (Washington, DC: Smithsonian Institu-
 tion Press, 1979), no. 155, p. 153.
Nancy Mowll Mathews and Barbara Stern
 Shapiro, *Mary Cassatt: The Color Prints*
 (Williamstown, MA: Williams College
 Museum of Art, 1989), no. 7, pp. 163–73.

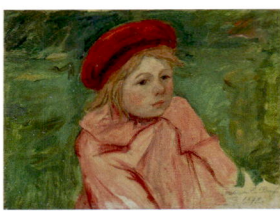

Little Girl in a Red Beret (Le béret rouge),
 1898
Oil on canvas
9½ × 13 inches

PROVENANCE
Estate of the artist
Mathilde Valet, Chateau de Beaufresne,
 France, 1927
Sold: Galerie A.M. Reitlinger, Paris, France,
 "Mathilde X" sale, May–June 1931, lot 2,
 illus. [as *Le béret rouge*]
Sold: Hôtel Drouot, Paris, France, May 4,
 1933, no. 43 [as *Le béret rouge*]
Acquavella Galleries, New York
Private collection, Texas, by 1979
Coe Kerr Gallery, New York, 1985
Private collection, 1985 (acquired from the
 above)
Sotheby's, New York, December 4, 2013,
 lot 39
The Macon and Joan Brock Collection of
 American Art, 2013

EXHIBITION HISTORY
Douane Centrale Exposition, Paris
 (stamped on the reverse).
American Impressionism, Coe Kerr Gallery,
 New York, November–December 1985,
 no. 8.

PUBLICATION HISTORY
Adelyn Dohme Breeskin, *Mary Cassatt:
 A Catalogue Raisonné of the Oils, Pastels,
 Watercolors, and Drawings* (Washington,
 DC: Smithsonian Institution Press, 1970),
 no. 103, p. 65.

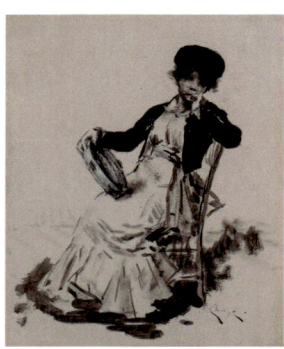

William Merritt Chase
American, 1849–1916
Spanish Roma Girl, ca. 1881–84
Ink and gouache on paper, mounted
 to card
18¼ × 13 inches
Promised Gift of the Macon and Joan Brock
 Collection of American Art

PROVENANCE
Moore's Art Gallery, New York, Chase sale,
 March 2–3, 1887, no. 18
Private collection, New York
Doyle, *American Paintings, Furniture &
 Decorative Arts*, May 5, 2021, lot 77
The Macon and Joan Brock Collection of
 American Art, 2021

EXHIBITION HISTORY
*Exhibition of Pictures, Studies, and Sketches
 by M. Wm. M. Chase, Under the Auspices
 of the American Art Association*, Boston
 Art Club, November 13–December 4,
 1886.

PUBLICATION HISTORY:
A Book of the Tile Club (Boston and New
 York: Houghton Mifflin and Co., 1887),
 p. 76.
Ronald G. Pisano et al., *The Complete Cata-
 logue of Known and Documented Work
 by William Merritt Chase (1849–1916)*,
 Vol. 1: *The Paintings in Pastel, Monotypes,
 Painted Tiles and Ceramic Plates, Water-
 colors, and Prints* (New Haven, CT, and
 London: Yale University Press, 2006),
 no. W.10, p. 74, illus.

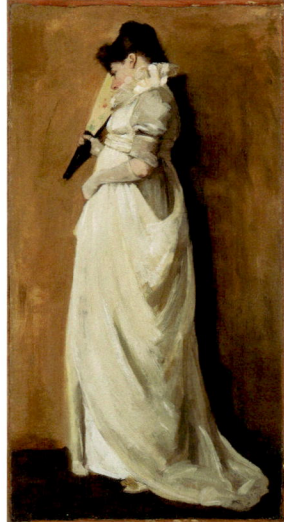

Woman in White Satin, ca. 1885
Oil on canvas, mounted on wood
22¹³⁄₁₆ × 11¹¹⁄₁₆ inches

PROVENANCE
John J. Bowden, Bayside, New York, 1949
George Guerry, New York, 1959
Mr. and Mrs. Leroy Davis, New York,
 1959–68
Terry Davis, New York, 1968–75
Mimi and Sanford Feld, 1975–2013
Sanford Feld, 2013–15
The Macon and Joan Brock Collection of
 American Art, 2015

EXHIBITION HISTORY
William Merritt Chase, Davis Galleries,
 New York, 1959, no. 15.
*American Paintings and Drawings from
 the Collection of Mr. and Mrs. Leroy
 Davis*, Everson Museum of Art, Syracuse,
 New York, 1960, no. 2.
*Selections from the Collection of Mimi and
 Sanford Feld*, Pennsylvania State Uni-
 versity Museum of Art, University Park,
 and Aspen Center for Visual Arts, Aspen,
 Colorado, 1981, no. 1.

PUBLICATION HISTORY
*Chase Centennial Exhibition: Checklist
 of Known Work by William M. Chase*
 (Indianapolis: John Herron Art Museum,
 1949).
Ronald G. Pisano, "Addendum Files"
 (unpublished) of *The Complete Catalogue of Known and Documented Work
 by William Merritt Chase (1849–1916)*
 (New Haven, CT, and London: Yale
 University Press, 2006), no. FAA.75.

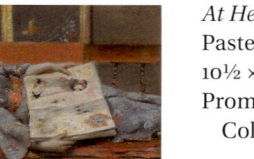

At Her Ease, ca. 1889
Pastel on panel
10½ × 16 inches
Promised Gift of the Macon and Joan Brock
 Collection of American Art

PROVENANCE
Private collection
Beard Galleries, Minneapolis, 1918
William Macbeth, Inc., New York, 1920

J. J. Gillespie Company, Fine Art Galleries,
Pittsburgh
Mr. Moorhead Benezet Holland, Pitts-
burgh, mid-1930s
Private collection by descent
The Macon and Joan Brock Collection of
American Art, 2015

EXHIBITION HISTORY
*Seventeenth Annual Chicago Inter-State
Industrial Exposition*, September 4–
October 19, 1889, no. 81.

PUBLICATION HISTORY
"Art Matters in Chicago," *Chicago Daily
Tribune*, October 20, 1889, p. 27.
Ronald G. Pisano et al., *The Complete Cata-
logue of Known and Documented Work
by William Merritt Chase (1849–1916)*,
Vol. 1: *The Paintings in Pastel, Monotypes,
Painted Tiles and Ceramic Plates, Water-
colors, and Prints* (New Haven, CT, and
London: Yale University Press, 2006),
p. 25, pl. 58.

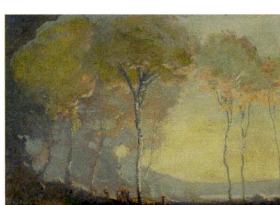

Arthur B. Davies
American, 1862–1928
Nymphs Rejoicing, ca. 1920–28
Oil on panel
21½ × 30 inches
Promised Gift of the Macon and Joan Brock
Collection of American Art

PROVENANCE
The Macon and Joan Brock Collection of
American Art, 2008

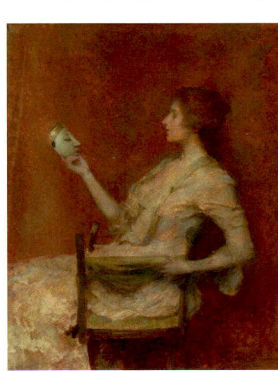

Thomas Wilmer Dewing
American, 1851–1938
The Mask, 1902
Oil on panel
20 × 15¾ inches
Promised Gift of the Macon and Joan Brock
Collection of American Art

PROVENANCE
From the artist to Frank J. Hecker, Detroit,
1902–27
To his son, Christian Henry Hecker,
Detroit, until 1963
To his wife Helen Stowe Hecker, Detroit,
until ca. 1979
To her granddaughter, Valeria Christian
Shatzel, Detroit, by 1979–97
Private collection
The Macon and Joan Brock Collection of
American Art, 2014

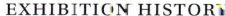

EXHIBITION HISTORY
*Fifth Annual Exhibition – Ten American
Painters*, Durand-Ruel Galleries, New
York, March 31–April 12, 1902, no. 8.
*Exhibition of Paintings by Ten American
Painters*, St. Botolph Club, Boston,
April 21–May 10, 1902, no. 8.

PUBLICATION HISTORY
*Pictures and Objects: Frank J. Hecker Inven-
tory* (Archives of American Art reel
D32, frame 925.
"Paintings Shown by Ten Americans, *New
York Herald*, March 31, 1902 p. 11.
Royal Cortissoz, "Art Exhibitions," *New
York Daily Tribune*, April 2, 1902 p. 9.
"Ten American Painters," *New York Times*,
April 2, 1902, p. 8.
"In the Galleries," *Art Interchange* 48
(May 1902): 111.
"List of objects from Frank J. Hecker
house given to his children at his death"
(5510 Woodward Avenue: Hecker Family
Archives, May 1928).
Lee Stephens Glazer, "A Modern Influence:
Thomas Dewing and Aesthetic Vision
at the Turn of the Century" (PhD diss.,
University of Pennsylvania, 1996), p. 277.
Deborah Davis, *Lowy. The Secret Lives of
Frames* (New York: Filipacc Publishing,
2007), p. 156.
Susan A. Hobbs, *Thomas Wilmer Dewing:
Beauty into Art, a Catalogue Raisonné*,
vol 1. (New Haven, CT, and London:
Yale University Press, 2018), no. 205
pp. 409–11.

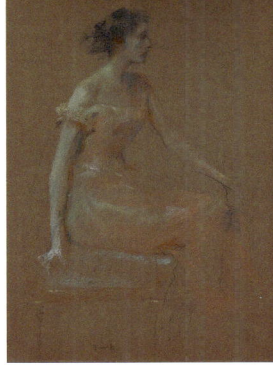

In Pink No. 1, 1910
Pastel, chalk, and graphite pencil on
brown paper
10¼ × 7 inches
Promised Gift of the Macon and Joan Brock
Collection of American Art

PROVENANCE
Anson Conger Goodyear, Buffalo, New
York, by purchase from Montross Gal-
lery, New York, probably 1911
Gift to his wife, Mary Forman Goodyear,
before 1940, the date per her son Stephen
Goodyear, who indicated that she likely
gave the pastel away
Private collection, Baltimore, after the
early 1980s
Doyle, New York, November 3, 2011, lot 301
The Macon and Joan Brock Collection of
American Art, 2012

EXHIBITION HISTORY
*Collection of Drawings Lent by Mr. and
Mrs. Anson C. Goodyear*, Buffalo Fine
Arts Academy, Buffalo, New York,
September 29–October 21, 1923, no. 27
[as *In Pink*].

PUBLICATION HISTORY
"May 17 1910 pastel no 11 finished framed &
sent to Montross named 'in Pink' May 31
1911 sold by Montross," Dewing Daybooks
(the artist's studio records, archived in
the papers of a descendant).
A. Conger Goodyear, Card File, Albright-
Knox Art Gallery, Buffalo, New York,
no. 37, unknown date.
"Collection of Drawings Lent to the
Albright Art Gallery by Mr. and
Mrs. Anson C. Goodyear," *Academy Notes*
(BFAA), vol. 18 (July–December 1923): 61,
illus. 58 in an installation.
Susan A. Hobbs, *Thomas Wilmer Dewing:
Beauty into Art, a Catalogue Raisonné*,
vol. 2 (New Haven, CT, and London:
Yale University Press, 2018), no. 469,
pp. 834–35.

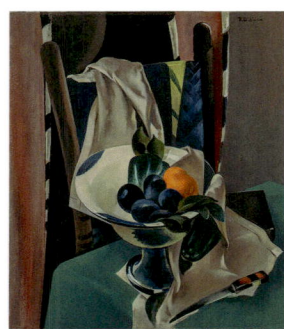

Preston Dickinson
American, 1889–1930
Still Life No. 1, ca. 1924
Oil on canvas
24 × 20 inches
Promised Gift of the Macon and Joan Brock
Collection of American Art

PROVENANCE
Daniel Gallery, New York
Ferdinand Howald, Columbus, Ohio, 1924
Columbus Gallery of Fine Arts, Columbus,
Ohio, 1931 (gift from the above)
Hirschl & Adler Galleries, New York
Andrew Crispo Gallery, New York (sold:
Sotheby's, New York, December 3, 1987,
lot 290, illus. in color)
Dr. Irwin Goldstein, New Jersey (acquired
at the above sale)
The Regis Collection, Minneapolis
Salander-O'Reilly Galleries, New York
Acquired by the former owner from the
above, 2005
Sotheby's, New York, November 20, 2014,
lot 29
The Macon and Joan Brock Collection of
American Art, 2014

EXHIBITION HISTORY
Paintings by Modern Americans, Daniel
Gallery, New York, 1924.
[Possibly] *Preston Dickinson*, Daniel
Gallery, New York, 1924.

Opening Exhibition, Gallery of Living Art,
New York University, New York, 1927–28.
Inaugural Exhibition, Columbus Gallery
of Fine Arts, Columbus, Ohio, 1931,
no. 74, illus.
*A Century of Progress: Exhibition of
Painting and Sculpture*, The Art Institute
of Chicago, 1934, no. 572, p. 76.
*Works from the Ferdinand Howald Collec-
tion*, Museum of Fine Arts, St. Peters-
burg, Florida, 1968.
The Ferdinand Howald Collection, Wilden-
stein & Co., New York, 1970, no. 54.
Paintings from the Howald Collection,
Dayton Art Institute, Dayton, Ohio, 1970.
*Six Centuries of Paintings from the
Columbus Gallery of Fine Arts*, Hopkins
Hall Art Gallery, Ohio State University,
Columbus, Ohio, 1973, no. 37.
*Modern Spirit: American Painting,
1908–1935*, Royal Scottish Academy,
Edinburgh, Scotland; Hayward Gallery,
London, 1977, no. 92, p. 62.
*Paris and the American Avant-Garde,
1900–1925*, Detroit Institute of Arts, 1980,
no. 6.
*American Modernism: The Shein Collec-
tion*, National Gallery of Art, Washington,
DC, May 2010–January 2011, no. 6, pp. 12,
52, 54–55, 124, 138, illus. in color p. 53.

PUBLICATION HISTORY
"The World of Art: Art in the House and in
the Galleries," *New York Times*, July 20,
1924, SM12.
Forbes Watson, "American Collections
No. 1—The Ferdinand Howald Collec-
tion," *Arts* 8, no. 2 (August 1925): 90, illus.
Columbus, Ohio, Bulletin 1 (1931), p. 11, illus.
"Preston Dickinson—Painter," *The Index
of Twentieth Century Artists* 3, no. 4
(January 1936): 510–11, 525.
Frank J. Roos, Jr., *An Illustrated Handbook
of Art History* (New York: Macmillan Co.,
1937), p. 273, illus. fig. C.
Marcia Tucker, *American Paintings in the
Ferdinand Howald Collection* (Colum-
bus, OH: Columbus Gallery of Fine Arts,
1969), no. 54, p. 39, illus.
William H. Gerdts and Russell Burke,
American Still-Life Painting (New York:
Praeger, 1971), p. 228, illus. fig. 16–11.
Ruth Cloudman, *Preston Dickinson 1889–
1930* (Lincoln, NE: Sheldon Memorial Art
Gallery, 1979), p. 28, illus. fig. 7, p. 29.
Richard Lee Rubenfeld, *Preston Dickin-
son: An American Modernist, with a
Catalogue of Selected Works* (PhD diss.,
The Ohio State University, 1985), vol. I,
pp. 137–38; vol. II, no. 95, pp. 420–21, illus.
fig. 96.

John Baker, *Henry Lee McFee and Formalist Realism in American Still Life, 1923–1936* (Lewisburg, PA: Bucknell University Press, 1987), p. 71.

"Catch a Rising Modernist," *ArtNews* (November 1988), p. 141, illus.

Michael O'Sullivan, "On Exhibit: Connecting Old and New Worlds," *Washington Post*, June 4, 2010, p. 37, illus. in color.

Stephen May, "American Modernism: The Shein Collection," *Antiques and the Arts Weekly*, June 4, 2010, p. 30, illus.

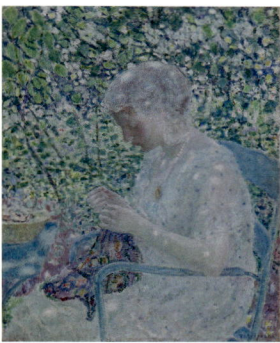

Frederick Carl Frieseke
American, 1874–1939
Girl Sewing, ca. 1917
Oil on canvas
32 × 26¼ inches

PROVENANCE
Warren Howell, San Francisco, until 1984
Gerald Wunderlich & Company, New York
From private collection to Hirschl & Adler Galleries, New York, 1986
Mr. and Mrs. Roy Furma, 1986
The Macon and Joan Brock Collection of American Art, 2009

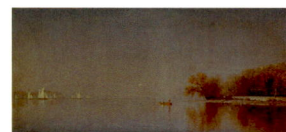

Sanford Robinson Gifford
American, 1823–1880
Tappan Zee, 1879–80
Oil on canvas
17¼ × 36¼ inches
Promised Gift of the Macon and Joan Brock Collection of American Art

PROVENANCE
Mr. Malcolm Graham
Miss Mary Douglass Graham, daughter of the above, by descent, ca. 1899
Samuel T. Hubbard, Yonkers, New York, 1914
By descent to the previous owner
Christie's, *American Art*, May 23, 2013, lot 46
The Macon and Joan Brock Collection of American Art, 2013

EXHIBITION HISTORY
A Memorial Catalogue of the Paintings of Sanford Robinson Gifford, N.A., exh. cat., The Metropolitan Museum of Art, New York, 1881, p. 45, no. 715.
Gifts of Art in Honor of Jeff Harrison, Chrysler Museum of Art, Norfolk, Virginia, November 17, 2017–March 25, 2018.

PUBLICATION HISTORY
Artist's notes, ca. 187?–3?, transcribed on S. R. Gifford, letter to Rev. O. B. Frothingham, New York, 1874.
John Ferguson Weir, *A Memorial Catalogue of the Paintings of Sanford Robinson Gifford, N.A.* (New York: The Metropolitan Museum of Art, 1881), p. 45, no. 715
I. Weiss, *Poetic Landscape: The Art and Experience of Sanford R. Gifford* (Cranbury, NJ: Associated University Presses, 1987), pp. 329, 333n7

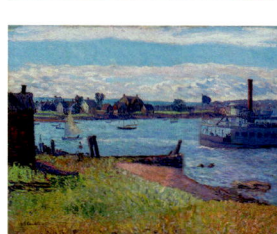

William James Glackens
American, 1870–1938
Wickford Harbor, Rhode Island, 1909
Oil on canvas
26 × 32 inches

PROVENANCE
Hirschl & Adler Galleries, New York
Montclair Art Museum, Montclair, New Jersey, 1956
Christie's, New York, May 19, 2005, lot 57
The Macon and Joan Brock Collection of American Art, 2009

EXHIBITION HISTORY
Seven/Eight: Paintings by the Canadian "Group of Seven" and the American "The Eight," The Heckscher Museum, Huntington, New York, June 18–August 1, 1982.
Personal Places: American Landscapes 1905–1930, Sarah Lawrence College Art Gallery, Bronxville, New York, February 16–April 24, 1983.
300 Years of Art in America: Masterworks from the Montclair Art Museum, Montclair Museum of Art, Montclair, New Jersey, September 1993–July 1994

PUBLICATION HISTORY
The American Painting Collection of the Montclair Art Museum (Montclair, NJ: Montclair Art Museum, 1977), p. 156, illus.
R. D. B. Carlisle, *A Jewel in the Suburbs: The History of the Montclair Art Museum* (Montclair, NJ: Montclair Art Museum, 1982), p. 60, illus.
Personal Places: American Landscapes, 1905–1930, exh. cat. (Bronxville, NY: Sarah Lawrence College Art Gallery, 1983), pp. 26–27, 71, illus.
Marilyn S. Kushner et al., *Three Hundred Years of American Painting: The Montclair Art Museum Collection* (New York: Hudson Hills Press, 1989), p. 189, no. 189, illus.

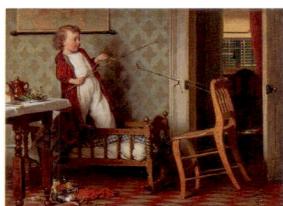

Seymour Joseph Guy
American, 1824–1910
The Big Catch (*Say! Not Too Fast!*), ca. 1862
Oil on canvas
9¼ × 12¼ inches

PROVENANCE
Skinner, *American & European Works of
Art*, February 1, 2013, lot 392
The Macon and Joan Brock Collection of
American Art, 2013

EXHIBITION HISTORY
[Possibly] National Academy of Design,
New York [as *Say! Not Too Fast!*], 1862,
no. 343.

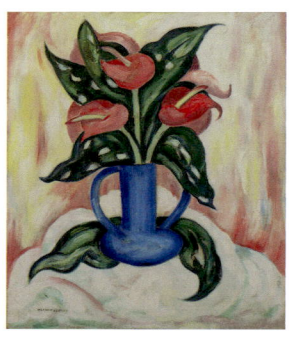

Marsden Hartley
American, 1877–1943
Volupté, 1919
Oil on canvas
24 × 20 inches
Promised Gift of the Macon and Joan Brock
Collection of American Art

PROVENANCE
Studio of the artist
Anderson Galleries, New York, 1921
Private collection, until 1997
Hollis Taggart Gallery, New York, 1997
Private collection
The Macon and Joan Brock Collection of
American Art, 2013

EXHIBITION HISTORY
*Marsden Hartley: New Mexico, 1918–1920,
An American Discovering America*,
Alexandre Gallery, New York, March 6–
April 19, 2003.

PUBLICATION HISTORY
*Seventy-five Pictures by James N. Rosenberg
and 117 Pictures by Marsden Hartley*
(New York: The Anderson Galleries,
May 17, 1921), lot 90 in auction.
Gail R. Scott, *Marsden Hartley: New Mex-
ico, 1918–1920, An American Discovering
America* (New York: Alexandre Gallery,
2003), p. 1, color illus.

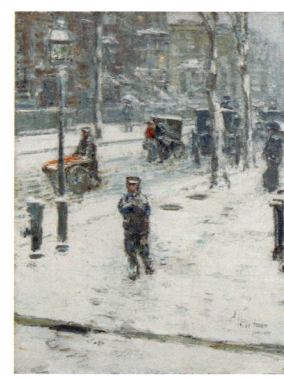

Childe Hassam
American, 1859–1935
Snowstorm, Fifth Avenue, New York, 1907
Oil on canvas
16⅛ × 12 inches
Promised Gift of the Macon and Joan Brock
Collection of American Art

PROVENANCE
Hirschl & Adler Galleries, New York
Sandy and Barbara Lewis, Short Hills, New
Jersey, 1983
Christie's, New York, June 5, 1997, lot 19
Private collection, until 2002
Vance Jordan Fine Art, New York, 2002
H. V. Allison & Co
The Macon and Joan Brock Collection of
American Art, 2011

EXHIBITION HISTORY
American Art from the Gallery's Collection,
Hirschl & Adler, New York, 1980, no. 71.
America's Best: 1820–1920, Museum at
Sunrise, Charleston, West Virginia, 1981,
no. 34.
*Childe Hassam: An American Impres-
sionist*, Adelson Galleries, New York,
November–December 1999, no. 58.

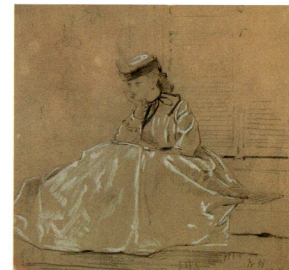

Winslow Homer
American, 1836–1910
Portrait of Elizabeth Loring Grant, 1866
Charcoal, chalk, and pencil on paper
10 × 10 inches
Promised Gift of the Macon and Joan Brock
Collection of American Art

PROVENANCE
The artist
Elizabeth Loring Grant, Belmont, Massa-
chusetts, gift from the above, 1866
Lena Wellington Grant Gibson (Mrs. Rich-
ard Gibson), Greenwich, Connecticut,
bequested from the above, 1921
Madelaine Grant Bufford (Mrs. John Henry
Bufford, Jr.), Newton Highlands, Massa-
chusetts, gift from the above
By descent to the previous owner
Christie's, *Important American Paintings,
Drawings and Sculpture*, November 28,
2007, lot 96
The Macon and Joan Brock Collection of
American Art, 2020

EXHIBITION HISTORY
*Building a Legacy: The Chrysler Collects
for the Future*, Chrysler Museum of
Art, Norfolk, Virginia, November 19,
2021–March 6, 2022.

PUBLICATION HISTORY
Lloyd Goodrich and Abigail Booth Gerdts, *Record of Works by Winslow Homer, 1867 through 1876*, vol. I (New York: Spanierman Gallery, LLC, 2005), p. 365, no. 290.

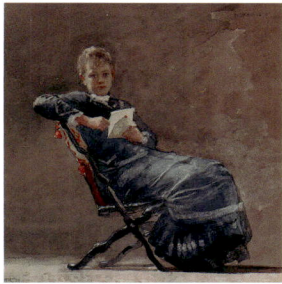

Girl with a Letter, 1879
Watercolor on paper
8½ × 8½ inches
Promised Gift of the Macon and Joan Brock Collection of American Art

PROVENANCE
Edward W. Hooper, Boston
Mabel Hooper La Farge (Mrs. Bancel La Farge), Boston, 1901
Thomas Sergeant La Farge, 1944
The Macon and Joan Brock Collection of American Art, 2020

EXHIBITION HISTORY
Loan Exhibition of Paintings by Winslow Homer, Museum of Fine Arts, Boston, February 8–March 8, 1911.
Centenary Exhibition of Works by Winslow Homer, Carnegie Institute, Pittsburgh, January 28–March 7, 1937, no. 133.
Oils and Watercolors by Winslow Homer, Whitney Museum of American Art, New York, October 3–November 4, 1944.
Winslow Homer, Worcester Art Museum, Worcester, Massachusetts, November 16–December 17, 1944, no. 28.
Early Winslow Homer, Covering Twenty-five Years from 1864 to 1889, Maynard Walker Gallery, New York, October 19–November 16, 1953, no. 15.
Winslow Homer: A Retrospective Exhibition, National Gallery of Art, Washington, DC, November 23, 1958–January 4, 1959; The Metropolitan Museum of Art, New York, January 29–March 8, 1959, no. 96.
Winslow Homer, Whitney Museum of American Art, New York, April 3–June 3, 1973; Los Angeles County Museum of Art, July 3–August 15, 1973; Art Institute of Chicago, September 8–October 21, 1973, no. 90.
Winslow Homer Watercolors, National Gallery of Art, Washington, DC, March 2–May 11, 1986; Amon Carter Museum, Fort Worth, Texas, June 6–July 27, 1986; Yale University Art Gallery, New Haven, Connecticut, September 11–November 2, 1986, no. 35 [as *Girl Seated*].

PUBLICATION HISTORY
Lloyd Goodrich and Abigail Booth Gerdts, *Record of Works by Winslow Homer, 1877 to March 1881*, vol. III (New York: Spanierman Gallery, LLC, 2008), no. 863, p. 265.

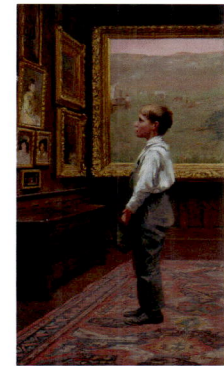

Helen Corson Hovenden
American, 1846–1935
In the Gallery, 1901
Oil on canvas
36 × 20 inches
Promised Gift of the Macon and Joan Brock Collection of American Art

PROVENANCE
Dennis Auction Service, July 8, 2011, lot 1019
Thomas Colville Fine Art
The Macon and Joan Brock Collection of American Art, 2011

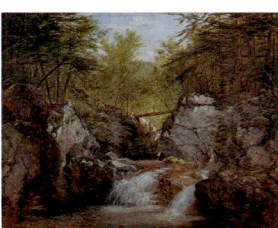

John Frederick Kensett
American, 1816–1872
Bash Bish Falls, ca. 1860
Oil on canvas
18 × 22¼ inches
Gift of the Macon and Joan Brock Collection of American Art, 2023.4.2

PROVENANCE
Hirschl & Adler Galleries, Inc., New York, until 1977
Charles and Alma Shoemaker, acquired from the above, until 2007
The Macon and Joan Brock Collection of American Art, 2022

EXHIBITION HISTORY
John F. Kensett. An American Master, Los Angeles County Museum of Art, July–September 8, 1985.

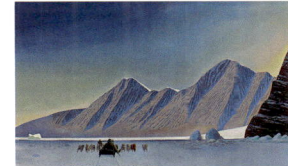

Rockwell Kent
American, 1882–1971
Sledging, ca. 1832–35
Oil on canvas, mounted on plywood
40 × 60 inches

PROVENANCE
From the artist to his son, Gordon Kent, until 2009
To the artist's grandson, David Kent
The Macon and Joan Brock Collection of American Art, 2016

EXHIBITION HISTORY
Distant Shores: The Odyssey of Rockwell Kent, Norman Rockwell Museum, Stockbridge, Massachusetts, June 24–October 22, 2000; Appleton Museum of Art, Ocala, Florida, November 18, 2000–January 28, 2001; Terra Museum of American Art, Chicago, February 24–May 20, 2001; Anchorage Museum of History and Art, Anchorage, Alaska, June 17–September 23, 2001.

Rockwell Kent: The Mythic and the Modern, Portland Museum of Art, Portland, Oregon, 2005.
The Lost Generation: Paintings, Driscoll Babcock Galleries, New York, March 11–April 23, 2016.

PUBLICATION HISTORY
Constance Martin, *Distant Shores: The Odyssey of Rockwell Kent* (Chesterfield, MA: Chameleon Books, 2000) pp. 36, 94, illus.

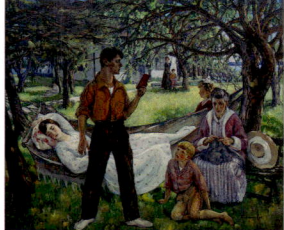

Leon Kroll
American, 1884–1974
Poetry Reading, Maine, 1918
Oil on canvas
45¾ × 52 inches

PROVENANCE
The artist to his daughter, Marie Kroll Rose
ACA Galleries, New York, 1994
The Macon and Joan Brock Collection of American Art, 2005

EXHIBITION HISTORY
31st Annual Exhibition of American Oil Paintings and Sculpture, Art Institute of Chicago, November 7, 1918–January 1, 1919, no. 122 [as *The Young Poet*].
Our Community Collects: From Durer to Warhol and Beyond, Chrysler Museum of Art, Norfolk, Virginia, September 21–December 31, 2011.

PUBLICATION HISTORY
Leon Kroll, *Leon Kroll: A Spoken Memoir*, ed. Nancy Hale and Fredson Bower (Charlottesville: University Press of Virginia, 1983), pl. 65.

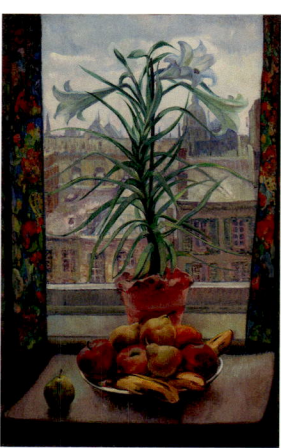

Still Life in the Studio Window, New York City, 1920
Oil on canvas
40 × 25 inches

PROVENANCE
Gift of the artist to his neighbor, New York
By descent through the family
Private collection, New York
The Macon and Joan Brock Collection of American Art, 2009

EXHIBITION HISTORY
Our Community Collects: From Durer to Warhol and Beyond, Chrysler Museum of Art, Norfolk, Virginia, September 21–December 31, 2011.

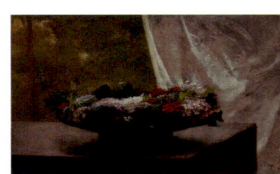

John La Farge
American, 1835–1910
Flowers in a Lacquer Bowl, 1861
Oil on canvas
13½ × 22½ inches
Promised Gift of the Macon and Joan Brock Collection of American Art

PROVENANCE
From the artist to his mother-in-law, Mrs. Christopher Grant Perry (Frances Sargeant)
By descent to the wife of the artist, Margaret
By descent to Mr. and Mrs. Bancel La Farge
By descent to Mary La Farge
By descent to her daughter
The Macon and Joan Brock Collection of American Art, 2016

EXHIBITION HISTORY
Thirty-Eighth Annual Exhibition, National Academy of Design, New York, 1863, no. 21.
An Exhibition of the Work of John La Farge, The Metropolitan Museum of Art, New York, March 23–April 26, 1936, no. 4.

PUBLICATION HISTORY
An Exhibition of the Work of John La Farge (New York: The Metropolitan Museum of Art, 1936), no. 4.
James L. Yarnall, *Nature Vivante: The Still Lifes of John La Farge* (New York: Jordan-Volpe Gallery, 1995), p. 66, pl. 1; p. 115, no. 5.

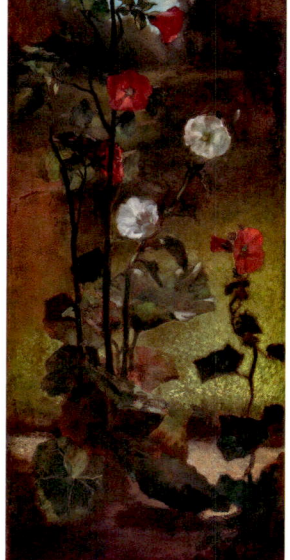

Hollyhocks, 1863
Encaustic on panel
34⅛ × 15⅝ inches
Promised Gift of the Macon and Joan Brock Collection of American Art

PROVENANCE
The artist
Sale: Messrs. Peirce & Company, Boston, *The Paintings of Mr. John La Farge, to be Sold at Auction*, November 20, 1878, lot 10
John Chandler Bancroft, Boston, acquired from the above
Mrs. R. L. Adlercron, Grantham, England, daughter of the above, 1901
Mrs. Christopher Blackie, Lincolnshire, England, daughter of the above, 1939
Sotheby's, New York, December 8, 1983, lot 191, sold by the above
The Jordan-Volpe Gallery, New York
Private collection, 1984
Sotheby's, American Art, May 18, 2016, lot 28
The Macon and Joan Brock Collection of American Art, 2016

EXHIBITION HISTORY

Thirty-Eighth Annual Exhibition, National Academy of Design, New York, April 14–June 24, 1863, no. 78.

Williams and Everett Gallery, Boston, February 1864.

Fall Exhibition, Brooklyn Art Association, Brooklyn, New York, December 7–11, 1869, no. 260.

Third Annual Exhibition, Yale School of the Fine Arts, New Haven, Connecticut, 1871, no. 65.

Annual Exhibition, Royal Academy, London, 1872, no. 230.

Cercle des Arts, Paris, 1872.

Centennial Commission International Exhibition, Fairmount Park, Philadelphia, 1876, no. 167.

First Exhibition, Society of American Artists, New York, March 6–April 5, 1878, no. 97.

Works of John La Farge, Carnegie Institute, Pittsburgh, March 27–April 10, 1901, p. 8, no. 89.

Les Amis: American Painters in France, 1865 to 1890, The Jordan-Volpe Gallery, New York, May 1984, no. 20.

John La Farge, National Museum of American Art, Smithsonian Institution, Washington, DC; Carnegie Museum of Art, Pittsburgh; Museum of Fine Arts, Boston, July 10, 1987–April 24, 1988, pp. 22, 257, no. 8, fig. 7, illus.

Nature Vivante: The Still Lifes of John La Farge, The Jordan-Volpe Gallery, New York, April 28–June 9, 1995, pp. 30–31, 54, 76, 118, 144, no. 13, pl. 11, illus.

Poetic Painting: American Masterworks from the Clark and Liebes Collections, Vance Jordan Fine Art, Inc., New York, October 29–December 7, 2001, pp. 4, 7, 17, 29–30, pl. 4, illus.

Variations on America: Masterworks from American Art Forum Collections, Smithsonian American Art Museum, Washington, DC, April 13–July 29, 2007, pp. 52–54, illus.

PUBLICATION HISTORY

"New Pictures at Williams & Everett's," *Boston Evening Transcript*, February 9, 1864, p. 1.

"Fresh Art in Boston," *Boston Evening Transcript*, February 18, 1864, p. 1.

"Art Notes," *New York Evening Post*, September 19, 1872, p. 1.

F. A. Walker, ed., *International Exposition, 1876: Reports and Awards Group XXVII* (Philadelphia, 1877), p. 30.

"Fine Arts: The Society of American Artists," *New York Evening Mail*, March 5, 1878, p. 4.

"Old and Young Painters," *New York Times*, March 17, 1878, p. 5.

"The Society of American Artists," *The World*, March 30, 1878, p. 5.

"Art and Artists," *Boston Evening Transcript*, November 21, 1878, p. 5.

"The La Farge Collection," *Boston Globe*, November 21, 1878, p. 4.

"Sale of Mr. La Farge's Paintings," *Boston Daily Advertiser*, November 21, 1878, p. 2.

"The La Farge Paintings," *Boston Post*, November 22, 1878, p. 3.

C. E. Clement, L. Hutton, *Artists of the Nineteenth Century and Their Works* (Boston, 1879), p. 30.

H. La Farge, *Catalogue Raisonné of the Works of John La Farge*, unpublished manuscript (1934–74), p. 36.

K. A. Foster, "The Still-Life Painting of John La Farge," *The American Art Journal*, no. 3 (July 1979): 32.

H. A. La Farge, "John La Farge and the 1878 Auction of His Works," *The American Art Journal* 15, no. 3 (Summer 1983) p. 15, fig. 11, illus.

Henry Adams, "Picture Windows," *Antiques* 3 (April 1934): 96, illus.

Henry Adams, "The Mind of John La Farge," *John La Farge* (New York: Abbeville Press, 1987), p. 22, illus.

James L. Yarnall, *John La Farge: Watercolors and Drawings*, exh. cat. Yonkers, New York: Hudson River Museum of Westchester, 1990), pp. 30, 108, no. 2, illus.

James L. Yarnall, *John La Farge in Paradise: The Painter and His Muse*, exh. cat. (Newport, RI: William Vareika Fine Arts, 1995), pp. 46, 47, 133, 155, fig. 74, illus.

"The Still Lifes of John La Farge at Jordan-Volpe Gallery April 28," *Antiques and the Arts Weekly*, April 21, 1995, p. 86, illus.

G. Glueck, "Gallery Watch," *New York Observer* 9, May 15, 1995, p. 3.

Kathleen Pyne, *Art and the Higher Life: Painting and Evolutionary Thought in Late Nineteenth-Century America* (Austin, TX: University of Texas Press, 1996), n.p., pl. 1, fig. 2.1, illus.

B. Gopnik, "Here and Now," *Washington Post*, July 1, 2007, p. N2

Elisabeth Hodermarsky et al. *John La Farge's Second Paradise: Voyages in the South Seas, 1890–1891* exh. cat. (New Haven, CT: Yale University Press, 2010), pp. 18–19, fig. 17, illus.

James L. Yarnall, *John La Farge: A Biographical and Critical Study* (Surrey, UK: Ashgate, 2012), pp. viii, 63–64, no. 34 illus.

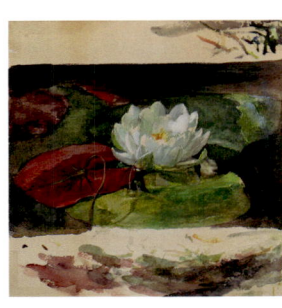

Water Lily with Green and Red Pads,
  ca. 1883
Pencil, watercolor, and gouache on heavy
  wove paper
Sight: 5½ × 9½ inches; sheet: 11¾ ×
  15½ inches
Gift of the Macon and Joan Brock Collection of American Art, 2023.4.3

PROVENANCE
The artist
Gifted from the above to Moritz Bernard
  Philipp, 1884
James Graham Gallery, New York, by the
  early 1970s
Sold from the above to a private collection,
  New England, until 2014
The Macon and Joan Brock Collection of
  American Art, 2022

EXHIBITION HISTORY
Annual Exhibition, Society of American
  Artists, National Academy of Design,
  New York, 1884, no. 54.
*Catalogue of a Collection of Oil and
  Water Color Paintings, by John La
  Farge*, Moore's Art Gallery, New York,
  March 26–27, 1884, lot 49.

PUBLICATION HISTORY
James Yarnall, *Nature Vivante: The Still
  Lifes of John La Farge* (New York: The
  Jordan-Volpe Gallery, Inc., 1995), p. 142,
  no. 76, illus.

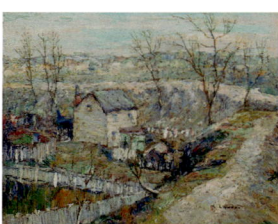

Ernest Lawson
American, 1873–1939
Squatter's Huts, Harlem River, ca. 1914
Oil on canvas
17 × 21 inches

PROVENANCE
Albert Eugene Gallatin, New York
Milch Galleries, Inc., New York
Sotheby's, New York, April 23, 2015, lot 94
Thomas Colville Fine Art
The Macon and Joan Brock Collection of
  American Art, 2016

EXHIBITION HISTORY
Ernest Lawson, Daniel Gallery, New York,
  February 1914.
*Paintings by Hayley Lever and Ernest
  Lawson*, Art Institute of Chicago,
  March 3–April 2, 1917, no. 2.

PUBLICATION HISTORY
"Ernest Lawson at Daniel Gallery," *American Art News* 12, no. 18 (Feb. 7, 1914): 6.
Albert Eugene Gallatin, *Certain Contemporaries; A Set of Notes in Art Criticism*,
  1916, illus.

Albert Eugene Gallatin, "Ernest Lawson,"
  International Studio 59 (July 1916):
  14, illus.
Guy Pène du Bois, *American Artists
  Series; Ernest Lawson* (New York:
  Whitney Museum of American Art, 1932),
  p. 11, illus.
Steven Nash, *Dallas Collects American
  Paintings, Colonial to Early Modern:
  An Exhibition of Paintings from Private
  Collections in Dallas* (Dallas: Dallas
  Museum of Fine Arts, 1982), p. 115.
Ross Barrett, "Speculations in Paint: Ernest
  Lawson and the Urbanization of New
  York," *Winterthur Portfolio* 42, no. 1
  (Spring 2008): 16, 20.

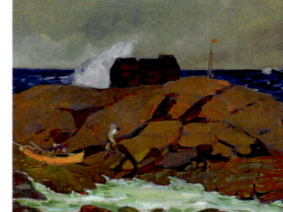

George Benjamin Luks
American, 1867–1933
Poverty Hump, Maine, ca. 1922
Oil on canvas
25 × 30 inches
Gift of the Macon and Joan Brock Collec-
  tion of American Art, 2021.25

PROVENANCE
Parke Bernet Galleries, New York, Sale
  catalogue, no. 1170, 1950, lot 357
Private collection, 1970 until 2009
Michael Altman Fine Art and Advisory,
  New York, 2009
Private collection, Pennsylvania
The Macon and Joan Brock Collection of
  American Art, 2021

EXHIBITION HISTORY
*Building a Legacy: Chrysler Collects for the
  Future*, Chrysler Museum of Art, Norfolk,
  Virginia, November 19, 2021–March 6,
  2022.

PUBLICATION HISTORY
Carl Little, "Henri, Bellows, and Luks: The
  Ashcan School in Maine," *Island Journal*
  37 (2021).

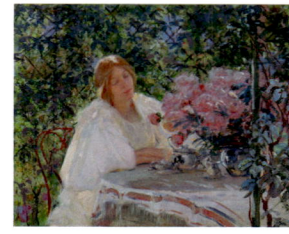

Mary Fairchild MacMonnies
American, 1858–1946
In the Garden, Giverny, ca. 1895
Oil on canvas
15 × 18 inches
Gift of the Macon and Joan Brock Collec-
  tion of American Art, 2023.4.6

PROVENANCE
Private collection, Massachusetts
The Macon and Joan Brock Collection of
  American Art, 2022

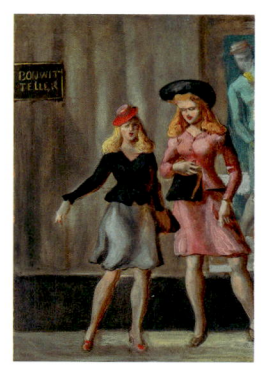

Reginald Marsh
American, 1898–1954
On Fifth, 1939
Tempera on panel
18½ × 12½ inches

PROVENANCE
The artist
Senator William Benton
Sotheby's Parke Bernet, New York, 1972
Private collection, New York
The Macon and Joan Brock Collection of
    American Art, 2005

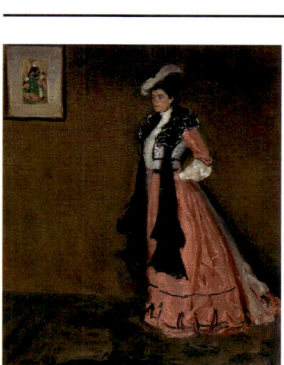

Alfred H. Maurer
American, 1868–1932
*Woman in Pink (Portrait of Roselle Fitz-
    patrick)*, 1902
Oil on canvas
16 × 12¾ inches

PROVENANCE
Salander-O'Reilly Galleries, New York
Hirschl & Adler Galleries, New York,
    1984–98
Private collection, California, until 2005
Private collection, to Hirschl & Adler
    Galleries
The Macon and Joan Brock Collection of
    American Art, 2012

EXHIBITION HISTORY
*Crosscurrents: Americans in Paris,
    1900–1940*, Hirschl & Adler Galleries,
    New York, 1993.
*Alfred Maurer: At the Vanguard of Modern-
    ism*, Addison Gallery of American Art,
    Andover, Massachusetts, April 25–July 31,
    2015; Crystal Bridges Museum of
    American Art, Bentonville, Arkansas,
    October 10, 2015–January 4, 2016.

PUBLICATION HISTORY
Elizabeth McCausland, *A. H. Maurer:
    A Biography of America's First Modern
    Painter* (New York: Published for the
    Walker Art Center by A. A. Wynn, 1951),
    p. 69.
*Crosscurrents: Americans in Paris,
    1900–1940* (New York: Hirschl & Adler
    Galleries, 1993), p. 47, no. 44.
Stacey B. Epstein, "Alfred H. Maurer:
    Aestheticism to Modernism, 1897–1916,"
    (PhD diss., City University of New York,
    2003), no. 11.
Stacey B. Epstein, *Alfred Maurer: At the
    Vanguard of Modernism* (Andover, MA:
    Addison Gallery of American Art, 2015),
    p. 35.

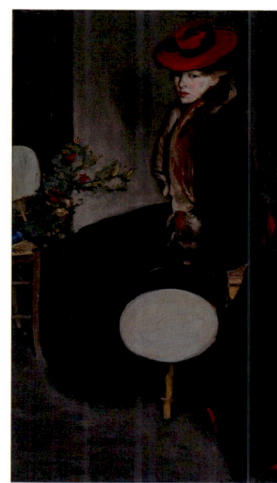

Seated Woman (Portrait of Jeanne Bloza),
    ca 1902–4
Oil on canvas
32 × 17¾ inches
Promised Gift of the Macon and Joan Brock
    Collection of American Art

PROVENANCE
The Macon and Joan Brock Collection of
    American Art, 2013

PUBLICATION HISTORY
Stacey B. Epstein, *Alfred Maurer: At the
    Vanguard of Modernism* (Andover, MA:
    Addison Gallery of American Art, 2015),
    pp. 15, 38.

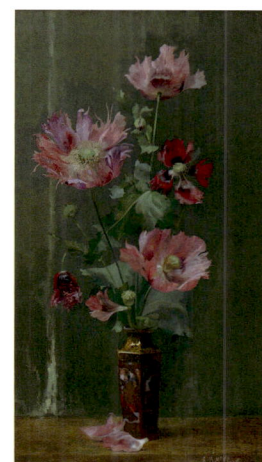

Alberta Binford McCloskey
American, 1863–1911
Poppies, 1901
Oil on canvas
30 × 16 inches
Gift of the Macon and Joan Brock Collec-
    tion of American Art, 2023.4.11

PROVENANCE
Private collection, California
Shannon's Fine Art Auctioneers, Milford,
    Connecticut, October 26, 2006
Private collection, New York
Sotheby's, New York, May 24, 2023,
    lot 1062
The Macon and Joan Brock Collection of
    American Art, 2023

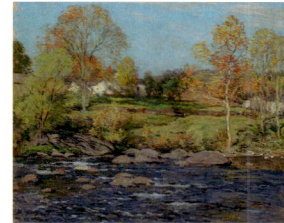

Willard LeRoy Metcalf
American, 1858–1925
October Morning No. 1, 1910
Oil on canvas
21⅛ × 29 inches
Promised Gift of the Macon and Joan Brock
    Collection of American Art

PROVENANCE
Private collection
The Macon and Joan Brock Collection of
    American Art, 2009

EXHIBITION HISTORY
*Our Community Collects: From Dürer to
    Warhol and Beyond*, Chrysler Museum
    of Art, Norfolk, Virginia, September 2–
    December 31, 2011.

PUBLICATION HISTORY
Elizabeth de Veer and Richard J. Boyle,
    *Sunlight and Shadow: The Life and Art of
    Willard L. Metcalf* (New York: Abbeville
    Press, 1987), p. 236, fig. 273, and cover.

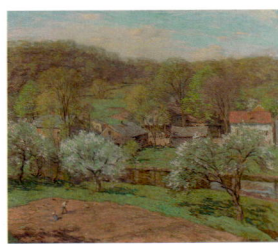

The Village in Late Spring, 1920
Oil on canvas
29¼ × 33½ inches

PROVENANCE
M. Knoedler & Co., New York
Milch Galleries, New York
Hirschl & Adler Galleries, New York
Private collection, Tennessee (acquired
    from the above), 1971
Sotheby's, *American Paintings, Drawings &
    Sculpture*, May 22, 2008, lot 86
The Macon and Joan Brock Collection of
    American Art, 2008

EXHIBITION HISTORY
Willard LeRoy Metcalf: A Retrospective,
    Hunter Museum of Art, Chattanooga,
    Tennessee, April–May 1977, no. 44, p. 7,
    illus. p. 52.
*American Impressionism: The Beauty
    of Work*, Bruce Museum of Arts and
    Science, Greenwich, Connecticut,
    September 2005–January 2006.

PUBLICATION HISTORY
The International Studio (1920s), illus.
Elizabeth de Veer and Richard J. Boyle,
    *Sunlight and Shadow: The Life and Art of
    Willard L. Metcalf* (New York: Abbeville
    Press, 1987), p. 248, illus., fig. 292.

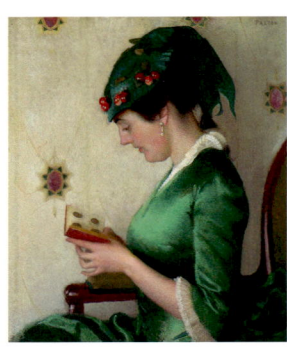

William McGregor Paxton
American, 1869–1941
The Green Princess or *The Album*, ca. 1913
Oil on canvas
30 × 25 inches
Promised Gift of the Macon and Joan Brock
    Collection of American Art

PROVENANCE
The artist's wife, Mrs. William M. Paxton
    (Elizabeth Okie), Boston
Vose Galleries, Boston, 1978
Hammer Galleries, New York [Grand
    Central Art Galleries, Inc., 1983]
Private collection, Atlanta
The Macon and Joan Brock Collection of
    American Art, 2015

EXHIBITION HISTORY
109th Annual Exhibition, Pennsylvania
    Academy of the Fine Arts, Philadelphia,
    February 8–March 29, 1914, no. 331.
*William McGregor Paxton, N.A.: Memorial
    Exhibition of Paintings*, Museum of Fine
    Arts, Boston, November 19–December 14,
    1941, no. 1.
William McGregor Paxton, N.A.: 1869–1941,
    Vose Galleries, Boston, from Novem-
    ber 17, 1979, no. WP-36.

*Before 1948: American Paintings in Georgia
    Collections*, Georgia Museum of Art,
    Athens, Georgia, January 15–March 14,
    1999, no. 34.
*William McGregor Paxton and Elizabeth
    Okie Paxton: An Artistic Partnership*,
    Dixon Gallery and Gardens, Memphis,
    Tennessee, April 28–July 14, 2019; Butler
    Institute of American Art, Youngstown,
    Ohio, August 18–November 10, 2019.

PUBLICATION HISTORY
109th Annual Exhibition (Philadelphia:
    Pennsylvania Academy of the Fine Arts,
    1914), no. 331.
Rebecca H. Whelen, "The 109th Annual
    Exhibition of the Pennsylvania Academy
    of the Fine Arts," *Book News Monthly*
    (April 1914): 369.
Ellen Wardwell Lee, *William McGregor
    Paxton (1869–1941)* (Indianapolis: India-
    napolis Museum of Art, 1979), p. 133.
William McGregor Paxton, N.A.: 1869–1941
    (Boston: Vose Galleries, Boston, 1979),
    p. 9, no. WP-36.
*19th and 20th Century European and
    American Paintings: The Gallery Collec-
    tion* (New York: Hammer Galleries, 1983),
    p. 30.
*Before 1948: American Paintings in
    Georgia Collections* (Athens, GA: Georgia
    Museum of Art, 1999), pp. 92–93, no. 34.
Donald D. Keyes, "American Paintings
    in Georgia Collections," *American Art
    Review* XI (February 1999): 187.
Jessica Todd Smith, "Is Polite Society
    Polite?: The Genteel Tradition in the
    Figure Paintings of William McGregor
    Paxton (1869–1941)" (PhD diss., Yale
    University, 2001), fig. 81.
Jane Ward Faquin, *William McGregor
    Paxton and Elizabeth Okie Paxton: An
    Artistic Partnership* (Memphis, TN:
    Dixon Gallery and Gardens, 2019).

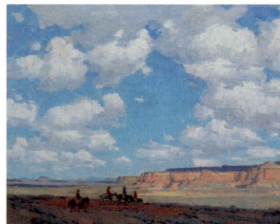

Edgar Alwin Payne
American, 1883–1947
Desert Skies, ca. 1917
Oil on canvas
28 × 34 inches

PROVENANCE
The Macon and Joan Brock Collection of
    American Art, 2008

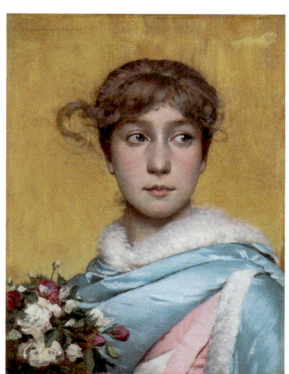

Charles Sprague Pearce
American, 1851–1914
Young Lady with Flowers, ca. 1875–80
Oil on canvas
13 × 10 inches
Promised Gift of the Macon and Joan Brock
Collection of American Art

PROVENANCE
Thomas Colville Fine Art, LLC
The Macon and Joan Brock Collection of
American Art, 2000

EXHIBITION HISTORY
*Our Community Collects: From Durer to
Warhol and Beyond*, Chrysler Museum
of Art, Norfolk, Virginia, September 21–
December 31, 2011.

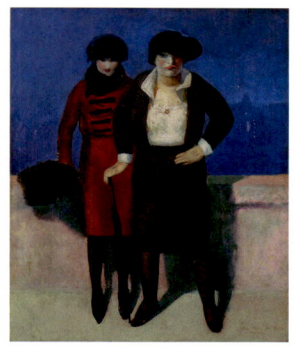

Guy Pène du Bois
American, 1884–1958
Protectrice, 1921
Oil on panel
25 × 20 inches

PROVENANCE
From the artist to his son, William Pène
du Bois
By descent to his wife, Willa Kim
The Macon and Joan Brock Collection of
American Art, 2017

EXHIBITION HISTORY
*Guy Pène du Bois, 1884–1958: Paintings of 20
Younger Years, 1913–1933*, James Graham
and Sons, New York, November 19–
December 14, 1963, no. 11, illus.
Guy Pène du Bois, 1884–1958, James
Graham and Sons, New York, March 17–
April 15, 1964, no. 27.
Guy Pène du Bois, 1884–1958, Parrish Art
Museum, Southampton, New York,
July 10–August 2, 1964, no. 23.

PUBLICATION HISTORY
*Guy Pène du Bois, 1884–1958: Paintings of
20 Younger Years, 1913–1933* (New York:
James Graham and Sons, 1963), no. 11,
illus.
Raphael Soyer, "The Lesson: The
Academy, the League, the Class-
room," *Arts Magazine* 42, no. 1
(September–October 1967): 36.

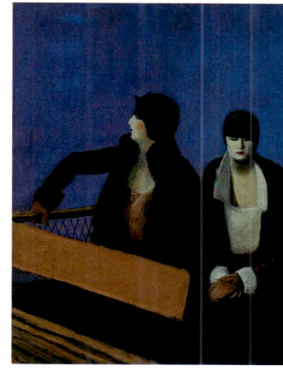

Bus Top (On Top of the Bus), 1924
Oil on panel
25 × 15 inches

PROVENANCE
From the artist to his son, William Pène
du Bois
By descent to his wife, Willa Kim
The Macon and Joan Brock Collection of
American Art, 2017

EXHIBITION HISTORY
*An Exhibition of Paintings and Drawings
by Guy Pène du Bois*, C. W. Kraushaar Art
Galleries, New York, November 3–5, 1925,
no. 2.
*Guy Pène du Bois, 1884–1958: Paintings of 20
Younger Years, 1913–1933*, James Graham
and Sons, New York, November 19–
December 14, 1963, no. 16, illus.
Guy Pène du Bois, 1884–1958, James
Graham and Sons, New York, March 17–
April 15, 1964, no. 25.

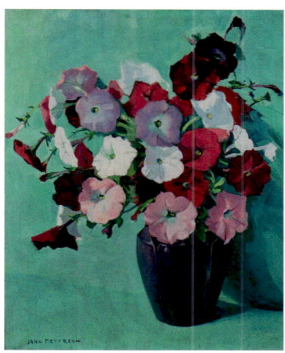

Jane Peterson
American, 1876–1965
Petunias, ca. 1932
Oil on canvas
30 × 24 inches
Promised Gift of the Macon and Joan Brock
Collection of American Art

PROVENANCE
Estate of the artist
By descent in the family of the artist
Sotheby's, New York, October 8, 2015, no. 38
The Macon and Joan Brock Collection of
American Art, 2015

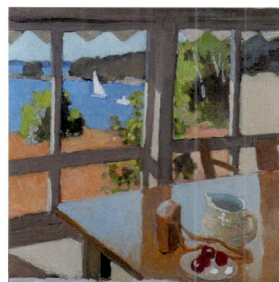

Fairfield Porter
American, 1907–1975
Still Life with White Boats, 1965
Oil on canvas
20 × 20 inches

PROVENANCE
Tibor de Nagy Gallery, New York
Stephen Booke
Mark and Janice Gold
Richard M. Thune Gallery, New York
The Macon and Joan Brock Collection
of American Art, 2013

EXHIBITION HISTORY
The Porter Family, Parrish Art Museum,
Southampton, New York, May 18–
July 13, 1980.

Fairfield Porter: Realist Painter in an Age of Abstraction, Museum of Fine Arts, Boston, January 12–March 13, 1983; Greenville County Museum of Art, Greenville, South Carolina, April 13–June 19, 1983; Cleveland Museum of Art, November 9–December 31, 1983; Carnegie Museum of Art, Pittsburgh, February 18–April 22, 1984; Whitney Museum of American Art, New York, May 31–August 19, 1984.

Figuration/Abstraction: Fairfield Porter/ Willem de Kooning, University Art Galleries, Wright State University, Dayton, Ohio, September 17–October 22, 1995.

PUBLICATION HISTORY

James R. Mellow, "New York Letter," *Art International* 13, no. 3 (1969): 57, illus.

Philip Ferrato, *The Porter Family* (Southampton, NY: Parrish Art Museum, 1980), p. 14; illus. 19, no. 11.

Kenworth Moffett et al., *Fairfield Porter: Realist Painter in an Age of Abstraction* (Boston: Museum of Fine Arts, Boston, 1982), pp. 55, color illus., 105, no. 74.

Davis Thomas, "Fairfield Porter: Poet of Penobscot Bay," *Down East: The Magazine of Maine* (August 1983): 99, color illus.

Betsy Aswad, *Family Passions* (New York: Dial/Doubleday, 1985), color illus. on dust jacket.

David Bergman and Daniel Epstein, *The Heath Guide to Literature*, 2nd ed. (Lexington, MA: D.C. Heath, 1986), cover.

Mary Elsie, *Family Life* (New York: Atheneum, 1987), color illus. on dust jacket.

John Updike, *Just Looking: Essays on Art* (New York: Alfred A. Knopf, 1989), p. 120.

Joan Ludman, "Checklist of the Paintings by Fairfield Porter," in *Fairfield Porter: An American Classic*, pp. 282–309 (New York: Harry N. Abrams, 1992), p. 299.

David Leach, *Figuration/Abstraction: Fairfield Porter/Willem de Kooning* (Dayton, OH: Wright State University, 1995), no. 10.

Jud Yalkut, "Figuration/Abstraction: Fairfield Porter/Willem de Kooning," Review of exhibition at Wright State University, *Dialogue: Arts in the Midwest* 18, no. 6 (November/December 1995): 20.

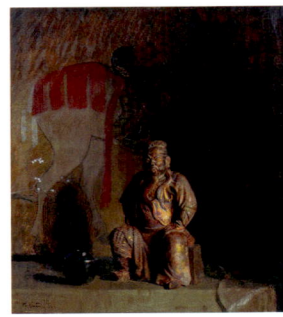

Hovsep Pushman
American, 1877–1966
In Silent Challenge, 1941
Oil on panel
25¾ × 23⅛ inches

PROVENANCE
Estate of the artist (Inventory no. 394)
The Macon and Joan Brock Collection of American Art, 1999

EXHIBITION HISTORY
Anderson Galleries, Chicago, 1941
Grand Central Art Galleries, New York, 1945
Findley Gallery, Chicago, 1951

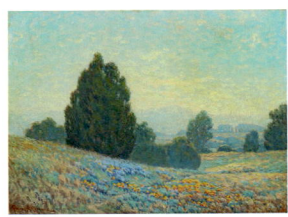

Granville Redmond
American, 1871–1935
Lupine and Poppies
Oil on canvas
18 × 24 inches

PROVENANCE
The Macon and Joan Brock Collection of American Art, 2007

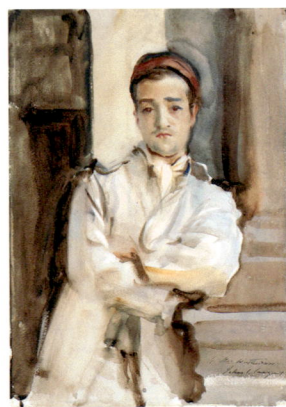

John Singer Sargent
American, 1856–1925
Spanish Convalescent, ca. 1903
Watercolor and pencil on paper
18 × 12 inches
Promised Gift of the Macon and Joan Brock Collection of American Art

PROVENANCE
Mrs. Flora Wertheimer, London
Conway Joseph Conway, by descent, 1922
Private collection, by descent, 1992
Richard Thune, Connecticut, acquired from the above, 2005
Acquired by the previous owner from the above
Christie's, American Art, December 4, 2013, lot 42
The Macon and Joan Brock Collection of American Art, 2013

EXHIBITION HISTORY
Loan Exhibition of Water Colours by the Late John S. Sargent, Claridge Gallery, London, July 1925, no. 13.
John Singer Sargent and the Edwardian Age, Leeds Art Galleries at Lotherton Hall, Leeds, England, April 5–June 10, 1979, no. 81.
Americans in Spain: Painting and Travel, 1820–1920, Chrysler Museum of Art, Norfolk, Virginia, February 12–May 16, 2021; Milwaukee Art Museum, June 11–October 3, 2021, no. 47.

PUBLICATION HISTORY

Loan Exhibition of Water Colours by the Late John S. Sargent, exh. cat. (London: Claridge Gallery, 1925), n.p., no. 13.

Richard Ormond, *John Singer Sargent: Paintings, Drawings, Watercolors* (London: Phaidon Press, 1970), p. 250.

James Lomax and Richard Ormond, *John Singer Sargent and the Edwardian Age*, exh. cat. (London: National Portrait Gallery, 1979), p. 95, no. 81, illus.

Stephanie L. Herdrich and H. Barbara Weinberg, *American Drawings and Watercolors in The Metropolitan Museum of Art: John Singer Sargent* (New York: The Metropolitan Museum of Art, 2000), p. 393.

Richard Ormond and Elaine Kilmurray, *John Singer Sargent: The Complete Paintings, Volume 7, Figures and Landscapes, 1900–1907* (New Haven, CT: Yale University Press, 2012), pp. 112, 114, 139, 345, no. 1269, illus.

Brandon Ruud and Corey Piper, *Americans in Spain: Painting and Travel, 1820–1920* (New Haven, CT: Yale University Press, 2021), p. 98, no. 47.

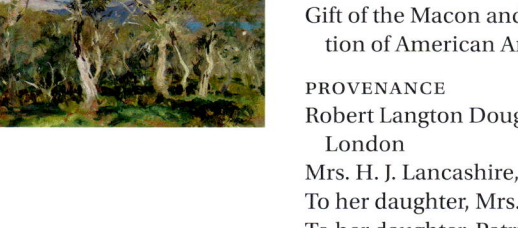

Olives at Corfu, 1909
Oil on canvas
22 × 28 inches
Gift of the Macon and Joan Brock Collection of American Art, 2023.4.1

PROVENANCE
Robert Langton Douglas (1864–1951), London
Mrs. H. J. Lancashire, Boston
To her daughter, Mrs. Lila Southgate
To her daughter, Patricia Southgate (1928–1998)
Hirschl & Adler Galleries, New York, 1984
Mr. and Mrs. Douglass Carmichael, Washington, DC
The Macon and Joan Brock Collection of American Art, 2022

EXHIBITION HISTORY
Exhibition of Works by the Late John S. Sargent, R.A., Royal Academy of Arts, London, January 14–May 13, 1926, no. 307.

PUBLICATION HISTORY
Evan Charteris, *John Sargent* (London: William Heinemann, 1927), p. 290.

Charles Merrill Mount, *John Singer Sargent: A Biography* (New York: W. W. Norton, 1955), p. 449, no. K092; 1957 ed., p. 359, no. K092.

Richard Ormond and Elaine Kilmurray, *John Singer Sargent: The Complete Paintings, Volume 8, Figures and Landscapes, 1908–1913* (New Haven, CT: Yale University Press, 2014), pp. 8, 114, no. 1520.

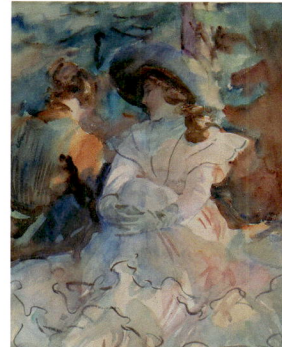

Ladies in the Shade: Series, 1912
Watercolor and pencil on paper
21 × 15¾ inches
Promised Gift of the Macon and Joan Brock Collection of American Art

PROVENANCE
The artist
Estate of the above
Christie, Manson & Woods, London, *Pictures and Water Colour Drawings by J. S. Sargent, R.A. and Works by Other Artists*, July 24 and 27, 1925, lot 9
M. Knoedler & Co., New York, acquired from the above
The Widener Family, Philadelphia
By descent to the previous owner
Christie's, *Important American Paintings, Drawings and Sculpture*, May 17, 2011, lot 55
The Macon and Joan Brock Collection of American Art, 2011

EXHIBITION HISTORY
Watercolor: An American Medium, Chrysler Museum of Art, Norfolk, Virginia, February 12–June 23, 2019

PUBLICATION HISTORY
Richard Ormond and Elaine Kilmurray, *John Singer Sargent: The Complete Paintings, Volume 8, Figures and Landscapes, 1908–1913* (New Haven, CT: Yale University Press, 2012), pp. 121, 198–99, 375, no. 1512.

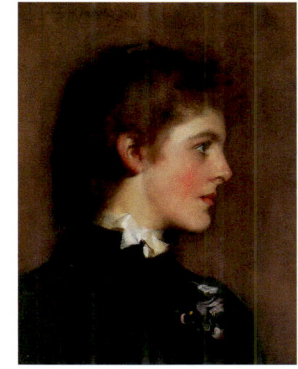

James Jebusa Shannon
British, 1862–1923
Portrait of a Young Woman, ca. 1889
Oil on canvas
18 × 14 inches

PROVENANCE
The artist to Lady Florence Shannon
To the artist's daughter, Kitty Shannon
To the artist's granddaughter, Julia Gibbons
The Macon and Joan Brock Collection of American Art, 2015

EXHIBITION HISTORY
Seeking Beauty: Paintings by James Jebusa Shannon, Debra Force Fine Art, New York, May 1–June 14, 2014

PUBLICATION HISTORY
Barbara Dayer Gallati, *Seeking Beauty: Paintings by James Jebusa Shannon*, (New York: Debra Force Fine Art, 2014), pp. 18–19.

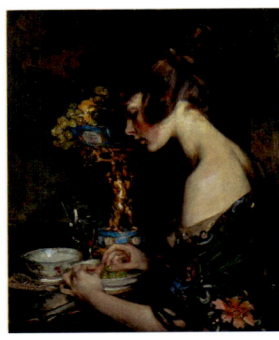

The Sèvres Vase, ca. 1910
Oil on canvas
30 × 25 inches
Promised Gift of the Macon and Joan Brock
    Collection of American Art

PROVENANCE
The artist's estate to his daughter, Kitty
    Shannon Keigwin, and her husband,
    Walter Skarrat Keigwin
By descent to their daughter, Julia Keigwin
    Gibbons
The Macon and Joan Brock Collection of
    American Art, 2015

EXHIBITION HISTORY
Autumn Exhibition, Walker Art Gallery,
    Liverpool, 1923, no. 295.
*Paintings of the Late James J. Shannon,
    R.A.*, Leicester Galleries, London, 1923,
    no. 28.
Autumn Exhibition, Walker Art Gallery,
    Liverpool, 1928, no. 970.

PUBLICATION HISTORY
*James Jebusa Shannon: Biographical and
    Inventory Information* (Guilford, CT:
    Thomas Colville Fine Art, 2015), pp. 14–16.

Charles Sheeler

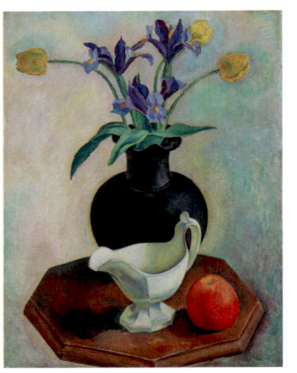

American, 1883–1965
Yellow Tulip, Blue Iris, 1925
Oil on canvas
24 × 18⅛ inches
Promised Gift of the Macon and Joan Brock
    Collection of American Art

PROVENANCE
Mrs. Frances M. Pollak, New York
Private collection, Massachusetts,
    by descent
Michael Altman Fine Art & Advisory
    Services, New York
Adelson Galleries, New York
Avery Galleries, Bryn Mawr, Pennsylvania
The Macon and Joan Brock Collection of
    American Art, 2013

EXHIBITION HISTORY
*Charles Sheeler: Paintings, Drawings, and
    Photographs*, The Museum of Modern
    Art, New York, 1939. Extended loan to
    Worcester Art Museum, Worcester,
    Massachusetts, 1979–96.
*Counterpoint to Abstraction: American
    Realism, 1920–1950*, Worcester Art
    Museum, Worcester, Massachusetts,
    August 28–November 4, 1991.

PUBLICATION HISTORY
*Charles Sheeler: Paintings, Drawings, and
    Photographs* (New York: The Museum of
    Modern Art, 1939), p. 47, pl. 17, illus.

L. N. Dochterman, "The Stylistic Devel-
    opment of the Work of Charles Sheeler"
    (PhD diss., State University of Iowa, 1963),
    p. 283.
Carol Troyen and Erica Hirshler, *Charles
    Sheeler: Paintings and Drawings* (Boston:
    The Museum of Fine Arts, Boston, 1987),
    p. 106, fig. A.

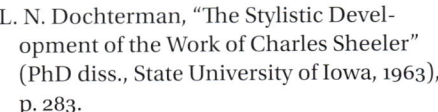

Abbott Handerson Thayer

American, 1849–1921
Profile of a Girl (Alice Rich), 1917
Oil on panel
24 × 18 inches
Promised Gift of the Macon and Joan Brock
    Collection of American Art

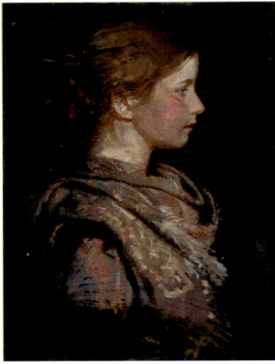

PROVENANCE
Estate of Abbott H. Thayer, ca. 1923
The Macon and Joan Brock Collection
    of American Art, 2009

EXHIBITION HISTORY
*La Femme: The Influence of Whistler and
    Japanese Printmakers on American Art,
    1880–1917*, Grand Central Art Galleries,
    New York, October 26–December 30, 1983.
*Our Community Collects: From Durer to
    Warhol and Beyond*, Chrysler Museum
    of Art, Norfolk, Virginia, September 21–
    December 31, 2011.

PUBLICATION HISTORY
Nathaniel Pousette-Dart, *Distinguished
    American Artists: Abbott H. Thayer*
    (New York: Frederick A. Stokes, 1923).
*La Femme: The Influence of Whistler and
    Japanese Printmakers on American Art,
    1880–1917* (New York: Grand Central Art
    Galleries, 1983).

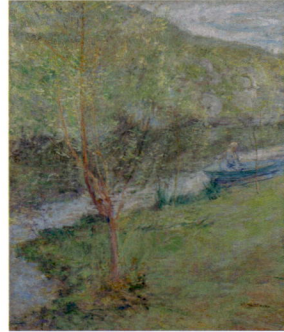

John Henry Twachtman

American, 1853–1902
Spring, ca. 1898
Oil on canvas
30⅛ × 25 inches
Promised Gift of the Macon and Joan Brock
    Collection of American Art

PROVENANCE
George F. Of, New York, by 1901
Kennedy Galleries, New York, by 1966
Campanile Galleries, Chicago
Dr. and Mrs. Robert B. Smythe, New
    Orleans, by 1971
Christie's, New York, December 3, 1982,
    lot 158
To private collection, 1982
Sotheby's, New York, March 6, 2019, lot 120
The Macon and Joan Brock Collection of
    American Art, 2019

[Probably] *First Exhibition: Ten American Painters*, Durand-Ruel Galleries, New York, March 31–April 16, 1898, no. 36 [as *Early Spring*].

[Probably] *An Exhibition of Paintings by Ten American Painters*, St. Botolph Club, Boston, April 25–May 14, 1898, no. 46 [as *Early Spring*].

Exhibition of Paintings by J. H. Twachtman and His Son, J. Alden Twachtman, St. Botolph Club, Boston, February 26–March 13, 1900, no. 11.

Exhibition of the Works of John H. Twachtman, Art Institute of Chicago, January 8–27, 1901, no. 13.

Exhibition of Paintings by John Twachtman, Columbus Art School, Columbus, Ohio, February 1901.

Paintings and Pastels by John H. Twachtman, Durand-Ruel Galleries, New York, March 4–16, 1901.

Exhibition of Sixty Paintings by Mr. John H. Twachtman, Formerly Resident in Cincinnati, Cincinnati Art Museum, April 12–May 16, 1901, no. 36.

John Henry Twachtman: A Retrospective Exhibition, Cincinnati Art Museum, October 7–November 20, 1966, no. 45.

New Orleans Collects: A Selection of Works of Art Owned by New Orleanians, New Orleans Museum, November 14, 1972–January 9, 1973, no. 179.

In the Eye of the Beholder: South Florida Collectors' Choice, Museum of Art, Fort Lauderdale, Florida, December 11, 1986–January 25, 1987.

Hidden Treasures: American Paintings from Florida Collections, Orlando Museum of Art, Orlando, Florida, January 4–February 23, 1992, no. 57.

John Twachtman (1853–1902): A "Painter's Painter," Spanierman Gallery, New York, May 4–June 24, 2006.

PUBLICATION HISTORY

"American Painters Display," *New York Times*, March 30, 1898, p. 6 [as *Early Spring*].

"The Art World: Ten American Painters at the Durand-Ruel Gallery," *New-York Commercial Advertiser*, March 30, 1898, p. 7 [as *Early Spring*].

J[ohn] C. V[an] D[yke], "Ten American Painters," *New York Evening Post*, April 1, 1898, p. 7 [as *Early Spring*].

"Art News and Notes," *Standard Union* (Brooklyn), April 2, 1898, p. 6 [as *Early Spring*].

"Exhibitions of the Week," *Chicago Times Herald*, January 12, 1901, part 4, p. 7.

"Twachtman's Painting—To Be Exhibited at Mr. Fauley's Studio Next Week," *Columbus Journal* (Ohio), January 27, 1901.

John Douglass Hale, "Life and Creative Development of John H. Twachtman," 2 vols., PhD diss., Ohio State University, 1957. Ann Arbor, MI: University Microfilms, 1958, vol. 2, p. 495 (catalogue G, no. 586).

"Painting: The Quiet American," *Time* 88, October 14, 1966 p. 92 illus. in color [as *Spring*].

Lisa N. Peters, "Catalogue," in *John Twachtman (1853–1902): A "Painter's Painter,"* exh. cat. (New York: Spanierman Gallery, 2006), pp. 170–71.

Lisa N. Peters, "Twachtman and the Equipoise of Impressionism and Tonalism," in *John Twachtman (1853–1902): A "Painter's Painter,"* exh. cat. (New York: Spanierman Gallery, 2006), p. 48.

Lisa N. Peters, *John Henry Twachtman Catalogue Raisonné* (Greenwich, CT: Greenwich Historical Society, 2021), http://jhtwachtman.org.

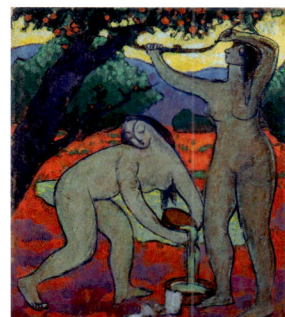

Max Weber
American, 1881–1961
Two Female Figures, ca. 1908
Oil on board
27 × 24 inches
Gift of the Macon and Joan Brock Collection of American Art, 2023.4.7

PROVENANCE
Estate of the artist
Bernard Danenberg Galleries, New York
Private collection, Long Island, New York
Joan Michelman, New York
Private collection, Texas
DuMouchelles Fine Arts Auctioneers, June 17, 2022, lot 01001
The Macon and Joan Brock Collection of American Art, 2022

EXHIBITION HISTORY
Max Weber: The Years 1906–1916, Bernard Danenberg Galleries, New York, May 12–30, 1970, no. 18.

PUBLICATION HISTORY
Alfred Warner, *Max Weber* (New York: Abrams, 1975), pl. 17.

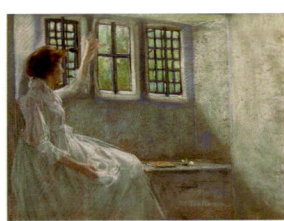

Julian Alden Weir
American, 1852–1919
The Window Seat, 1889
Pastel, charcoal, and pencil on paper
Sight: 13¼ × 17½ inches
Gift of the Macon and Joan Brock Collection of American Art, 2023.4.4

PROVENANCE
The artist
By descent through the artist's family to his granddaughter
Private collection, Atlanta, acquired directly from the above, 2004
The Macon and Joan Brock Collection of American Art, 2022

EXHIBITION HISTORY
Society of Painters in Pastel Fourth Exhibition, H. Wunderlich & Company, New York, 1890, no. 22.
J. Alden Weir: An American Impressionist, The Metropolitan Museum of Art, New York, October 13, 1983–January 8, 1984, pp. 170–71; p. 302, pl. 21, illus.
J. Alden Weir: A Place of His Own, The William Benton Museum of Art, University of Connecticut, Storrs, Connecticut, June 4–August 18, 1991.
Embracing Elegance 1885–1920: American Art from the Huber Family Collection, Hood Museum of Art, Dartmouth College, Hanover, New Hampshire, June 11–September 4, 2011, pp. 14, 26, 90–91, 106, no. 30, fig. 11, illus. (This exhibition traveled to High Museum of Art, Atlanta, September 24–November 27, 2011.)

PUBLICATION HISTORY
"Painters in Pastel," *New York Times*, May 5, 1890, p. 4.
"Gallery and Studio: The Fourth Exhibition by Painters in Pastel," *Brooklyn Daily Eagle*, May 11, 1890, p. 6.
"The Pastel Exhibition," *Art Amateur* 23 (June 1890): 4.
William H. Gerdts, *American Impressionism* (New York: Abbeville Press, 1984), p. 50, illus.

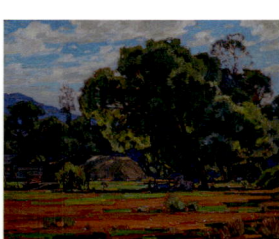

William Wendt
American, 1865–1946
Mountain Willow, 1927
Oil on canvas
25 × 30 inches

PROVENANCE
The Macon and Joan Brock Collection of American Art, 2008

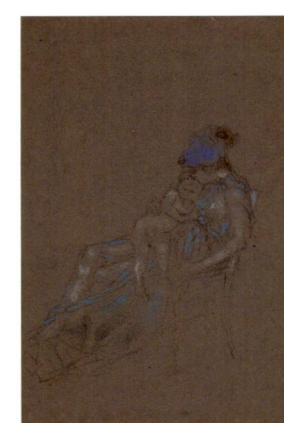

James McNeill Whistler
American, 1834–1903
Mother and Child, ca. 1890
Pastel on brown paper, laid down on board
11 × 7⅛ inches
Gift of the Macon and Joan Brock Collection of American Art, 2023.4.10

PROVENANCE
John H. Wrenn, by 1904
By family descent to a lady
Sale: New York, Sotheby's, December 2, 1982, lot 14
Private collection, Washington, DC
Sally Engelhard Pingree, Washington, DC
The Macon and Joan Brock Collection of American Art, 2022

EXHIBITION HISTORY
The Works of Whistler, The Memorial Exhibition, Copley Society of Boston, February 1904, no. 115.
Notes, Harmonies and Nocturnes: Small Works by James McNeill Whistler, M. Knoedler & Company, New York, November 30–December 27, 1984, no. 45.
James McNeill Whistler: A Retrospective Exhibition, The Tate Gallery, London, October 12, 1994–January 8, 1995, no. 176; Musée d'Orsay, Paris, February 6–April 30, 1995; National Gallery of Art, Washington, DC, May 28–August 20, 1995.
Songs on Stone: James McNeill Whistler and the Art of Lithography, The Art Institute of Chicago, June 6–August 30, 1998, cat. no. 98.

PUBLICATION HISTORY
Margaret F. MacDonald, *James McNeill Whistler: Drawings, Pastels and Watercolours, A Catalogue Raisonné* (London and New Haven, CT: Yale University Press, 1995), pp. 464–65, no. 1282.

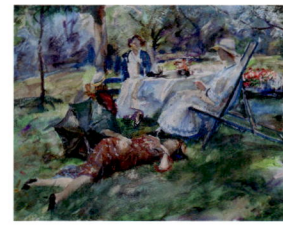

John Whorf
American, 1903–1959
Siesta, ca. 1925
Watercolor on paper
15 × 20¾ inches
Gift of the Macon and Joan Brock Collection of American Art, 2023.4.5

PROVENANCE
Margaret Brown Gallery, Boston
Galleries Maurice Sternberg, Chicago, 1990
Mr. and Mrs. David Wintermann, until 2007
The Macon and Joan Brock Collection of American Art, 2008

EXHIBITION HISTORY

Watercolor: An American Medium, Chrysler Museum of Art, Norfolk, Virginia, February 12–June 23, 2019.

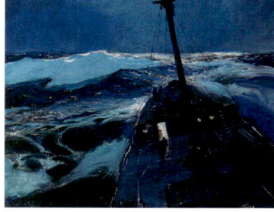

Southern Cruiser (Maritime Nocturne with Ship in Rough Water), ca. 1930
Oil on canvas
28 × 36 inches
Promised Gift of the Macon and Joan Brock Collection of American Art

PROVENANCE

Private collection, Los Angeles
Avery Galleries, Bryn Mawr, Pennsylvania
The Macon and Joan Brock Collection of American Art, 2014

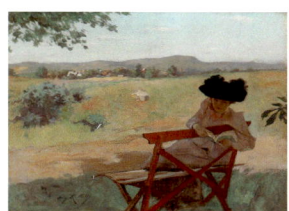

Irving Ramsay Wiles
American, 1861–1948
Sunshine and Shadow, ca. 1895
Oil on panel
13½ × 16½ inches
Promised Gift of the Macon and Joan Brock Collection of American Art

PROVENANCE

Private collection, New York
Andrew Crispo Gallery, New York
Thyssen-Bornemisza Collection, Lugano, Switzerland
Phillips, de Pury and Luxembourg, 2002
The Macon and Joan Brock Collection of American Art, 2002

EXHIBITION HISTORY

American Impressionism, Andrew Crispo Gallery, New York, 1979, no. 44.
America and Europe: A Century of Modern Masters from the Thyssen-Bornemisza Collection, Art Gallery of South Australia, Perth, Australia; Art Gallery of South Australia, Adelaide, Australia; Queensland Art Gallery, Brisbane, Australia; National Gallery of Victoria, Melbourne, Australia; Art Gallery of New South Wales, Sydney, Australia; National Art Gallery, Wellington, New Zealand; Auckland City Art Gallery, Auckland, New Zealand; Robert McDougall Art Gallery, Christchurch, New Zealand, 1979–80, no. 16.
Maestri Americani della Collezione Thyssen-Bornemisza, Vatican Museums, Rome; Villa Malpensata, Lugano, Switzerland; 1983–84, nos. 59 and 57.
American Masters: The Thyssen-Bornemisza Collection, Baltimore Museum of Art; Detroit Institute of Arts; Marion Koogler McNay Art Institute, San Antonio; IBM Gallery of Arts and Sciences, New York; San Diego Museum of Art; The Society of the Four Arts, Palm Beach, Florida, October 28, 1984–April 13, 1986, no. 59.
Mestres Americans del segle XX de la Thyssen-Bornemisza Collection, Palau de la Virreina, Barcelona, 1988, no. 81.
Two Hundred Years of American Painting from the Thyssen-Bornemisza Collection, Hyogo Prefectural Museum of Modern Art, Kobe, Japan; Nagoya City Art Museum, Nagoya, Japan; Bunkamura Museum of Art, Tokyo; Hiroshima City Museum of Contemporary Art, Hiroshima, Japan; January 5–August 25, 1991, no. 26.
Les Impressionistes Américains, Fondation de l'Hermitage, Lausanne, Switzerland, 2002, no. 59.

PUBLICATION HISTORY

Barbara Novak, *The Thyssen-Bornemisza Collection: Nineteenth-Century American Painting* (London: Vendome Press, 1986), pp. 294–95, no. 102.

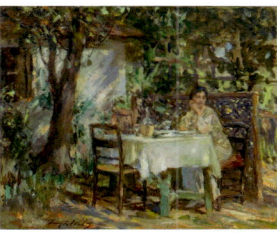

A Summer Day, ca. 1932
Oil on canvas
15 × 18 inches

PROVENANCE

The Macon and Joan Brock Collection of American Art, 2017

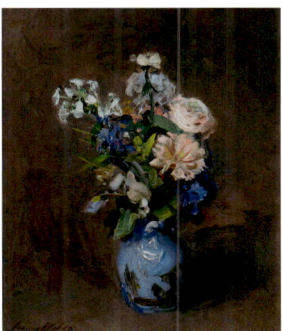

Bouquet in a Blue Vase, ca. 1930s
Oil on canvas
18 × 15 inches

PROVENANCE

The Macon and Joan Brock Collection of American Art, 2016

List of Contributors

LLOYD DEWITT, PhD, is the Senior Curator and Irene Leache Curator of European Art, Chrysler Museum of Art.

JR (JENNIFER R.) HENNEMAN, PhD, is the Director, Petrie Institute of Western American Art and Curator of Western American Art, Denver Art Museum.

STEPHANIE L. HERDRICH, PhD, is the Associate Curator of American Painting and Sculpture, The American Wing, Metropolitan Museum of Art.

SUSAN A. HOBBS, PhD, is the Director of the Thomas Wilmer Dewing Catalogue Raisonné.

LEO MAZOW, PhD, is the Louise B. and J. Harwood Cochrane Curator of American Art, Virginia Museum of Fine Arts.

ERIN MONROE is the Krieble Curator of American Paintings and Sculpture at the Wadsworth Atheneum Museum of Art.

CAROLYN SWAN NEEDELL, PhD, is the Richard and Carolyn Barry Curator of Glass, Chrysler Museum of Art.

LAUREN PALMOR, PhD, is the Associate Curator of American Art, Fine Arts Museums of San Francisco.

JENNIFER STETTLER PARSONS, PhD, is Associate Curator at the Florence Griswold Museum, Old Lyme, Connecticut.

CHELSEA PIERCE, PhD, is the McKinnon Curator of Modern and Contemporary Art, Chrysler Museum of Art.

COREY PIPER, PhD, is the Brock Curator of American Art, Chrysler Museum of Art.

SCOTT A. SHIELDS, PhD, is the Ted and Melza Barr Chief Curator and Associate Director, Crocker Art Museum.

TASHAE SMITH is the Andrew W. Mellon Curatorial Fellow, Chrysler Museum of Art and Hampton University Museum.

Acknowledgments

This catalogue would not be possible without the generosity of Macon and Joan Brock, who built a collection with great diligence and earnest intention to be made available for public enjoyment and education. Joan Brock has been instrumental in realizing the tremendous gift of the Brock Collection to the Chrysler Museum of Art and in bringing this publication to life. I am grateful for all the time and energy she has devoted to this project and for sharing these exceptional works of art with me and many others who will come to know them at the Chrysler and in the pages of this catalogue. At the Chrysler I am appreciative of the leadership of the Museum's Macon and Joan Brock Director and CEO Erik H. Neil, who has been instrumental in realizing this catalogue. Wayne F. Wilbanks, chairman of the Museum's Board of Trustees, has also been a steadfast supporter, along with the entirety of the Board.

I owe a debt of gratitude to the esteemed group of authors who shared their insights and expertise across the pages of this volume. I appreciate their keen interest in exploring and studying this collection and making American art accessible to a wide audience. Beyond those who wrote for the catalogue, many others contributed research and assistance to help build this volume. Special thanks are due to Nicole Amoroso, Eric Baumgartner, William Coleman, Thomas Colville, Bethany Dobson, Debra Force, Rob Leith, Kathy Lett, Glenn Peck, Lisa N. Peters, Michael Preble, Ray Redfern, Kirstin Ringelberg, Richard Rosello, and Jonathan Stuhlman. John Wadsworth carried out the mammoth task of photographing the bulk of the collection, along with the assistance of Zachary Varos and Joshua Solomon. Additional photography was provided by Ashley Kerr and the Chrysler's Ed Pollard. Gina Broze diligently tackled the image permissions. I am appreciative of the entire team at Marquand Books, who have made the process of working on this publication a great pleasure. Melissa Duffes's keen editing has greatly refined the text, while Ryan Polich's design of the catalogue has marvelously conveyed the remarkable beauty of the Brock Collection. I am thankful for Adrian Lucia and Keetra Fuerle's guidance of the project, along with the co-ordination of publication details by Jeremy Linden and Leah Finger.

At the Chrysler I have been grateful to work with a spirited team of professionals who have all had a hand in bringing this catalogue and the related exhibition to fruition. Debbie Ramos expertly coordinated the administration of the project, and Dana Fuqua provided valuable oversight, along with Lona Hyde and Christina Jenkins in the Museum's finance department. Melanie Neil oversaw the registration for the project, and her longstanding work on the Brock Collection was fundamental in compiling the wealth of information included in the catalogue's checklist. Chief registrar Devon Dargan and conservator Mark Lewis also supported aspects of the exhibition and gift of the Brock Collection. Ed Pollard offered vital assistance with images, and preparators Anita Pope, Garth Fry, and Rachel Greggs coordinated the movement and installation of the artworks. My curatorial colleagues Lloyd DeWitt, Carolyn Swan Needell, Chelsea Pierce, and Seth Feman all provided valuable insight and advice along the way. Cassie Rangel provided much-appreciated design input for both the catalogue and exhibition, and Ashley Cove Mars, Megan Frost, and Mattie Ruedimann coordinated the communications details of the project. In development Liz Hamilton offered key support for many different areas of the catalogue and exhibition. In the education department, Stacey Shelnut-Hendrick, Emily Shield, and Emily Cayton built impactful programs to support the exhibition, while Liz Weir tracked down countless library resources to aid in research.

I must reiterate my appreciation to Macon and Joan Brock, who supported the Chrysler Museum of Art over many years and transformed its American art program in the process. Their endowment of the Brock Curator of American Art position helped bring me to the Chrysler, and the establishment of the Macon and Joan Brock Fund for American Art has elevated the Museum to a leader in the field. In my time at the Chrysler, Joan Brock has shown immeasurable kindness to my family and me, for which I am most thankful. Lastly, I am grateful for the opportunity to have enjoyed this special collection so many times with my family, and I appreciate all their support through this project and many others.

COREY PIPER
Brock Curator of American Art

Index

This book was published in conjunction with the exhibition *A Shared Vision: The Macon and Joan Brock Collection of American Art* presented at the Chrysler Museum of Art, Norfolk, VA, from December 8, 2023, to March 10, 2024.

Library of Congress Cataloging-in-Publication Data

Names: Piper, Corey, editor. | Chrysler Museum, organizer, host institution.
Title: A shared vision : the Macon and Joan Brock collection of American Art / Corey Piper, editor ; with contributions by Lloyd DeWitt, JR (Jennifer R.) Henneman, Stephanie L. Herdrich, Susan A. Hobbs, Leo Mazow, Erin Monroe, Carolyn Swan Needell, Lauren Palmor, Jennifer Stettler Parsons, Chelsea Pierce, Corey Piper, Scott A. Shields, Tashae Smith.
Other titles: Shared vision (Chrysler Museum)
Description: Norfolk, VA : Chrysler Museum of Art, [2023] | Includes bibliographical references and index.
Identifiers: LCCN 2023018621 | ISBN 9781737183792 (hardcover)
Subjects: LCSH: Art, American—19th century—Exhibitions. | Art, American—20th century—Exhibitions. | Brock, Macon, 1942–2017—Art collections—Exhibitions. | Brock, Joan (Joan P.)—Art collections—Exhibitions. | Art—Private collections—United States—Exhibitions.
Classification: LCC N6510 .S525 2023 | DDC 709.7309/034—dc23/eng/20230523
LC record available at https://lccn.loc.gov/2023018621

Published by the Chrysler Museum of Art
chrysler.org

Distributed by the University of Virginia Press
upress.virginia.edu

Produced by Marquand Books, Seattle
marquandbooks.com

Edited by Melissa Duffes
Designed by Ryan Polich
Typeset in Utopia and Utile Display by Brynn Warriner
Proofread by Ivy Long
Indexed by Dave Luljak
Color management by I/O Color, Seattle
Printed and bound in China by Artron Art Group

DETAILS
p. 2: John Singer Sargent, *Ladies in the Shade: Abriès*, 1912 (p. 74)
p. 4: Willard LeRoy Metcalf, *October Morning No. 1*, 1910 (p. 105)
p. 8: Preston Dickinson, *Still Life No. 1*, ca. 1924 (p. 133)
p. 12: George Bellows, *Upper Broadway*, 1907 (p. 117)
pp. 20–21: John Leslie Breck, *Apple Trees in Bloom*, ca. 1890–93 (p. 95)
p. 168: Sally Michel Avery, *Autumn*, 1956 (p. 161)